CM

On the Reliability of Economic Models

Recent Economic Thought Series

Editors:

Warren J. Samuels
Michigan State University
East Lansing, Michigan, USA

William Darity, Jr.
University of North Carolina
Chapel Hill, North Carolina, USA

On the Reliability of Economic Models

Essays in the Philosophy of Economics

edited by
Daniel Little
Colgate University

Kluwer Academic Publishers
Boston/Dordrecht/London

Distributors for North America:
Kluwer Academic Publishers
101 Philip Drive
Assinippi Park
Norwell, Massachusetts 02061 USA

Distributors for all other countries:
Kluwer Academic Publishers Group
Distribution Centre
Post Office Box 322
3300 AH Dordrecht, THE NETHERLANDS

Library of Congress Cataloging-in-Publication Data
On the reliability of economic models : essays in the philosophy of
   economics / edited by Daniel Little.
      p.   cm. — (Recent economic thought series)
   Includes bibliographical references and index.
   ISBN 0-7923-9494-1
   1. Economics—Philosophy.   2. Economics—Mathematical models
—Philosophy.   3. Reliability.   I. Little, Daniel.   II. Series.
   HB72.05   1995   94-27547
   330'.01—dc20   CIP

Contents

Contributing Authors

Daniel Little
Associate Dean of Faculty
Colgate University
Hamilton, NY 13346

James Woodward
Division of Humanities and Social
  Sciences
California Institute of Technology,
  101-40
Pasadena, CA 91125

Nancy Cartwright
Department of Philosophy, Logic,
  and Scientific Method
London School of Economics
Houghton Street
London WC2A 2AE
United Kingdom

Cristina Bicchieri
Department of Philosophy
Carnegie Mellon University
Pittsburgh, PA 15213

David Schmidtz
Department of Philosophy

BGSU
Bowling Dreen, OH 43403-0222

Margaret Schabas
Department of Philosophy
York University
North York, Ontario M3J 1P3
Canada

Harold Kincaid
Department of Philosophy
University of Alabama at
  Birmingham
Birmingham, AL 35294

Kevin Hoover
Department of Economics
University of California–Davis
Davis, CA 95616-8578

Barton L. Lipman
Department of Economics
University of Pennsylvania
Philadelphia, PA 19104

Jeffrey Baldani
Department of Economics

Colgate University
Hamilton, NY 13346

A. W. Coats
Department of Economics
Box 90097
Duke University
Durham, NC 27708-0097

Marina Bianchi
Universita degli studi di Roma
Rome, Italy

Lance Taylor
Department of Economics
New School For Social Research
66 West 12th Street
New York, NY 10011

On the Reliability of Economic Models

1 INTRODUCTION: CURRENT ISSUES IN THE PHILOSOPHY OF ECONOMICS

Daniel Little

Philosophy of Science and Economic Theorizing

This volume represents a contribution to the philosophy of economics with a distinctive point of view. The contributors to the volume have not by and large taken up the general and abstract issues that have usually occupied philosophers in their discussions of the philosophy of economics in the past. Instead, they have selected particular areas of economics and have probed these areas for the philosophical and methodological issues that they raise: for example, the meaning of causal ascriptions in econometrics, the reliability of large economic models, the status of the assumptions of rationality that go into the public goods argument, the explanatory import of equilibrium analysis, and the role of experiment in economics. The primary essays are written by philosophers, who were invited to concentrate on philosophical issues that arise at the level of the everyday theoretical practice of working economists. Commentary essays have been provided by working economists, who were asked to respond to the philosophical arguments from the standpoint of their own disciplines. The volume thus represents something of an "experiment" in the philosophy of science, striving as it does to explore methodological issues across two research communities. The fruits of the experiment are available for the reader's own assessment; but it is the editor's judgment that these exchanges between philosopher and economist have been fruitful indeed.

The purpose of the volume is very specific: to stimulate a discussion of the epistemology and methodology of economics that works at the level of detail of existing "best practice" in economics today. The contributors have been asked to design their contributions in such a way as to stimulate productive conversation between philosophers and economists on topics in the methodology of economics. Collections in the philosophy of economics that are currently available focus on very general philosophical issues—falsifiability, realism, the status of economic laws, and so forth. However, a more detailed level of analysis is likely to be more fruitful for working economists.

The rationale for this approach to the philosophy of economics is that philosophy of science ought to be useful for the scientific practitioner. It is the editor's conviction that the social sciences raise important philosophical problems, and that adequate analysis of these problems can actually facilitate the theoretical and empirical work of the social scientist. But it is evident that these advantages can be realized only if the philosopher takes seriously the details and techniques of the social science with which he or she is concerned. And the working social scientist will find the results of the philosopher's inquiry useful and worthwhile only to the extent that the philosopher's analysis gives adequate expression to real problems in the practice of the social scientist.

Economics is no exception to these observations. The science of economics raises myriad difficult philosophical problems: What is the status of economic generalizations? What counts as evidence for economic hypotheses? How do economists explain events in the real world? In what sense do economic circumstances exert causal influence on other factors? What evidence gives us reason to believe a causal ascription in economics? How are economic models to be empirically evaluated? What is the status of predictions premised on economic models?

There is no question, then, that economics as a science raises difficult and important philosophical issues—problems which repay the careful analysis made possible by a philosopher's training. There is little question either that the way in which these problems are resolved has consequences, not only for philosophy but for the science of economics as well. One has only to think of the mischievous consequences that early twentieth-century philosophy had on the methodology of psychology in the form of radical behaviorism, to recognize that bad philosophy leads to bad science.

The Essays

The reader will find the following essays dense in detail and rich in analytical insight. It will be useful to have a brief sketch of the topics that emerge from these essays.

The first two essays by James Woodward and Nancy Cartwright represent challenging discussions of problems of causal reasoning in econometrics. Woodward focuses on the idea of a "structural" or autonomous relationship as being fundamental to our understanding of a causal relationship between two or more variables. As a first effort, Woodward defines an autonomous relation in these terms: "if [the equation] is autonomous, the relationship expressed by the equation—its functional form, its coefficients and so on—will remain unaltered under some relevant classes of changes." (p. 12). Woodward provides a philosophical analysis of the suitability of understanding causality in econometrics in terms of the notion of autonomy. Perhaps Woodward's most significant conclusion is that "econometric techniques take domain-specific causal information as inputs and combine these with statistical evidence to yield conclusions about causal relationships expressed in structural equations." In other words, the causal relations cannot be extracted directly from the data; it is necessary to have a hypothesis about the underlying causal mechanisms in order to extract the structural equation.

Nancy Cartwright's essay, "Causal Structures in Econometrics Models," focuses on related issues. Cartwright's central point is that econometrics ought not be led to a theory of causation out of a bad social ontology. Her concern is with the idea that facts about causal relations are simply facts about probabilities of association among variables. She argues that there are good philosophical reasons for doubting the stability and depth of such probabilities—in the natural sciences as well as in econometrics. Instead, she urges econometrics to conceive of its subject matter in terms of causal structures embodying causal powers and capacities. She argues as well that econometrics is no more able than any other area of science to provide an algorithm for arriving at a good explanation; in econometrics the upshot of this observation is that causal analysis cannot be done mechanically, guided by standard statistical tests. On Cartwright's view, what econometrics permits is a form of controlled experimentation for economists. Cartwright considers the issues of autonomy and invariance raised by Woodward and maintains that the more fundamental issue is the causal structure within which a set of economic processes takes place.

Kevin Hoover's commentary on these two econometrics essays provides a thoughtful and detailed discussion of both essays. Hoover takes up the important topic of the status of laws within economics (both Cartwright and Woodward deny that even strongly supported econometric findings constitute laws of the variables in question). And he offers illuminating discussion of the role of economic theory in causal judgments in econometrics, the problem of measurement, and the issue of how to identify an underlying causal structure.

Christina Bicchieri takes on the central idea of a Nash equilibrium within game theory in her essay. The foundational concept of game theory is the notion of a Nash equilibrium: a combination of strategies each of which is each player's best (or as good) reply to each other strategy. An outcome is explained (and predicted) if it is a Nash equilibrium: such an outcome will be stable because no player has an incentive to alter his or her strategy. Bicchieri raises a series of important difficulties with this concept as a basis for explanations of outcomes, beginning with the question of how players might reach a Nash equilibrium. Her concerns proceed from the "epistemic foundations" of a Nash equilibrium: that is, the assumptions we are forced to make about players in order for the Nash equilibrium to have a genuine explanatory role. Her central result is that the bare assumption that the players are rational and know the structure of the game does not entail that they will arrive at the equilibrium. She arrives at the skeptical conclusion that "the epistemic conditions required for a given strategic profile to be a Nash equilibrium . . . are seldom met in a static context . . . in such cases, we must be prepared to admit that Nash equilibrium has no particular claim on us." The best hope she offers for the salience of Nash equilibrium is in the dynamic case, in which repeated interactions permit learning. In this case the players can eventually converge on equilibrium through updating of their beliefs.

Barton Lipman's discussion of Bicchieri's essay provides useful commentary on the significance of game theory within the discipline of economics. Briefly, it is Lipman's view that game theory provides a framework from which to analyze the significance of institutions in competitive markets. Lipman's most telling comment on Bicchieri's approach is his suggestion that her desiderata concerning a justification of Nash equilibrium are too idealized. Lipman would settle for a set of beliefs and assumptions specific to a context that would permit players to arrive at an equilibrium position; whereas Bicchieri typically assumes that what we need are purely formal and context-independent assumptions about the participants' beliefs that are sufficient to entail convergence on the equilibrium. Lipman is persuaded that there are no such assumptions; he argues, however, that we can do second-best by attributing context-dependent assumptions to the players. Lipman proposes that we should ask, "In a real-world setting . . . what would we predict" about the outcome of a game of a given structure? He also expresses skepticism, however, about Bicchieri's notion that learning might improve the availability of Nash equilibria.

David Schmidtz introduces the topic of experimentation in economics in his essay on public good provision. He details experimental efforts to test the behavioral assumptions underlying public goods analysis and the prisoners' dilemma. The experimental results are clear: participants in controlled public good problems provide positive though suboptimal levels of contribution to the public good. How are we to interpret these results? Schmidtz breaks the prisoners' dilemma into an assurance problem and an exploitation problem. Schmidtz maintains that these problems have independent effects on decision makers—with the result that altering a public goods problem in a way that addresses one or the other ought to result in a change in behavior. And this is what experiments incorporating a money-back guarantee show, according to Schmidtz: by eliminating the assurance problem, the money-back guarantee induces participants to contribute. Schmidtz concludes that the experiments he describes permits us to probe rather accurately the decision-making rules employed by actual subjects (in contrast to the sparse abstraction of the rationally-self-interested utility maximizer of microeconomic theory). Jeffrey Baldani's insightful commentary piece draws out points of contrast and continuity between Schmidtz's argument and that of Christine Bicchieri. Baldani focuses on the logical issues raised by experimental economics: What assumptions in fundamental microeconomic theory are amenable to testing through the sorts of experiments described by Schmidtz? Baldani doubts that experimentation in economics could serve the function of calibrating quantitative parameter values, and he suspects that many areas of economics are complex enough to defy experimentation. Baldani concludes that the most valuable contribution of experimentation is in probing the effects of alternative institutional arrangements on economic behavior.

Margaret Schabas shifts our attention to problems of reasoning about economic history. The "new economic history," cliometrics, is the focus of her analysis. The new economic history applies the analytical framework of neoclassical economics to processes of economic change in the past. Schabas reviews the problems of data paucity and the framing of counterfactuals that have received much attention in the past several decades in debates over cliometrics, and then focuses her attention on the suitability of neoclassical models in economic history. Is it reasonable to use linear models and Cobb-Douglas production functions in modeling historical economies? Is the notion that economic history represents a series of neoclassical equilibria a sustainable one? Schabas gives sustained attention to the arguments constructed by Fogel and Engerman (1974) in *Time on the Cross* concerning the economics of American slavery. Her central criticism focuses on the lack of correspondence between the abstract and general assumptions of microeconomic theory—agents possessing complete, transitive, and continuous preferences, simple Cobb-Douglas production functions—and the complex and changing economic arrangements to which these assumptions are applied. Her essay concludes by linking some of the methodological characteristics of cliometrics to recent work in the philosophy of science on the status of law and rationality in historical explanations. A. W. Coats's commentary piece offers a defense of the new economic history against some of Schabas's criticisms. Coats argues that most work in this area is less ruthlessly abstractive than Schabas's account would suggest and that the field is in better shape than Schabas would allow.

Harold Kincaid puts forward a different concern for specificity within economic analysis in his treatment of the theory of the firm. The focus of Kincaid's analysis is the use of optimality explanations in the theory of the firm: such and so characteristic of the firm is explained on the basis of the assertion that the trait is optimal and maximizes profitability, self-interest, efficiency, or other economic features. Kincaid's essay, more than any other in the volume, focuses as well on problems of the empirical confirmation of economic models; he provides an admirably clear exposition of Bayesian confirmation theory. Kincaid examines several recent neoclassical theories of the firm—a transaction cost theory, a principal-agent theory, and an implicit contract theory—and argues persuasively that the empirical basis for accepting any of these theories is weaker than initially appears. Kincaid's point is not that these theories are discredited but rather that the right sort of empirical data have not been presented on the basis of which to evaluate them. Marina Bianchi provides a thoughtful discussion of both the epistemic and the substantive issues raised by Kincaid's argument. Her discussion complements Kincaid's, in that she attempts to assess the transactions costs theory of the firm on the grounds of its theoretical cogency rather than its direct empirical support. In line with the conclusions of several of the essays in the volume, she argues that the abstract analysis of the firm based on rational agents arriving at efficient outcomes must be supplemented with more detailed analysis of the specific circumstances and arrangements within which the firm took shape.

Finally, Daniel Little's essay examines some methodological issues raised by computable general equilibrium (CGE) models in macroeconomics. A CGE model is designed as a multisectoral representation of a functioning economy; it is aimed at assessing the effects of a variety of policy interventions (changes in tariffs, energy prices, taxes, and so on). The CGE simulation is often described as a way of performing "experiments" in macroeconomics. Little attempts to identify some of the epistemic problems raised by such models. The essay lays out a framework of evaluation in terms of which one might undertake to assess the credibility of the results produced by a CGE simulation. Issues of abstraction and the correspondence between models and the world arise again in this context. Lance Taylor's commentary piece provides a spirited discussion of some of the assumptions of Little's piece; he doubts, for example, that CGE models are often put forward as assertively as Little assumes. Taylor's view is that a typical CGE model is no stronger, and usually no weaker, than the underlying body of theory upon which it rests. So undertaking to assess the independent empirical warrant of the model is fruitless.

Themes

As is evident from these brief descriptions, there is a wide range of topics included in the essays below. But several themes emerge from most or all of the essays. A central theme in the volume is the epistemic status of economic models, hypotheses, and theories. The authors of the essays in this volume concern themselves with problems of assessing and interpreting the results of various areas of economics. How reliable are various economic techniques? What implicit assumptions are being made in applying a given economic model to a particular empirical case? How do data limitations constrain the evaluation of hypotheses in economic history? How appropriate are the behavioral assumptions of the model? To what extent have contextual institutional factors been adequately represented within the analysis? To what extent do arbitrary features of the framework affect the analysis in particular cases? How sensitive are outcomes to variations in the values of parameters? These questions make up what one might call the epistemology of economics; and the essays included in this volume offer philosophically insightful frames of analysis in efforts to formulate answers to them.

A related theme involves the issue of how best to understand the relation between an abstract and highly simplified model, on the one hand, and the textured and complex reality to which it is asserted to correspond. Economists employ models for a variety of purposes, with greater and lesser ambition. Most ambitiously they use models to simulate the behavior of existing economies to provide a basis for predictions. At the other end of the spectrum, models are used to explore the dynamics of multiple theoretical assumptions; on this use, it is the overall behavior of the model rather than its predictive consequences of the model that is of central interest. In what sense can the literally false model succeed in explaining the concrete reality? Is there a credible sense in which we may say that economic models correspond to economic reality?

Third, many of the essays focus attention on the behavioral assumptions of neoclassical economics: the abstract assumption of the rational self-interested agent. This assumption is unavoidably central to economic theorizing; at the same time, it is evident that the theory corresponds only weakly to actual human psychology. So how does this lack of correspondence affect the credibility of theorizing based on it?

A related theme in the volume is the need for greater specificity in economic analysis—whether in analyzing historically specific institutions, the firm, or developing economies. These points converge with a number of developments in the recent economics literature itself—institutional economics, increased attention to transaction costs, and attention to the importance of market imperfections, incomplete information, and problems of incomplete rationality.

Finally, many of the essays raise problems in the logic of confirmation that find a priori formulation in the philosophy of science literature but that are applied with detail and finesse to particular areas of economic reasoning in the essays below. If economics is a science, it needs to explain, and it needs to be grounded in some appropriate way on empirical evidence. But in almost all of the essays below, it emerges that the problem of confirmation of economic theory and economic model continues to be unresolved—both within the economics profession and among those philosophers who have observed economic theorizing over the years.

In short, there is ample room for productive exchange between philosophers and economists. But it is apparent that philosophers will succeed in entering into fruitful debate with economists only to the extent that they take seriously the particular details of current practices and controversies in economics. Philosophers of physics have learned this lesson well in the past several decades, and extremely fruitful interactions have occurred between philosophy and contemporary physics, Philosophers of economics must likewise link their work to specific technical details in problematic areas of economics.

The philosophers who have contributed to this volume fit the bill admirably for this perspective. Each has taken up an issue that arises directly out of current economic research. And each has treated the subject matter in sufficient detail to make the results of interest to the working economist. Equally, the economists who have provided commentaries to the philosophers' essays have taken up the challenge of considering with seriousness and attentiveness the philosophical problems raised in the philosophers' essays. There is a genuine sense of productive conversation that emerges out of these essays, and it is the hope of this editor that these conversations will stimulate continuing productive relationship between economics and philosophy.

References

Fogel, Robert William, and Stanley L. Engerman. (1974). *Time on the Cross: The Economics of American Negro Slavery.* (Boston: Little, Brown.)

2 CAUSATION AND EXPLANATION IN ECONOMETRICS

James Woodward

Econometric and causal modeling techniques are widely used to test causal claims both within economics and in many other areas of social sciences. My aim in this essay will be to suggest, in a rough and preliminary way, one perspective on how we should understand and evaluate these techniques. Section 2.1 reviews, very quickly, the basic apparatus of linear models. Sections 2.2 and 2.3 then discuss the idea that I take to be the key to the causal interpretability of such models—the idea of a structural or autonomous relationship. I attempt to locate this idea within a more general philosophical framework and to defend the conception of causation and explanation it embodies against various challenges. Sections 2.4 and 2.5 then explore the status of the various sorts of causal assumptions that serve as inputs to econometric techniques—assumptions about which variables to include, about causal ordering, and about the distribution of the error term. I discuss what sort of causal knowledge such input claims represent and how we can assess such claims. Section 2.6 explores similar questions concerning the output of econometric techniques—the structural models themselves.

2.1

In a linear regression model, one assumes that a dependent variable Y is a function of a set of independent variables, $X_1, X_2 \ldots X_k$ and an error term U. Assuming that we have T observations of the values of Y and T corresponding observations for the values of $X_1 \ldots X_k$, we have a set of T linear equations of form

$$Y_i = B_0 + B_1 x_{1i} + B_2 x_{2i} + \ldots B_k x_{ki} + u_i, \, i = 1, 2 \ldots T. \qquad (2.1)$$

We can summarize these in matrix form as

$$\mathbf{Y} = \mathbf{XB} + \mathbf{U} \qquad (2.2)$$

where $\mathbf{Y}$ is a $T \times 1$ column vector of observations on the dependent variable, $\mathbf{X}$ a $T \times K$ matrix of observations on the independent variables, $\mathbf{B}$ a $T \times 1$ column vector of the regression coefficients, and $\mathbf{U}$ an $T \times 1$ vector of the error terms. A standard result then shows that under certain assumptions regarding the distribution of the error term, the ordinary least squares (OLS) estimator

$$b = (\mathbf{X} \, \mathbf{X})^{-1} \, \mathbf{X} \, \mathbf{Y} \qquad (2.3)$$

will be a best linear unbiased estimator of the vector $\mathbf{B}$.

A regression equation, when interpreted causally, corresponds to a very simple structure. Each of the explanatory variables is assumed to exert a fixed causal influence, represented by the regression coefficient, on the dependent variable, but the independent variables are assumed to exert no causal influence on one another, nor is there any reciprocal causal influence back from the dependent variable to any of the independent variables. However, many of the systems that are of interest in economics and in other areas of social science have a more complicated causal structure involving reciprocal causal relationships or direct causal relationships between the explanatory variables themselves. To model such relationships one must use systems of simultaneous equations, rather than a single equation as in a regression model. Suppose that we have such a system of equations with M endogenous variables and K exogenous variables and as before T observations. If we let $\mathbf{Y}$ be a $T \times M$ matrix representing the observations on all endogenous variables (the ith row of which corresponds to the ith observation on all endogenous variables) and $\mathbf{X}$ be a $T \times K$ matrix representing the observations on all exogenous variables, then we can write the general form of a simultaneous equation model as

$$\mathbf{Y}\boldsymbol{\Gamma} + \mathbf{XB} + \mathbf{U} = \mathbf{O}, \qquad (2.4)$$

where $\boldsymbol{\Gamma}$ and $\mathbf{B}$ are coefficient matrices and $\mathbf{U}$ is as before the error vector.

While there are thus a number of distinctive difficulties that arise when trying to estimate coefficients in a system of simultaneous equations, the fundamental epistemological problem is the same as with regression models: to infer values for the coefficients in the model on the basis of observational information that consists of facts about statistical relationships (variances and covariances) among measured variables. As is well known (and as we shall see in more detail below) this cannot be done either for ordinary regression models or for simultaneous equation models without a good deal of additional information.

2.2

Discussions in the econometrics literature frequently draw a contrast between the use of systems of equations to represent "empirical associations" and to represent "structural" or "autonomous" relationships (see Fox, 1984: 63ff). In this section I want to explore this contrast, which like a number of other writers, I take to be crucial to issues about the causal interpretability of such equations.[1] There are many discussions of structure and autonomy and closely related notions in econometrics, but a still very illuminating point of departure is Haavelmo's classic early monograph (1944). Haavelmo introduces the idea of autonomy by means of often-quoted mechanical analogy (1944: 27–28, emphasis in original):

> If we should make a series of speed tests with an automobile, driving on a flat, dry road, we might be able to establish a very accurate functional relationship between the pressure on the gas throttle (or the distance of the gas pedal from the bottom of the car) and the corresponding maximum speed of the car. And the knowledge of this relationship might be sufficient to operate the car at a prescribed speed. But if a man did not know anything about automobiles, and he wanted to understand how they work, we should not advise him to spend time and effort in measuring a relationship like that. Why? Because (1) such a relation leaves the whole inner mechanism of a car in complete mystery, and (2) such a relation might break down at any time, as soon as there is some disorder or change in any working part of the car. We say that such a relation has very little autonomy, because its existence depends upon the simultaneous fulfillment of a great many other relations, some of which are of a transitory nature. On the other hand, the general laws of thermodynamics, the dynamics of function, etc., etc., are highly autonomous relations with respect to the automobile mechanism, because these relations describe the functioning of some parts of the mechanism *irrespective* of what happens in some *other* parts.

Haavelmo (1944: 28–29, emphasis in original) then suggests the following, more formal characterization of autonomy:

> Suppose that it be possible to define a *class* Ω, of *structures*, such that *one member or another* of this class would, approximately, describe economic reality in *any*

practically conceivable situation. And suppose that we define some nonnegative *measure* of the "size" (or the "importance" or "credibility") of any subclass, W in Ω, including itself, such that, if a subclass contains completely another subclass, the measure of the former is greater than, or at least equal to, that of the latter, and such that the measure of Ω is positive. Now consider a particular subclass (of Ω), containing all those—and only those—structures that satisfy a particular relation "A." Let W_A be this particular subclass. (E.g., W_A might be the subclass of all those structures that satisfy a particular demand function "A.") We then say that the relation "A" is *autonomous* with respect to the subclass of structures W_A. And we say that "A" has a *degree* of autonomy which is the greater the larger be the "size" of W_A as compared with that of Ω.

Although this characterization is far from transparent (how exactly does one go about measuring the "size" of W?), the underlying idea is perhaps clear enough. In the most general sense the degree of autonomy of a relationship has to do with whether it would remain stable or invariant under various possible changes or "interventions." The larger the class of changes under which the relation would remain invariant—the more structures in W compatible with the relation—the greater its degree of autonomy. Standard examples of physical laws—the laws of thermodynamics or the Newtonian gravitational law—are highly autonomous in this sense. Given a system of two masses, the Newtonian gravitational law will continue to truly characterize their mutual gravitational attraction under an extremely wide class of changes in the system—under changes in the distance between the masses, under changes in their shape or temperature, under the addition of other masses to the system and so on. By contrast, the relationship (call it R) between the pressure on the gas pedal and the speed of the car in Haavelmo's example is far less autonomous. (R) may hold stably for some particular car if the experiment of depressing the pedal is repeated in very similar circumstances, but (R) will be disrupted by all sorts of changes—by variations in the incline along which the car travels, by changes elsewhere in its structure (e.g., the removal of the wheels or spark plugs), and so on. (R) is thus relatively fragile or nonrobust in the sense that it is dependent on certain very specific background conditions.

Applying this idea to a single equation like (2.2), we can say, then, that if (2.2) is autonomous, the relationship expressed by the equation—its functional form, its coefficients and so on—will remain unaltered under some relevant classes of changes, including at a minimum, changes in the values of the independent variables in (2.2) and changes in the value of the error term. However, Haavelmo's remarks (and in particular his reference to relationships that remain stable irrespective of what is happening in the other parts of a system) suggest a further implication of the notion of autonomy, which we can bring out most clearly by considering a system of simultaneous equations like (2.4). Suppose that it is possible to intervene in such a way as to separately change each of the coefficients in (2.4). Then if the relationships described in (2.4) are autonomous, each of the coefficients should be invariant under interventions that produce changes in any of the other coefficients. To illustrate, consider the following elementary example, drawn from Duncan (1975). Suppose that the true structural model (the model that captures the autonomous relations) for some system is

$$X_3 = b_{31} X_1 + b_{34} X_4 + U \qquad (2.5)$$
$$X_4 = b_{42} X_2 + b_{43} X_3 + V.$$

Then the following model (2.6) will be "observationally equivalent" to (2.5), in the sense that it will have exactly the same solutions and imply the same facts about statistical relationships among the measured variables:

$$X_3 = a_{31} X_1 + a_{32} X_2 + U' \qquad (2.6)$$
$$X_4 = a_{41} X_1 + a_{42} X_2 + V',$$

where $a_{31} = \dfrac{b_{31}}{\Delta}$ $a_{32} = \dfrac{b_{34} b_{42}}{\Delta}$ $a_{41} = \dfrac{b_{43} b_{31}}{\Delta}$ $a_{42} = \dfrac{b_{42}}{\Delta}$ $U' = \dfrac{U + b_{34} V}{\Delta}$ V'

$= \dfrac{b_{34} U + V}{\Delta}$ $\Delta = 1 - b_{34} b_{43}.$

Despite their observational equivalence, there is, as Duncan notes, an important difference between (2.5) and (2.6). Each of the coefficients in (2.6) is a "mixture" of several of the coefficients in (2.5). Since (2.5) is by assumption a structural model, each of the coefficients in (2.5) can change without any of the other coefficients in (2.5) changing. But since the coefficients in (2.6) are mixtures of the coefficients in (2.5), if one of the a's in (2.6) changes, this would presumably mean that one or more of the b's in (2.5) had changed, which would mean in turn that a number of the other coefficients in (2.6) would change as well, since each b is involved in the expression for several a's. In short, if (2.5) is structural, (2.6) will not be structural: the coefficients in (2.6) will not be stable or invariant under changes in the other coefficients. In this sense the b's are, as Duncan (1975: 153) puts it "more autonomous" than the a's.

Why does it matter whether a relationship is autonomous? According to both Haavelmo and subsequent discussion, autonomous relationships are causal in character and can be used to provide explanations. By contrast, relationships that are nonautonomous are noncausal. They can be used to describe or represent a body of data but not to provide explanations. It is because or to the extent that we regard the identification of causal connections and the provision of explanations as an important goal of theory construction that notions like autonomy and structural invariance matter.[2]

The notions of autonomy and invariance, at least in the forms that they take in econometrics, have received relatively little attention from philosophers of science.[3] It is natural to ask whether there is some philosophically defensible rationale for associating autonomous relationships with causal or explanatory relationships in the way described. In this section I want to explore this issue in more detail. In part my motive will be simply to locate autonomy and related notions in a more general philosophical perspective and to set the stage for my discussion in Sections 2.5 and 2.6. But in addition there is a more immediate practical reason for this part of my discussion. Although the importance of asking whether a relationship is structural or autonomous is recognized in a good deal of econometric discussion, this recognition is by no means universal. Many econometrics texts concentrate solely on issues of statistical estimation and have little to say about autonomy and invariance. There is an influential conception of causation, due to Clive Granger and discussed below, which is fundamentally different from the conception implicit in the notion of autonomy. Moreover, if one looks outside economics, to the use of econometric techniques in sociology and political science, one often finds that little attention is paid to the question of whether estimated relations are autonomous: indeed it seems fair to say that the importance of this question is not even appreciated in much of this research. It is thus of considerable normative importance for econometric practice to try to understand what conception of causation and explanation is implicit in the notion of an autonomous relationship.

We may begin by noting that the idea that causal relationships must be invariant or autonomous relationships fits naturally with what philosophers will recognize as a *manipulability theory* of causation. The manipulability theory is the theory defended by philosophers like Gasking (1955) and Von Wright (1971), that causes are potential handles or devices for manipulating or bringing about their effects. Put very roughly the idea is that if C causes E, then if it is possible to manipulate C, this should be a way of manipulating or changing E. The manipulability conception does not provide a successful reductive analysis of causation since notions like "manipulation" (and even more clearly, "possible manipulation") are already causal in character. Nonetheless this conception is, in my view, far from unilluminating. Among other things, it provides a nontrivial constraint on causal relationships: if the relationship between C and E is such that even it were possible to manipulate C, this would not be a way of changing E, then we ought to reject the claim that this relationship is causal. As we shall see below, by no means all conceptions of causality satisfy this constraint. More generally, as I also hope to illustrate in more detail below, thinking of causal claims in terms of their implications for various hypothetical experiments or manipulations can play an important heuristic role in clarifying what such claims mean and in assessing competing procedures for making causal inferences.[4]

One can think of the manipulabity theory as providing a rationale for the claim that causal relationships must be autonomous relationships because, as the econometrics literature emphasizes, at least in typical social scientific contexts autonomous relationships are precisely those relationships that can in principle be exploited for purposes of manipulation and control. If the relationship between C and E will remain invariant under some significant class of changes (including, crucially, changes in C itself and changes elsewhere in the system of which C and E are a part), then we may be able to avail ourselves of the stability of this relationship to produce changes in E by producing changes in C. If, on the contrary, the relationship between C and E is not autonomous, so that relevant changes in C itself or in background circumstances will simply disrupt the previously existing relationship between C and E, we will not be able to make use of this relationship to bring about changes in E by manipulating C.[5]

A standard macroeconomic illustration of this idea involves the Phillips curve, which describes the historically observed inverse relationship or "tradeoff" between unemployment and inflation in many western economics from the midnineteenth to midtwentieth centuries. According to some Keynesian economic models, this relationship will be at least approximately invariant for many policy interventions of the sort Western governments might undertake. If so, this relationship is one that governments might be able to exploit for purposes of manipulation and control. For example, governments might be able to lower the unemployment rate by introducing measures that lead to a higher level of inflation.

The burden of an influential critique developed by Lucas (see Lucas, 1976) and others is that it follows from fundamental microeconomic assumptions that the Phillips curve is highly nonautonomous. According to this critique, increasing inflation can reduce unemployment only if employers or employees mistake an absolute increase in prices for a higher relative price for the goods or labor they are attempting to sell and this is not a mistake they will make systematically or over the long run. As soon as economic agents come to expect a general increase in the price level or as soon as they realize that they have mistaken an increase in the general price level for a favorable shift in relative prices, unemployment will return to its original level. The result of tolerating inflation will thus not be to permanently reduce unemployment but rather simply disrupt the relationship postulated in the Phillips curve. Put more abstractly, the point is that as the expectations of economic agents change, so will the Phillips curve in a way that renders it relatively noninvariant. Because of this, the Phillips curve cannot be exploited for policy purposes and hence does not represent a lawful or causal relationship.

It is also natural to think about the importance of autonomy in the context of systems of simultaneous equations in terms of manipulability conception of causation. If I know that the true system of structural relations is represented by

(2.5), then if, for example, I wish to alter the relationship between X_1 and X_3, I can intervene to change b_{31}[6] and because (2.5) is structural, the result of this will not be to produce any changes elsewhere in the system (2.5), which may under-cut the result I am trying to achieve. By contrast, the coefficients in (2.6) are, as it were, entangled with each other in a way that makes the relationships described in (2.6) unsuitable for purposes of manipulation and control. Suppose one wishes to alter the relationship between X_1 and X_4 in (2.6) by altering the value of the coefficient a_{41} (or suppose some natural change occurs that produces this result). As I have noted, to accomplish this result, one or more of the b's in (2.5) would have to be different. However, not knowing the true structural model (2.5), one will not know exactly how the coefficients in (2.6) were dif-ferent in such a way as to produce this change in a_{41}. Moreover, each of these b's is involved in the expression for several a's, and the exact way in which the a's depend on the b's is unknown to someone who possesses only the model (2.6). Thus, while we may expect that if a_{41} were to change, some of the coef-ficients in (2.6) would probably change as well, it will be impossible to say (in the absence of knowledge of the true structural model) which coefficients will change and exactly how they will change. Clearly this makes (2.6) in compari-son with (2.5) an unsuitable instrument for manipulation and control. This in turn makes it plausible to suggest, on a manipulability theory of causation, that (2.5) captures genuine causal relationships in a way that (2.6) does not.

Another way of putting essentially the same point is this: There is a hypo-thetical experiment connected with (2.5) which is unproblematic and well de-fined, and, associated with this experiment, a counterfactual claim with an unambiguous truth value. If, say, I intervene to change the value of b_{31}, it is clear from the independence of the coefficients in (2.5) how this change will ramify through the system and thus what the result of this change will be. By contrast, the hypothetical experiment associated with changing a'_{41} to, say, a'_{41} will be indeterminate and not well defined. The result of this experiment will depend upon how this change in a'_{41} has been produced, and without knowing this (i.e. without knowing how the true structural coefficients have changed so as to produce this change in a'_{41},) one can't say what the result of this experiment would be. Relatedly, one will be unable to evaluate counterfactuals of the form: If a'_{41}, were to change to a'_{41}, the result would be such and such. Thus, if one thinks that associated with any true causal claim there ought to be an unambigu-ous counterfactual with a determinate truth value, (2.6) will again seem, in comparison with (2.5) to be a defective representation of causal relationships.[7]

I want to suggest, then, that the notion of causation implicit in the notion of a structural model and in the idea that causal relationships must be autonomous relationships is roughly that captured by the manipulability theory: the mark of a causal relationship is that it should in principle be exploitable for purposes of manipulation and control. When one worries about whether the relationship between inflation and unemployment represented by the Phillips curve or the apparent association between growth in the money supply and inflation is a mere correlation instead of a genuine causal relationship, it is this question about whether one of these variables in these relationships might potentially be used to manipulate the other that is really at issue. Given this manipulability conception of causation and the connection between manipulability and autonomy we then have an obvious rationale for associating autonomous relationships with causal or explanatory relationships.

In addition to the connection between autonomy and manipulability, there are other reasons for thinking that the importance assigned by econometrics literature to the discovery of autonomous or invariant relationships is not misguided. One finds in many areas of scientific practice outside of economics and econometrics a similar association lawful or causal relationships with those relationships that are autonomous or invariant. For example, one of the features of fundamental physical laws most emphasized by physicists themselves (but very largely ignored in philosophical discussion, at least until recently) is that laws must satisfy various symmetry requirements. Such symmetry requirements are in effect invariance requirements. They amount to the demand that laws express relationships that remain invariant under certain kinds of transformations or changes—for example, under spatial or temporal translations or under translation from one inertial frame to another. Moreover, it is widely—and I think correctly—believed that the discovery of laws is an important goal of theorizing in physics and that appeals to laws play an important role in physical explanation. While I think that is a mistake, for reasons that will emerge below, to think of fundamental relations in economics as laws of nature, the importance attached in the natural sciences to the discovery of invariant relationships suggests that the idea that one finds in the econometrics literature that relationships that are causal or nomological or particularly suitable for constructing explanations ought to be invariant relationships is by no means an eccentric or isolated idea, unconnected to ideas of good scientific methodology outside of economics and the social sciences. Instead it is a very natural and plausible idea that is widely accepted in many areas of scientific investigation.

We can get a further grip on what is distinctive about the notion of causation implicit in talk of autonomous relationships by contrasting this notion with a well-known conception of causation associated with Clive Granger. Granger's definition applies to stochastic systems and in particular to stationary time series. The basic idea is that Y_t causes X_{t+1} "if we are better able to predict X_{t+1} using all available information then if the information apart from Y_t had been used" (1969: 376). Slightly more precisely, Granger proposes the following "causality definition:" Y_t causes X_{t+1} if Prob $(X_{t+1} \in A/\Omega_t) \neq$ Prob $(X_{t+1} \in A/\Omega_t - Y_t)$ for some set A where Ω_t, is the set of all observable events available up to time t and $\Omega_t - Y_t$ is this set minus information exclusively in the sequence Y_{t-j}, ≥ 0 (1988: 10).

To make this observation operational, the reference to "all observable events available" must be replaced by some more manageable subset of observational information, and the reference to the complete conditional probability distribution of X_{t+1} must be replaced by a few moments of this distribution. When so operationalized Granger's proposal is that if the variance of the forecast error of an unbiased linear predictor of X based on all past information is less than the variance of the corresponding prediction based on all past information except for past values of Y, then Y causes X. This in turn suggests a simple test for causality, which somewhat imprecisely expressed is this: regress X on a number of lags of itself and a number of lags of Y. If the coefficients on the lagged values of Y are zero, Y does not Granger cause X.

The basic idea behind Granger's theory is that causes should carry information about their effects: information about the cause should improve one's ability to predict the effect. The idea is very similar to Patrick Suppes's well-known probabilistic theory of causation (Suppes, 1970), and both theories seem to suffer from very similar defects. To begin with, Granger's characterization applies only to nondeterministic systems, since in deterministic systems there is no residual variance that knowledge of the cause can reduce (that is, no improvement in predictability that knowledge of the cause can provide). As Zellner (1984: 54ff) notes, the idea that a different notion of causation is required for deterministic and indeterministic systems is implausible and by itself suggests that Granger's characterization does not capture the ordinary notion of cause. By contrast, the controllability conception of causation and the associated conception of autonomy apply equally well to both deterministic and stochastic systems. Second, on Granger's characterization, causal relationships are relative to a body of a data or a set of measured variables: causal conclusions will vary depending upon what is included in the set of available information. By this I do not mean simply that what causal conclusions it is reasonable to believe will depend upon available evidence: this will presumably be the case for any defensible theory of causal inference. Rather, on Granger's theory, causation is itself an information-relative notion: one variable may cause another relative to a certain information set but not relative to some other, larger information set, just as (or because) a variable may improve one's ability to predict a second variable relative to one information set, but not relative to a larger information set. By contrast, the manipulability notion of causality exhibits no such information relativity.

In general, it seems clear that Granger's conception of causality and the manipulability conception are very different notions. It seems quite possible that knowledge of X might improve one's ability to predict Y (indeed might even improve predictability relative to "all other information in the universe" besides X) and yet that manipulating X might not be a way of manipulating Y but might rather destroy the correlation on the basis of which we use X to predict Y. On a manipulability theory a correlation of this sort will be regarded as nonautonomous or "accidental." It is also apparent that X can cause Y in the manipulability sense even though X does not Granger cause Y. Suppose, for example, that the relation

$$Y_t = X_{t-1} + U \tag{2.7}$$

is autonomous and that X is steadily increased by the same amount (e.g., by 1 unit) in every time period. Then knowledge of the value of X will not allow us to predict the mean value of Y any more accurately than we would be able to predict its given just past values of Y and thus X will not Granger cause Y. Nonetheless, ex hypothesi, X is used to control Y.

The difference between Granger causation and the notion of causation associated with the manipulability theory and with autonomy is also acknowledged in the econometrics literature. Both Cooley and Leroy (1985) and Hoover (1988) give examples involving economic theory in which X is used to control Y even though X does not Granger cause Y. Hoover also notes that distinct but observationally equivalent models (see below pp. 22 ff) may yield exactly the same claims about Granger causality but different claims about the results of various possible manipulations—further evidence for the distinctness of Granger causality and the manipulability conception. Hoover comments that "clearly, Granger causality and causality as it is normally analysed [the manipulability conception] are not closely related concepts" (1988: 174) and that "Granger-causality and controllability may run in opposite directions" (1988: 200). Granger (1990) also distinguishes his account of causation from the controllability or manipulability conception and explicitly rejects the latter. He writes (1990: 46), "The equivalence of causation and controllability is not generally accepted, the latter being perhaps a deeper relationship. If a causal link were found and was not previously used for control, the action of attempting to control with it may destroy the causal link." The contrary view for which I have been arguing is that an alleged causal link between C and E which is such that any attempt to control E by controlling C destroys the link is not a causal relationship. The notion of Granger causation illustrates my earlier suggestion that although manipulability theories do not provide a reductive definition of causation, they nonetheless provide a useful constraint on any acceptable definition of causation. In rejecting the idea that if C is a cause of E, then if it is possible to manipulate or control C, this must be a way of manipulating or controlling E, it seems to me that Granger's approach has abandoned an idea that is so central to the common sense notion of causation that what we are left with is not causation at all.

2.3

With this background let us now look at autonomy and related notions as they figure in econometric investigation more detail. The first point to note is that autonomy and invariance have modal or subjunctive or counterfactual import. This is apparent in Haavelmo's original discussion. He insists that there is "clearly a difference" between what he calls "the actual persistence" of a relationship which "depends upon what variations *actually occur*" and the "degree of autonomy of a relationship," which "refers to a class of *hypothetical* variations in structure, for which the relationship *would be* invariant" (1944: 29, emphasis in original). Haavelmo's idea, I take it, is that it is perfectly possible for a relationship to be highly nonautonomous—in the sense that it would break down if any one of very large number of possible changes in background structure were to occur—and yet for the relationship to persist over some substantial period of time because, as it happens, those changes don't occur. The Phillips curve before 1970 is arguably a case in point. Autonomy has to do not (just) with what *actually* happens but also with what *would* happen if, perhaps contrary to fact, various changes were to occur.

The idea that claims about causal and lawful connections have counterfactual import has of course also been a central theme in philosophical discussion and several recent discussions of autonomy have explicitly noted this connection.[8] However, the relationship between causal and nomological claims and counterfactuals suggested by the notion of autonomy seems to me to interestingly different from the relationship standardly assumed in philosophical discussion. Oversimplifying considerably, philosophers tend to think of laws and causal generalizations as universally quantified conditionals of form

$$\text{All } As \text{ are } Bs. \tag{2.8}$$

They have generally supposed that if (2.8) is a law, it must support counterfactuals of the form

$$\text{If } X \text{ were to be an } A, \text{ then X would be a } B. \tag{2.9}$$

As I understand it, the counterfactual test associated with the notion of autonomy is importantly different from this. In asking whether (2.8) is autonomous or possesses a significant degree of autonomy, we ask the following counterfactual question (or really, set of questions).

$$\begin{array}{l}\text{If initial and background conditions were to change} \\ \text{in various ways, would (2.8) continue to hold?}^9\end{array} \tag{2.10}$$

To see the difference between (2.9) and (2.10), suppose that a generalization of form (2.8) is true but highly nonautonomous: it holds only because a very large number of very specific initial and background conditions happen to obtain and would break down if those conditions were to change at all. If, in this sort of case, one had good reason to think that these initial and background conditions would persist, one might also think that (depending on one's theory of counterfactuals) that the counterfactual claim (2.9) is true or at least that is not obviously false. One might think this because, for example, one believed that the possible worlds most similar to the actual world in which the antecedent of (2.9) is satisfied are worlds in which these initial and background conditions persist, so that if anything satisfied the antecedent of (2.9) in whose worlds it would also satisfy its consequent.[10]

To illustrate suppose that the generalization

$$\text{All ravens are black.} \tag{2.11}$$

is true in the actual circumstances, but highly nonautonomous: ravens of different colors would have resulted if the species had been subject to even slightly different selection pressures or if the genetic structure of some ravens were to change in small ways as a result of any one of a number of perfectly possible mutations. Under such a supposition the result of applying the counterfactual test (2.10) to (2.11)—

If initial and background conditions were to change
in various ways, (2.11) would continue to hold. (2.12)

—yields a counterfactual claim that is false. Still if one believed that these conditions making for the blackness of present ravens would persist, one might reasonably also believe that

If X were a raven (i.e., a descendant of present ravens),
then X would be black. (2.13)

Similarly, if one expected that the special conditions that made for the trade off between inflation and unemployment captured in the pre-1970 Phillips curve would persist, one might believe that the Phillips curve would support counterfactuals of form (2.9)—e.g., that it is true that

If inflation were to increase by such and such an amount,
unemployment would decrease by the amount specified
in the Phillips curve. (2.14)

However, one might also believe that Phillips curve itself is nonautonomous—that counterfactuals of form (2.10) for the Phillips curve are false.

We see, then, the test (2.10) associated with the notion of autonomy is a more stringent and demanding counterfactual test then the test (2.9) standardly imposed in philosophical discussion. Moreover, as I have tried to emphasize, (2.10)

is the counterfactual test suggested by an account of causation and explanation that ties causal and explanatory relationships to those relationships that can support manipulation and control. (It is (2.10) and not just (2.9) that is relevant to successful manipulation.) If we accept such an account, we also ought to accept the claim that the strong requirement of counterfactual import embodied in (2.10) associated with the notion of autonomy is an appropriate requirement to impose on causal and explanatory relationships.

The fact that autonomous or structural models have modal import of the sort just described has an important consequence: It generates an underdetermination problem that is crucial to understanding and evaluating the use of econometric techniques to make causal inferences. Suppose that we put aside statistical problems having to do with inferring from sample to population and assume that we have accurate population information about means, variances, covariances, and so on. This statistical information has to do with what has actually happened, with the patterns of association that have so far occurred in this population. However, as we have emphasized, structural models have implications not just for what has actually happened—and, indeed, not just for what will happen, assuming that present background conditions persist—but for what would happen under various counterfactual conditions including changes in those background conditions. It is thus not surprising that in the absence of relevant changes in background conditions a large number of different structural models will be, as the econometrics literature claims, "observationally equivalent" in the sense that we will be unable to distinguish among them just on the basis of available statistical data: they will imply exactly the same probability distribution for all values of variables so far measured. (For reasons that I have relegated to a footnote, I caution that this is a different notion of "observational equivalence" than the notion standardly discussed by philosophers. The problem of determining which model from among a set of observationally equivalent models is the correct structural model is also *not* the Goodmanian inductive problem of determining whether a present pattern of statistical association will persist into the future.)[11] Such models will nonetheless differ about which relationships are autonomous or invariant and in consequence will make quite different predictions about what would happen if various hypothetical changes or interventions were to occur. These differences will be quite crucial if we are interested in manipulation and control, or if, relatedly, we are interested in explanation and the identification of causal relationships. A well-known economic example of this is the observational equivalence, discovered by Sargent (1976), of models in which there is a natural rate of unemployment and models which are inconsistent with this assumption. The two observationally equivalent systems of equations (2.5) and (2.6) above can also be used to illustrate the same point. If (2.5) is the correct structural model, then if one intervenes to change b_{31}, this will not result in changes in any of the other structural coefficients in (2.5). By contrast, if (2.5) is not structural (if instead (2.6) is structural) we may expect that a change in b_{31} will be associated with changes in the other coefficients in (2.5).

More generally, consider again a system of structural equations of form

$$Y\Gamma + XB + U = O. \tag{2.4}$$

If Γ is nonsingular, then we can always transform (2.4) into the reduced form of the system (2.15), in which each nonlagged endogenous variable appears in only one equation and on the left side of that equation, and only so-called predetermined variables (exogenous or lagged endogenous variables) appear on the right side:

$$Y = X\Pi + V \text{ where } \Pi = -B\Gamma^{-1} \text{ and } V = -U\,\Gamma^{-1}. \tag{2.15}$$

These reduced form equations (2.15) will be observationally equivalent in the sense described above to the original structural system (2.4). Moreover, if for each equation in (2.15) the error terms satisfy the usual distributional requirements, we can use ordinary least squares to arrive at unbiased estimates of the reduced form coefficients. One can thus think of the reduced form equations as representing whatever observational information is present in the original system (2.4). However, in general, a large number of different structural models will have the same reduced form equations. Indeed any nonsingular transformation of a structural model will yield a new model with the same reduced form equations, even though the causal relationships postulated in the new model will of curse be quite different from those in the original model. We thus cannot infer just from the observational information embodied in the reduced form equation which structural model is correct. To select and estimate the correct structural model we must make use of additional assumptions, the character which will be discussed in more detail in Sections 2.4 and 2.5.

The underdetermination of the correct structural model by available observational information is thus a quite general feature of the use of structural models. We also see that it is a concern with finding autonomous relationships that creates this underdetermination problem. If all that mattered in econometrics was finding an accurate description of or "an empirically adequate" representation of the data, one could ignore the problem of identifying the correct structural model and simply estimate the associated reduced form equations. The extensive attention given to the "identification problem" (the problem of finding and estimating the correct structural model from a set of observationally equivalent candidates) is a reflection of the fact that econometric investigation often has other goals—in particular the discovery of causal and explanatory relationships having the sort of modal import I have described.

The general point that facts about observed patterns of statistical dependence fail to determine which of a number of competing structural models is correct has a number of additional implications. To begin with, it follows that there will be no purely statistical or formal test for whether a given relationship is autonomous or structural. Since autonomy has to do with how some relationships would behave under various hypothetical changes, an equation may fit the observed data very well—may do very well on various statistical tests of goodness of fit (F-tests, t-tests, and so on), may exhibit a high R^2 value and so on—and yet fail to represent an autonomous relationship. Indeed, as we shall see below, the search for autonomous relationships may rationally lead a researcher to prefer less well fitting models to models that are better fitting or more empirically adequate (see Section V). Given that a variety of different structural models will typically be consistent with the same observed patterns of statistical association, it also should be clear that it is a mistake to think of structural models as "Humean" attempts to translate or reduce causal claims to claims about such patterns. It is equally a mistake to suppose, as several recent philosophical discussions do, that structural models embody a conception of explanation according to which explanation is simply a matter of subsumption under patterns of statistical association ("explanation by correlation" as Peter Railton, 1981, has called it). On the conception of causation associated with the idea of a structural relationship, the distinctive feature of a causal relationship is *not* the presence of a correlation per se or even of a correlation that persists when we statistically control for various possible confounding variables, but rather the presence of a correlation that is stable or invariant under some class of changes. This is a modal or subjunctive claim that (or so I would argue) cannot be cashed out just in terms of facts about covariances, partial correlation coefficients, conditional probabilities and the like.[12] It is perfectly true that a substantial portion of social scientific practice consists in nothing more than the search for patterns of correlation, partial correlation, and so on, with no accompanying argument that the relationships in question are structural or autonomous. But if my discussion so far is correct, such practices, insofar as they claim to yield causal conclusions or to furnish explanations, lack any serious methodological rationale.

If claims about autonomous or structural relations are underdetermined by statistical evidence in the way I have described, it becomes a serious question how we can we possibly assess such claims. As intimated above, the usual strategy adopted in the econometrics and causal modeling literature is to combine available statistical evidence with substantial amounts of prior background knowledge in an attempt to single out a particular structural model as correct.[13] By "background knowledge" I mean, for example, the sorts of considerations that justify the inclusion of certain variables in a system of equations, or that justify setting certain coefficients within those equation equal to zero, or that justify some hypothesis about causal ordering or various claims about the distribution of the error term. These are (or will include) the "identifying restrictions" used in conventional econometric practice to support the choice of one structural model over other observationally equivalent competitors. As we shall see in Sections 2.4 and 2.5 much of this background knowledge will be causal in character: it will take the form of domain specific information about causal capacities and mechanisms.

There is a final feature of autonomy that will be important for our subsequent discussion. This is that autonomy is a *relative* notion: a relationship will be autonomous or nonautonomous always relative to a particular class of changes or interventions. A relationship can be highly autonomous under some set of changes and yet can breakdown completely under some different set of changes. In understanding and assessing causal relationships we thus need to specify the changes over which the relationship is claimed to be invariant and consider whether the evidence supports that particular claim. Among relationships that possess some degree of autonomy, we can imagine a spectrum or continuum of possibilities, depending upon the size of the domain or class of changes over which the relationship is invariant. At one extreme are fundamental physical laws, which are invariant under a very large class of changes and which, if they break down at all, do so only under extreme conditions. We may contrast these with relationships that possess a much smaller degree of autonomy: relationships that are invariant or roughly so under fairly restricted class of changes, but will break down completely under many interventions outside of this class. The automotive relationship (R) described by Haavelmo is of this kind. Although less autonomous than physical laws, (R) is not entirely lacking in autonomy, since provided that the appropriate background conditions (having to do with the rest of the engine, the incline, and so on) remain constant, (R) will be invariant under many of the changes we might most naturally be interested in. For example, (R) will be stable for different levels of pressure on the pedal within some allowable range and across a number of different times and places and for many possible changes in the environment external to the car. One indication that it is appropriate to think of (R) as autonomous over a limited domain is that it can be exploited for purposes of manipulation and control: (R) is not a spurious correlation or accidental coincidence. It is just that the range of cases in which it can be so used is much narrower than the range of cases over which we expect a fundamental physical law to be invariant.

I will try to show below that the idea of a relationship that is invariant or roughly so under some limited class of changes but breaks down outside this class is a very useful tool for thinking about the status of generalizations in economics and the other social sciences and their role in supporting causal claims and providing explanations. Philosophers of science, guided largely by what they take to be the example of physics, have frequently supposed that laws of nature must underlie or somehow be associated with every true causal claim and that explanation consists in derivation from such laws. Much of the most influential recent philosophical work on these subjects has moved a surprisingly short distance away this picture.[14] However, if—as I have suggested—we think of laws as precisely formulated exceptionless generalizations that are invariant over an extremely wide class of changes, there seem to be few if any plausible candidates for laws in economics or in the other social sciences. For example, it seems likely that virtually any economic generalization purporting to describe features of the operation of contemporary market economies will break down under some possible set of governmental interventions or institutional changes. Thus even if it is true that an increase in the rate of growth in the money supply causes inflation, this causal relationship will be disrupted if, say, the government intervenes in the economy by freezing all prices at their present levels.

If constructing explanations and identifying causes requires possession of laws, it looks as though the social sciences, including economics, contain little genuine causal or explanatory knowledge. A better way of thinking about these matters, it seems to me, is to sever this supposed connection between cause and explanation on the one hand and laws on the other. My alternative suggestion, which I think fits much better with actual practice in economic and the other social sciences is this: what is crucial in identifying causal relationships and constructing explanations is not the discovery of laws per se but rather the discovery of invariant or autonomous relationships. Laws are just one kind of invariant relationship. Generalizations can be sufficiently invariant or autonomous to support causal claims and to figure in explanations even if they are not invariant enough or sufficiently precise or exceptionless to count as laws. Most of the generalizations likely to be discovered in the social sciences including, I shall suggest below, those that figure in econometric models are of this character. They are generalizations that, like the example given in previous paragraph, may be invariant or roughly so within some limited class of changes or circumstances but that we have no reason to suppose will continue to hold outside of these changes or circumstances. My view is that provided that we are within the scope of invariance of those claims we can nonetheless legitimately interpret them as causal relationships (we can, for example make use of them for purposes of manipulation and control) and we can use them to provide explanations.

2.4

I said above that on the most common and plausible understanding of econometric and causal modeling techniques, drawing reliable causal conclusions on the basis of statistical data requires that such data be combined with various kinds of domain-specific causal assumptions. In arriving at a satisfactory understanding of how causal modeling techniques work, and the kinds of causal inference they will support, we thus need an understanding of the status of these input assumptions—of what sort of causal knowledge they represent and of how they figure in causal inference. In this section I want to describe some examples of these assumptions. This will, I hope, introduce some concrete detail into what has hitherto been a rather abstract discussion. Section 2.5 will then take up, in a more general and analytical way, the question of the status and reliability of these assumptions.

I begin with an example designed to illustrate the role of assumptions about which variables it is appropriate to include in a structural model. As the expression (2.3) for the least squares estimator of B in the linear regression model (2.2) makes explicit, one can alter the coefficient of any variable in (2.2) by the addition or deletion of other variables, as long as these variables exhibit a nonzero correlation with the original variables in the equation. Given a finite body of data—and of course this is the only kind of data we will ever has access to—it is very likely that we will always be able to find such additional, correlated variables. Depending upon which variables we choose to include in the regression equation the causal conclusions that follow will vary enormously—or, to put the matter in another way, without some strong independent justification for including certain variables in the equation and not others—we will not be entitled to draw any causal conclusions.

A striking illustration of this point can be found in Edward Leamer (1983). Leamer shows that depending on which variables one includes in a regression equation one may obtain quite different results about the deterrent effect of the death penalty. For example, if one includes a suitable set of socioeconomic variables (such as unemployment rate and family size), it will follow that each additional execution *causes* about twelve additional murders. If one omits these socioeconomic variables and focuses instead mainly on variables purporting to measure extent of deterrence (such as conditional probablility of conviction for murder, given commission) one can obtain a deterrent effect of 22.56 murders *prevented* per execution. This illustrates how, by beginning with different premises about causally relevant factors, one can reach quite different conclusions about the causal effect of capital punishment on the murder rate, given the same body of statistical data.

Even when we have identified the causally relevant variables to be entered into a structural model, we need to make a further set of assumptions about which variables causally affect which others. These are assumptions about "causal ordering"—about causal direction and independence. The importance of these assumptions should be clear from our earlier observations that there are many transformations of a system of structural equations that will fail to preserve the

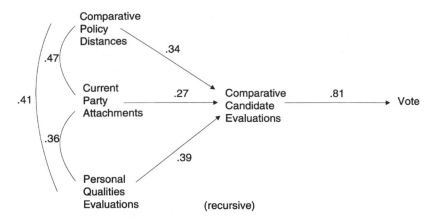

Figure 2.1. A recursive model of candidate evaluation and voting behavior

causal ordering of the original system but will nonetheless yield a system that is "observationally equivalent" to the original. As a specific illustration, consider Figures 2.1 and 2.2, which describe simplied versions of two models of candidate evaluation and voting behavior. Here the coefficients are so-called standardized regression coefficients—reflecting changes in the variables measured in standard deviation units. Although both models are estimated from largely the same statistical data, the structural coefficients vary considerably—for example, the policy position variable plays a more important role in determining candidate evaluation in the second model than in the first, and of course all of the reciprocal linkages are omitted in the first model. Indeed, the authors of the second model (Page and Jones, 1979: 106) claim that "virtually all past voting studies have erred by ignoring the possibility of reciprocal causal effects among the central variables of the electoral process." Page and Jones attempt to motivate their model by providing various theoretical extrastatistical rationales for the assumption of reciprocal causal influence. For example, in connection with the relationship between perceived policy position and voting intention they write (1979: 114)

> Clearly, citizens may tend to vote for the candidate to whom they feel closest on matters of public policy. Yet it seems to us quite possible—in fact likely—that citizens whose initial vote intentions may be formulated on non-policy grounds, can and do convince themselves that the candidates they prefer stand closer to them on the important issues. Just such a pattern is suggested by social-psychologists' studies of "projection" or selective perception"; it also follows theoretically from the rational calculus of citizens operating with less than perfect information. Lacking other evidence,

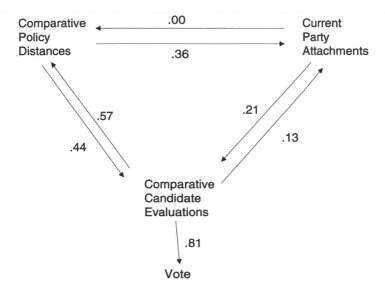

(non-recursive--after Page and Jones, but simplified)

Figure 2.2. A nonrecursive model of candidate evaluation and voting behavior (after Page and Jones but simplified)

voters might reasonably infer that a candidate who agrees with them on most matters also would agree with them on any new policy matter that comes up. Thus perceived policy distances may be consequences as well as causes of intended votes.

We thus see again that drawing causal conclusions from statistical data requires extensive use of other causally loaded assumptions and that which conclusions one gets out of such data depend very much on which such assumptions one is willing to make.

Let me conclude this section with some more general observations. In each of the above cases providing support for a particular structural model requires appealing to considerations that rule out or at least undercut the plausibility of other (perhaps observationally equivalent) competing models. As a number of writers have observed, one can think of the use of econometric techniques in nonexperimental contexts as attempts to achieve, by statistical analysis and explicit modeling and calculation, the kind of systematic elimination of alternatives that is achieved in real experiments by design (that is, by the causal structure of one's experiment). Indeed, as our remarks on the connection between causation and manipulation suggest, the whole idea of a structural model is to simulate the outcome that would be produced by a certain experimental intervention but without actually performing this intervention. While it would be unduly pessimistic to adopt the view of some commentators that it is virtually never possible to do this successfully, I do not, in my subsequent discussion, want to understate the epistemological difficulties facing such inferences in many nonexperimental social scientific contexts. At bottom, the problem is that statistical data and background causal information in such contexts are often simply not powerful enough to permit the convincing ruling out of competing alternatives that is central to successful causal inference. For example, virtually all of the independent variables considered by Leamer have (in the terminology I will adopt in Section 2.5) the capacity to affect the murder rate and are thus plausible candidates for inclusion in a regression model. Background information about capacities thus does not tell us which of the many different competing models considered by Leamer is correct. Similarly, while it is certainly possible that, as Page and Jones claim, voting intention and perceived policy position may be reciprocally causally related, it is also quite possible that causation may run only from perceived policy position to voting intention and not vice versa. The current state of social scientific knowledge does not strongly favor one of these possibilities over the other. Similar remarks can be made about other kinds of background causal assumptions that are required for model identification. For example, background knowledge will often not justify any particular set of assumptions regarding the distribution of the error term, and yet model specification is often extremely sensitive to such assumptions.[15]

The material that follows in Sections 2.5 and 2.6 is thus emphatically *not* intended to suggest that with proper attention to background causal facts about capacities and mechanisms, econometric and causal modeling techniques will always yield secure causal conclusions. I think that what Christopher Sims says about many of the identifying restrictions assumed in the estimation of large scale macroeconomic models—namely, that they are "incredible" (Sims, 1980)—holds as well for many econometric applications elsewhere in economics and the other social sciences. My object in what follows is only to argue we are *sometimes* justified in drawing causal conclusions from nonexperimental data and in understanding the conclusions themselves and the information that functions as input to them when this is the case.

2.5

I have suggested that econometric techniques take domain-specific causal information as inputs and combine these with statistical evidence to yield conclusions about causal relationships expressed in structural equations. But how should we understand the various kinds of causal information that figure in this process? What does it mean to claim that some independent variable is causally relevant to a dependent variable and thus a potential candidate for inclusion in a structural equation, and what sort of evidence would show this claim to be correct? And what about the resulting equation itself: what sort of causal knowledge does it represent? Is a correctly specified structural equation like a law of nature but, as it were, more local in scope—a sort of minilaw as several writers have suggested (see Section 2.6)? Or would it be more appropriate to adopt some quite different picture of the causal information such an equation provides?

Let me begin by summarizing the general picture defended in the next two sections. On my view, the prior causal knowledge that enters as input into a structural model is information about *causal capacities* and *mechanisms*[16]—information about the power or ability of various factors to produce characteristic effects or about the detailed behavior of such factors when they produce these effects. In social scientific contexts, claims about capacities and mechanisms rarely take the form of laws, when these are understood as quantitatively precise or exceptionless generalizations. Instead such claims are typically qualitative, exception ridden, and imprecise.[17] But although imprecise, such claims are nonetheless general in the sense that it is built into the idea of a causal capacity or mechanism that they must be capable of operating over a wide range of different circumstances and conditions. To take a natural scientific example: if smoking has the capacity to produce lung cancer and the mechanism by which it does this involves the inhalation of smoke into the lungs and resulting damage to lung tissue, then it must be the case that smoking is able to produce this effect and by means of the above mechanism for people in many different populations and background conditions. We can thus think of qualitative relationships expressed in this capacity claim as satisfying a weak sort of invariance requirement, in the sense that we may reasonably expect the capacity of smoking to produce lung cancer (and the associated mechanism by which this effect is produced) to be stable or invariant across some interesting range of changes in background conditions, even though there may not be some exact quantitative law linking smoking and lung cancer that is similarly stable or invariant. I shall argue that similar weak invariance requirements ought to be satisfied by the social scientific capacity claims that serve as inputs to structural models.

When we estimate a structural model, our interest is typically not (or not just) in establishing a capacity claim, but rather in establishing a claim about (what I shall call) the *causal role* of different factors in some particular population. Such causal role claims are claims about the *relative importance* of various factors in this population in bringing about some effect of interest. The difference between a capacity claim and a causal role claim is roughly the difference between the claim that some cause *can* produce some effect and the claim that it actually *is* at work in some particular population producing an effect of a certain magnitude. The claims that smoking plays an important role in causing lung cancer in the American population or that some proportion of lung cancer deaths in the United States populations is due to smoking or that such and such an decrease in smoking among Americans would cause such and such decrease in lung cancer are all causal role claims. Obviously, even if smoking has the capacity to cause lung cancer, it is a further what quantitative causal role smoking plays in the American population. It is questions of this latter sort that structural models are typically intended to answer.

Consider another illustration. It seems fairly uncontroversial that the death penalty has the capacity to deter murder in the sense that it can deter (and has deterred) some would-be murderers. As I see it, this capacity claim is *not* what Leamer is trying to establish when he estimates the various regression models described above. Instead this capacity claim is *assumed* when one enters a variable measuring incidence of the death penalty as an independent variable in the regression model: estimating the model doesn't provide evidence for or test this claim. The questions that Leamer attempts (unsuccessfully) to answer when he estimates his regression models are rather questions about the relative importance of the death penalty as a deterent. That is, Leamer is interested in such questions as the following: Does execution have a large or small effect on the murder rate, and can we arrive at a rough quantitative estimate of magnitude of this effect? How does the influence of the death penalty compare with other possibly relevant variables such as poverty and unemployment? These are questions about the causal role of the death penalty in a particular population. We thus need something like the distinction between capacity and role if we are to understand the difference between the causal information that serves as input to a structural model and the causal claim represented by the estimated model itself.

While capacity claims in the social sciences are typically qualitative and imprecise, when we estimate a structural equation we arrive at a quantitatively precise relationship with particular numerical values for the estimated coefficients. In my view, it is simply an empirical fact that in economics and the other social sciences the quantitative relationships embodied in structural equations often hold only for the population or particular background circumstances for which they are estimated and fail to hold exactly in other populations or background circumstances. That is, while qualitative capacity claims are often invariant or roughly so across different populations or significant changes in background conditions, the quantitative coefficients in structural models typically are not. Such coefficients are rather population specific. If smoking has the *capacity* to cause lung cancer, it should exhibit this same capacity in many different populations. However, from the fact that smoking plays a certain quantitative *causal role* in causing lung cancer in the American population, we cannot infer that it is playing a similar quantitative causal role in other populations. In view of this fact and our earlier claims about the relationship between causality and invariance, we face an obvious question about how to understand such population-specific relationships: how, if at all, are they to be interpreted causally? One possible answer (an answer implicit in a great deal of econometric discussion) is that if the coefficients and exact functional forms embodied in structural equations are not stable across different places, times, and populations, they do not tell us about genuine causal relationships at all. Rejecting this answer as embodying a requirement on causal relationships that is too demanding, I suggest instead an alternative account that allows us to regard such relationships as genuinely causal, even though population specific.

I turn now to a more detailed discussion of the notions of a causal capacity and of a causal mechanism and of how such information figures as in econometric reasoning. Section 2.6 will then take up the issue of the status of the output of such techniques—the structural equations themselves.

As I have suggested, capacity claims are claims about the power or ability of a kind of causal factor to produce a kind of effect. We make such claims when we contend, for example, that Xs are the sorts of occurrences that can cause Ys, or that Xs are "possible causes" of Ys, or that Xs are "potentially causally relevant" to Ys or that Zs and Ys are causally independent of each other or that if Xs and Ys are causally related, it must be that Xs that cause Ys and not vice versa. We appeal to such claims about capacities and mechanisms when we try to justify or criticize the causal background assumptions discussed in Section 2.4. For example, a necessary condition for it to be appropriate to include a variable representing the unemployment rate in the regression equation estimated by Leamer is that the unemployment rate have the capacity to influence the murder rate. Similarly the resolution of the disagreement between the causal model (2.16) and the competing model (2.17) will largely turn on whether is it true that, as Page and Jones claim, candidate evaluation has the capacity to affect perceived policy position or whether it is instead true, as previous theorists implicitly assumed, that candidate evaluation lacks this capacity.

While some capacities studied in the natural sciences operate in accord with precise quantitative laws, we usually do not know how to formulate social scientific capacity clims as laws. Typically such claims tell us that some causal factor can produce some effect and perhaps a bit about the conditions under which the effect will or will not be produced and about the mechanism or modus operandi (see below) by which the effect is produced, but they do not state precise conditions under which the effect will always be produced. Thus, while we know that the presence of a effective principal in a school or favorable parental attitudes can boost scholastic achievement, and that within a certain range, per pupil expenditure has little effect on achievement (for discussion, see Chubb and Moe, 1990) these claims, at least as presently formulated, are far too imprecise and exception ridden to count as laws. Similarly, while economic theory tells us that demand curves are typically (but not always) downward sloping, it will not prescribe a specific functional form or specific numerical values for the parameters characterizing the demand curve for some particular good in some particular market. It may be possible to use econometric techniques to estimate these parameters and to ascertain the shape of a particular demand curve, but—to anticipate a point to which I return in Section 2.6—there commonly will be no theoretical reason to expect this particular curve to remain stable or invariant across many plausible changes in economic conditions. In this respect, the estimated curve contrasts sharply with functional relationships in, say, physics, where it *is* plausible to expect that specific functional forms and parameters will be highly invariant—where the parameters appearing in fundamental equations are genuine constants.

Information about causal capacities (including social scientific capacities) will often include more than just the bare fact that some cause can produce a certain effect. There are usually general facts to be discovered about the conditions or circumstances in which a cause has the capacity to produce an effect and about the conditions that prevent or interfere with the production of the effect. Similarly, empirical investigation will often provide further information (again typically in a somewhat loose and gappy form) about the qualitative behavior of the cause or about the results of altering its magnitude or intensity or about the direction or sign of its effect. In addition to this, causal capacities typically also have a characteristic *mechanism* or *modus operandi*—a distinctive pathway or intervening causal chain by which they produce their effects. In the context of econometric such knowledge is quite important because it can yield important constraints on the choice of structural models: it can suggest plausible directions for elaborating such models and predictions and additional patterns we ought to expect to find in the data if the model is correct, and it can allow us to identify certain modifications in our models as involving data mining (see below) or as objectionably ad hoc. Causal arguments in the social sciences often rely heavily on complex statistical considerations and neglect the role of such qualitative considerations about the behavior or capacities and mechanisms, but I believe that this is a mistake: it is frequently the latter rather than the former that are most decisive in establishing causal conclusions. The reason for this is that detailed exploitation of qualitative information about capacities and mechanisms is often much more effective at ruling out alternative explanations than purely statistical considerations.

Given that capacity claims in the social sciences usually do not take the form of exceptionless laws, is there nonetheless a way of making sense of the idea that they invoke invariant relationships? Roughly, my idea is this: if C has the capacity to cause Es, then, we should expect an association between Cs and Es that persists over a range of changes in circumstances. Here association means simply that Es occur more frequently in the presence of Cs than in their absence, when other factors causally relevant to Es are controlled for. And what is required is not that this association always appears whenever C is introduced, but that it appears sufficiently frequently and across a sufficiently different background circumstances to rule out the possibility that the association has some other explanation besides the existence of a direct causal relationship between C and E. Such a qualitative association between C and E can be stably present across a range of different circumstances, even though the quantitative details of the association—the exact level of the frequency increase, the functional form of the association, the conditions under which it appears, and so on—vary considerably across those circumstances. The presence of such an association can either be established nonobservationally or, in appropriate cases, by experiment. When such an association is present, I shall say that the capacity claim satisfies a weak invariance requirement.

Consider, as an illustration, the much-discussed question of whether the historically observed decline in voter turnout as measured as a percent of voters among the eligible electorate could have been caused by various sorts of institutional changes (changes in registration requirements, introduction of the secret ballot, extensions of the franchise, removal of compulsory voting laws, and so on) or whether it is instead the case, as some writers have claimed, that institutional changes cannot produce a substantial decline in turnout and that the decline is due instead to a decrease in interparty competition (for discussion, see Niemi and Weisberg, 1984: 23 ff). A number of studies show that an association between such institutional changes and reduced turnout is a common pattern both across time in the case of the United States and across many different countries. For example, the introduction of registration laws and the secret ballot in the late nineteenth century United States was accompanied by a sharp decline in turnout. A decline in turnout also occurred both when the franchise was extended to women and to eighteen-year-olds. Moreover, in cases involving franchise extension the usual pattern of change is fairly robust: typically turnout is sharply reduced when an extension first occurs, gradually increases as new voters become more experienced, but fails to return completely to its previous level. In my view, this is exactly the sort of stability of behavior that makes plausible the general claim that institutional changes have the capacity to lower voter turnout. Even if there were a number of cases in which relevant institutional changes occurred and failed to reduce turnout, this capacity claim might be correct as long as the required association between institutional change and turnout is sometimes present and as long as we can rule out alternative interpretations according to which this association is noncausal (including the interpretation that ascribes the association to chance or coincidence.)

As a second illustration, consider the series of experiments carried out in different American states in the 1970s to test the effects of a negative income tax or income maintenance program on labor market participation. (Stafford, 1985). Although the effects detected differ significantly in quantitative magnitude depending on the population studied, in most cases there is a broadly similarly qualitative pattern: the negative income tax has a relatively small effect on the labor-market response of primary wage earners and a considerably more substantial effect on secondary wage earnings. In addition the availability of income support increases the rate of marital separation and divorce in some but not in all cases. In my view such experiments show convincingly that income maintenance programs have the capacity to lower labor-market participation and to increase rates of marital separation. They thus make it justifiable to construct structural models with direct causal connections between these variables.

Finally, consider the rationale for assuming a reciprocal causal influence between perceived policy position and voting intention enunciated by Page and Jones in the passage quoted on page 28. Page and Jones do not claim that there exists a credible general theory specifying conditions under which voting intention always affects perceived policy position or allowing one to predict the quantitative magnitude of this effect. What they instead claim is that voting intention has the capacity to produce this effect—a claim that they support by appeal to social-psychological experiments and by appeal to commonsense psychological generalizations, concerning the inferences that potential candidates with imperfect information "might" make. Here again, we can think of this capacity claim as embodying general causal knowledge and as satisfying a weak kind of invariance claim, in the sense that if this capacity claim is true, we may expect that voting intention can or may influence perceived policy position across some nontrivial range of circumstances or background conditions. But what is invariant in this case is not some law or precise generalization linking these variables, but rather, as I have sought to show, a claim that is far looser and more qualitative.

Some readers may worry that weak invariance is such a vague and permissive requirement that it excludes few if any capacity claims. Although I lack the space for detailed discussion, I believe that this is far from the case: in fact, many candidates for structural models rest on capacity claims that fail to be even weakly invariant. As an illustration consider Christopher Jencks's (1992) discussion of whether, in our terminology, socioeconomic inequality has the capacity to cause crime. Jencks begins by citing a well-known study (Blau and Blau, 1982) that shows a strong correlation at present between inequality and crime in 125 American cities. However, when Jencks looks at other populations, places, and times, he finds not just that the coefficients in structural models linking these variables vary (in my view, one should expect this even if inequality has the capacity to cause crime) but that there apparently isn't any qualitative association at all between inequality and crime that is stable or consistent across such changes. Thus, for example, a decrease in inequality in the United States in the 1960s was accompanied by a significant increase in crime, and an increase in inequality in the 1980s by a decline in crime. Comparisions across countries and worldwide comparisions over time in the nineteenth century also seem to show no stable pattern of response of the crime rate to inequality. Jenks (1992: 118) concludes that "Crime rates depend on how people respond to economic inequality rather than on the actual level of inequality, and these responses appear to vary with the historical circumstances—a polite way of saying that we have no clear idea what determines people's responses."

The character of Jenck's investigation is just what we would expect if to show that inequality has the capacity to cause crime, one needs to show that the relationship between these variables is weakly invariant. Finding evidence against such invariance, Jencks concludes that inequality per se does not cause crime. If this is correct, Blau and Blau's original structural model lacks the kind of capacity-based rationale it needs for the inclusion of inequality and crime. (For further discussion illustrating the nontrivial character of weak invariance, see my remarks on data mining below.)

I said above that detailed information about the mechanism or modus operandi by which a capacity operates serves as an important constraint on the choice of a structural model. Consider Eric Veblen's (1975) investigation of the effects of favorable news coverage by the Manchester *Union Leader* on New Hampshire elections during 1960–1972. Veblen begins by regressing a variable (vote difference) measuring the difference between the vote for the *Union Leader* candidate in Manchester (where the *Union Leader*'s circulation is large) and the vote for this candidate outside of the Manchester area (where the newspaper's circulation is low) against a variable (slant) designed to measure the number of favorable news stories a candidate receives. Veblen finds that the prima facie effect of favorable coverage is quite large: a change from below to above average slant is associated with a 22 percent increase in the vote for the *Union Leader*'s candidate.

However, as Achen (1982) remarks, this gross correlation is not by itself overwhelmingly persuasive. There are many other possible explanations for why favorable coverage might be correlated with vote besides the possibility that the former variable causes the latter: perhaps, for example, the direction of causation runs the other way, with the *Union Leader* endorsing only candidates who are popular in Manchester. Veblen's claim that the *Union Leader* is influencing election outcomes is convincing because he is able to show that, as Achen

(1982: 20) puts it, "the data behaves in detail as if the effect were present." This is a matter of exploiting relevant qualitative information about the behavior of capacities and mechanisms. For example, one such piece of qualitative information is this: on the basis of what we know about how newspapers influence votes we expect that if the *Union Leader*'s coverage has indeed influenced the vote, there should be a gradient effect. That is the magnitude of this influence should be larger in areas of the state where the circulation of the *Union Leader* is greater. This is just what Veblen finds: the increase in vote with favorable coverage in different areas is roughly proportional to the circulation of the *Union Leader* in those areas. Similarly, if the association is causal, it seems reasonable to expect that it will be greater in primaries, where determinants of the vote such as party identification are absent, than in the general election where such factors are known to influence voting quite strongly. It is another qualitative fact about electoral behavior "know[n] from many previous studies" that "voters in primary elections are far more volatile than those in general elections" (Achen, 1982: 20). Here again this is the pattern one finds. Moreover, the presence of this pattern helps to rule out other, competing possible explanations of the vote besides the explanation proposed by Veblen. For example, if the *Union Leader* only supports those candidates whom the electorate is predisposed to support, it is hard to understand (without a good deal of ad hoc contrivance) why the increase in vote for favored candidates should be proportional to the *Union Leader*'s circulation in different parts of the state.

As a final illustration of the role of information about capacities and mechanisms as inputs to structural equations, consider the notion of "data mining." As we have already noted, for any body of data there typically will be many variables correlated with the dependent variable of interest. If a researcher searches through this data, mechanically entering various combinations of these correlated variables into his model, he will often be able to obtain equations that fit the data very well and that "explain" (in the sense of having a high R^2 value) a high portion of the variance in the dependent variable. Nonetheless, textbooks and other methodological discussions typically sharply criticize this practice as "data mining" or "data snooping." We are told that decisions about which variables to include in the model or which causal ordering to adopt must instead be based on "substantive" or "theoretical" considerations. For example, Herbert Asher (1983: 10–11) writes that if the inclusion of variables is not based on such considerations, "the application of causal modeling techniques may become a mindless attempt to find the best fit to the data, regardless of whether the final result is substantively and theoretically plausible. One should not allow the testing and revising of models to become an enterprise completely determined by statistical results devoid of theoretical underpinning." Unfortunately, these methodological prescriptions are rarely accompanied by an account of what "substantive" or "theoretical" considerations are needed to justify decisions about the inclusion of variables or about causal order. To the extent that this issue is discussed at all, there is a widespread tendency to suppose that what is crucial is simply whether the model being tested is formulated prior to any detailed analysis of the data: on this conception, avoiding data mining is simply a matter of not "peeking" at the data before constructing one's model (see, for example, Cliff, 1983, and Zeisel, 1982, and for cogent criticism of this idea, Glymour, Scheines, Spirtes, and Kelly, 1987).

Although I lack the space for detailed discussion, I believe that this "temporal" interpretation of the prohibition against data mining is misguided: it rests on claims about the existence of a sharp distinction between discovery and justification and about the superior evidential force of temporally novel predictions that are increasingly discredited within philosophy of science. Instead, I believe that the notions of a causal capacity or mechanism form a natural framework for isolating what is objectionable about data mining. On the conception I favor to engage in data mining is to employ a model that lacks any plausible rationale in terms of what is known about capacities or mechanisms in the domain under investigation—for example, to include an independent variable in a model simply to increase fit, even when there is no independent reason to think that the variable has the capacity to affect the dependent variable. Formulating one's model after looking at the data may make it easier or more tempting to do this, but this fact about the order of formulation is certainly not sufficient and is not strictly speaking necessary for data mining to occur. As long as there is a capacity-based rationale for including a variable in one's model, or for reaching a certain conclusion about causal order, it doesn't matter whether the model is formulated after looking at the data.

Putting the matter this way suggests that what is really at issue in connection with data mining has to do with the behavior of one's model outside the present data set—that is, with whether the relationships postulated in the model are autonomous or invariant in at least the weak sense described above. To incorporate X into a model with Y as the dependent variable, there must be some reason to think that the relationship between X and Y will persist under some relevant set of changes in background conditions. To include X even when there is no reason to suppose that such an invariance requirement is satisfied is to open up the serious possibility that one's model succeeds by exploiting an accidental, noninvariant association between X and Y that just happens to be present in this particular body of data. As it is sometimes put, one "capitalizes on chance." In Stanley Lieberson's suggestive analogy (1985: 97ff), proceeding this way is like flipping a number of fair coins ten times each, noting the varying numbers of heads produced, and then finding features of the coins (such as date or discoloration) that are correlated with and thus "explain" this variation. With enough ingenuity one usually can find such correlated features, but there is no reason to think the correlations will persist in any form when the coins are flipped again under different circumstances. That is, there is no reason to think that the correlations represent relationships that are autonomous or invariant even in the weak sense appropriate to social scientific capacities. We thus see that to make sense of the notion of data mining we need something like the weak notion of invariance described above.[18]

I conclude this section by drawing attention to a further consequence of this way of looking at matters. It is perfectly possible—indeed in many cases likely—that, at a given level of analysis and among explanatory variables we are able to identify, only a limited number of such variables (or none at all) will be (even weakly) invariantly related to some dependent variable of interest. If, as I have argued, explanation has to do with finding invariant relationships, we thus may be able to explain relatively little about the behavior of the dependent variable. Of course, we can add additional variables whose inclusion is unsupported by invariant relationships into our model, but although this may yield a better fit with or a more complete or descriptively accurate representation of the data, it will also yield a less good (because misleading) explanation. We thus see how, as I suggested above, an interest in description and the accurate curve fitting is not only distinct from, but may actually conflict with, a interest in finding autonomous, explanatory relationships. Contrary to what is suggested by a great deal of social scientific practice, if we are interested in explanation, we may rationally prefer models that fit less well to better fitting competitors.

2.6

I turn now to the output of econometric techniques—the structural equations themselves. What sort of causal knowledge do they represent? I suggested above these equations provide information about the causal role of various factors in particular populations, with the coefficients in structural models serving as quantitative measures of the relative importance of these factors. In this section I want to develop this idea in more detail. For a variety of reasons, including expository convenience, I shall focus on regression equations, although I believe that much of what I have to say will transfer to the more general case of systems of simultaneous equations. I begin with a conception of the causal significance of such equations that is very different from the conception that I defend— namely, that regression equations represent laws of nature. Understanding the inadequacies of this conception will help to prepare the way for my alternative conception.

A number of writers defend such a law-based conception. For example, Herbert

Blalock (1964: 51, emphasis in original) tells us straightforwardly that *"It is the regression coefficients which give us the laws of science"* and that regression equations, when interpreted causally, "involv[e] causal laws" (1964: 44).[19] Similarly, Arnold Zellner (1984: 38) defends the view that the notion of cause in econometrics is the notion of "predictability according to a law or set of laws" with the apparent implication that when equations are interpreted structurally, they embody such a law-based conception. Related views are defended by the philosophers Paul Humphreys (1989) and Richard Scheines (1987).

While I do not wish to claim that econometric investigations never uncover quantitative relationships that are lawful (or at least stable across changes in populations and circumstances), I think that such achievements are relatively rare. The more usual pattern is that the quantitative relationships discovered in econometric investigation are far less stable. If we wish to interpret such relationships causally, we thus need to interpret the notion of a structural relationship in such a way that it does not require the kind of invariance characteristic of physical laws. While I lack the space to argue for this large claim in detail, here are some relevant considerations.

First, empirical investigation often shows that when the same linear model is estimated even on very similar but different populations, there is significant instability or nonconstancy in the coefficients. Consider the negative income tax experiments described in Section 2.5. While there is, as we noted, a broadly similar pattern of labor-market response in most of these experiments, the coefficients representing the quantitative values of these effects vary in nontrivial ways across the different populations studied. For example, estimates of uncompensated wage elasticity for the entire population of U.S. adult males range from −0.19 to −0.07 and estimates of income elasticity range from −0.29 to 0.17. Estimates of uncompensated wage elasticity from two negative income experiments (Gary, and Seattle-Denver) yield values of 0 (Gary), −0.06 (short-run, Seattle-Denver), and 0.02 (long-run, Seattle-Denver). Estimates of income elasticity from these two experiments yield values of −0.05, and −0.08, respectively. Labor-market response also varies significantly for members of different ethnic groups and varies as well with marital status and gender (for discussion see Stafford, 1985: especially 104–112).[20]

Upon reflection, this variability is not surprising. Plainly, the effect of the negative income tax on labor-market participation itself depends upon a number of background characteristics of the population under study: these have to do with general attitudes toward work, the availability of other social welfare services, the availability of various employment opportunities, the existence of certain differentiated sex roles, and so on. Similar background characteristics probably affect the divorce rate. Such characteristics vary somewhat across the different populations studied, and, for reasons I will try to make clear below, it will not always be possible to control or adjust for them by entering them explicitly into one's model as additional variables. For this reason alone, it is reasonable to expect that the estimated coefficients will also vary across different populations in the contemporary United States. Of course, they would probably vary even more if the model were estimated on culturally very different populations. No one seriously supposes that there is a law of nature relating levels of income support to labor-force participation.

Similar conclusions follow for the other examples we have considered. Veblen estimates that a move from relatively neutral to highly favorable coverage by the *Union Leader* in a primary election changes a candidate's vote by 19 percent and that in a general election the difference is 14 percent, but, as both Veblen (and Achen, 1982, commenting on Veblen) make clear, these are results about the causal influence of a particular newspaper in a particular population. It would be absurd to suppose that these quantitative estimates can play the role of constants in a universal law concerning the influence of newspapers on election results.

The variability and instability of the coefficients in typical structural models is acknowledged by a number of contemporary econometricians and causal modelers. For example, Thomas Mayer (1980) describes a number of empirical studies of consumption functions, investment functions, money supply, and demand functions, all of which seem to suggest considerable coefficient instability. While this instability derives in some cases from correctable methodological lapses, Mayer (1980: 168) acknowledges that in many cases it results from what he describes as the "more general problem that behavioral parameters are not as stable as those in the natural sciences." Failure of stability is also acknowledged in many methodological treatises. For example, Newbold and Bos (1985: 11) write

> There is a crucial distinction between much physical scientific and social scientific theory. In the physical sciences, theory often suggests the presence of *physical constants*, yet only rarely is this truly the case in the social sciences. For example, we know that if a heavy object is dropped to the ground today in Champaign, Illinois, it will accelerate at a rate of approximately 32 feet per second. Moreover, the rate of acceleration would be very nearly the same in Melbourne, Australia, today or in Champaign, Illinois in twenty years time. It is very difficult to think of any social scientific theory that strongly asserts the existence of such a physical constant. In economics, theories of the consumption function and of consumer demand are well developed. It is not, however, asserted as a result of such theories, that the marginal propensity to consume is the same in the United States as in Australia, or that the elasticity of demand for coconuts is the same in Champaign as in Melbourne.

In a similar vein Johnston (1992: 53) writes in an overview of recent work in econometrics

One impression which surfaces repeatedly in any perusal of applied work is the *fragility* of estimated relationships. By and large these relationships appear to be time specific, data specific and country or region specific. . . . Should one expect, for example, a stable demand function for apples? If so, would one expect that function to encompass the behavior of Eve in the Garden of Eden and that of her present-day sisters, such as the Newport Beach Matrons strolling the aisles of the up-scale super markets in Southern California? The question need only be posed to provide the answer.

As is well known, this sort of skepticism about the invariance of estimated econometric relationships across populations and across changes in time and place has been expressed almost from the inception of econometrics: classic sources are Keynes's famous review (1973) of Tinbergen's (1939) and Lionel Robbins (1949) discussion of Dr. Blank and the demand curve for hearing.

Finally, there is a more systematic reason for expecting that coefficients in many structural models will not have the strong kind of invariance characteristic of laws. For a causal capacity to produce some characteristic effect typically requires the presence of certain background conditions—what philosophers have called a causal field (see Mackie, 1965). To take a hackneyed example, short circuits have the capacity to cause fires, but they will do so only when oxygen is present and no automatic sprinkler system is operative. Similarly, an increase in the money supply may cause inflation, but only assuming a causal field in which free markets, various legal and governmental institutions, and so on are present.

Since the causal field contains factors that are causally relevant to the dependent variable, the question arises of how, if at all, one might represent the role of these in a structural model. In might seem that a natural approach would be to incorporate those factors from the causal field that we can explicitly identify into the model as additional independent variables and use the error term to represent the role of additional unenumerated factors from the causal field (see Hoover, 1990). However, there is a basic difficulty with this strategy: causal field variables typically do not contribute in a linear or even additive way to the value of the dependent variable. We thus cannot capture their role by treating them as additional independent variables to be added to a structural model. Nor can we summarize their influence by means of an additive error term. Instead the field variable interact with the other independent variables in the model in highly unsystematic and unpredictable ways. Many field variables are more like necessary conditions for the presence of a stable relationship between the dependent and independent variables than like additional explanatory variables that make a fixed, quantitative contribution to the dependent variable, independent of the values of the other explanatory variables. Consider, for example, the capacity of the *Union Leader* to influence election results. Obviously, endorsements by the

Union Leader or any other newspaper will produce such results only given certain background conditions—democratic institutions, an educated newspaper reading electorate, and so on. In the absence of such a causal field, newspaper endorsements would probably have very different results from those produced in New Hampshire. It is also likely that the precise quantitative relationship that Veblen finds between favorable coverage and increase in vote depends upon a variety of more specific background features of the New Hampshire context— for example, on the general political attitudes of New Hampshire voters, including their attitudes toward the *Union Leader* itself. It is easy to imagine that in another population, the effect of favorable news coverage by the largest circulation local newspaper might be quite different. For example, the dominant newspaper in Southern California, the relatively liberal *Los Angeles Times*, is strongly disliked by many voters in conservative Orange county. One would guess that editorial endorsements and favorable news coverage by this newspaper would have a quantitatively smaller positive effect—if indeed the effect is positive at all.

We do not know how to capture the influence of these various elements in the causal field by representing them as one or more independent variables to be added on to Veblen's regression equation. To capture the influence of the causal field variables in this way, we would need to suppose, not just (as Veblen argues) that, given these background elements, there is a stable approximately linear relationship between favorable coverage and increased vote in New Hampshire, but that there is a similar relationship between variables representing the presence of democratic institutions and the political attitudes of the New Hampshire electorate and increased vote, holding favorable coverage constant. This second supposition seems to be to make doubtful sense. Instead democratic institutions and political attitudes are better conceptualized as part of a set of background institutions against which favorable coverage affects vote in a stable way. To employ a familiar (but nonetheless defensible) distinction, democratic institutions and political attitudes are not in this context *causes* of the vote but rather *conditions* that must be present for favorable coverage to causally affect the vote.

Similarly, while it makes sense to ask what the effect of money supply on inflation is, given a causal field consisting of background market and governmental institutions like those in the contemporary United States, it seems doubtful that there is some constant stable effect of money supply on inflation that would be the same, even if the above causal field variables were at quite different levels. And it seems even more misguided to try to represent the role of these background institutions in terms of variables that make a stable independent causal contribution to the level of inflation, regardless of the level of other variables in the model. It seems wrong-headed to ask what effect the presence of a market economy in which the government controls the money supply has on inflation, holding everything else fixed, although it does make sense to ask what effect money supply has on inflation, assuming the existence of this institutional background.

If this is correct, it follows that we cannot treat the causal field variables as a distinct independent causal influences that enter additively into a structural model. Instead, the causal field represents the only partially articulated background conditions across which (one hopes) the structural model will be valid. Moreover, because of this, the coefficients on the other variables that we can legitimately enter into our model will reflect the influence of these causal field variables and will vary as relevant parts of the causal field vary. We should thus expect that coefficients in structural models often will be unstable across changes in the causal field and that we will be unable to extend or modify such models (for example, by adding causal field variables) in a way that will remove this instability.[21]

One possible response to this instability is that one should look elsewhere for genuinely invariant relationships. Thus it might be argued that if the effects of favorable news coverage on vote are unstable across time and place, this just shows that one needs to dig down to a deeper level to find the genuinely structural relationships that underlie and explain these more transitory patterns. Similarly, a number of writers (see Sargent, 1981; Cooley and Leroy, 1985) suggest that if the relationships in some economic model are unstable, this merely shows that genuinely invariant relationships must be sought at a different level—in a suitably developed microeconomic theory that specifies principles governing the behavior of individual agents taking only preferences and technology as given.[22]

For several reasons this response is unsatisfying. First, as we have argued, it is not clear that there are enough social scientific generalizations with the desired invariance characteristics. If we insist that all genuine causal relationships must be invariant over very wide changes in background circumstances, we run the risk of being forced to conclude that there are few if any causal relationships for social scientists to discover. Second, as a number of the above examples illustrate, many applications of econometric techniques make no pretense of uncovering relationships that are invariant in the very strong sense under discussion and yet it seems implausible to conclude, on this ground alone, that the relationships in question lack any causal significance. For example, it seems plausible that the relationship between favorable coverage by the *Union Leader* and increased vote is a causal or explanatory relationship even though the associated regression coefficients are presumably specific to a definite time and place.

Taken together, these considerations make it plausible to look for an alternative way of thinking about the significance of structural equations—an alternative that allows us to see such equations as having causal or explanatory significance, although they do not have the kind of invariance characteristic of laws of nature. The alternative conception I favor has three basic features. First, many structural models have what I shall call a contrastive structure and represent attempts to explain the actual variation of some quantity of interest in a particular population. Second, the coefficients in such models are quantitative estimates of the weight or relative importance of different causal factors contributing to this variation. Third, we can think of such models as possessing a restricted kind of invariance or autonomy, which warrants us in thinking of them as causal or explanatory.

To illustrate these features, I begin with a thought experiment due to Stanley Lieberson (1985: 99ff). Suppose that a variety of different objects (a feather, a piece of paper, a cannonball, and so on) in a population P_1 fall through the earth's atmosphere. The objects encounter different forces due to air resistance and thus take different amounts of time to reach ground, despite the fact that each is subject to the same constant gravitational force G. Time of fall is taken to be the dependent variable and is regressed against a number of candidate explanatory variables (object density and so on), including some measure of the gravitational force. Assume that the resulting equation is correctly specified: the explanatory variables are indeed causally relevant to the time of fall and the error term satisfies the usual distributional conditions. What will the results of this exercise be? Since G is constant, the regression coefficient for G will be zero. It will be the other variables in the equation, which actually vary in P_1 that will have nonzero coefficients and that will be identified as contributing to the explanation of the dependent variable.

This example illustrates what I mean by the claim that structural models typically explain actual variation in some specific population. What is explained in the above equation is not really the absolute time of fall for various objects but rather *differences* in the rate of fall for different objects. A satisfactory explanation for why some particular object takes, say, ten seconds to reach the ground surely ought to mention the gravitational force to which the object is subject but this, even though it is theoretically fundamental, is omitted from the regression equation. The regression equation identifies factors such as surface area that vary for different objects in P_1, and what it claims is that these variations partly explain the differences in time of fall for different objects in P_1. That is, the equation really addresses a kind of comparative or contrastive question—roughly, something like this: given that all of the objects are subject to a common set of background conditions (a constant gravitational force and so on), why do some objects like feathers fall more slowly than others like common ball? The answer provided by the equation presupposes the existence of this common background condition and addresses itself to explaining the variation in the population that occurs given the condition, rather than to explaining the occurrence of the condition itself.[23]

We can further bring out what is distinctive about this form of explanation by considering a particular falling feather F in P_1. There will, of course, be a detailed causal story about why F falls as it does, which will mention the gravitational force incident on the F the role of air resistance and so on. This story will be, in Elliott Sober's (1988) useful terminology, "local": it will have to do just with the forces incident on F and not with what happens to other objects in P_1. This story will be the same regardless of the population to which F belongs and regardless of the variation that happens to occur elsewhere in P_1.

By contrast, the regression equation itself and the sort of explanation it provides will be highly sensitive to nonlocal factors having to do with what is happening elsewhere in the population of which F is a member. Consider a different population P_2 consisting entirely of falling feathers, all similar to F, but falling in gravitational fields of different strength. If we estimate the same regression equation on P_2 the coefficient for G will be nonzero, and gravity will emerge as a rather important cause of variation in time of fall in P_2 even though the local causal story about F will be the same whether it belongs to P_1 or P_2. We can think this shift in population from P_1 to P_2 as amounting to a shift in contrastive focus—instead of asking why F falls at a different rate from other objects in P_1 subjected to the same gravitational field, we now ask, in estimating the regression equation on P_2, the quite different question of why F falls at a different rate from other objects in P_2 that are subject to varying gravitational fields. Not surprisingly, we find this different question demands a different explanation by way of answer. This example illustrates how the notion of causal importance is a population-relative notion: how important or influential a cause is will depend upon the range of variation we wish to use the cause to account for, and this in turn will be determined by the population in which we are interested. If—as I have been trying to argue—regression coefficients are measures of causal importance, it should be either surprising or disturbing that they similarly vary from population to population and are not fixed as a matter of law.

For Lieberson, these logically distinctive features of regression techniques illustrate their superficiality and methodological limitations. Clearly, gravitational force is the most theoretically fundamental factor at work in P_1 and perhaps the only factor whose causal contribution we know how to describe by means a law, yet its role is entirely missed when we estimate the regression equation on P_1. A better methodological strategy, according to Lieberson, would be to look for analogues of the gravitational force law in the social world. That is, one should look for the fundamental factors and laws governing social structures and social change, recognizing that because these will make the same unvarying contribution to all social structures, they may account for little of the actual variation in those structures and may not be discoverable by the use of regression techniques. But whether this is good advice depends on what sorts of questions we are interested in (what we want to explain) and on whether such fundamental lawful relationships are actually there to be discovered. I have already argued that it is unlikely that we will find social scientific anologues to the gravitational force in social science. I think that it is also true (no doubt in part for this reason) that in the social sciences we are often most interested in explaining actual change or variation in the sense illustrated by the above example. We are interested, for example, in why some candidates receive more votes than others, why some schools are more effective at educating than others, why the murder rate is higher in some states than others, and so on. Given these interests and the difficulty of discovering fundamental lawful relationships, the project of trying to explain actual variation does not seem to be misguided. It is this project and not the discovery of social laws to which regression techniques are addressed.

We can further explore what is involved in the idea of explaining actual variation by considering an additional example, also due to Lieberson (1985: 110ff). Suppose that a researcher regresses a variable measuring rates of criminal violence in major U.S. cities against a measure of socioeconomic inequality for those cities and finds a positive coefficient. That is, when one compares American cities, the crime rate is systemically higher in cities with greater inequality. Assuming for the sake of argument (contrary to what our discussion on p. 36 appears to suggest) that inequality has the capacity to cause violence and that the regression equation is otherwise correctly specified, we might think of this result as providing at least a partial explanation of the variation in the crime rate (why the crime rate is higher in some cities than others) in terms of variation in the level of inequality across cities. It seems clear, however, that both the explanans and explanandum of this explanation are tied to a particular population (U.S. cities). Even if it is correct that variations in the level of inequality partially explain variations in the crime rate across American cities, it does not follow that variations in the level of inequality will play a similar causal role in explaining variations in the crime rate across the units in some different population.

To make the point vivid, suppose with Lieberson that our researcher now attempts to explain variations in the crime rate across cities in a country that is very different from the contemporary United States (such as contemporary Iran) or that he attempts to explain variations in the crime rate across different countries (such as the United States, Japan, and Iran). Lieberson claims (and it seems intuitively clear) that a regression of crime rate against socioeconomic inequality should not be expected to yield the same results for these new populations as the original regression estimated on U.S. cities. It may be that although there is a substantial positive relationship between crime and inequality in Iran, the numerical value of the regression coefficient will be quite different from the coefficient for U.S. cities. Or it may be that there is little correlation between crime and inequality in Iran, and that by far the most important variables in explaining variations in crime across Iranian cities are ethnic or cultural or religious differences. A similar result is even more likely in the case of the comparison across countries envisioned above.

As Lieberson notes, we would expect these different regressions to give identical answers only if we believe these is no nation effect per se—no unique effect associated with the United States, Iran, or any other country. The fact that no researcher seriously supposes that he could satisfactorily explain variations in the level of violence among U.S. cities or between the United States and Iran by carrying out an investigation confined just to Iranian cities is an indication that no one really expects the regression coefficient to be stable across all of these different populations. Here again, I want to suggest that there is nothing very mysterious or surprising about this conclusion. When—as we were supposing—variations in the level of inequality contribute to variations in the crime rate across different American cities, they do so against the background of a causal field F that contains many other conditions that we know are relevant to the level of crime in the United States. (These conditions are complex and multifaceted. They are in part cultural: American attitudes toward violence are different than those of inhabitants of other countries. In part, they have to do with easy availability of guns in the United States, and so on.) If the causal field F were different, the effect of inequality on violence might well be different. Thus, the coefficient that results from regressing crime rate against inequality for American cities reflects the fact that the regression is being carried out in a population in which the particular causal field F is present—what the coefficient reflects is not some fixed contribution of inequality to violence that is invariant across all possible causal fields, in the manner of a physical constant, but (at best) the distinctive effect of inequality in F.

Reverting to our earlier notion that structural models explain contrasts or differences, assuming the presence of a certain stable background, we can say that the original regression equation tells us about the effect of inequality on crime assuming or presupposing the presence of the causal field F. The equation thus represents an attempt to answer something like the following question: assuming the presence of this same field F in all American cities, why do these cities nonetheless differ in crime rate, and how much, if any, of this difference can be attributed to differences in the level of inequality? Since we know that the causal field for Iran is very different from F (different cultural attitudes toward violence and so on), it is hardly surprising that the corresponding question for Iran (that is, what accounts for the variations in crime in different Iranian cities) and the corresponding regression of crime rate on inequality should produce a quite different result.

We thus see that there is a close interconnection among all of the themes explored in this section. The plausibility of the suggestion that regression equations explain actual variation in particular populations is linked to the idea that such equations presuppose a particular causal field associated with that population. This in turn is closely linked to the idea that the regression coefficients themselves reflect the influence of such particular fields and should not be expected to be stable across different fields or populations. Alternatively, we can think of the idea of explaining variation given a causal field as an attempt to isolate a notion of explanation appropriate to regression equations, given that the coefficients of such equations cannot be expected to be stable or invariant across many changes in population or background conditions.

I began this essay by asserting close connection between (a) causal or explanatory relationships and (b) relationships that are invariant or autonomous and that can be exploited for purposes of manipulation and control. We have seen, however, that the coefficients in many structural equations in the social sciences are not invariant across (extensive) changes in background conditions or populations. If such equations nonetheless convey causal information and provide explanations, then we must either abandon the connection between (a) and (b) or find some alternative way of thinking about invariance that allows us to see such equations as satisfying an invariance condition. I want to conclude, not very surprisingly, by advocating the second alternative. Recall that invariance and autonomy are relative notions: a relationship can be invariant with respect to one class of changes but not with respect to another class and can be locally stable under a restricted set of background conditions and break down very sharply outside of this set. My suggestion is that we should think of the coefficients in structural models as embodying such local or population-bound invariant relationships—relationships that are stable with respect to certain changes within a particular population or causal field, but that need not remain stable outside of these. Such models will identify relationships that can be used for manipulation or control (and thus respect the demands imposed by a manipulability theory of causation), but the circumstances over which they are so usable will be restricted to a particular population or set of background conditions.

Consider a bivariate regression equation

$$Y = aX + U \tag{2.16}$$

estimated on a population P with background causal field F. I suggest that if (2.16) represents a genuine causal relationship, then it must be the case that changing X for various particular individuals within P should not disturb the relationship represented by (2.16)—that is, the result of changing X by ΔX for some randomly selected individual i should genuinely be that the expected value of Y for that individual changes by $a \Delta X$. The coefficient in (2.16) thus should be invariant under changes in the value of X and in the value of U, as long as one remains within F and P. Thus, if, for example, the regression relating crime and inequality in American cities is genuinely causal, altering the level of inequality in any particular city in the American population should not by itself alter the relationship expressed in the equation, as long as we remain within the assumed causal field. Other things being equal, this intervention instead should change the expected value for the crime rate. This stability and the possibility of intervention it brings may disappear if we move to another population or disturb the causal field on which the relationship depends, but as long as we don't do this, the relationship ought to be invariant in the way described.

As these remarks suggest, one central problem with many structural models is that, even in the absence of the more obvious kinds of specification error, the scope of invariance of such models is often unknown. Because we are unable to explicitly model the influence of the various conditions impounded in the causal field and because the structural coefficients will be sensitive, in unknown ways, to these influences, we often are unable to identify just when a change in causal field will lead a structural model to break down. As a result the causal interpretation of the model will be ambiguous. The relationship between inequality and crime described above provides one illustration of this. For another, consider the relationship (V) between news coverage and the *Union Leader* vote discovered by Veblen. Although it is plausible that the relationship (V) is causal, there are important limitations on the scope of invariance of V, and Veblen's investigation leaves these unknown. For example, it seems plausible that various socioeconomic events such as a large-scale depression might sharply shift voter's political preferences so as to disrupt V. Similarly, if the *Union Leader* began endorsing liberal Democrats, it seems unlikely this would cause an increase in their votes in accordance with V. But while it thus seems apparent that V depends on various background conditions, Veblen's analysis tells us little about the details of this dependence. Because the range of condition over which V is invariant is left under, the causal claim represented by V is also left unclear. To clarify the meaning of V we would need to specify the scope of its invariance more precisely or—what comes to the same thing—spell out in more detail the hypothetical manipulations V will or will not support. I believe that a similar sort of sensitivity to unknown background conditions is typically present when structural models are used in the social sciences, and this is one reason that, even when such models can be interpreted causally, one needs to exercise care in deriving policy recommendations from them.[24]

My general conclusion, then, is that structural models do sometimes tell us about causal relationships, even when those relationships lack the kind of invariance characteristic of physical laws. Such models convey causal information because (or to the extent that) they identify relationships that are stable under restricted classes of changes and that will support limited interventions. Nonetheless the causal information so conveyed is typically vague because the scope of invariance of such models is left imprecise. One of the virtues of the account of causation sketched in this chapter is that is allows us both to appreciate the sense in which linear models are causally interpretable and to recognize some of the limitations of the causal knowledge such models provide.[25]

Notes

1. I claim no originality at all for the material in this section, which, in my view, merely restates ideas that have long been prominent in econometric discussion. Nonetheless the picture of econometric techniques that follows is, I believe, interestingly different, at least in emphasis from the conceptions defended in other recent philosophical treatments (for relevant discussion see, for example, Cartwright, 1989; Glymour, Scheines, Spirtes, and Kelly, 1987; Humphreys, 1989). The writer whose views about the significance of autonomy and its connection to causality are closest to my own is probably Kevin Hoover. I have learned a great deal from the material on econometrics in his recent papers (1990, 1991) and from his book on macro economics (1988). A superb historical study of the notion of autonomy, together with references to more recent related ideas, like the notion of "super exogeneity" (Engle, Hendry, and Richard, 1983) and the notion of "deep parameters" (Cooley and LeRoy, 1985) can be found in Alderich (1989). A philosophically sensitive discussion can also be found in Duncan (1975).

Finally, I should forthrightly acknowledge the obvious point (which can hardly escape the reader's attention) that the examples I choose to illustrate the application of econometric techniques derive largely from sociology and political science rather than economics. I wish that there was some intellectually reputable explanation for this, but I am afraid it is due to simple ignorance of economic theory.

2. This association of autonomous relationships with those that can be used to provide explanations is explicit in Haavelmo and other early writers. For example, Haavelmo (1944: 27, emphasis in original) claims that when one sets up a simultaneous system of general autonomous relationships like those in general equilibrium theory: "We conceive of a *wider set of possibilities* that might correspond to reality, were it ruled by one of the relations only. The simultaneous system of relations gives us an *explanation* of the fact that out of this enormous set of possibilities only one particular one actually emerges." Similarly, Frisch (1938: 17, emphasis in original, quoted in Alderich, 1989) writes that "The higher this degree of autonomy the more *fundamental* is the equation, the deeper is the insight which it gives us into the way in which the system functions, in short the nearer it comes to being a *real explanation*. Such relations are the essence of 'theory.'" For a more general philosophical defense of this idea, which ties explanation in general (and not just causation) to the discovery of relationships that are invariant and hence relevant to manipulation, see Woodward (forthcoming c).

3. The general idea that lawful and causal relationships must be invariant has, however, received significant philosophical attention. Space precludes a detailed discussion, but a classic source is Skyrms (1980). In particular, Skyrms's notion of resiliency is in many respects similar to Haavelmo's

notion of autonomy, although the former is developed within a subjective probability framework that Haavelmo does not share. For brief additional discussion and some references, see Woodward (1992), and for a striking application of the general idea that causal relations must be invariant relations see Arntzenius (1990).

4. Recent philosophical discussion of the manipulability theory has tended to be unsympathetic. This assessment contrasts sharply with the views of econometricians and statisticians, who explicitly endorse the manipulability conception and have found it analytically useful (see, for example, Lieberson, 1985; Hoover, 1988; Holland, 1985). As should be apparent from my remarks above, I side with the latter but lack the space to defend this position here.

5. This connection between invariance, manipulability and causation is explicitly noted in Hoover (1988: 173).

6. A natural question—put to me by Dan Little—is what this talk of intervening to change coefficients (which is very common in discussions of structural equations; see, e.g., Duncan, 1975) means? Are not the coefficients supposed to be constants? Perhaps Haavelmo's automotive analogy can be helpful here. Think of the coefficients as representing the operating characteristics or the causal structure of different parts of the car. Particular values for various coefficients thus characterize the functioning of the carburetor, fuel pump, and so on in a particular car. As long as one confines oneself to just varying the depression of the gas pedal, all the coefficients remain unchanged. But one can also intervene in the internal mechanism of the car to change coefficients individually: one might clean the carburetor, cause or repair a leak in the fuel pump, and so on. The car thus has, at any given time, a determinate causal structure—represented by a set of structural equations with determinate coefficients—but we nonetheless can intervene to change individual features of this causal structure. As I put it below, this causal structure and the coefficients associated with it are invariant under certain kinds of changes, but not others. Incidentally, the fact that such talk of changing coefficients is assumed to be intelligible in econometric discussion is additional evidence against the thesis, rejected in Section VI, that structural equations represent laws of nature.

7. Still another way of putting the motivation for associating causal interpretability and autonomy in the way I have described is this: If, the relation between X_3 and X_1 in the first equation in (2.5) is a genuine causal relationship and describes a real causal mechanism, then it should make sense to think in terms of doing something that affects just this relationship or mechanism and none of the other relationships specified in (2.5). Altering b_{31} alone should be an allowable hypothetical experiment, even if it is not one that we may in fact be able to carry out, and the result of this experiment should not depend upon what causal relationships hold elsewhere in the system: causal relationships should be in this sense modular or context—independent rather than dependent in an indeterminate and holistic way on the other relationships and mechanisms holding elsewhere in the system.

8. See, for example, Alderich (1989).

9. The distinction between the two counterfactuals (2.9) and (2.10) and the relevance of the latter to the assessment of lawfulness is emphasized in Aardon Lyon's unjustly neglected work (1977). For further discussion see Woodward (1992).

10. I recognize that these remarks raise a number of complex issues about the truth conditions for counterfactual conditionals that I lack the space to explore here. I hope to discuss them more systematically in a later paper.

11. One may distinguish two different notions of "observational equivalence" that have figured prominently in recent philosophical discussion. According to the first conception, two theories are "observationally equivalent₁," if they make exactly the same predictions about what will be observed under all physically possible circumstances. This conception has figured importantly in recent philosophy of physics: for example, it is in this sense that it is frequently claimed that certain theories that postulate a flat spacetime and a separate gravitational potential are "observationally equivalent"

to theories that do not postulate a separate gravitational potential but rather build the potential into the curvature of spacetime.

The second conception (perhaps less frequently described as a matter of observational equivalence but nonetheless arguably classifiable under that rubric) is this: Suppose one has a fixed mechanism that generates a stream of observational data and two competing hypotheses H_1 and H_2 concerning what that data will be like. If, because of an observer's present statiotemporal location, data have not yet been generated that will distinguish which of H_1 or H_2 is correct, but if such data eventually will be generated by the mechanism in question (even without any changes in the mechanism or interventions by the observer), then there is a sense in which H_1 and H_2 are at present "observationally equivalent" for that observer. It is in this sense that it is sometimes claimed that the hypothesis that all diamonds are grue and the hypothesis that all diamonds are green are "observationally equivalent." Let us call this conception "observational equivalence$_2$." Although the green and grue hypotheses are "observationally equivalent$_2$," they certainly make different predictions about what would be observed in some physically possible circumstances and hence are not observationally equivalent$_1$: indeed all the observer has to do is wait and she will have access to the observations that will observationally distinguish them.

The sense in which different structural models with the same reduced form equations are "observationally equivalent" is different from either of the two previous senses. On the one hand, models like (2.5) and (2.6) are clearly not observationally equivalent$_1$. As we have noted, if an experimenter intervenes in such a way as to alter b_{31}, (2.5) and (2.6) certainly make different predictions about what will be observed. More generally (2.5) and (2.6) make different predictions about what will be observed if the mechanism generating the data for these models changes in various ways. On the other hand, (2.5) and (2.6) are also not observationally equivalent$_2$. Unlike the case of green and grue, if no change occurs in the mechanism generating the data for (2.5) and (2.6), no observations will be produced that will enable us to distinguish between them. As I say above, the point at which (2.5) and (2.6) differ is in their modal or subjunctive content. They don't necessarily make different predictions about what *will* happen (this depends on whether the data-generating mechanism happens to change). They rather differ in what they predict about that would happen if various possible changes were to occur in the data-generating mechanism. The green and grue hypotheses, by contrast, do differ about what will happen. Let us call this third notion "observational equivalence$_3$." The difference between observational equivalence$_2$ and observational equivalence$_3$ corresponds to the difference between the two counterfactual tests (2.9) and (2.10) distinguished on p. 20 above. It is observational equivalence$_3$ which is distinctively at issue when one makes causal inferences. This notion deserves more attention from philosophers than it has hitherto received. For additional discussion, see Woodward (1992).

12. Many philosophers will resist these claims. I acknowledge that they raise a number of complex issues, concerning the interpretation of probability and its relation to causation that I lack the space to discuss. But the fact that a number of different structural models, embodying different claims about which relationships are invariant, are consistent with the same probability distribution among measured variables is a prima facie reason for thinking that invariance is not going to be definable in terms of facts about conditional probabilities, partial correlations, and the like. To put this in the context of standard probabilistic theories of causation: to characterize causation one needs the notion of stable or invariant conditional probabilities, not just conditional probabilities.

13. This is certainly not the only possible strategy for resolving the underdetermination problem. An alternative strategy is not to rely on specific background knowledge, but instead on some highly general principle of inductive inference or theory—choice that, among all those models that reproduce the observed data and are "empirically adequate," selects one or some small set of such models as best. For example, the selected model(s) might be the simplest model(s) according to some general criterion of simplicity or the model (or models) that best explains the observed data best

according to some general theory of explanation. I take this to be essentially the strategy adopted by the philosopher Clark Glymour and his collaborators in their book *Discovering Causal Structure* (1987). A related strategy is to rely on a few highly general domain-independent principles connecting statistical information and causal claims. This strategy is pursued by Spirtes, Glymour and Scheines in their impressive recent book (1993) and also by the computer scientist Judea Pearl in his work on Bayesian belief networks (1989). Space preludes discussion of such approaches, but if we accept the idea that causal relationships are structural or autonomous relationships in the sense described above, the obvious question to ask about these approaches is what grounds we have for believing that the inductive inference procedures they advocate will reliably select (according to some reasonable criterion of reliability), from the class of empirically adequate models, the model that imbodies the true structural relationships in the domain under investigation or that the true structural model should be among those selected if several models are selected. That is, they face the question of why some model, that is simplest according to their favored conception of simplicity or some model that explains the best according to their favored conception of explanation or some model that satisfies the general principles connecting causes and statistics should be the one that in fact captures the autonomous or invariant relationships in the domain under investigation. For additional discussion of this point in connection with Spirtes, Glymour and Scheines, 1993, see Woodward forthcoming a. I might add that lurking in the background here is a very important and much more general question about science. Does successful inductive inference primarily work by exploiting highly general domain independent methodological rules governing theory choice or do such principles play a very limited role, with the constraints on theory—choice instead being provided by large amounts of domain specific background knowledge? Like Glymour and Pearl, traditional philosophy of science opts for the former alternative. I favor the latter.

14. For example, many probabilistic theories of causation (see Humphreys, 1989) in effect require that causes increase the probability of their effects in a lawlike manner. See Woodward (1994) for discussion.

15. While background knowledge or theory may provide some (albeit incomplete) guidance about which variables to include and about causal ordering, the way that the error terms in a structural model happen to be distributed is an idiosyncratic consequence of the totality of causal factors that happen to be at work in the relevant population. At least in many cases this distribution is not fixed by general theoretical considerations. As Mason (1991: 339) puts it, "Social Scientists rarely, if ever, have theory for the stochastic parts of the specification." Anyone with more than a passing familiarity with the econometric and causal modeling literature will recognize the correctness of the complaints of critics (see Freedman, 1991) that standard textbook conditions regarding the error term (absence of correlation with explanatory variables, homoscedascity, and so on) are often simply assumed without serious argument or evidence and that causal conclusions are often sensitive to the violation of such assumptions.

16. For a more detailed discussion of the notion of a causal capacity, see Woodward (1993a).

17. The idea that general relationships in the social sciences are likely to be qualitative and exception ridden, rather than quantitatively precise and exceptionless, is defended at some length in Achen (1982). Achen's discussion has been an important stimulus for the ideas in this section.

18. Berk (1991: 320) writes, "A good theory and its implied causal model should be essentially reproducible in a wide variety of settings with a wide variety of subjects." My view is that whether this is correct depends crucially on the way in which the notion of reproducibility is understood. If we demand that the quantitative values of the coefficients in a structural model be stable across different populations or background conditions, then (for reasons I describe in Section 2.6), we will reject many legitimate structural models as unreproducible. A better way of formulating the demand for reproducibility is in terms of the notion of weak invariance. On this conception, a model is reproducible if the qualitative mechanisms or capacities it invokes are operative across a range of

different circumstances. In the case of Veblen's study, for example, we should not demand that the quantitative values of the structural coefficients be reproducible—that the effect of editorial slant on vote gain be the same of different newspapers in different settings or even that this effect should be exactly the same in the case of the *Union Leader* from election to election. Instead, the kind of reproducability we should expect to find, if the relationship described by Veblen is genuinely causal, is that capacities and mechanisms Veblen invokes should exhibit qualitatively similar behavior across a range of similar settings and populations. That is, support for Veblen's analysis will take the form of evidence that other newspapers can and do substantially influence the vote in other circumstances, that their influence has been greater in primaries and so on.

19. In a more recent discussion Blalock (1991: 330) adopts a quite different view of the status of regression coefficients which is much closer to the position advocated below: "The 'constants' appearing in regression equations are much more realistically considered as variables, particularly as one attempts to increase the scope of one's generalizations."

20. In an extremely interesting recent paper, Nancy Cartwright (1991) also makes use of a group of studies (apparently identical in a number of cases to those cited by Stafford) of labor market behavior among U.S. adult males to make a different but perhaps related point about coefficient instability. Cartwright is struck by the fact that when different econometricians attempt to estimate the same parameters on what is apparently the same population (in her example, income and wage elasticities estimated on the entire U.S. male population), they obtain values that while qualitatively similar, nonetheless differ quantitatively in substantial ways. These differences result from different choices for functional forms, different empirical measures for key variables, and so on. This coefficient variability across different models estimated on the same population is different from the coefficient variability across populations that I emphasize above. I regret that I lack the space to explore the relationship between Cartwright's discussion and my own.

21. To reiterate a point made in passing above: It is no part of my argument that the coefficients in structural models are *never* invariant across significant changes in background conditions. My point is rather than in many cases they are not so invariant and that it makes sense to ask what causal interpretation, if any, can be given to a structural model in such cases. The remarks that follow are intended to apply to (illustrate characteristic features of) structural models with noninvariant coefficients.

22. For an illustration of this dialectic, see the well-known exchange between Koopmans (1947) and Vining (1949). Koopmans critizes the statistical practices of the National Bureau Economic Research regarding the modeling of business cycles on the grounds that they are not motivated or informed by microeconomic relationships that are truly invariant across large changes in background conditions. Vining objects that no one has discovered plausible examples of such relationships. I do not think that the dialectical situation is fundamentally different today.

23. Kevin Hoover discusses this example extensively in his comments, and, while an endnote is obviously an inappropriate place to try to respond, several brief clarificatory remarks are in order. Hoover points out that if one tries to estimate an equation of form (2.4) $T = \alpha + \beta D + \gamma G + \varepsilon$, where G measures the gravitational force on each falling object and G is indeed constant (and there is no measurement error in G), then it is false that, as I claim in the text above, γ will be zero. Instead, the coefficient γ will be undefined because the $X X^{-1}$ matrix in the coefficient estimator cannot be inverted. While Hoover is clearly correct about this, I want to make it clear that this mistake is entirely my own and not, as might be supposed from my discussion, Stanley Lieberson's. Lieberson's discussion makes no reference to estimating a specific regression equation such as (2.4) but merely notes that conventional causal modeling techniques are in effect techniques for identifying factors that explain variation or differences. Lieberson points out that if it should turn out that, say, differences in the density and shape of objects fully account for all of the differences between velocity of fall of different objects, a researcher using standard causal modeling techniques will be fully

satisfied "because all of the differences among the objects under study have been accounted for." There thus will be no motivation for introducing a measure of gravitational force like G into the analysis, since G, as a constant, will be of no help in accounting for additional variation in time of fall. As remarked above, Lieberson (1985: 100) takes this to be a defect of causal modeling techniques; he objects that "there must be something faulty with our procedures if we can approach such a problem without even considering gravity itself."

While my claim that $\gamma = 0$ is mistaken, it seems to me that the more general claim made by both Lieberson and me that causal modeling techniques, including regression techniques when interpreted causally, are explanations of differences is unaffected by this mistake. Hoover's conclusion that with no measurement error in G, the regression (2.4) can't be run, is still a reason, although a different reason from the one I give in the text above, for thinking that regression techniques are inappropriate for identifying the causal or explanatory significance of a constant factor like G and a reason for thinking that such techniques are best construed as attempts to explain contrasts in the value of the dependent variable in the sense claimed in my text. (Lieberson and I, of course, take different views of the value of this explanatory project.)

Hoover apparently wishes to deny that regression and other causal modeling techniques are ever properly contrued as providing explanations. This is an issue that can be addressed only in the context of a general theory of explanation. Since I obviously can't provide such a theory here, let me just reaffirm that on my view there is a perfectly natural and straightforward sense of explanation in which, assuming that the relevant regression equations are correctly specified, differences in density help to explain differences in rates of fall in the above example, and differences in favorable editorial coverage of candidates by the *Union Leader* help to explain differences in the votes those candidates receive. I agree with Hoover that regression techniques are sometimes used in a nonexplanatory way simply to observe or detect phenomena that then become candidates for theoretical explanation, but often, as in the Veblen example, the clear intention of those who use such techniques is to provide explanations. For a conception of explanation that can be naturally extended to cover such cases, see Woodward (1979, 1984, forthcoming b).

24. If I have understood him correctly, the idea that regression coefficients have an implicit contrastive structure is suggested in Holland (1985). I do not know, however, whether he would agree with the way I have tried to unpack this idea. Achen (1982) also argues that regression equations are attempts to measure relative causal importance, although I believe that his account of what this means is different from mine. For additional discussion of the notion of constrastive explanation see Woodward (1984) and the references therein.

25. In several recent papers, Kevin Hoover (1990, 1991) describes an ingenious methodology for testing causal claims that relies on facts about the stability of coefficients in regression equations under various sorts of interventions and then applies this methodology to testing claims about the causal direction between money and prices. Suppose that there is a observed association between money (M) and prices (P). Suppose also that there are interventions in the process generating this association and that we can identify these as either interventions in the process that determines M or in the process that determines P. Hoover argues that if prices causes money, then one would expect the coefficient in a (correctly specified) regression of money against prices to be stable under interventions in the price-determination process but not under interventions in the money-determination process. One would expect just the reverse pattern of stability if money causes prices. Using this methodology, Hoover (1991: 419) arrives at what he describes as a "somewhat surprising result: the evidence supports the view that prices cause money and not that money causes prices." What is the relationship between Hoover's methodology and the skepticism about stability of regression coefficients expressed in my discussion above? I fully agree that *if* one is able to unambiguously identify interventions in the processes that determine M and P and no other interventions occur during the period examined that affect the relationship between M and P (and there is no specification error),

then this procedure can indeed be used to disambiguate the causal direction between M and P. But while I am not competent to assess the evidence in the particular example at hand, I think that if my discussion above is correct, we ought to be sceptical about whether the antecedent of the above conditional is often satisfied in social scientific contexts. Instead a very common situation will be this: X_1 causes Y at least within a certain population on set of background conditions, but when one regresses Y against X_1 using data from a extended period of time or from larger populations, there is considerable coefficient instability because of changes in the causal field or background conditions against which X_1 causes Y—changes that we may not be able to recognize or to describe in a systematic way. In such cases requiring coefficient stability under changes in the process by which X_1 is determined may give a misleading result about whether X_1 causes Y. In the language of this chapter it seems perfectly possible that money has the capacity to cause (and often does cause) prices, even though the causal role (and hence the coefficients in a regression) of money on prices varies over time and across place, depending on changes in institutional framework and so on. Such instability is not by itself evidence against the claim that causation runs from money to prices.

References

Achen, C. (1982). *Interpreting and Using Regression*. Beverly Hills: Sage Publications.

Alderich, J. (1989). "Autonomy." In N. de Marchi and C. Gilbert (eds.), *History and Methodology of Econometrics*. Oxford: Oxford University Press.

Arntzenius, F. (1990). "Physics and Common Causes." *Synthese* 82, 77–96.

Asher, H. (1983). *Causal Modeling*. Beverly Hills: Sage Publications.

Berk, R. (1991). "Toward a Methodology for Mere Mortals." *Sociological Methoodology*, 315–324.

Blalock, H. (1964). *Causal Inference in Non-Experimental Research*. Chapel Hill: University of North Carolina Press.

———. (1991). "Are There Really Constructive Alternatives to Causal Modeling?" *Sociological Methodology*, 325–336.

Blau, J. and Blau, P. (1982). "The Cost of Inequality: Metropolitan Structure and Violent Crime." *American Sociological Review* 47, 114–129.

Cartwright, N. (1989). *Nature's Capacities and their Measurement*. Oxford: Oxford University Press.

———. (1991). "Replicability, Reproducibility and Robustness: Comments on Harry Collins." *History of Political Economy* 23, 143–155.

Chubb, J., and T. Moe. (1990). *Politics, Markets and America's Schools*. Washington, DC: Brookings.

Cliff, N. (1983). "Some Cautions Concerning the Application of Causal Modeling Methods." *Multivariate Behavioral Rsearch* 18, 115–126.

Cooley, T., and S. LeRoy. (1985). "Atheoretical Macroeconomics: A Critique." *Journal of Monetary Economics* 16, 165–178.

Cornfield et al. (1959). "Smoking and Lung Cancer: Recent Evidence and a Discussion of some Questions." *Journal of the National Cancer Institute* 22, 173–203.

Duncan, O. (1975). *Introduction to Structural Equation Models*. New York: Academic Press.

Eatwell, J., M. Milgate, and P. Newman. (1990). *Econometrics*. New York: Norton. First published in *The New Palgrave: A Dictionary of Economics*.

Engle, R. F., D. R., Hendry, and F. J-F. Richard. (1983). "Exogeneity." *Econometrica* 51, 277–304.

Fox, J. (1984). *Linear Statistical Models and Related Methods*. New York: John Wiley.

Freedman, P. (1991). "Statistical Models and Shoe Leather." *Sociological Methodology*, 291–314.

Frisch, R. (1938). "Statistical Versus Theoretical Relations in Economic Macrodynamics." Mimeo dated July 1938. In R. Frisch (ed.), (1948), *Autonomy of Economic Relations*, collection of mimeo articles issued by the University of Oslo.

Gasking, D. (1955). "Causation and Recipes." *Mind* 64, 474–487.

Glymour, C., R. Scheines, P. Spirtes, and K. Kelly. (1987). *Discovering Causal Structure*. Orando: Academic Press.

Granger, C. W. J. (1969). "Investigating Causal Relations by Econometric Models and Cross-Spectral Methods." *Econometrica* 37, 424–438.

Granger, C. W. J. (1988). "Causality Testing in a Decision Science." In B. Skyrms and W. Harper (eds.), *Causation, Chance and Credence*, Vol. I. Dordrecht: Kluwer Academic Publishers.

———. (1990). "Causal Inference." In J. Eatwell, M. Milgate, and P. Newman (eds.), *Econometrics* (from *The New Palgrave: A Dictionary of Economics*). New York: Norton.

Haavelmo, T. (1944). "The Probability Approach in Econometrics." *Econometrica* 12 (Supplement).

Hanushek, E., and J. Jackson. (1977). *Statistical Methods for Social Scientists*. New York: Academic Press.

Holland, P. (1985). "Statistics and Causal Inference." Program Statistics Research Report No. 85-63 Educational Testing Service, Princeton, NJ.

Hoover, K. (1988). *The New Classical Economics*. Oxford: Basil Blackwell.

———. (1990). "The Logic of Causal Inference: Econometrics and the Conditional Analysis of Causation." *Economics and Philosophy* 6, 201–234.

———. (1991). "The Causal Direction Between Money and Prices." *Journal of Monetary Economics* 27, 381–423.

Humphreys, P. (1989). *The Chances of Explanation*. Princeton: Princeton University Press.

Iyengar, S., and D. Kinder. (1987). *News That Matters*. Chicago: University of Chicago Press.

Jencks, C. (1992). *Rethinking Social Policy*. Cambridge: Harvard University Press.

Johnston, J. (1992). "Econometrics: Retrospect and Prospect." In J. Hey (ed.), *The Future of Economics*. Oxford: Blackwell.

Keynes, J. M. (1973). *Collected Works* (vol. 14). London: Macmillan.

Koopmans, T. (1947). "Measurement Without Theory." *Review of Economics and Statistics* 31, 161–172.

Leamer, E. (1983). "Let's Take the Con out of Econometrics." *American Economic Review* 79, 31–43.

Lieberson, S. (1985). *Making It Count: The Improvement of Social Research and Theory*. Berkeley: University of California Press.

Lucas, R. E. (1976). "Econometric Policy Evaluation: A Critique." In K. Brunner and A. Meltzer (eds.), Carnegie-Rochester Conference on Public Policy supplementary series to the *Journal of Monetary Economics* (vol. 1). Amsterdam: North Holland.

Lyon, A. (1977). "The Immutable Laws of Nature" in *Proceedings of the Aristotelian Society 1976–7*. London: Compton Press, 107–126.

Mackie, J. C. (1965). "Causes and Conditions." *American Philosophical Quarterly* 2, 245–264.

Mason, W. M. (1991). "Friedman is Right as Far as He Goes But There is More. It's Worse. Statisticians Could Help." *Sociological Methodology* 21, 337–351.

Mayer, T. (1980). "Economics as Hard Science: Realistic Goal or Wishful Thinking?" *Economic Inquiry* 18, 165–178.

Newbold, P., and T. Bos. (1985). *Stochastic Parameter Regression Models*. Beverly Hills: Sage.

Niemi, R., and H. Weisberg. (1984). "What Determines Vote." In R. Niemi and H. Weisberg (eds.), *Controversies in Voting Behavior*. Washington, DC: Congressional Quarterly.

Page, B., and C. Jones. (1979). "Reciprocal Effects of Policy Preferences, Party Loyalties and the Vote." *American Political Science Review* 73, 1071–1090.

Pearl, J. (1989). *Probabilistic Reasoning in Intelligent Systems*. San Mateo, CA: Morgan Koufman.

Railton, P. (1981). "Probability, Explanation and Information." *Synthese* 48, 233–256.

Robbins, L. (1949). *An Essay on the Nature and Significance of Economic Science*. London: Macmillan.

Sargent, T. (1976). "The Observational Equivalence of Natural and Unnatural Rate Theories of Macroeconomics." *Journal of Political Economy* 84, 631–40.

Scheires, R. (1987). *Causal Models in Social Science*. Unpublished Ph.D. Dissertation, University of Pittsburgh.

Sims, C. (1980). "Macroeconomics and Reality." *Econometrica* 48, 1–49.

Skyrms, B. (1980). *Causal Necessity*. New Haven: Yale University Press.

Sober, E. (1988). "Apportioning Causal Responsibility." *Journal of Philosophy* 85(6), 303–318.

Stafford, F. (1985). "Income-Maintenance Policy and Work Effort: Learning From Experiments and Labor-Market Studies." In J. Hausman and D. Wise (eds.), *Social Experimentation*. Chicago: University of Chicago Press.

Suppes, P. (1970). *A Probablistic Theory of Causality*. Amsterdam: North Holland.

Tinbergen, J. (1939). *A Method and Its Applications to Investment Activity*. Geneva: League of Nations.

Veblen, E. (1975). *The Manchester Union-Leader in New Hampshire Elections*. Hanover, NH: University Press of New England.

Vining, R. (1949). "Koopmans on the Choice of Variables." *Review of Economics and Statistics* 31, 77–86.

Von Wright, G. H. (1971). *Explanation and Understanding*. Ithaca: Cornell University Press.

Weisberg, *Controversies in Voting Behavior*. Washington, DC: Congressional Quarterly.

Woodward, J. (1979). "Scientific Explanation." *British Journal for the Philosophy of Science*, 41–67.

———. (1984). "A Theory of Singular Causal Explanation." *Erkenntnis* 21, 231–262.

———. (1992). "Realism About Laws." *Erkenntnis* 36, 181–218. Reprinted in D. Ruber, ed. (1993). *Explanation* (Oxford Readings in Philosophy). Oxford: Oxford University Press, 246–274.

———. (1993a). "Capacities and Invariance." In J. Earman, A. Janis, G. Massey, and N. Rescher (eds.), *Philosophical Problems of the Internal and External Worlds: Essay Concerning the Philosophy of Adolph Grünbaum*. Pittsburgh: University of Pittsburgh Press, 283–328.

———. (1994). "Review Essay of Humphreys' *The Chances of Explanation*." *British Journal for the Philosophy of Science* 45, 353–374.

———. (Forthcoming a). *A Theory of Explanation*.

Woodward, J. (forthcoming b). "Causal Modeling, Probabilities and Invariance." To appear in the proceedings of a conference entitled "Causality in Crisis? The New Debate About Causal Structures in the Social Sciences" held at Notre Dame University, 1993.

Zeisel, Hans. (1982). "Disagreement Over the Evaluation of a Controlled Experiment." *American Journal of Sociology* 88, 378–389.

Zellner, A. (1984). *Basic Issues in Econometrics*. Chicago: University of Chicago Press.

3 CAUSAL STRUCTURES IN ECONOMETRICS

Nancy Cartwright

3.1. Introduction

There has recently been a renewal of interest among economists, especially econometricians, in deep versus shallow parameters, autonomous versus confluent equations, and fundamental versus phenomenological laws. What is at stake in these concerns is not the truth of various findings of economics but rather their range of reliability. The worry is that the parameters that we can measure are shallow, while the laws that we can establish are, in the terms of one of the founders of econometrics, Ragnar Frish, *confluent*, or as philosophers would say *phenomenological*. Only deep parameters and fundamental or autonomous laws are sure to hold come what may. (I take it that in econometrics, "Come what may" means, "Hopefully over the next one to five years, through a range of relatively minor policy changes we might envisage making.") The idea is that we can measure only shallow parameters and confluent or reduced-form equations, whereas what we need for stability are autonomous or fundamental laws determined by deep parameters. So (if that's the case) the empirical methods of economics are no good at finding out what we need to know in order to make predictions about what will happen in changing circumstances. The very possibility of forecasting is threatened and with it the hope for rational policy formulation.

Whether consciously or not, these discussions proceed, I shall argue, within a highly confined philosophical frame. They presuppose a universe of dead, pellet-like events, succeeding one after the other—a universe whose laws govern uniformities of coexistence and succession among these events. I believe that this is a fundamentally mistaken ontology, especially for economics. We live in a world of continuously unfolding causal processes, and if information about these processes can be usefully summarized in claims about general relations between economic variables, these will be claims about causal powers and causal structures.

What I want to do here is to pry apart two very different sources of worries about the stability of economic equations. One is epistemological. It is the one that I think worries—and ought to worry—econometricians. It is this worry that lies behind concerns about misspecification: perhaps, indeed with all probability, we are operating with the wrong choice of variables or at the wrong level of analysis. The other worry is one we are led to by adopting what I believe to be inappropriate ontology. This is not a case-by-case worry, responsive to the characteristics of the particular situation, not a reasoned diffidence about how well we have modeled its causal structure. Rather it is a global worry that arises in every case as long as we conceive of the underlying laws as laws of association rather than laws about causal powers and causal possibilities. It arises because we think about probabilities and not about causal structures.

I shall argue that these ontology-based worries are unfounded and we should brush them out from the interstices of our other problems so that we can proceed more clearly with the questions that matter. These are problems that get described by the misleading, technical sounding label *misspecification*. Causal inference in economics is extraordinarily difficult, just like all the other kinds of serious scientific inference. In order to make the tiniest step forward, we must deploy a great mass of already well-established information. When our causal input is shaky to begin with, the causal conclusions we draw will be of suspect reliability. That is a problem of absolute centrality that we must, and do, focus on. But we do not need to add to it problems generated by stripping down our ontology. I will argue in this chapter against the standard ontology that begins and ends with probabilities. Not only is there far more in the world than probabilities and associations; probabilities themselves have a faint grasp on reality. Usually they arise from the operation of some stable arrangement of underlying causal relations. It is the causal relations that are primary; the probabilities, when they exist at all, are derivative.

3.2. So What Is Causality?

You will notice that I talk about causality without defining it. That is deliberate. Econometricians are wont to offer a large number of definitions but (I take it) to believe in none. I suggest we proceed differently. The *Concise Oxford English Dictionary* tells us that "to cause" is to effect, to bring about, or to produce. At this very general level of discussion where we have in mind no particular subject matter, no specific phenomena, no designated problem to solve, we should, I think, leave it at that.

Most econometric characterizations are best thought of not as definitions of causality but rather as tests. I say this in part with the lessons of operationalism in mind. We do not want to turn the legitimate requirement that we devise operations that will test our hypotheses into the suffocating demand that these operations double as definitions. More important, I want to underline the peculiarity of offering some single precise statistical test for a notion of such abstractness and generality.

Causes make their effects happen. That is more than, and different from, mere association. But it is not one single different thing. One factor can contribute to the production or prevention of another in a great variety of ways. There are standing conditions, auxiliary conditions, precipitating conditions, agents, interventions, contraventions, modifications, contributory factors, enhancements, inhibitions, factors that raise the number of effects and those that only raise the level, and so on. Some think they can see a central simple form lying behind this tangle of causal concepts. This seems to involve the idea of a causally active factor operating against a relatively stable causal field. I take this to be what motivates various philosophical theories of probabilistic causality, for instance the theories of Patrick Suppes, Wolfgang Spohn, and Clark Glymour, as well as the closely related idea of Grainger-causality and the work of Herbert Simon.

But we must be wary: even if there is a central causal notion, we should not expect there to be a single probabilistic test or set of tests for it. The appropriate test for a causal relation between two factors in a given situation will depend both on the structure of the causal network in which the relation is embedded and also on the specific nature of the causal processes involved. Causal inference is a highly individual, case-by-case matter, just like the rest of science. There is no template for an experiment in genetics or a conclusion in cosmology. Similarly, there is no universal tool for testing claims about causality.[1]

3.3. Identifiable Models and Controlled Experiments

To see the importance of the contrast between causes and probabilities, let us look at a toy two-variable model. In this section I explain why we give the toy model a causal interpretation. In the next I raise a worry that undermines this interpretation. Finally I want to show how that worry grows out of a fundamentally *a*causal point of view, a point of view that takes the probability function rather than a causal structure to be God's favored way of imposing order on nature.

In her book *The History of Econometric Ideas* Mary Morgan (1990: 9) claims that the early econometricians were excited and optimistic about the discipline they were developing because they believed that their new statistical techniques provided "a substitute for the experimental method." We can understand the force of this claim very simply by looking at a two-variable model taken from Kevin Hoover (1990) involving a simple process in which money causes price:

$$M = v \tag{3.1}$$

$$P = \alpha M + \xi, \tag{3.2}$$

where v and ξ are random error terms. The usual econometric task is to estimate α. In the nice case when v and ξ are uncorrelated, α can be identified: $\alpha = <MP>/<M^2>$. So $\alpha \neq 0$ if and only if M and P are correlated. Can we draw any causal conclusions from this fact?

The surest way to find out about the causal connection between M and P is to conduct a controlled experiment. The experiment requires a control variable that can be used to change the distribution in M. If the distribution in P changes correspondingly, we conclude that M causes P; if not, in the simple two-variable case we conclude that M does not cause P. The characteristics of the control variable are crucial. It must satisfy two important conditions: the control variable must be a known cause of M and we must be assured that it varies independently from all causes of P operating at the same time except M.

Look back again at equations (3.1) and (3.2). Can we use v as a control variable for an experiment testing the effects of M on P? That depends on what we know about v and ξ. In particular it depends on what we know about the causal relations between v and ξ on the one hand and those between v and P on the other. In the case we were considering, v and ξ are independent by hypothesis. That's a good start. But what do v and ξ represent? We know that we can always write equations representing the same statistical information as (3.1) and (3.2) with "error" terms independent by construction. That is clearly not enough: v and ξ must not represent mere residuals; they must stand for causes of M and P, respectively. In that case v will satisfy the two conditions I described for a control variable. It represents a known cause of M that varies independently of the alternative causes of P. So v can be used to conduct a controlled experiment.

From equation (3.2) it is clear that changes in the distribution of M that are not associated with corresponding changes in ξ will be followed by changes in the distribution of P if and only if $\alpha \neq 0$. But we have already been reminded that α can be identified from the population data in the situation where v and ξ are independent of each other. So just by looking at population statistics we can tell what outcomes would be observed in a controlled experiment.

This is a very powerful result. Utilizing the idea of the controlled experiment, we see how we can infer a causal structure from an identifiable linear system, just as the founders of econometrics maintained. But we can do so only under very special conditions. In our simple two-variable case we had to presuppose that ξ was known to represent the omitted causes of P and that it varied independently of v, the control variable. We would need to know this in any case if we did wish to run a controlled experiment. The gain is that if we have equations (3.1) and (3.2) we do not need to run the experiment ourselves; nature runs it for us.[2]

3.4. Failures of Autonomy for Probabilistic Relations

Now turn to the worries of the well-known paper by Engle, Hendry, and Richard (1983) about the autonomy or stability of econometric parameters when other parameters are being manipulated. Their worries come out immediately if we change notation and think about matters not from the point of view of the equations, but rather in terms of the parameters of the underlying distribution in P and M. For simplicity let us take this to be bivariate normal with covariance matrix $\Omega = \{\omega_{ij}\}$:

$$
\begin{aligned}
D(M) &\sim N(0, \sigma_v^2) \\
D(P) &\sim N(0, \sigma_p^2) \\
D(P/M) &\sim N(M, \sigma_p^2) \\[6pt]
\sigma_v^2 &= \omega_{mm} \\
\sigma_p^2 &= \omega_{pp} \\
\alpha &= \omega_{pm}/\omega_{mm} \\
\sigma_\xi^2 &= \omega_{pp} - \omega_{pm}^2/\omega_{mm}.
\end{aligned}
$$

Consider again our hypothetical controlled experiment. We are going to change the distribution in M by changing $\sigma_v^2 = \omega_{mm}$. What will happen? As Engle, Hendry, and Richard point out, we do not know. Will α stay the same or not? What about $D(P)$ (ω_{pp})? Even if we assume that after the shift the distribution is still bivariate normal, the new parameters will be entirely unsettled. Notice $\alpha = \omega_{pm}/\omega_{mm}$. Nature might be very concerned with pure unnormalized joint expectations and hence fix it that $<MP>$ (ω_{pm}) is invariant. Under these conditions α must change. Or it could be that the joint expectation varies in just the right way to keep α fixed. Or a multitude of other possibilities. The current bivariate normal—which is all the probabilistic information one has about M and P—does not tell us what new distribution will obtain. That is because from the probabilistic point of view we are not dealing with a bivariate distribution in $D(M, P)$ alone, but rather with a distribution in three variables $D(M, P, F)$, where F represents the behavior of the control variable. (I use F because, following Hoover, I envisage the Federal Reserve as the agent responsible for changes in monetary policy.)

So we are really looking at two different marginal distributions from the perspective of the larger joint distribution:

$$D_{\text{old}}(M, P) = D(M, P/F = 0)$$
$$D_{\text{new}}(M, P) = D(M, P/F = 1).$$

The point is that there is no reason to assume that

$$D(P/M, F = 0) = D(P/M, F = 1).$$

3.5. How Causes Can Help

Or is there? That is the crucial question. From the purely probabilistic point of view there is none. But we do not live in a universe in which probabilities are all there is. Indeed, I do not think that the probabilities are primitive. The most realistic models begin with causal structures—fixed arrangements of causal relations like those studied by Stroz and Wold. The probabilities are generated from these. And within a causal structure there can be very good reasons for taking the marginal conditional densities to be the same.

At this point I want to switch to the notation of the philosophers because I think the ideas are more transparent there. Philosophical accounts like those of Patrick Suppes usually consider yes-no events rather than continuous variables, and they begin with some theoretically given probability distribution rather than with empirically generated statistics. They do so in order to focus on the single issue of the relation between causes and probabilities, temporarily laying aside sticky questions about statistical inference.

Again we are going to consider a two-variable toy model. We want to know whether or not the two variables in the model, C and E, are related as cause and effect. The probabilistic theory of causality tells us that (for this simple two-variable case) C causes E iff $P(E/C) > P(E/-C)$. The rationale is this. Look at the standard expansion of the probability of E:

$$P(E) = P (C/E) P(E) + P(C/-E) P(-E).$$

If indeed $P (E/C)$ is greater than $P(E/-C)$ then, it seems, if you increase $P(C)$, you will increase $P(E)$. And that is just what we expect in the assumption that C causes E. But is this really the case? That depends on how we envisage proceeding. If we want to go around a population and collect instances of E's, a very good way to do so is to collect instances of C's and wait. (This will for

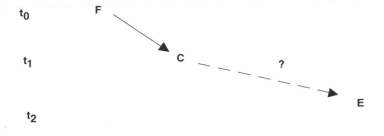

Figure 3.1   A three-event model

instance be more effective than picking individuals at random.) But in most cases where we are interested in causal reasoning, this is not what we have in mind. What we want to establish is whether or not changing the level of C will be reflected in a change in the level of E. This is a question we cannot answer using the simple argument above. Why? For the same reason we have already seen. The old $P(E)$ is a marginal probability over an old joint distribution, and you cannot change the probability of E without changing that joint distribution. As before, this is achieved by manipulating some "control variable." Call it F. So the old distribution in E and C is really a conditional distribution, conditional on the assumption that the "control variable" is not acting, while the new distribution is a conditional distribution where the "control variable" is acting. That is,

$$P_{old}(C, E) = P(C, E/F = 0)$$
$$P_{new}(C, E) = P(C, E/F = 1).$$

Again, from the probabilistic point of view there is no reason to assume that

$$P(E/C, F = 0) = P(E/C, F = 1).$$

But probabilities are not all there is. In my view probabilities are a shadow of our underlying causal structure. The question of which are fundamental, causes or probabilities, matters because reasoning about causal structures can give us a purchase on invariance that probabilities cannot provide. Think again of our three-event model (C, E, F) in terms of its causal structure. It looks like Figure 3.1. The hypothesis we are concerned with is whether C at t_1 causes E at t_2 in a toy model with very limited possibilities: (1) F at t_0 causes C at t_1 and (2) C is the only candidate cause for E at t_1.[3] In this case the invariance we need is a simple consequence of a kind of Markov assumption: a full set of intermediate causes screens off earlier causes from later effects.

What justifies this Markov-like assumption? It is causal reasoning throughout.

We suppose that causes are connected with their effects by temporally continuous processes, and at each point between the causes and the effect there is some feature that carries the entire influence of the cause towards the effect. We also assume that the causes at each point in the chain have what I have before called a "fixed capacity" (Cartwright, 1989) toward the given effect: they operate in the same way from occasion to occasion and from context to context. In the philosopher's model of yes-no events, the strength of this capacity is measured by the number of effects the cause on average produces; in models with continuous variables, strength will be reflected not only in the probability of the effect but also in its level.

I do not want to insist that either of these assumptions are necessary features of a causal structure. Quantum mechanics, for instance, provides a case where we have good reason to think causes do not propagate by temporally continuous processes (Chang and Cartwright, 1993). I also believe that processes may be so bound to their background context that we cannot assign to them any stable capacity that could be relied on under different circumstances, or on different occasions. Nevertheless, a Markov type assumption is very often a reasonable one to make about particular underlying causal structures we are studying, both in economics and elsewhere; and when it can be made, the worries we have generated about invariance in our simple two-variable model can be met. When we consider larger worlds with richer sets of possibilities, the problems, of course, become far more complicated. This is especially true when we turn not to toys but to real-life models where we are bound to have omitted large numbers of causally relevant variables. But the point is that at any stage we will have a far more powerful set of tools to work with if we keep firmly in mind that the probabilities we look at are generated by causal structures that impose serious constraints on them.[4]

How then should we think about Haavelmo's worries about autonomy and invariance? Haavelmo tells us that we need to find fundamental equations and not just confluent or phenomenological ones. I think, by contrast, that that depends, as Engle, Hendry, and Richard point out, on what kinds of manipulation we plan to undertake. Haavelmo illustrated with the example of the automobile throttle. Charting the relationship between the amount the gas pedal is depressed and the acceleration the car undergoes leaves the whole inner mechanism of the car a mystery he tells us. But if the project is to make cars go faster or slower, this is exactly the information we need: stepping on the throttle causes the car to accelerate; governors in the throttle mechanism will prevent too much acceleration; and sophisticated governors can be overriden in emergency situations. If, on the other hand, the project is to set up a new causal structure (as certainly Haavelmo's mentor Frisch would have liked) (Andrig, forthcoming), then indeed we do need a different kind of causal information.

The Lucas (1976) critique too is often cast as a concern about deep or fundamental relations versus shallow or confluent ones. But this is a misdescription. What Lucas raises are the ordinary questions one always needs to ask about causal relations. (As I understand it, this is Kevin Hoover's interpretation as well.) We can think about the lessons he urges in the simple two-variable example of money and price. In this case the "exogeneous variable" v represents something like government deliberation. If Lucas is right, then v does not satisfy the conditions for a control variable. A control variable for testing the effects of money on price should have no way to affect price other than via the money supply. But on Lucas's account, the deliberations of the government can, and usually will, affect prices directly via their effects on individual expectations. In this case, the observed relations between price and money, which we imagine to be expressed in equations (3.1) and (3.2), do not serve as a natural experiment. We are not here experiencing, as some have suggested, a special problem about interventions that uproot the basic causal structure and undermine invariances that we might otherwise have relied on. We are instead dealing with the ordinary, well-known, and difficult problem that we need a lot of knowledge about our causal structures in the first place if we hope to use the simple tools of statistics to generate new information about them. If indeed individual expectations are a major omitted factor, then it is no surprise that we may draw mistaken conclusions from regressing price on money alone.

The immediate conclusion I want to draw is that the early econometricians were right. In very special cases econometrics can substitute for the experimental method. Section 3.3 showed how, in a simple toy world where only two causal factors are allowed. Here I hope to have shown that worries about invariance of the kind raised in Section 3.4 need not undermine that conclusion. The conditions under which we can draw causal conclusions from econometric data are very restricted. In order to do so we must already know a great deal about the causal structure that we are investigating. Each case needs thinking about on its own. But in general, when we have good reason to think that nature is running an experiment for us, we will also be in a position to assume the invariances we need in order to use our causal conclusions to formulate policy and initiate change.

3.6. Conclusion

There are a special set of worries about the stability of parameters that we do not need burden ourselves with. These are worries that arise when we artificially restrict our ontology. Or perhaps, better put, they arise from a view about laws of nature that is too associationist. There will be, I know, philosophical reservations; I want to take up an econometric matter.

It is very possible that the variables one considers, and attempts to discover a relationship between, are not part of the causal structures at work in the domain under study. So hypotheses—like a Markov assumption—about causal structures will not provide any purchase on invariances. I think that is David Hendry's (1988, 1993) view. He urges us to think locally about the kinds of invariances we might be able to expect in the particular cases across the particular range of manipulations we might be making. That is a good idea; but I have a worry about it. Haavemo's groundbreaking work on the probabilistic approach provided econometrics with a logically secure foundation, both on the theory side—for the formulation of typical econometric models—and on the testing side—legitimizing standard methods of statistical inference. Since then econometrics standardly supposes that we draw our data from an underlying probability distribution. This is an assumption which I am not very sanguine about.

In *The Logic of Statistical Inference* Ian Hacking (1965) urges that propensities and frequencies are obverse sides of the same phenomenon. Propensities give rise to frequencies; frequencies are the expression of propensities. This is a point of view that I want to endorse. A chance set-up may occur naturally, or it may be artificially constructed, either deliberately or by accident. But in any case, probabilities are generated by chance setups, and their characterization must necessarily refer back to the chance setup from which they arise. We can make sense of the probability of drawing two red balls in a row from an urn of a certain composition with replacement; but we cannot make sense of the probability of 6 percent inflation in the United Kingdom next year without an implicit reference to a specific social and institutional structure to serve as the chance setup that generates this probability. The originators of social statistics followed this pattern, and I think rightly so. When they talked about the iron law of probability that dictated a fixed number of suicides in Paris every year or a certain rising rate of crime, this was not conceived as an association between events laid down by natural law like the association between force and acceleration, but rather as an association generated by particular social and economic structures and susceptible to change by change in these structures.

A fundamental problem about economic theory is that very often it does not provide enough secure information about the causal structures we are studying to allow us to find out more. Still, we tend to assume that we can at least help ourselves to a probability distribution over the variables we are interested in. That is a claim I find suspicious. Consider Haavelmo's automobile example again. The car engine is a good case of a stable causal structure that can be expected to give rise to a probability distribution over the events of the the cooperating causal processes that make it up. That is why it can make sense to ask about the conditional expectation of the acceleration given a certain level of the throttle. But in social and economic contexts we are more likely to ask questions like "What is the probability that one automobile accelerates a certain amount given a fixed acceleration in an approaching car?" which may have no answer. There is no gigantic chance setup spewing out autos and drivers in a systematic pattern. We may treat the problem as if it were sampling with fixed probability from the outcomes of different chance setups, but that too would most probably be a great misrepresentation.

I realize that it may nevertheless prove to be a useful fiction. In that case, trying to figure out the invariances of this imposter may be a way to find out useful information about the underlying causal structures. But if it is so, it is an indirect and nontransparent way, and ultimately we would like some kind of representation theorem that shows that any recommended strategy produces results tracking those fixed by the causal structures. The real caution I want to urge is that we not fall into the trap of taking probabilities for granted. A probability distribution as it functions in scientific theory is a nomological item. It is not part of the data, but a putative law of nature that (depending on your view) summarizes, governs, or generates the data. You shouldn't think that the probabilistic approach avoids ontology. It just chooses one ontology over another. To my mind it makes the wrong choice.

I can summarize the overall conclusion very briefly then: when you are studying causal structures, you have a purchase on invariances beyond that available from pure probabilities. And if you are not studying causal structures, you may well not have the probabilities to begin with.

Notes

1. Several illustrations of this are given in Cartwright (1989). The case of the so-called "common-cause" criterion and its application to quantum mechanics is pursued in Cartwright (1993) and in Chang and Cartwright (1993: 169–190).

2. This argument is spelled out in more detail in Cartwright (forthcoming).

3. If the hypothesis that C causes E is false, then changes in E will be spontaneous, which is a natural feature of any probabilistic model.

4. Spirtes, Glymour, and Scheines (1994), for example, produce a powerful set of results for causal structures that satisfy a very strong condition that combines a conventional Markov assumption with an assumption that rules out standard product/by-product relations.

References

Andvig, J. (1988). "From Macrodynamics to Macroeconomic Planning: A Basic Shift in Ragnar Frisch's Thinking?" *European Economic Review* 32, 495–502.

Cartwright, N. (1989). *Nature's Capacities and Their Measurement.* Oxford: Oxford University Press.

————. (1993). "Marks and Probabilities: Two Ways to Find Causal Structure." In F. Stadler (ed.), *Scientific Philosophy: Origins and Developments*. Dordrecht: Kluwer.

Cartwright, N. (forthcoming). "Probabilities and Experiments." *Journal of Econometrics.*

Chang, H., and N. Cartwright. (1993). "Causality and Realism in the EPR Experiment." *Erkenntnis* 38, 169–190.

Engle, R., D. Hentry, J.-F. Richard. (1983). "Exogeneity." *Econometrica* 51, 277–304.

Hacking, I. (1965). *The Logic of Statistical Inference*. Cambridge: Cambridge University Press.

Hendry, D. (1988). "Encompassing." *National Institute Economic Review* (August), 88–92.

————. (1993). *Econometrics: Alchemy or Science?* Oxford: Blackwells∕

Hoover, K. (1990). "The Logic of Causal Inference." *Economics and Philosophy* 6, 207–234.

Lucas, R. (1976). "Econometric Policy Evaluation: A Critique." In *The Phillips Curve and Labor Markets*. New York: Elsevier.

Morgan, Mary. (1990). *The History of Econometric Ideas*. Cambridge: Cambridge University Press.

Spirtes, P., C. Glymour, and R. Scheines. (1994). *Causation, Prediction and Search*. Berlin; New York: Springer Verlag.

Kevin D. Hoover

Comments on Cartwright and Woodward: Causation, Estimation, and Statistics

In work over the past several years, Nancy Cartwright has paid economics the compliment—unusual for a philosopher—of taking the taking econometrics seriously as a source of causal analysis. Her chapter in this book continues to mine this vein. And now James Woodward has joined the excavation with a rich and insightful chapter. As an economist, I am pleased to think that my profession may have something to teach philosophers; but more than that, I am hopeful that the systematic scrutiny of philosophers of this caliber will raise the level of causal analysis in empirical economics. I am sympathetic to the approaches of both Cartwright and Woodward. And I am flattered to have my own work figure so largely in their analyses. Anyone familiar with that work will recognize at once the depth of my debt to Nancy Cartwright—especially to her *Nature's Capacities and Their Measurement.* I am less familiar with James Woodward's work. The evidence of his chapter suggests that the loss is mine and that remedy is in order. Woodward stresses the importance of "contrastive explanations" in his chapter. While recognizing that the common ground between Woodward, Cartwright, and me is far broader and more fertile that the contested ground, it is nevertheless more enlightening and—if I may speak like an economist— offers more value-added if I try to follow Woodward and examine and explain the contrasts between my own views and his and those of Cartwright. My comments on Woodward are restricted to the chapter in this book; my comments on Cartwright refer more generally to her work on causality in economics.[1]

Taking Linear Models Seriously

Woodward's project is to make sense of linear econometric models as part of causal explanations. He concludes that, since estimated econometric models cannot be interpreted as exceptionless generalizations quantitatively invariant across a wide range of changing circumstances, they cannot be regarded as natural laws. This does not rule them out, however, a sources of information about causation in the economy. Econometric models can, Woodward believes, provide reliable, qualitative information, as well as context-specific quantitative

75

information, about the manner and action of causes in the economy when they are bolstered by other sorts of knowledge—particularly by knowledge about causal capacities. Indeed, Woodward goes further: econometric models may provide contrastive explanations of particular economic events by assigning quantitative importance to the various causal factors responsible for them. More generally, Woodward argues that economic knowledge is not analogous to knowledge in, say, physics—precise and fine-grained. Rather, it is often the imprecise, highly variable, coarse knowledge of causal capacities. Coarse knowledge, as Woodward so persuasively argues, is knowledge nonetheless.

Woodward appears optimistic about the possibilities for causal knowledge in economics, once the role of linear econometric models is rightly understood. Cartwright's chapter, in contrast, is more world weary and ends on a decidedly pessimistic note. Cartwright had hoped to use econometrics as a substitute for experimentation in economics. In *Nature's Capacities* she viewed econometrics as having a method for getting causes from probabilities. In this chapter, she surveys the attempts of several economists to determine what collateral knowledge one must bring to linear econometric models to succeed in this quest. She concludes that either one must have deep theoretical commitments or a "detailed acquaintance with particular cases." Cartwright recognizes that this conclusion undermines her hope for a shortcut to causal conclusions. She does not acknowledge the degree to which it also changes the necessary direction of research: the question now becomes how do we obtain either the theoretical certitude or the detailed acquaintance with particular cases that might support causal conclusions from linear models. There is no hint of where to begin. Perhaps this is because her overall conclusion is even more stunningly pessimistic. Is there even the degree of invariance needed to support something like Woodward's coarse economic knowledge? Is there any sound justification in the nature of the real-world economy for invoking probability distributions as the statistical techniques of econometrics requires? What guarantee is there that there are *stable capacities*—the sheet anchor of both her own and Woodward's analyses of causality?

The Existence and Direction of Causation

One might mean different things by "getting causes from probabilities." There are at least three issues. First, does a particular causal relationship exist, and what is its direction? Second, given that one factor causes another, what is the strength of the association? Third, what is the explanation for the causal connection? Although, Cartwright's work seems principally directed toward the second question, the problem of measurement, it is not wholly restricted to that.

Woodward's chapter also deals with measurement, although the question of causal explanation also looms large. In both chapters, these question are conflated. The reason, I believe, has to do with an unstated equivocation over the term *model*. A model might be a kind of theory—in particular, a precisely specified theory. An econometric model is not a theory but a template for organizing observable economic data. To speak about an econometric model as if it were in itself an economic theory generates confusion.

If econometric models are in fact theories, then it is plausible—as Woodward, citing Arnold Zellner, Herbert Blalock, Paul Humphreys, and Richard Scheines, notes—to think that the individual regression equations are laws of science. Woodward quite rightly rejects that view, but without, it seems, rejecting the view that econometric models themselves are something more than templates for organizing data. Rather, Woodward rejects the lawlikeness of the regression equation because he takes a rather high view of what constitutes a law. A law for Woodward is a highly autonomous relationship, invariant under a wide range of changing background conditions. And although he does not say it in so many words, Woodward implies that laws must be precisely quantified. The instability of econometric estimates across different samples and through time in itself suggests that they are not laws in this sense.

The difficulty with Woodward's view is that the distinction he draws is one of degree and not of kind. The law of gravity is, to be sure, more autonomous than an economic estimate that a 1 percent increase in the price results in a 0.5 percent decrease in the sales of toothpaste. Nevertheless, just how many exceptions and qualifications are allowed before a law ceases to be a law? Do even the laws of physics qualify? Woodward and Cartwright differ on this point. In a striking passage that I have frequently quoted, Cartwright (1989: 8) writes: "It is hard to find [laws] in nature and we are always having to make excuses for them: why they have exceptions—big or little; why they only work for models in the head; why it takes an engineer with a special knowledge of real materials and a not too literal mind to apply physics to reality." Indeed, where Woodward takes a high view of laws, Cartwright (1983: essay 4) has been willing to take the laws of physics down a peg by regarding them as purely instrumental, despite her own realism with respect to capacities, and to argue for affirmative action for phenomenal laws—precisely the sort of nonautonomous relationships found in economics or in Haavelmo's example of the relationship between the speed and the throttle-setting of a car.

Cartwright (1989: ch. 5) considers the idea that laws might be idealizations. How this squares with her instrumental interpretation of laws is an interesting question.[2] If we regard laws as idealizations, it is not obvious that economics does not have laws as strict as those of physics. Once the perturbing influences of changing tastes and imperfect markets can be assumed away, a law such as the substitution effect is always negative (that is, compensating for induced income changes the demand for any good falls when its price rises) is perfectly autonomous and invariant. Of course, such an economic law fails on the criterion that the relationships be quantitatively precise; for how large the substitution effect will be depends on the precise tastes of the consumers. This criterion is implicit in Woodward's account, but there does not seem to be an argument for it. Again, it is not clear just how much quantitative precision is needed to make a law. What is clear, however, is that if laws are idealizations, econometric models are not laws; they do not succeed in abstracting from perturbing factors. Even if laws are not idealizations, it is still not clear that economics has no laws. While every textbook cites theoretical exceptions (such as Giffen goods) to the law of demand (that is, quantities sold fall when prices rise), there are few concrete instances of such exceptions.

For Woodward, economics is not the domain of laws. Instead, he argues that we should look for other kinds of invariant relationships. Causal structures, underpinned by causal capacities, are the sort of things he has in mind. But this raises a question, never really adequately answered by Woodward or Cartwright: just what is a causal capacity? Woodward wants to distinguish causal capacities from minilaws—locally invariant relationships—and to acknowledge that "claims about capacities and mechanisms rarely take the form of laws or quantitatively precise or exceptionless generalizations. Instead such claims are typically qualitative, exception-ridden, and imprecise." Nevertheless, Woodward requires that a causal capacity be able to produce its effect "in many different populations and background conditions." It is not clear how such a criterion of robustness distinguishes capacities *in kind* from laws—especially from "minilaws." And it would seem to miss part of the point about capacities, certainly implicit in Cartwright's discussion, as well as elsewhere in Woodward's. A capacity manifests itself only in some circumstances and not in others, and differently from circumstance to circumstance. The plastic explosive C-4 can be burned or used as a baseball and will not explode. It will explode only when triggered in a certain way. It has the capacity to explode but only in quite particular circumstances. Some research suggests that asbestos particles have the capacity to cause asbestosis but only when present in conjunction with another aggravating factor—in particular, tobacco smoking. These examples suggest that robustness against a wide range of circumstances cannot be the critical criterion of the existence of a capacity. They also suggest that capacities need not manifest themselves linearly. Sometimes there is a proportionality between cause and effect, but nonlinear or threshold relationships also obtain. To cite one of Woodward's own examples, the classic Phillips curve in economics is nonlinear, with the tradeoff between higher inflation and lower unemployment becoming more severe as unemployment rates decline. The linear model is the most common one in econometrics, but limited-dependent variables models, switching models, threshold models, systems with cross-equation restrictions, and other forms of nonlinear models are more and more frequently used. There is a danger in making a fetish of linearity and of providing a causal analysis that depends fundamentally upon it.

While I question whether robustness in the sense that Woodward has used it is an essential part of causal capacities, I do believe that he is right to look for some form of invariance, and that his analysis in terms of counterfactual conditionals is on the right track. Woodward draws a distinction about counterfactuals that is essential to econometrics. A law of the form "All As are Bs" need not sustain the counterfactual "If X were to be an A, then X would be a B." Rather, it sustains a counterfactual such as "If certain collateral conditions were to change, the law would continue to hold." This analysis can be carried over from exceptionless laws to the sort of relationships found in econometrics that hold only in particular circumstances and within some margin of error. To illustrate, imagine that an estimated Phillips curve takes the form

$$\pi = (\alpha/U)\gamma + \varepsilon, \tag{1}$$

where π is the rate of inflation, U is the rate of unemployment, α and γ are estimated parameters, and ε is a random error term. Equation (1) is the analogue of the universal statement "All As are Bs." It cannot, however, sustain the first type of counterfactual; since, having estimated such a relationship, it will be a rare event if any future π is precisely $(\alpha/U)\gamma$; that is the message of the error term. Thinking that it must sustain an analogue to the first type of counterfactual has forced econometricians to concentrate on the minimization of the error (that is, on goodness of fit or high R^2). Unfortunately, this is a standardless measure: how high an R^2 is (or, equivalently, how many and how large exceptions to the rule are) permitted if a relationship is to be regarded as almost universal? Woodward rightly points out that this is the wrong criterion, appealing to the wrong sort of counterfactual. It is not the fit, but the stability of a relationship such as equation (1) to new data that supports the causal interpretation. In the context of equation (1), it is easier to see my point about causal capacities. Woodward seems to say that higher unemployment has the capacity to lower inflation according to equation (1) if such a relationship remains invariant to changes in many possible background conditions. I argue instead that some relationships (such as the explosiveness of C-4) will hardly be invariant to even slight changes in background conditions yet, nonetheless, have a causal capacity to act according to the relationship. To assert that there is a capacity of unemployment to cause inflation according to equation (1) is to say that there exist some (possibly narrowly restricted) set of background conditions in which changes in other background conditions that result in changes in unemployment are related to changes in inflation according to equation (1). Thus, it is the robustness of equation (1) to variations in U, rather than to arbitrary background conditions that marks it off as causal. Of course, if equation (1) were highly sensitive to changing background conditions, it would not be practically important—not because it does not represent a true causal capacity, but because we would rarely find ourselves in the circumstances usefully to exploit that capacity. An airplane has the capacity to fly, but that is useless if we do not have fuel. Woodward makes a telling point when he says that often it is not the capacities that are of interest, but what actually happens in particular circumstances.

Measurement

Woodward does not have a lot to say about the existence and direction of causes. And while Cartwright does discuss ontology in her chapter, in most of her work she has, like Woodward, spent relatively more time considering issues related to the measurement of causes. "Getting causes from probabilities" in this context means assigning the appropriate strength to causal factors. In this, they stand in the mainstream tradition of econometrics that has focused on estimation and its problems above all things.

Unless causal direction is established, measurement of causal strengths is surely not possible. Obvious as this may seem, it is a point often ignored by practicing empirical economists. So why do Cartwright and Woodward concentrate so much on measurement issues? The answer appears to be that they are too willing to take economists at their words; and, when economists pay attention to causal direction at all, they look to economic theory to supply the causal structure so that measurement is the only thing left to do. Economists are often in the thrall of theory, and Cartwright and Woodward seem willing to be mesmerized as well.

What is economic theory? Cartwright has little to say on this point. Woodward illustrates through examples, such as the Phillips curve. More telling are his examples from other disciplines: the example of party preferences, party loyalty and the vote, and the example of the effect of newspaper endorsements on voting behavior. Woodward writes as if these were theories in need of quantification. Yet neoclassical economists get rather sniffy about political scientists and sociologists precisely because they do not regard these as examples of theory. Economists typically think of a theory as a derivation under special pertinent assumptions of economic behavior from primitive axioms of economic psychology. Theory, for Cooley and LeRoy (1985), for example, must involve economic agents maximizing utility functions subject to budget constraints. By *primitive*, economists mean fundamental, but the underlying psychology is primitive in a pejorative sense as well.

Even if we restrict our attention to theory such as is acceptable to neoclassical economists, we still have a problem of determining causal direction. To take one example, Hoover and Sheffrin (1992) demonstrate that in the relationship between government expenditures and taxes, every causal direction is theoretically possible: taxes to spending, spending to taxes, or mutual causation. Settling the question is logically prior to measuring causal strengths. This explains why my project is very different from Cartwright's. I want to find empirical inputs, not theoretical inputs, quasi-experiments, not metaphysics, to help identify causal direction. After causal structure is understood, the econometrics of obtaining accurate estimates of causal strengths is pretty clearly worked out in Engle, Hendry, and Richard (1983) under the heading "weak exogeneity" (see Pratt and Schlaifer, 1984).

Like Cartwright, Woodward is willing in principle to put aside theory as an essential element in causal understanding in favor of other domain-specific knowledge. Unfortunately, his most detailed account of the use of such knowledge comes close to a being simply a watered-down version of the probabilistic theory of causality (Suppes, 1970) that he is ready to dismiss elsewhere. A causal capacity in Woodward's view must manifest itself in a wide range of circumstances when other relevant factors are controlled for. This is very like Suppes's test for the genuineness of a prima facie cause or to Salmon's (1984) account of "screening". Salmon, however, saw the need for some other criterion of causal efficacy. One is needed here as well.

Cartwright (1983) speaks of the "efficacy of causes," and in *Nature's Capacities*, as well as in her chapter here, she turns to theory to provide assurances of efficacy. In the Cowles Commission program—to which she give a limited endorsement—it is theoretical understanding that makes it possible to use a model as a substitute for experiments. Here our beliefs about causal structure determine the outcomes of thought experiments using econometric models. But causal structure is a property of the world independent of our beliefs about it. We need, therefore, an account of how those beliefs are best acquired. Woodward's chapter seems to suffer from similar problems, especially in the section in which he apparently endorses Leamer's view that our beliefs about reality should determine what independent variables we include or exclude from regression equations.[3] The difficult problem is not the measuring of causal strengths but knowing what to measure.

Explanation

Woodward comes close to thinking of linear models themselves as theories. He explicitly refers to them as providing explanations. This, I believe, is a misapprehension: econometric models do not explain.

There are two views of the role of econometrics, or, perhaps, there are two roles for econometrics. Hoover (1994b) draws a contrast between "econometrics-as-measurement" and "econometrics-as-observation." Although the terminology is my own, Morgan (1990) demonstrates in her contrast between the econometrics of demand and the econometrics of business cycles, that the distinction has a long history in econometric practice. Econometrics-as-measurement sees the function of econometrics as the quantification of fully articulated theoretical structures. As I have argued already, the difficulty in the measurement strategy is in finding an empirically justified way of providing the necessary articulation. Econometrics-as-observation regards econometric estimates not as direct measurements—which may be valid or invalid, good or bad, ways of determining causal strengths—but as instruments, methods of processing economic data, that may be revealing or unrevealing about features of the economic world that we wish to know about. A parallel might be in microscopy in which stains and filters are used to alter the image received by the observer. Sometimes such alterations are quite useless; other times they are quite revealing; in all cases, they are genuine observations. My contention is that virtually all practical econometrics is econometrics-as-observation, and that the principal task of the econometrician is to find ways to make econometric observations more revealing. It is more to the point that theory should explain econometric observations than that econometric observations should quantify theory. To have an estimated econometric model is to know that certain economic variables are related in certain ways; it is not to know why they are related in those ways. This is why econometric models are not, absent theory, explanatory.

Woodward speaks of linear econometric models as explanations. But he is well aware of certain distortions that such models are subject to in practical applications. He therefore qualifies his view of econometric models to suggest that they provide *contrastive* explanations. To use his own example, drawn from Stanley Lieberson, Woodward considers estimating the time to fall through a fixed distance of different objects as providing a contrastive explanation of their *relative* rates of fall, which depend on the varying air resistance that they display, as opposed to an explanation of their absolute rate of fall, which also depends on the acceleration due to gravity. As reported by Woodward, Lieberson argues that a regression that included a measure of the force of gravity would find a zero coefficient since that force does not vary in the sample. The root problem is well known in econometrics and is sometimes referred to as the problem of *nonexcitation* (see Engle, Hendry, and Richard, 1983: 285): one cannot estimate accurately the influence of a factor, even if that factor is crucially important, if it shows no variation over the sample.

Woodward's detailed account (and his interpretation of Lieberson) nevertheless seems flawed. Suppose that the distance each object falls is given by the standard formula for an object falling in a vacuum modified by a factor related to the density of the object and an error term to account for other independent factors:

$$x = 0.5gt^2d^{2\theta}e^{2\varepsilon,} \qquad (2)$$

where x is the distance of fall (assumed constant in Woodward's example), g is the constant of acceleration due to gravity at the earth's surface, t is time of fall, d is the density of the falling object, θ is the parameter determining the relationship between density and rate of fall, ε is a random error term (both θ and ε are scaled by 2 for notational convenience), and e is the base of natural logarithms. Equation (2) can be linearized by taking logarithms of both sides and rearranged so that time is the dependent variable. The form of the regression equation would then be

$$T = \alpha + \beta D + \varepsilon, \qquad (3)$$

where $T = \log(t)$, α is the estimate of $-0.5 \log (2x/g)$, $D = \log(d)$ and β is the estimate of $-\theta$.

Woodward looks to β to provide the contrastive explanation of the differential falling times of different objects. One should note, however, that the constant α can be unpacked to give an estimate of g so long as one knows x and is committed to the accuracy of equation (2) as a description of the truth. This is a simple example of how theory provides identification and permits the measurement of a theoretically articulated system. Unfortunately, theory is rarely so straightforward as this. Suppose, however, that we had physical measurements of the force of gravity acting on each object. These would, within measurement error, be constant. Nevertheless, suppose that we entered them into a modified regression equation:

$$T = \alpha + \beta D + \gamma G + \varepsilon, \qquad (4)$$

where $G = \log(g')$ and g' is the measured value of g for each object. Were there absolutely no measurement error in G, then rather than γ being zero as Woodward suggests, the regression could not be run at all because the $\mathbf{X'X}$ matrix in the coefficient estimator formula (see Woodward's equation (2.3)) could not be inverted owing to perfect collinearity between G and the constant. One could omit the constant; but, in that case, γ in equation (4) without a constant would simply equal α in equation (3). If the constant were included and G was measured with error, the standard errors of estimate for γ would be extremely large, not indicating an effect of zero, but of an indeterminable value.

Were one's commitment to the theory of gravity sufficiently secure (for whatever reason) and were an independently measured value of g available, a regression with a modified dependent variable would provide the best estimate of β:

$$T' = \beta D + \varepsilon, \tag{5}$$

where $T' = T + 0.5 \log (2x/g)$.

The point of this detour into elementary econometrics is partly to correct an error, but it is also to illustrate that regressions are not explanations, contrastive or otherwise, but data-based calculations, that may help us observe facts for theoretical interpretation. The *explanation* for the behavior of falling objects is the theory of gravity modified by a theory of air resistance: here that is summarized in equation (2). Woodward wants to say that a regression such as equation (3) explains the differences in the rates of fall for different objects (it is because of the differences in their densities), but not their rate of fall per se. I want to say, absent a theoretical account, that the regression merely describes a correlation, and, at best, suggests factors that may be important in the explanation. Nevertheless, a perfectly adequate account must explain not just the correlation in equation (3), but those in equations (4) and (5) and in other repackagings of the data. These observational regressions place a constraint on what can be an adequate theory. And since we are not given theories (especially in neat forms like equation (2)) by nature, a fruitful empirical strategy seeks to place as many systematic constraints on theory as possible. Consider a simple example. If instead of estimating equation (3), we estimate

$$T = \beta D + \varepsilon, \tag{6}$$

that is, equation (3) with the intercept term, α, omitted, we force the regression line to go through the origin. Statistical examination of the estimated values of ε will now show them to be systematically heteroscedastic rather than random with a uniform variance. Furthermore, equation (6) will systematically mispredict the times to fall of objects, especially those outside the range of densities for which equation (6) was estimated. These statistical properties cry out that factors other than densities are important; although they do not, in themselves, point to which other factors are omitted. But equation (6) is not a false explanation: densities are important. Nor is it an invalid regression: one would have to assume that the purpose of the regression was to quantify a cause; and, even then, one could only judge validity against the standard of already knowing equation (2), which *ex hypothesi* who do not know. Like equations (3)–(5), equation (6) is an observation, it just happens to be one that, if we may keep to the analogy of microscopy, is out of focus. An adequate explanation would explain why equation (6) has the properties it has.

Reading regressions as explanations reflects, I think, a confusion of epistemology and ontology. The properties of an estimated regression are dictated by the data, which, in turn, is determined by the way the world is. By thinking of regressions as explanations, Woodward seeks to make them conform to a priori theory. Thus, in his discussion of Leamer's analysis of capital punishment and in his strictures against datamining, Woodward argues that, since what regressions seem to imply in the way of explanations depends on what variables are included, variables should be included only if there is a "plausible rationale" for their being causally important, an "independent reason to think that the variable has the capacity to affect the dependent variable." This cannot be right; thinking a thing does not make it so.

The inclusion or omission of a variable will not bias the estimates of the coefficients of other variables unless it is correlated with those variables. In finite samples, of course, a correlation can be spurious and transitory, as it is in Lieberson's example of coin flipping cited by Woodward. This is why it is good procedure, a good method of ensuring the focus of a regression, to check for subsample stability of coefficient estimates or to test for stability of estimates against entirely new data. But if a correlated variable continues to be important after taking steps to guard against spurious correlation, then it cannot simply be excluded from the regression because we do not know why it should be important. What is called for, instead, is further investigation. Reichenbach's common-cause principle suggests that correlations arise because of omitted causal links (Reichenbach, 1956; also see Cartwright, 1989: 24 *passim*). No science could make progress if lack of understanding of causal mechanisms were itself grounds to dismiss the existence of causal mechanisms: there is a confusion here between the explanation and the thing-to-be-explained.

As noted earlier, Woodward's conception of what constitutes a theory is not so narrow as is typical for neoclassical economists. Equation (2) may summarize a theory, but, for Woodward, a much looser link (such as newspaper endorsements cause changes in voter loyalties) also constitutes a theory. Loose theories seem much easier to map onto linear regression equations. It then appears possible to measure the strength of a particular causal factor. But once one acknowledges that these estimates vary according to what other variables are included, and that what to include is critically a matter of a priori theory, Leamer's view that the only good estimate of causal strength is one that is robust to changes in the other included factors in the regression appears attractive. In contrast, once one commits to the view that the causal structure of the world is independent of our knowledge of it, then this notion of robustness to misspecification seems decidedly odd. A regression can measure an effect directly only if it articulates the world in a way that recapitulates the way the world is. If it is specified some other way, there is no reason at all to believe that the estimate of the coefficient of interest should not be altered in a, perhaps, uninterpretable manner. The estimate of β will be different in equation (3) and equation (6), but if the world is in fact as described in equation (2), the estimate from equation (3) will be close to the truth, and that in equation (6) far from it. The failure of the estimates to agree is no argument against the estimate in equation (2). It may not be possible to know in advance which regression, if either, should form the basis for measurement, but that merely suggests that we must devote considerable attention to learning more about causal structure through deeper investigation and spend some time thinking about the statistical evidence for whether or not our regressions are "in focus."[4]

Representation and Reality

Woodward questions my account of what a representation of causal structure should look like. I would like to conclude by clarifying some of the issues he raises.

The causal field includes irrelevant background conditions, standing conditions that do not change or that act as boundary conditions marking out the range of applicability of a causal relationship, and variables that simply are not the focus of our interest. Irrelevant field conditions can simply be ignored, but relevant ones may or may not be known and enumerated. In general relevant variables cannot be ignored even if they are not enumerated when seeking an interpretable regression. Even in the example of the falling objects discussed above, ignoring the force of gravity and the distance of the drop as in equation (6) ensures that β is not a good measure of θ, the true parameter governing the importance of density in equation (2). But sometimes factors can be ignored. Any factor that is uncorrelated with other causal determinants can be left out of a regression equation without biasing the estimates of the coefficients of the remaining factors. Omitting such a variable simply means that the residual error of the regression equation will be greater. Woodward objects to my impounding these field variables in the random error term because, he says, such "variables typically do not contribute in a linear or even additive way to the value of the dependent variable."

In *Nature's Capacities*, Cartwright argues that a stochastic system can be sensibly thought to possess a well-defined causal order only if it has a canonical representation in which the random error terms are mutually independent. If a variable does not contribute in a way consistent with Cartwright's stricture then, I agree with Woodward that it cannot be impounded in a random error term that is taken to represent the causal field. But, in fact, I was careful not to say otherwise. Woodward cites an illustrative example for which I point out (Hoover, 1990: 226) that "[t]he random error terms . . . are taken to be adequate summaries of the influence of field variables." But, I continue, "whether a variable may be legitimately impounded in the causal field depends on its causal relationship to the variables which command our immediate interest" (that is, whether or not it is correlated with those variables, so that impounding it in the error term would violate Cartwright's stricture). In this passage (1990: 226–227) and another (1990: 221–223) I discuss precisely which field variables must be explicitly dealt with in an econometric model and which may be impounded. Random variables may in special circumstances represent field variables, but they may also be unobservable variables of direct interest or related to variables of direct interest in such a manner that they must be accounted for (such as latent causal factors) (see Glymour, Scheines, Sprites, and Kelly, 1987).

So the difference between Woodward and me on this point comes down to the adverb *typically*: how typical is it that unenumerated factors enter into the determination of the dependent variable in nonlinear, nonadditive ways? Surely Woodward is correct with respect to what might be regarded as boundary conditions: for examples, the long-term institutional structure of a particular national economy. This is probably the major factor in ensuring that measured causal structures in economics are local and cannot be transferred except in broad brush manner from one particular economy to another. Of course, this point is not limited to economics. Equation (3) above might provide an excellent quantification of the parameters in equation (2) at sea level, yet be hopelessly inaccurate for similar measurements made in the Himalayan uplands, where the where both the force of gravity and the air density are substantially different. Recognizing the locality of causal structures in economics does not rule out, however, that many other factors may be legitimately impounded in the error terms. Here the proof of the pudding is in the eating. If the error terms show all the properties of randomness, independence and local stability that make them fulfil Cartwright's stricture, then we have substantial evidence that the field assumptions are fulfilled. I discuss these conditions in the section of Hoover (1990) entitled "Misspecification of the Causal Field." If these conditions are not fulfilled, as they are not for example in an estimate based on equation (6) above, which shows both serial correlation of the estimated errors and predictive failure, then what is called for is further empirical investigation. The factors that contribute to the misspecification of the causal field must be isolated and accounted for. My own experience in econometrics is that this is often easier than Woodward pessimistically suggests. And that is surely a good thing because regressions that fail to fulfil these specification conditions are difficult to interpret theoretically and certainly provide not a hope of obtaining accurate measurements of causal strengths, which is the prey that both Woodward and Cartwright are stalking.

Cartwright's and Woodward's chapters are important and stimulating. If I have discussed them in an unremittingly critical mode that is only because of the importance that I attach to the issues they raise and to the provocativeness of their own discussions of those issues. We stand mostly on common ground, but the contested ground represents the work to be done or, at the least, the work that *we* can do.

Notes

1. This strategy is necessitated by the fact that the version of Cartwright's paper contained in this book is very different from the one for which this comment was originally drafted over a year earlier. Cartwright's views—or at least her current expression of them—are now even closer to views that I would endorse. But how do you catch a moonbeam? I have edited the current version just enough to remove any confusing references. I hope that what remains will have its own independent interest even if it less than squarely confronts Cartwright's current chapter.

2. See Hoover (1994a). Nowak (1980), for example, regards idealizations as essences.

3. See Hendry and Mizon (1990) for a rebuttal to Leamer's view, and Pratt and Schlaifer (1984) for a more general discussion of the difficulties of obtaining accurate structural measurements when important variables are omitted from regression equations.

4. Cartwright (1991: 151–154) offers an explicit argument against the criterion of robustness against misspecfication. The general message that coefficient estimates are not robust to changes in functional form is implicit in the discussion of weak exogeneity in Engle, Hendry, and Richard (1983). McAleer, Pagan, and Volcker (1985) and Hendry and Mizon (1990) provide specific rebuttals to Leamer's methodology; while Hendry (1983, 1988) and Hendry and Richard (1982, 1987), provide an alternative statistical approach.

References

Cartwright, Nancy. (1983). *How the Laws of Physics Lie.* Oxford: Clarendon Press.

———. (1989). *Nature's Capacities and Their Measurement.* Oxford: Clarendon Press.

———. (1991). "Replicability, Reproducibility, and Robustness: Comments on Harry Collins." *History of Political Economy* 23, 143–156.

Cooley, Thomas F., and Stephen F. LeRoy. (1985). "Atheoretical macroeconometrics: A Critique." *Journal of Monetary Economics* 16(3) (November), 283–308.

Engle, Robert E., David F. Hendry, and Jean-Francois Richard. (1983). "Exogeneity." *Econometrica* 51(2), 113–127.

Glymour, Clark, Richard Scheines, Peter Sprites, and Kevin Kelly. (1987). *Discovering Causal Structure: Artificial Intelligence, Philosophy of Science, and Statistical Modeling.* Orlando: Academic Press.

Hendry, David F. (1983). "Econometric Modelling: The Consumption Function in Retrospect." *Scottish Journal of Political Economy* 30, 193–220.

————. (1987). "Econometric Methodology: A Personal Perspective." In Truman F. Bewley (ed.), *Advances in Econometrics* (vol. 2). Cambridge: Cambridge University Press.

————. (1988). "Encompassing." *National Institute Economic Review* (August), 88–92.

Hendry, David F., and Grayham Mizon. (1990). "Procrustean Econometrics: Or Stretching and Squeezing Data." In Clive W. J. Granger (ed.), *Modelling Economic Series: Readings in Econometric Methodology*. Oxford: Clarendon Press, 1990.

Hendry, David F., and Jean-François Richard. (1982). "On the Formulation of Empirical Models in Dynamic Econometrics." *Journal of Econometrics* 20, 3–33.

————. (1987). "Recent Developments in the Theory of Encompassing." In B. Cornet and H. Tulkens (eds.), *Contributions to Operation Research and Econometrics, The XXth Anniversary of CORE*. Cambridge, MA: MIT Press.

Hoover, Kevin D. (1990). "The Logic of Causal Inference: Econometrics and the Conditional Analysis of Causation." *Economics and Philosophy* 6(2), 207–234.

————. (1991). "Six Queries About Idealization in an Empirical Context." In Bert Hamminga and Neil B. De Marchi (eds.), *Idealization VI: Idealization in Economics. Poznan Studies in the Philosophy of Science and the Humanities*, vol. 38, 43–54. Amsterdam: Rodopi.

————. (1994). "Econometrics as Observation: The Lucas Critique, Causality and the Nature of Econometric Inference." *Journal of Economic Methodology* 1(1) (June), 65–80.

Hoover, Kevin D., and Steven M. Sheffrin (1992). "Causation, Spending and Taxes: Sand in the Sandbox or Tax Collector for the Welfare State?" *American Economic Review* 82(1) (March), 225–248.

McAleer, Michael, Adrian Pagan, and Paul A. Volcker. (1985). "What Will Take the Con Out of Econometrics? *American Economic Review* 75, 292–307.

Morgan, Mary. (1990). *The History of Econometric Ideas*. Cambridge: Cambridge University Press.

Nowak, Leszek. (1980). *The Structure of Idealization: Towards a Systematic Interpretation of the Marxian Idea of Science*. Dordrecht: Reidel.

Pratt, J. W., and Robert Schlaifer. (1984). "On the Nature and Discovery of Causal Structure." *Journal of the American Statistical Association* 79(385) (March), 9–24, discussion 25–33.

Reichenbach, Hans. (1956). *The Direction of Time*. Berkeley: University of California Press.

Salmon, Wesley C. (1984). *Scientific Explanation and the Causal Structure of the World*. Princeton: Princeton University Press.

Suppes, Patrick. (1970). "A Probabilistic Theory of Causality." *Acta Philosophica Fennica*, Fasc. 24.

4 THE EPISTEMIC FOUNDATIONS OF NASH EQUILIBRIUM

Cristina Bicchieri

4.1. Introduction

In the last twenty years or so game theorists have devoted much effort to the development of so-called refinements of Nash equilibrium. However, too little attention has been paid to the very basic question of how a Nash equilibrium comes about. A Nash equilibrium (Nash, 1951) is a strategy profile in which each player's strategy is a best reply to the others' strategies. The problem is that nothing in the definition of Nash equilibrium entails that players will in fact play their equilibrium strategies. It is quite possible that an equilibrium is played by chance, but for the concept of Nash equilibrium to have predictive value it must be the case that players choose an equilibrium rather than happen upon one. A traditional game-theoretic argument for the predictive significance of equilib-rium points asserts that a process of reflection about what other rational players should expect, and accordingly should do, will lead to one of the equilibrium points, so that rational agents who understand the game and think it through thoroughly before choosing their action should play in this way, even if the game is played only once.[1]

The above argument presupposes that there is a match between what players do and what other players expect them to do. What needs to be specified then are the epistemic conditions that make this match possible. For example, it might be assumed that players have common knowledge of the strategies that are actually played (Aumann and Brandenburger, 1991).[2] In this case the strategies must be in equilibrium, but we are presupposing here what we wanted to explain. Another possibility is to explore the predictive power of the assumption that players know the structure of the game and are rational (that is, they maximize expected utility). As I shall argue, in many nontrivial cases knowledge of the game being played and self-evident principles of rationality are not sufficient to guarantee that an equilibrium will be attained. In such cases, it is usually further assumed that the structure of the game and players' rationality are common knowledge. Yet even when common knowledge is present, there are games in which this much knowledge is not sufficient to infer a correct prediction of the opponents' choices.

Since playing a Nash equilibrium involves correct expectations on the part of the players, one might impose the additional epistemic requirement that the beliefs that players hold about the strategies of others are common knowledge. I shall argue that common knowledge of beliefs is an implausible assumption. Moreover, the assumption does not guarantee that players will end up with correct expectations if they have mutually inconsistent beliefs to begin with. If we want to maintain that Nash equilibrium is a good prediction of how the game will be played, we must explain how rational players come to have correct beliefs in the absence of any conclusive evidence about how other players are going to choose. Presumably, correct beliefs are the result of a rational procedure such as, for example, Bayesian updating from so-called priors. Players, that is, may learn to play an equilibrium through repeated interactions, and what has to be made explicit is the dynamics of such interactions and the conditions under which the learning process converges. The purpose of this chapter, however, is not that of providing a dynamic analysis. It is rather an attempt to state the epistemic conditions required for a given strategy profile to be a Nash equilibrium. My conclusion is that these conditions are seldom met in a static context such as the one depicted by one-shot games; in such cases, we must be prepared to admit that Nash equilibrium has no particular claim on us.

4.2. Mutual Rational Beliefs

Consider the case of the isolated agent facing nature: time and resources are scarce, and there may be risk or uncertainty about future states of the world. Bayesian decision theory tells us how such an agent will decide when facing different circumstances: he has preferences, has beliefs (including probabilistic assessments), and is rational, in that he aims at maximizing expected utility.

Suppose now we introduce other agents into our agent's environment and make them interact. Is a theory of their interaction reducible to a theory of the isolated agent? One might wonder why there needs to be any difficulty here. After all, the only difference between a natural environment and a social environment is just the presence of other people; rational choice looks the same in both cases. Imagine Robinson Crusoe, alone on his island, deciding whether to spend the afternoon cutting wood or, allowing himself to be lazy, taking a bath, napping, and eating bananas later on. He prefers the second alternative but worries that tomorrow it might rain, in which case he would be better off under a roof built with the wood he could cut today. To be uncertain about the rain simply means assigning subjective probabilities to the possible states of tomorrow's weather, and to be rational means to maximize expected utility with respect to this probabilistic assessment.

Now think of a different scenario. Robinson has met Friday, so his environment has changed; there is nature with all its uncertainties, but now Robinson has got a companion. He still faces a choice between industry and laziness, with an important difference. If Friday were to cut the wood, Robinson could be lazy without worrying. Alas, Friday is on the other side of the island, and Robinson cannot communicate with him until tonight. To dramatize the problem, let us suppose that the two friends were never before in a 'similar situation, so they cannot rely on past experience to solve their coordination problem. Let us assume further that Robinson knows Friday is facing the same dilemma. Indeed, suppose both know one of four things can happen: either one cuts the wood while the other rests, both cut the wood, or both rest. In this setting, there is no independent best choice that each of them can make, and because the other's expected choice is relevant to one's own decision, each wants to know what the other is planning to do.

Since Robinson is uncertain as to what Friday will do, he should assess a subjective probability distribution for Friday's choice of action. Then if he is rational, he will proceed to maximize his expected utility. I will assume throughout that actions and states are independent, in that the probability of a state is not conditional on one's act. In our example, dependence does not mean that Robinson's choice causally affects Friday's choice, since they choose independently and simultaneously. Dependence would rather mean that Robinson sees his choice as a strong clue to Friday's choice, so that he would assign a high subjective probability to Friday's doing whatever it is that he does (Jeffrey, 1965: 16). If Robinson and Friday were clones, then the hypothesis that one's action is evidence for what the other's choice will be would not be too extravagant. What I am assuming instead is that the two friends are different people who find themselves in symmetrical situations, so there is no reason to use one's choice of a given course of action as a relevant piece of information in calculating the likelihood of another's choice.

It is important to understand that Robinson's aim is not just that of making a guess about Friday's behavior and acting accordingly; he wants to make a very good guess, he wants to predict as accurately as he can Friday's behavior so as to "coordinate" with him. Robinson could well consider Friday's possible actions as among the possible states of the world. But how would he assess the probability of each such state? Friday is a human being and as such is capable of strategic reasoning and of forming goals and expectations that will influence his choice. Robinson knows that Friday is trying to solve a strategic problem analogous to his own, and he cannot hope to solve his own strategic problem without putting himself in Friday's shoes and trying to decide what he would do if he were in Friday's place. In order to assign probabilities to Friday's choices of action, Robinson needs to have a theory (however rudimentary) of Friday's behavior, and since Friday's choice will presumably be guided by his beliefs and desires, Robinson will first need to have some ideas about them. Each of the two friends is like a chess player who has to decide what move to make and tries to imagine how the opponent will respond to each possible move and what the opponent may think he himself will do after each possible move on his part. The analogy with chess is imperfect because Robinson and Friday are not taking turns but rather are choosing simultaneously. More important, they are trying to coordinate their actions, whereas chess players are not. The crucial similarity is rather that each party engages in strategic analysis, trying to figure out what the other will do by putting himself into the opponent's position.

Although we seldom know for sure other people's preferences and values, and whether the alternatives they face are those that we perceive as alternatives, as long as we believe that their choice is constrained by the situation they are in, we can try to anticipate their choice by imagining ourselves in that position, endowed with those very goals and options. And this is just what Robinson and Friday are doing. Our story can be greatly simplified by having each know that the other, besides facing the same options he does, has the same preferences he has, in that each prefers to be idle if the other works, but each prefers to work rather than risking being unsheltered on a rainy day. Let us take for the time being Robinson's side, with the understanding that Friday is involved in a similar reasoning process, and let us analyze the logic being employed one step at a time. Putting L for lazy and I for industrious, Friday's preference ranking can be expressed thus:

L, I Friday rests and Robinson works.
I, I Both work.
I, L Friday works and Robinson rests.
L, L Both give way to laziness.

The top of the list is Friday's most preferred option, followed by the other options in decreasing order of preference. An easy way to order preferences over outcomes is by means of numbers (let us call them utiles), so Robinson may couple each alternative with a number. That number has only ordinal significance: it represents the option's ranking in the list and not how much, or with what intensity, Friday enjoys that outcome.[3] Thus we can write $L, I = 4$; $I, I = 2$; $I, L = 2$; $L, L = 1$. This ranking would have little meaning without a further assumption: Friday is rational, and hence he will try to get as much as he can out of the circumstances. Since he is not acting under certainty (Robinson is now part of his environment), for him to be rational means trying to maximize his expected utility. To do so, he has to sum the utiles he can get by performing a given action weighted by the probabilities of his friend's choices and then choose that action that gets him the highest expected value. We further assume that both friends know that to be rational means to maximize one's expected utility.

In order to decide how well Robinson (R) can infer Friday's (F) behavior from what he knows about him, let us review Robinson's information:

(i) R knows F is rational.
(ii) R knows all of F's possible actions.
(iii) R knows F's preferences over outcomes.

What Robinson knows makes him predict that Friday would certainly allow himself to be lazy just in case he *expects* Robinson to cut the wood. But propositions (i)–(iii) tell Robinson nothing about Friday's expectations. Propositions (i)–(iii) do not let Robinson infer anything specific about Friday unless he makes some further assumption about Friday's knowledge, or the evidence from which he reasons about Robinson. Were he to think that Friday is completely ignorant about Robinson's available choices, preferences, or rationality, Robinson would have to conclude that Friday is at a loss in trying to guess Robinson's choice. In this case Friday's inability to predict Robinson's choice would make Robinson unable to predict Friday's choice, too. As a matter of fact, Robinson needs to make the following assumptions to proceed toward predictability:

(iv) F knows that R is rational.
(v) F knows all of R's possible actions.
(vi) F knows R's preferences over outcomes.

Now suppose that Robinson knows (iv)–(vi). Is he any better off in terms of predictive ability? Now he can see that Friday faces the same predicament he faced before since Friday is also trying to guess what Robinson will do. But it is also quite evident that from (iv)–(vi) alone Friday cannot infer Robinson's choice, since he has no way to tell what Robinson's predictions about him might be. For example, if Friday does not know that Robinson knows that he is rational, his actions will be based on a calculation that would not exclude the case where Robinson's choice reflects the possibility that Friday is not rational. Since Friday is including this case in his calculation, so must Robinson (who is again vicariously replicating Friday's reasoning). So both may still have to analyze what would happen if Friday were not rational. To avoid this, Friday must have additional knowledge; in particular, he will have to know propositions (i)–(iii). Hence a further assumption is needed:

(vii)   Both F and R know (i)–(vi).

Does (vii) make a difference? Note that (vii) says only that both friends know (i)–(vi), but nothing has been said to the effect that each knows that the other knows (i)–(vi). Put yourself in Friday's place and try to infer what you can from your information about Robinson. Friday knows Robinson is rational by (iv) and also knows that Robinson knows that he is rational by (i) and (vii). But does Friday know that Robinson knows that Friday knows that Robinson is rational? The question is cumbersome but not vacuous. Since Friday does not know whether Robinson knows that he knows that Robinson is rational (assumption (iv)), his actions will be based, as in the preceding case, on a calculation including the case in which Robinson does not know (iv). That is, Friday cannot rule out the case in which Robinson believes that he thinks Robinson is irrational. Irrationality here means behavior that flies in the face of one's best interest as determined by one's preference ranking. In our example, it may mean that Robinson errs in predictable ways: his evaluations of the situation may be systematically wrong, he may be a person with poor self-control, or else he may make his choice depend on circumstances that have nothing to do with the choice setting, as when one lets an oracle decide for him.

To be sure, Robinson can replicate Friday's reasoning, and since Friday's putative belief that Robinson is irrational would make it harder for him to forecast Robinson's future behavior, Friday's likely difficulty in predicting in turn affects Robinson's ability to make a reliable prediction. Note, again, that Friday is not alone in including the case in which Robinson does not know (iv) in his calculation. Even if Robinson knows (iv), he does not know whether Friday knows that he knows it, hence he has to assess what Friday would do if he were to doubt that Robinson knows (iv). Thus both may have to analyze what would happen were Robinson not to know (iv). A similar argument applies to the symmetric case in which Robinson does not know that Friday knows (i).

It is not too difficult to see that providing both of them with knowledge of

(vii) does not solve the predictability problem, which reappears at higher levels of knowledge. With n levels of mutual knowledge of rationality, it will still be the case that each will be uncertain as to the other's n-th level knowledge of his rationality; to dispel the uncertainty, a further, $n + 1$-th level of mutual knowledge of rationality must be added. To eliminate the nuisance of calculating what a less than fully rational player would do, we may want to assume that (i)–(vi) are *common knowledge*:

(viii)   (i)–(vi) are common knowledge among F and R.

Simply stated, common knowledge of p among a group G means that each member of G knows p, and each knows that each knows p, . . . and so on ad infinitum (Lewis, 1969). Common knowledge of rationality, preferences, and strategies may facilitate the task of predicting an opponent's strategy but, as I shall argue, does not guarantee that the resulting prediction will be correct.

How does one reason from the above assumptions to a solution to the Robinson-Friday predicament? By now we know that none of the parties can solve his own strategic problem without solving the other's at the same time. But is the information available to them sufficient to identify a unique course of action for each? Given propositions (i)–(viii), what Robinson now knows for sure is that Friday will cut wood only if he expects Robinson not to, since in this case to cut wood will be Friday's best reply to Robinson's choice. That is, were Friday to assign probability 1 to the event that Robinson chooses to rest, he would maximize his expected utility by working. If for some reason it was obvious that Robinson would choose to be lazy, then it would be obvious what Friday's response would be, since Friday's rationality, options, and preferences are by assumption common knowledge. Since in this context a truly obvious mode of behavior must be obvious to both parties, each would assign probability 1 to the other doing the obvious thing. In this case, a solution would be reached, in the sense that the two friends would succeed in coordinating their actions to their mutual satisfaction.

Alas, Robinson's choice is anything but obvious. Indeed, Friday can predict with confidence that Robinson will be lazy only if he is reasonably convinced that Robinson expects him to be industrious. And why should he? After all, what one does depends on what one believes the other is choosing, which in turn depends on what the other thinks one is going to do. A person's choice may be unpredictable like the weather, but for different reasons. Someone is unpredictable not because he chooses randomly or is incapable of forming a plan and sticking to it, but because his choice depends on what he expects you to choose, which in turn depends on what you expect him to choose. There seems to be no way to ground these mutual expectations other than referring to another, higher-level expectation, and what the prospective choosers may be left with is just an infinite regress of expectations.

A crucial feature of all kinds of strategic interaction is that what it is rational to do depends on what one expects other agents will do. I have discussed elsewhere (Bicchieri, 1987, 1993) what can happen when a large number of agents expect something to occur, whether inflation, a stock market crash, or the victory of a political candidate. Expectations can be self-fulfilling or self-defeating, and this is because they are causally relevant to the final outcome. When large numbers are involved, one may well be aware that the final outcome depends on the aggregate choices of a multitude of people, so that one's individual choice has negligible effect on the final outcome, and the best one can do is try to guess correctly what the majority choice will be. Small numbers involve expectations about others' actions as well, but in addition there is awareness that one's choice matters, in that other people have expectations about one's own choice and these expectations are to be taken into account. Could one take other people's expectations as exogenously given, the problem of strategy choice would be simple: one would choose the strategy that maximizes one's expected utility under the assumption that all other agents act in accordance with his expectation. If these mutual expectations are not given, then the problem arises of which beliefs a rational individual ought to have who expects every other agent to act rationally, and to hold equally rational expectations about everyone else. This problem has been appropriately termed by Harsanyi one of mutual rational expectations (Harsanyi, 1965: 450). As we shall see, when rational choice depends on beliefs about other agents' beliefs, it may be difficult to specify a uniquely best course of action because of the indeterminacy of those beliefs.

Note well that expected utility maximization in an interactive setting is no different from expected utility maximization in the purely decision-theoretic context. Weather is certainly no more predictable than people, and in both cases one can do no better than optimizing in light of one's priors. In the decision-theoretic approach, one predicts the behavior of other agents first and then solves his decision problem. A fundamental difficulty with this approach is that to assess his subjective probability distribution over Friday's actions, Robinson should try to imagine himself in Friday's situation. In so doing, he may realize that Friday cannot determine his optimal course of action without assessing his subjective probability distribution over Robinson's possible actions. And so Robinson may come to understand that he cannot predict Friday's behavior until he has some idea of what Friday expects him to do, which is precisely the problem he started with. In an interactive context such as this, Robinson would try to solve his and Friday's decision problems simultaneously.

What Robinson and Friday are after is a solution to the strategic problem they face. Their goal is not just that of choosing in a rational manner, given arbitrary priors: they want their choices to coordinate in the right way so that they can build a shelter without a waste of effort. To this end, just saying that the actors have some internally consistent beliefs does not say much. In particular, we would expect these beliefs to be consistent with what the actors know about each other. The problem, then, is to analyze what relationship there is between beliefs, knowledge of the opponent, and the kind of predictions we would make about the actors reaching a solution. As I argued before, a solution to a strategic problem is always a mutual solution: each participant knows that the outcome is the joint result of everybody's choice, so each makes his choice conditional on the others' choices. And this, I have argued, requires more than simple knowledge of the other agents' rationality, preferences, and available actions; it requires a conjecture of what it is that others believe. Evidently one's guess may be wrong, and so the ensuing expectation about another's choice will be faulty. In this case, however, we cannot say that a solution to the strategic problem has been achieved. Let me make this point very clear with an example. Suppose that Robinson expects Friday to be lazy. Then he chooses to be industrious, fearing that they will be left unsheltered on a rainy day. And if Friday likewise expects Robinson to be lazy, he will proceed to cut the wood himself. Both make a rational choice based on expectations that turn out to be wrong and the joint outcome is a disappointment to both, for it is not necessary that both cut wood in order to build a shelter, and each would have been better off by remaining idle if the other were known to do the work.

Is there a pair of expectations they can have about each other that will lead them to choices that confirm those expectations? Yes, if Robinson expects Friday to be lazy, he is content with working, and if Friday expects Robinson to work he is content with being lazy. Notice that if the roles are reversed, in that it is Friday who is expected to be industrious, and Robinson lazy, we still have a case of fulfilled expectations. In both cases the joint outcome of their choices will be satisfactory to both, since they succeed in coordinating and cutting just the right amount of wood that is needed to build the shelter. Our story then has two solutions in which the parties succeed in coordinating their actions. More generally, we may say that a solution to Robinson and Friday's coordination problem is a combination of actions that has the property that if they both make the corresponding choices—each expecting the other to do so—each has behaved correctly in accordance with his expectations and each has confirmed the other's expectations. If we assume that Robinson and Friday are trying hard to coordinate their choices, it becomes clear how important it is that they have the right expectations about each other. But where do these expectations come from? In our example we have supposed that Robinson and Friday are rational, have two available actions each, and a preference ordering over outcomes. We have even assumed they have common knowledge of all of the above. And yet they

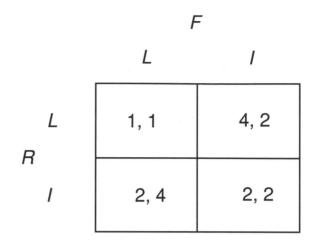

Figure 4.1

cannot correctly predict each other's choice on this basis alone. But if they cannot correctly predict each other's action they may not reach a solution and we, the theorists who are observing them, will not be able to predict the outcome either.

A general point to be made is that seldom in a strategic context can beliefs be determined solely on the basis of the payoffs involved and of hypotheses like rationality or common knowledge of rationality. Of course, one may know things about the other parties that are not written down in the model, so perhaps one can predict the opponents quite well. But what we are interested in is whether what is generally specified in a model of strategic interaction is enough for the parties correctly to infer what the others will do, as well as for the theorist to predict that a specific solution will obtain. My concern in what follows will thus be with the scope of predictions based on rationality and common knowledge of rationality alone. I shall subsequently handle more complex cases in which common knowledge of beliefs is called forth in order to get a solution.

4.3. Game-Theoretic Reasoning

Let us now look at how the story that began this chapter is approached through game theory. The choices faced by Robinson and Friday can be put in strategic (normal) form as shown in Figure 4.1. The two *pure strategies* available to each player are L (being lazy) and I (being industrious). Each combination of strategies results in a pair of payoffs, one for each player, denominated in units of utility. For each pair of payoffs, the first is the payoff of Robinson, and the second is Friday's. More formally, we say that a normal form game is completely defined by three elements: a list of players $i = 1, \ldots, n$; for each player i, a finite list of pure strategies $S_i = \{s_{ij} \in S_i: j = 1, \ldots, m\}$ that i might employ; a payoff function u_i that gives player i's payoff $u_i(s)$ for each n-tuple of strategies $(s_1, \ldots, s_n)$, where $u_i: \overset{n}{\underset{j=1}{X}} S_j \to R$. We customarily denote all players other than some given i as $-i$. For reasons I shall discuss later, a player may want to randomize over his pure strategies; a probability distribution over pure strategies is called a *mixed strategy*. Each player's randomization is assumed to be statistically independent of that of his opponents, and the payoffs to a mixed strategies profile are the expected values of the corresponding pure strategy payoffs.[4] We denote with Σ_i the space of player i's mixed strategies, where $\sigma_i(s_i)$ is the probability that σ_i assigns to pure strategy s_i. The set of pure strategies to which σ_i assigns a positive probability is called the *support* of σ_i. Finally, player i's payoff to profile σ, denoted as $u_i(\sigma)$, is defined as

$$\sum_{s \in S} \left\{ \prod_{j=1}^{n} \sigma_j(s_j) \right\} u_i(s)$$

The matrix in Figure 4.1 depicts a static simultaneous-choice environment: each player picks a strategy independently and without communicating with the other, and the outcome is the joint result of these two strategies. Another point, not illustrated in our matrix, is that the game is one of *complete information*, in that the players know the rules of the game and other players' payoffs. In the example of Robinson and Friday, I have further assumed that they have common knowledge that both possess this information. It turns out that sometimes we do not need to make this additional assumption. There are games in which a few rounds of the "I know that you know that I know . . ." assumption are enough to imply a solution, and there are games in which a player does not even have to consider the opponents' payoffs in order to decide what is best for him. In this latter case all the information that is relevant to a player's choice is contained in the matrix representation, so if he has a reason to prefer one strategy over another, this reason must be clear by looking at the matrix alone. For example, if a player has a strategy that she would be satisfied with having chosen no matter what the others chose, this fact must be reflected in her payoffs. In this case there is an endogenous argument (that is, an argument that takes as its sole premise the structure of the game) that concludes in favor of picking a particular strategy as the 'obvious' choice. If we draw up a modified version of Figure 4.1, we have an example of what we mean by an endogenous argument (see Figure 4.2).

This matrix differs from Figure 4.1 in an important way. Whatever Friday

$$F$$

	L	I
L	1, 1	4, 2
I	2, 4	5, 2

R

Figure 4.2

does, Robinson is better off by being industrious rather than lazy. We can modify our original story and explain the new payoffs by saying that Robinson has a work ethic that makes him equally appreciate his own and others' working habits, whereas he gets annoyed at the sight of laziness, and this is why the combination (I, L) gets him only a payoff of 2. We say that I is a *strictly dominant* strategy, in that it guarantees Robinson a better payoff than any other strategy, irrespective of Friday's choice. If instead a strategy guarantees a player payoffs that are greater or equal to the payoffs of any other strategy, that strategy is only *weakly dominant* for him.

   More formally, given strategy sets $S_1, \ldots, S_n$, let S_{-i} denote the set $S_1 \times \ldots \times S_{i-1} \times S_{i+1} \times \ldots \times S_n$. For any finite set S, let $\Sigma(S)$ be the set of probability distribution over S, where $\sigma \in \Sigma(S_{-i})$ is a subjective probability distribution of player i over the strategy profiles of the opponents. Let s_i^*, range over the set of pure strategies S_i and let $u_i (s_i^*, s_{-i})$ be i's utility for playing s_i^*, given that his opponents play the strategy profile s_{-i}. We say that a strategy s_i is strictly dominated for player i if there exists some (randomized) strategy $\sigma_i \in \Sigma(S_i)$ such that

$$(*) \quad \sum_{s_i^* \in S_i,} \sigma_i (s_i^*) \, u_i (s_i^*, s_{-i}) > u_i (s_i, s_{-i}) \text{ for all } s_{-i} \in S_{-i},$$

whereas a strategy s_i is weakly dominated if there exists a $\sigma_i \in \Sigma(S_i)$ such that (*) holds with weak inequality, and the inequality is strict for at least one s_{-i}. Since a rational player will choose a strategy s_i^* such that

$$\max_{s_i^* \in S_i} \sum_{s_{-i} \in S_{-i}} \sigma(s_{-i}) \, u_i (s_i^*, s_{-i}),$$

and a strategy s_i is strictly dominated for player i if there is no probability assessment σ_i to which s_i is a best reply, if one knows that a player is rational one can immediately rule out some of his strategies, as they are not best replies to any probabilistic assessment over the opponents' strategies. In Figure 4.2, strategy I is the obvious course of action for Robinson. He would reach this conclusion even without knowing Friday's payoffs or that Friday is a rational decider. Friday, on the other hand, has to decide on the basis of his expectation of Robinson's choice. If he knows Robinson's payoffs, as well as the fact that Robinson is a rational decider, he assesses zero probability that L will be played. Then his obvious response is L, which is the best he can do against Robinson's expected choice of I. If we think the players will think through the game in this way we can predict that the outcome will be (I, L).

What I have just described is an iterated dominance argument. We begin by eliminating one strictly dominated strategy for one of the players, and if we believe that the opponent is rational and knows the other player's payoffs and rationality, we may infer that he will figure out what the first player is choosing. Now we may discover that in this reduced game we are able to eliminate some of the opponent's strategies on the ground that they are dominated, too. When we further reduce the game, the first player may have more dominated strategies that we proceed to eliminate, and we continue the process until all dominated strategies have been eliminated. Sometimes iterated dominance succeeds in reducing the set of available strategies for each player to a singleton. In this case we can predict that the unique resulting profile of undominated strategies is the solution to the game. Note that to complete each step of the iteration it is sufficient to add a new level of the "I know that you know . . . that I know my opponent's payoffs and rationality" assumption. As the number of iterations grows larger, our prediction becomes less and less robust because it is vulnerable to small changes in players' information. For example, even if you know that your opponent is rational, you may not be so sure that he thinks much of your rationality, or else you may doubt that your opponent knows that you regard him as rational, and so on. In each case, your choice will depend on your probability assessments, which may or may not lead you to choose in a way consistent with iterated elimination of dominated strategies. To simplify things, game theorists suppose that rationality and payoffs are common knowledge, and for the time being we will retain this assumption.

Formally, the process of iterated deletion of strictly dominated strategies proceeds recursively as follows: suppose there are only two players, i and j, and let S_i be the initial set of pure strategies of player i. Because player i will have probabilistic beliefs about the opponent's strategies, she will only consider the strategy subset $S_i \supseteq S_i^1$ that contains all those strategies that are best replies to some $\sigma \in \Sigma(S_j)$, i.e. $S_i^1 = \{s_i \in S_i: s_i$ is a best reply to some $\sigma \in \Sigma(S_j)\}$. But

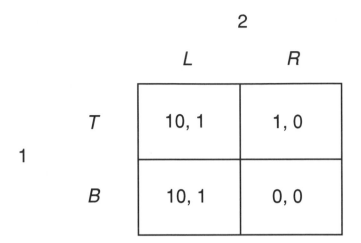

Figure 4.3

player i knows that player j is rational, too, so she predicts that j will choose only actions that are best replies to some probabilistic assessment by j—that is, j will choose strategies $s_j \in S_j^1$. And since rationality is common knowledge, any probability distribution of i will assign zero probability to any $s_j \notin S_j^1$. If some of j's strategies are thus ruled out, the set of i's possible strategies gets further restricted to $S_i^2 = \{s_i \in S_i^1 : s_i$ is a best reply to $\sigma \in \Sigma(S_j^1)\}$, and rational player i should then choose a strategy that belongs to the set S_i^2. Since rationality is common knowledge, each player will replicate the other's reasoning and consequently restrict her choice set up to the point at which no further reduction is possible. Because we have assumed the set of pure strategies to be finite, there must be a number n such that, for all $m \geq n$, $S_i^m = S_i^n \neq \emptyset$.

Thus far I have only considered iterated elimination of strictly dominated strategies. The case of weakly dominated strategies is less straightforward. For one, it is not true that a weakly dominated strategy cannot be a best reply to any beliefs. In fact, for any weakly dominated strategy (that is not strictly dominated) there is always some belief for which the strategy is a best reply. Putting the point differently, weak dominance that is not strict means that there is at least one choice on the part of an opponent that makes one indifferent between the weakly dominated strategy and other strategies. That it is more difficult to justify the choice of a weakly dominated strategy is illustrated by Figure 4.3.

In Figure 4.3, T weakly dominates B, but common knowledge of rationality implies that player 2 is expected to choose L (which strictly dominates R), and this makes 1 indifferent between T and B, since both strategies are best replies to L. The choice of T is justified only by the belief that either player 2 is not rational, or that he might make a mistake and play R instead. To make player 1 choose prudently, we should either drop the assumption that rationality is common knowledge, or else we may wish to include assumptions to the effect that—due to some sort of random noise—what one does does not always coincide with what one decides to do. This example shows how the analysis of some games is very sensitive to small uncertainties about the behavioral assumptions players make, as well as to the amount of information they have about the structure of the game and their mutual rationality. I shall return to this important point presently.

Now if we turn to Figure 4.1 it is easy to determine that there is no dominant strategy for either player, and so there is no "obvious course of action" for the players to follow. In this case rationality and common knowledge of rationality cannot recommend a specific strategy as the "obvious choice" for each player. And since one's expectation about the opponent's strategy choice cannot be grounded on the assumptions made in the model, it is difficult to imagine how the players could predict with any accuracy each other's choice. Because one can make many conceivable conjectures about the opponent's choice, it is possible that the joint outcome will turn out to be an unpleasant surprise for both. If Robinson believes that Friday plays I with probability 1 he will respond with L. And if Friday believes that Robinson will play I with probability 1, he will pick L, too. But (L, L) is the worst outcome for both, since if they refrain from work they will be exposed to the likely injuries of rain the following day.[5] The pair of expectations I have just described are individually plausible, but they jointly lead to choices that do not bear those expectations out.

4.4. Consistent Beliefs

We may well ask whether imposing rationality conditions on players' beliefs would yield further restrictions on their strategy sets, thereby enabling them correctly to predict each other's choice, as well as facilitating our forecast of the outcome of the game. To illustrate this point, consider the game shown in Figure 4.4.

Neither player in Figure 4.4 has a dominated strategy, and so we cannot use an iterated dominance argument to solve the game. How might the players reason to an outcome? If Row were to expect Column to choose left with probability 1, then her best reply would be top, and if Column were to expect row to pick top with probability 1, then his best reply would be left. This only establishes that (T, L) can be a solution to the game; it does not tell why a player ought to assign probability 1 or, for that matter, any other probability to the

Column

		L	C	R
	T	10, 4	4, -1	4, -1
Row **M**		2, 1	5, -1	2,20
	B	2, 1	3, 2	50,0

Figure 4.4

opponent's choosing that particular strategy. A further element in the players' reasonings needs emphasizing: if Row assigns a probability equal (or very close) to 1 to left being played, one way to justify her belief is to show that it is consistent with a putative belief she attributes to Column that justifies his choice of left. For example, if Row believes that Column will play left with probability 1, Row must also believe that Column expects Row to play top with probability 1 (since, by assumption, Column is rational), and further believe that Column believes that Row expects Column to play left with probability 1 . . . and so on in an infinite series of expectations. We are simply requiring that one's beliefs about the opponent's choice and the conjectures supporting it must be *consistent* with each other. This is not a surprising requirement, in that we usually expect of a rational agent that he has consistent beliefs. In the single-agent case, this means that one cannot believe that p and not p at the same time, and that one cannot believe p but disbelieve what p entails. In a strategic environment, beliefs are about other people's actions and the beliefs that induce them to act in one way or another. For example, one cannot consistently believe that a player is rational and does not choose his best reply, given the putative beliefs about other players' choices one imputes to him. Thus defined, consistency is an internal matter: one's beliefs about other players can be consistent and yet wrong.

So far I have been assuming that players' beliefs are rational in the following sense: a player's belief should be logically coherent and consistent with his overall belief system, and he ought to use all the information conveyed by the game situation in forming his beliefs. Note that belief consistency thus defined is not a unique feature of the attractive outcome (T, L) since it does not refer to players' *actual* beliefs, but only to their beliefs as they are *conjectured* by another player. For example, suppose that in our game Row believes that Column will play C with probability 1. Then she must also believe that Column assigns probability 1 to Row choosing B, since C is a best reply to B only, and Column is known to be rational. But Column must then also believe that Row expects R to be chosen with probability 1, since B is a best reply to R only, and Row is known to be rational. Then Column also believes that Row believes R is played with probability 1 because Row believes that Column expects her to choose M with probability 1, a choice in turn justified by Row's belief that Column plays C with probability 1. The original conjecture of Row is perfectly consistent with the nested beliefs she attributes to Column in order to justify her expectation that Column will pick C. In a game situation, an *internally consistent conjecture* can be defined as follows: if player i has some belief about player j, then he must believe his belief is among the possible beliefs that j has about i himself (Tan and Werlang, 1986).

Belief rationality thus interpreted, coupled with the assumption that the structure of the game and the rationality of the players are common knowledge, implies the restrictions on play embedded in the concept of *rationalizability* (Pearce, 1984; Bernheim, 1984). The idea is that a rational player will use only those strategies that are best replies to his beliefs about the strategies of the opponents. Since payoffs and rationality are common knowledge, one should not have arbitrary beliefs about the opponents' strategies, which can only be best replies to the beliefs one imputes to them; in turn, the opponents' beliefs that justify their strategy choices should not be arbitrary, which leads to the infinite series discussed above. More formally, suppose there are only two players, i and j, and let $\sigma \in \Sigma(S_j)$ denote player i's belief over j's choice of strategy. Setting $\Sigma(S_i) = \Sigma^0(S_i)$, we can recursively define $\Sigma^n(S_i) = \{\sigma_i \in \Sigma^{n-1}(S_i): \sigma_i$ is a best reply to some $\sigma \in \Sigma^{n-1}(S_j)\}$. The rationalizable strategies for player i are those strategies that belong to the intersection of all sets of strategies that survive after each round, that is

$$R_i = \bigcap_{n=0}^{\infty} \Sigma^n(S_i).$$

The rationalizability criterion is completely adequate if our aim is that of rationally justifying a strategy choice on the part of a player. If in addition we want to predict a player's choice, that criterion is often too weak. Rationalizability, while necessary for a rational solution, is hardly sufficient. In the absence of dominated strategies, we can rationalize every strategy profile. Since we want to restrict the evidence on which the epistemic rationality of the players is grounded to the game situation, we know that in the absence of dominance players' epistemic states are unrestricted. Therefore every alternative is optimal with respect to some epistemic state. To understand why prediction and justification need not coincide, let us replicate in detail the practical syllogism that provides a player with a decisive reason for selecting a specific strategy.[6] To keep things simple, the example is that of the two-person game of Figure 4.1, but the same reasoning can be easily extended to an n-person game. Also, the beliefs considered are *firm beliefs*, which means that whenever a player firmly believes that p, his subjective probability for p is 1. Below is a duplicate of the matrix in Figure 4.1.

Each player has two pure strategies (L_r and I_r for player R, and L_f and I_f for player F). By assumption, the structure of the game and players' rationality are common knowledge. A strategy profile can be rationalized by showing each player's practical inference that concludes in favor of doing his part in that strategy combination. For example, the profile ($L_r I_f$) can be rationalized as the outcome of two practical inferences, one by player R and the other by F. Let us interpret the symbols below as follows:

(i) $L_r | B_r I_f$ R plays L_r given his belief that F plays I_f.
(ii) $B_r L_f$ R believes that F plays L_f.
(iii) $B_r(L_f | B_f I_r)$ R believes that F plays L_f given that F believes that R plays I_r.
(iv) $B_r(B_f L_r)$ R believes that F believes that R plays L_r (loop belief).

Player R's practical syllogism (A^r) can be thus illustrated:

p_1^r R knows that F will choose a best reply to the strategy he believes R is playing.
p_2^r Player R knows that $L_r | B_r I_f$ and $I_r | B_r L_f$.
p_3^r Player R knows that $L_f | B_f I_r$ and $I_f | B_f L_r$.
p_4^r $B_r(B_f L_r)$.
c^r Player R chooses L_r.

The first premise lists player R's best replies to his possible beliefs about the opponent's choice. The second premise identifies the opponent's best replies to his possible beliefs about R's choice. And the third premise gives a loop belief: R expects F to expect him to play L_r, and hence by his second premise R must also expect F to choose I_f. It follows that he concludes in favor of strategy L_r. Similarly, F's practical syllogism (A^f) will be:

p_1^f F knows that R will choose a best reply to the strategy he believes F is playing.

p_2^f Player F knows that $L_f| B_f I_r$ and $I_f| B_f L_r$.

p_3^f Player F knows that $L_r| B_r I_f$ and $I_r| B_r L_f$.

p_4^f $B_f(B_r I_f)$.

c^f Player F chooses I_f.

Since by assumption the players have common knowledge of the structure of the game and of their rationality, premises p_1^r, p_2^r, p_3^r, p_1^f, p_2^f, p_3^f are common knowledge, too. Furthermore, a crucial premise in both arguments is each player's belief about the other player's conjecture about his own choice. How are the *loop beliefs* that appear in premises p_4^r and p_4^f justified? The criteria of belief rationality imposed so far only demand that if one expects a player to choose a given strategy, one must assign to that player beliefs to which that strategy is a best reply. For example, if $B_r(B_f L_r)$, consistency requires that player R also believes that $B_f(B_r I_f)$ (since L_r is only a best reply to R's belief that I_f is played). If so, R must further believe that $B_f(B_r(B_f L_r))$, and so on up to higher and higher levels of loop beliefs. Every new loop belief is justified both by common knowledge of rationality and by a further, higher-level loop belief. But an infinite iteration of loop beliefs can only rationalize the original loop belief, which remains ungrounded.

In our example the players are lucky. They start out with beliefs that are subsequently confirmed by the opponent's choice. But they might have been less fortunate, ending up with an outcome neither of them likes. For suppose that instead of p_4^f, player F has a different loop belief p_{4*}^f—namely, $B_f(B_r L_f)$. If so, F's choice will be to play L_f, but since by assumption player R still believes $B_f L_r$, the final outcome will be $(1, 1)$, a disappointment to both players. As in the former case, players' expectations are internally consistent, but they do not coordinate in the right way, and so they turn out to be wrong. Note that the practical inferences A^r and A^f that lead to the outcome $(4, 2)$ are *interconnected*, in that each player's choice is conditional upon his expectation about the opponent's choice. And the beliefs that appear in the last premise of each syllogism are *self-fulfilling*, in that a player's belief about what the opponent expects him to do induces him to behave in the expected way. But beliefs can be self-fulfilling in this sense without being correct, in that the belief one imputes to one's opponent may not coincide with his actual expectation. What distinguishes A^r and A^f from other plausible practical inferences is that in this case players' beliefs about the opponent's choice (and the opponent's beliefs supporting that choice) are correct, in that they coincide with the opponent's actual choice (and the opponent's beliefs that justify that choice).

The conclusion of each syllogism is the choice of a strategy that is the player's best reply to his conjecture about the opponent's choice. In the case of A^r and A^f, a player's best reply to the opponent's putative choice happens to be a best reply also to the opponent's actual choice. Thus a crucial feature of the pair of strategies $(L_r I_f)$ that result from A^r and A^f, respectively, is that each player's strategy is a best reply to the other's actual strategy. In playing $(L_r I_f)$, therefore, each player maximizes his expected utility and his choice is a best reply to the opponent's actual choice. In telling the story of Robinson and Friday, I pointed to the fact that both (I, L) and (L, I) were combinations of strategies in which the two friends were rational in the above sense and succeeded in coordinating their actions to their mutual satisfaction. I informally called those pairs of strategies solutions for the game, as they exemplify the idea that players choose rationally and that each player's choice is best against the opponent's actual choice. Again very informally, let us say that we require of a *solution* for the game that it be a combination of strategies, one for each player, such that each player does his best against the other players' choices. These considerations suggest a stability condition that beliefs about the opponents' choices must satisfy in order to support a solution for the game:

(C) If a player were to know the beliefs of the other players regarding his action, he would have no reason to change his beliefs about their actions.

When a player's beliefs lead to a unique action, a stable belief is also a correct belief.[7] For example, condition C is not satisfied by the beliefs appearing in premises p_{4*}^f and p_4^r. If each player were to know the belief of the other, he would have reason to revise his conjecture. Note that although a stable belief is always an internally consistent belief, the reverse need not be true. Premises p_{4*}^f and p_4^r, however, are in no way irrational, as internal consistency does not demand that we impose any substantive constraint upon beliefs.

So far I have established that the beliefs that support a solution are both internally consistent and correct. Since game theory purports to predict the behavior of rational players who choose in an interdependent manner, it is not surprising that it assumes that players, besides making rational choices, have rational beliefs, too. And we have seen that belief rationality usually means belief consistency. But even if we assume that belief rationality, too, is common knowledge among the players, we are not led to infer that they have correct beliefs. Nor can the players themselves infer what the correct beliefs would be, unless they are granted more evidence than common knowledge of payoffs and rationality alone. For the moment, we are left with a gap between our game-theoretic assumptions about the players and the solution (or solutions) for the game that we can easily identify but hardly predict as outcomes of actual play.

4.5. Justifications of Nash Equilibrium

Among the games we have looked at so far, only one was a good candidate for having an obvious solution—that is, a solution that we can confidently predict and the players themselves can identify as the obvious way to play the game. I am referring to the game in Figure 4.2, which was solved by an iterated dominance argument. Even if these arguments require fairly strong informational assumptions, the nice thing about them is that once you have accepted the assumptions, the conclusion about which profile of strategies will be played seems quite reasonable. Unfortunately all the other games we examined are not solvable by iterative elimination of dominated strategies. Let us turn to the game in Figure 4.4. Each strategy in this game is a unique best reply to some strategy be the other side, but in spite of this it might seem quite obvious to some of us that (T, L) will be played, since it has the unique feature, among all other possible strategy combinations, that players' expectations supporting it are both consistent and correct. If Row believes Column plays L, he will play T, and Column plays L exactly because he thinks Row plays T. Even so, the prediction of (T, L) seems questionable, since it is not really grounded on the customary assumptions we make about players' information and the structure of the game.

We may now ask: Had there been the possibility of communicating before playing the game, would Row and Column have been better off in terms of knowing what to do? We may imagine them discussing until they reach an agreement to follow a certain course of action (that is, to play a given pair of strategies). Afterwards they leave one another and communication is no longer possible between them; later each chooses his strategy in complete ignorance of the other's choice. The agreement, we must add, is not binding: there is no moral or material punishment for breaching it, and each player has the choice of breaching the agreement or keeping it. There are nonbinding agreements that have the following property: if one assumes the other party to be loyal, then one has every reason to be loyal himself. In other words, the agreement is *self-enforcing*. Can one envisage such agreements for the game in Figure 4.4? It is easy to check that if the players were to agree to play (T, L), then it would not be reasonable for either one to defect unilaterally. In fact, (T, L) is the only pair of pure strategies that is self-enforcing in the above sense. This is an example of *equilibrium analysis*. Each player is supposed to think "as if" he were not aware of strategic interdependence: considering a combination of other players' strategies as exogenously given, the player must seek to maximize his expected utility against them. To put it differently, to decide whether a combination of strategies is an equilibrium, a player must reason hypothetically and ask whether the fact that the other players play their part in that combination would induce him to modify his choice. For example, the strategy combination (M, C) of Figure 4.4 is not an equilibrium in that, were Column to expect Row to play M, he would do better by playing R instead of C. In this sense an agreement to play (M, C) would not be self-enforcing.

So far we have granted the possibility that players may meet before the play of the game with the aim of agreeing on a joint plan of action. It makes a big difference to the way the game is played if there exists a system for the enforcement of the contracts the players may enter into. Take again Figure 4.1. Here the players may enter a legal agreement to play the pair of strategies (I, I), with the understanding that whoever breaches the contract will pay a penalty. In this case, presumably the agreement is legally enforceable and therefore binding, and no player has an incentive to deviate from it. If the players are allowed to enter into binding agreements before the game is played, we say that the game is *cooperative*. In our examples we have allowed preplay communication but made no allowance for the existence of an enforcement mechanism that would make the terms of the agreement binding on the players. If preplay negotiation leads to an agreement, and there is no enforcement mechanism available, it becomes crucial to ask whether or not the agreement is self-enforcing, by virtue of being in the best interest of each player to adhere to. The games in which there exists no institution that makes an agreement among players binding are called *noncooperative*, and the standard solution concept for these games is called Nash equilibrium.

Informally, a *Nash equilibrium* (Nash 1951) specifies a set of strategies and beliefs such that each player's strategy is optimal given his beliefs about other players' strategies. As before, let $u_i(\sigma)$ be i's payoff if the strategy profile σ is played. Now define: σ_i^* is an equilibrium strategy for player i if and only if $u_i(\sigma_i^*, \sigma_{-i}^*) \geq u_i(s_i, \sigma_{-i}^*)$, for all pure strategies s_i belonging to the set S_i. A Nash equilibrium is a n-tuple of (mixed) strategies $\sigma_1^*, \ldots, \sigma_n^*$, one for each of the n players in the game, such that each σ_i^* is an equilibrium strategy.[8]

The Nash equilibrium is an appealing solution concept for noncooperative games for several reasons.[9] It captures an important feature of individual rationality that we have already sketched in our account of what is required of a solution. Being rational means maximizing one's expected utility under the constraint represented by what one expects other individuals to choose. Game theorists typically assign predictive value to Nash equilibrium; the best available explanation of the achievement of a Nash equilibrium in a given case is that each of the players knows what the others are going to do. It is for this reason that theorists who predict that a Nash equilibrium will be achieved also assume that players know what the others will do. But notice that knowledge of what others will do is not implied by the definition of Nash equilibrium. Therefore

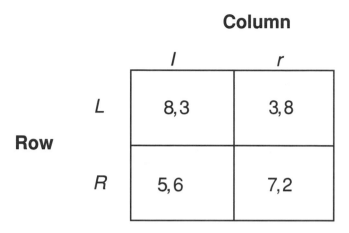

Figure 4.5

one wishing to explain the occurrence of a Nash equilibrium does well to explain how those correct beliefs are arrived at in the first place. I shall return to this point later.

Given the definition of Nash equilibrium, it is easy to verify that every self-enforcing agreement is a Nash equilibrium. Suppose two rational people are negotiating over how each of them will act in a given strategic situation and they settle on a joint course of action. If nobody can gain from deviating, the agreement will be honored. But the only agreement in which no player has an incentive to cheat is an agreement to play an equilibrium. Indeed, any agreement on a off-equilibrium pair of strategies would be self-defeating, as there would be at least one player who would profit from deviating, and therefore the agreement would be doomed. At this point, all we can say is that whenever a strategy profile is a good candidate for a self-enforcing agreement, that profile is a Nash equilibrium and a solution to the game. Notice that I did not say "the" solution. In Figure 4.1, for example, there are two such solutions—(I, L) and (L, I)—each of them equally likely to be chosen as the outcome of preplay negotiation. This example makes it quite clear that granting the possibility of preplay communication makes a big difference to the prospect of reaching a solution. There are cases, however, in which a self-enforcing agreement is not feasible, at least if we limit ourselves to pure strategies. Consider the game shown in Figure 4.5.

Is there a rational way to play this game? If it is rational for Row to play L, then it is rational for Column to respond with r. But if Column is expected to play r, then Row should play R. If Row plays R, however, it is better for Column to play l, and in this case Row should play L instead of R. No matter what one player does, if the other player anticipates this, her best response is something that would induce the first to change what he was doing. No pair of pure strategies can be a candidate for a self-enforcing agreement, since for any such pair one of the players has an incentive to defect from the agreement. Suppose instead that the players choose between their strategies randomly. For example, Row may play L with probability 4/9 and R with probability 5/9. Then if Column chooses l, she will have an expected utility of 3 (4/9) + 6 (5/9) = 42/9. If Column chooses r instead, she will net 8 (4/9) + 2 (5/9) = 42/9. In this case Column will be indifferent between l and r and will be willing to randomize between them. In fact, if she chooses l with probability 4/7 and r with probability 3/7, then Row will net 8 (4/7) + 3 (3/7) = 41/7 if he chooses L, and 5 (4/7) + 7 (3/7) = 41/7 if he chooses R. So Row will be indifferent between his two strategies and will therefore be content to randomize. In this game, there is an equilibrium in mixed strategies, where if Row randomizes between L and R with probabilities 4/9 and 5/9, respectively, then Column will randomize with any probabilities, since she will be indifferent between l and r. And conversely, if Column chooses to randomize with probabilities 4/7 and 3/7, then Row will be happy to respond with any probabilistic combination of L and R.

In a mixed-strategy equilibrium, the probabilities with which a player randomizes are determined by the opponents' payoffs, since the goal of randomization is that of creating some uncertainty about one's own choices and of making other players indifferent among the strategies over which they are randomizing. As the above example shows, in a mixed-strategy equilibrium a randomizing player has many best responses, since any randomization between the equally good strategies is a best response. In our case, any pure or mixed strategy for Row is a best response to Column playing (4/7, 3/7), but Column will only randomize against Row's choice of (4/9, 5/9). Consider now an agreement to play the game in Figure 4.5 with mixed strategies (4/9, 5/9) and (4/7, 3/7), respectively. Would the agreement be self-enforcing? Clearly if Row expects Column to randomize with probabilities (4/7, 3/7), he has no reason to stick to the agreement, since now any of his strategies is a best response. He does not, however, have any incentive to deviate from the agreement either. Indeed, a mixed-strategy equilibrium is a self-enforcing agreement only in the weak sense that the players are indifferent among all lotteries that consist of the actions taken from the support of the mixed strategy. For this reason it is hard to see how a mixed-strategy equilibrium can be an obvious solution to a competitive situation. It might be argued that we are considering only the naive interpretation of a mixed strategy as an action that is conditioned on the outcome of a lottery performed by the player before the game begins. Nevertheless, there are situations in which randomizing among strategies is a good practice. For example, people who play poker know that they have to be unpredictable in the right sort of way: they may bluff often enough to be called now and then, but not so much that they are always called. Poker, though, is a game that one plays over and over with the same opponents, whereas the games we are discussing are one-shot affairs. In a one-time confrontation and in the absence of a pure strategy equilibrium, there seems to be no decisive reason for randomizing, even if the players have entered an agreement to do so. As long as the opponents are expected to stick to the agreement, one has no incentive to comply and randomize with the agreed upon odds.

A different understanding of mixed strategies is the purification idea (Aumann et al., 1983). A player's mixed strategy is thought of as a plan of action that depends on certain private information that is not specified in the model. So even if to an outside observer behavior appears induced by randomization, it is in fact deterministic, and the mixed strategy can actually be described as a pure strategy in which the player's action depends on some private piece of information about payoffs or available actions. A problem with this interpretation of mixed strategies is that if there are reasons behind the choices one makes, they should be included in the model, since they are likely to be payoff relevant. A better specification of this idea answers the objection by making the player's private information payoff relevant, in that a player's mixed strategy consists in uncertainties in the minds of other players as to the real values of his payoffs (Harsanyi, 1973).[10] That is, a player does not randomize between two strategies with probabilities—say, 5/9 and 4/9; it's just that the opponent attaches probability 5/9 to the event that he has payoffs such that he will pick the first strategy and probability 4/9 to the event that he has different payoffs, in which case he would choose the second strategy. Though the purification idea answers the objection that players do not usually choose by throwing dice, its drawback is that it does not enhance predictability. We could run an experiment ten thousand times and observe a player picking the same strategy every time without ever contradicting the assumption that what we observe is a mixed-strategy equilibrium, under either interpretation of that notion.

By now we have established that if preplay communication is allowed and the players succeed in reaching an agreement on how to play, and the agreement is self-enforcing, then that agreement must be a Nash equilibrium. Preplay negotiation, when it is successful, solves the problem of how players come to have beliefs that are both correct and consistent. If people do talk beforehand, they can avoid being mistaken about each other's expectations because once they reach an agreement they can be quite sure about what it is that each of them believes. Arguments involving iterated dominance do equally well, once it is assumed that the structure of the game and players' rationality are common knowledge. Since a strictly dominant strategy is a best reply to any strategies the other players pick, when a player has a dominant strategy he need not have any belief about the opponents' choices. And in the case of iterated dominance, the only restriction on players' epistemic states we need to impose is an assumption of common knowledge of rationality.

So when repeated deletion of strictly dominated strategies yields a unique strategy profile, this profile must necessarily be a Nash equilibrium. The proof is straightforward. Let $(s_1^*, \ldots, s_n^*)$ be the unique strategy profile resulting from iterated elimination of strictly dominated strategies. Suppose for reductio that there exists a player i and strategy $s_i \in S_i$ such that $u_i(s_i, s_{-i}^*) > u_i(s_i^*, s_{-i}^*)$. Then if one round of elimination was sufficient to yield the unique profile, s_i^* must dominate all other strategies in S_i, which is impossible if s_i is a better response to s_{-i}^* than is s_i^*. More generally, suppose that s_i is strictly dominated at some round by s_i', which is in turn eliminated at a later round because it is strictly dominated by $s_i'', \ldots$, which gets finally eliminated by s_i^*. Because s_i^* belongs to the undominated strategies of i at each round, by transitivity s_i^* must be a better response to s_{-i}^* than s_i, a contradiction.

We now have a better idea of what the justification of a Nash equilibrium demands. A necessary and sufficient condition for Nash equilibrium is that each player's strategy is a best reply to the opponents' strategies. But this coordination of individual plans can be attained by chance even by "idiot" players. What we want are conditions that justify Nash equilibrium as a prediction of how a game will be played. A necessary condition is then that strategies be best replies to some set of beliefs, and a sufficient condition is that beliefs about other players' strategies are both consistent and correct. In games without dominance or preplay communication, this restriction on beliefs seems rather artificial, especially since the equilibrating mechanism generating this property of belief sets is left unexplained. These constraints on beliefs would be completely satisfactory were game theory just bound to define what an equilibrium is and the conditions under which it would reasonably arise. Given the definition of Nash equilibrium, the best explanation of the achievement of a given equilibrium is that there exists a set of stable beliefs, in the sense defined by condition C. Yet an alleged aim of game theory is to prescribe actions that will bring about an equilibrium, which means providing a *unique* rational recommendation on how to play. If the task of the theorist were limited to pointing to a set of rational actions, the players might never succeed in coordinating their actions, since different agents might follow different recommendations. Thus a unique rational action for every player must be recommended, together with a unique belief about the behavior of other players that justify that action. Furthermore, the unique rational belief in question must be shown to be held by any player who is rational in an appropriate sense. For to say that the attainment of a Nash equilibrium is explained by a configuration of consistent and correct beliefs is still just part of a description of how an equilibrium is attained and gives remarkably little guidance as to what to expect actual players to do.

A common way to justify equilibrium play is to claim that since an important feature of game theory is that it must be public, it can only recommend equilibrium strategies, or else it would be self-defeating. To understand why, let us turn to the game in Figure 4.4, and let us suppose that there is a theory of the game that recommends to the players a maximax strategy. This means that a player must identify, for each strategy, the maximum possible payoff and subsequently choose the strategy having the largest maximum. If that theory is common knowledge, it is common knowledge that Row should play B and Column should play R. But if Column expects Row to play B he has an incentive to deviate from the recommended course of action and play C instead, which guarantees him a better payoff (if Row behaves according to the theory). Therefore a theory that prescribes maximax behavior will be self-defeating. Given that the other players behave according to the theory, at least one of the players has a motive to deviate from the theory because its recommendation is not optimal for him.

It is hard to assess the force of the suggestion that if game theory is to be publicly adopted it can recommend only Nash strategies as rational choices for the players (in which case it will be self-fulfilling). When multiple equilibria are present we need a unique recommendation of play for each player or else, as I already pointed out, players may not succeed in coordinating their choices. But then a theory that simply recommends Nash strategies is too weak and the very concept of Nash equilibrium has to be refined in order to identify one equilibrium as "the rational way to play." I will come back to this point later. When there exists a unique Nash equilibrium in mixed strategies, we have seen that the players have no incentive to play according to the required odds.[11] We must conclude that it is only when there is a unique equilibrium in pure strategies that this consideration has force. But for it to be a convincing justification of Nash equilibrium, it is necessary that the players know game theory, or that they manage to be advised by a game theorist on how to play, and in both cases the resulting advice must be common knowledge among them.

Each justification of Nash equilibrium so far mentioned is an attempt to justify the assumption that players are able correctly to infer each other's strategy and compute a best reply. In the case of preplay communication, as well as when consulting a game theorist, the players are told what the other players plan to do, and if what they are told to do (or themselves propose to do) is a best reply to what the opponents are expected to do, there is no reason for them to deviate from the intended (or recommended) course of action. A player can see that the same reasoning applies to every other player, so he can be reasonably sure about the opponents' expectations and choices. In these justifications of equilibrium play, communication and counsel are mechanisms that ground players' mutual expectations and lead them to converge to an equilibrium.

In the absence of such mechanisms, we are left with common knowledge of payoffs and rationality, and we have already seen how rarely this succeeds in completely pinning down choices. It is even rarer to have a player's choice completely determined by his own rationality with no need to consider choices by other players. Rationality alone determines a player's action only when she has a dominant strategy; common knowledge of rationality does the trick only when successive elimination of dominated strategies eliminates all but one strategy for each player. In most games neither of these occurs, so there is no clear-cut prescription for how to act. We may conclude that for Nash equilibria to have a claim on us, we have to assume (rather gratuitously) that players have expectations supporting the Nash profile. In a sense, a Nash equilibrium is just a consistent prediction of how the game will be played: if all players predict that a particular equilibrium will occur, then no player has an incentive to play differently. But a consistent prediction is not necessarily a good prediction. The fact that a given combination of strategies is a Nash equilibrium is a necessary but not a sufficient condition for predicting it as the outcome of rational play.[12]

4.6. Focal Points

Some would argue that even when multiple equilibria are present players may be able to coordinate on a particular equilibrium by using information that is abstracted away by the normal form representation of the game. Some Nash equilibria are particularly compelling for one reason or another, and, the argument goes, it takes little thought to see that they are "the obvious choice" for the players. A telling example is the division of $100 among two players. Each must independently propose a way of splitting the money and if the total amount proposed is equal to or less than $100 each gets the amount she proposed, whereas if the total is greater than $100 both get nothing. There are many possible equilibrium points: "I get $60 and you get $40" is one, but so is "I get $100 and you get nothing." In fact, there are 101 Nash equilibria, if we restrict the proposals to integers. But most of us, when asked to suggest a way to split the dollars, immediately propose a 50-50 share, for reasons that have to do more with symmetry and simplicity than equity.

Consider next two games that have multiple equilibria and are thought to possess qualitative features that make one of the equilibria unique. I want to argue that in both cases, unless we add further assumptions, the players may not succeed in correctly predicting each other's behavior and consequently there is no compelling reason to favor one equilibrium strategy over the others.

Of the two pure strategy equilibria in Figure 4.6 (B, R) and (T, L), the second is the most attractive for both players, since it guarantees each of them a payoff of 9, which is better than (8, 8). Since (T, L) is uniquely Pareto optimal, should

Column

	L	R
T	9, 9	0, 8
B	8, 0	8, 8

Row

Figure 4.6

the players expect one another to play it?[13] To answer this question, let us follow the reasoning of Row (which is symmetrical to that of Column), remembering that both the structure of the game and rationality are assumed to be common knowledge among the players.

Row may thus reason: "Since Column is rational, she will aim at maximizing her expected utility, given her beliefs about my strategy choice. She knows that I am rational, so she expects me to choose the strategy that maximizes my expected utility, given my beliefs about her choice. She will choose L only if she expects me to choose T, but the only reason why I would choose T is my expectation that she will choose L. How can I be sure she will play L? That is, how can she be sure that I will play T?" That (T, L) is the equilibrium with greater payoffs for both players does not make it individually rational to choose it, unless one is sure enough that the other player is aiming at it, too. This reasoning may seem counterintuitive, since in Figure 4.6 one would expect the players to have no trouble in coordinating their expectations at the best equilibrium point (T, L). To be of any use, this intuition should be captured by the formal model of the game as a description of what players know. For example, if it were common knowledge that equilibrium points with greater payoffs for all players should be preferred in equilibrium selection, then coordination of expectations would follow.

Another reason for this further common knowledge specification is that in games like the one in Figure 4.6 other reasonable conjectures are possible. For example, an equilibrium may have better payoffs for both players, but be riskier than another equilibrium.[14] Indeed, (B, R) risk dominates (T, L), in that for either player to choose the strategy associated with (T, L) is a much riskier choice than to choose the strategy associated with (B, R). For in choosing T (L) the player risks obtaining a payoff of zero; whereas if he chooses B (R) he cannot obtain less than 8. There is then good reason to expect the players to lend some weight to this factor in forming their subjective probabilities concerning the other player's behavior. Since the game is symmetrical, we may just consider next the reasoning of Row.

First, Row has to consider the losses incurred if he deviates from either equilibrium point. In Row's case, a deviation from (T, L) involves a loss of 1 $(9 - 8)$, and a deviation from (B, R) involves a loss of 8 $(8 - 0)$. Let us call these losses, respectively, a and b. Row will choose T if the probability p of Column playing L is such that $9p \geq 8p + 8$ $(1 - p)$. If instead p is such that $8p + 8$ $(1 - p) \geq 9p$, he will select B. Then B is a best reply if Row thinks that Column may shift to R with probability greater than $1/9$, and T is a best reply if he thinks that Column may shift to L with a probability greater than $8/9$. Column can easily replicate Row's reasoning, but all he knows as to the value of p is that it must be equal or greater than $\dfrac{b}{a+b}$ for Row to play T. Unless Row's and Column's probability assessments are common knowledge among them, there is no reason to expect coordination of expectations and equilibrium play.

Pareto optimality is the prototype of a qualitative feature that may make an equilibrium compelling.[15] But anything else focussing players' attention on one particular equilibrium may create a situation in which all players expect this equilibrium to occur and thus implement it. Schelling (1960) has called it the focal-point effect. Qualitative features that make an equilibrium unique, symmetry, or equity considerations can all have a focal-point effect. Figure 4.7 shows a case in which Schelling would make a focal-point argument to lend plausibility to a particular equilibrium as the likely outcome of the game.

Among the three equilibria (T, L), (M, C), and (B, R), Schelling (1960: 296) argues that only (M, C) calls itself to our attention, by virtue of having a different payoff from the other equilibria. It is certainly possible that if two people are made to play the game several times and happen initially to coordinate on (M, C), then they will keep playing it, presumably because they expect each other to follow the precedent. In fact, experimental evidence shows that if similar games are repeated over and over by the same players, there will be convergence to one equilibrium because of learning and adaptation (Roth and Schoumaker, 1983). But if the game is one-shot, I want to argue that nothing in its structure gives us reason to expect the players to see (M, C) as a focal point. Even if Row thinks that (M, C) stands out because of the different payoffs, he has no reason to believe Column to think likewise.[16] And even if he knows that

Column

		L	C	B
Row	T	2, 2	0, 0	0, 0
	M	0, 0	1, 1	0, 0
	B	0, 0	0, 0	2, 2

Figure 4.7

Column considers (M, C) special, this is not a sufficient reason to play his part in it, since unless it is common knowledge that both players consider (M, C) a focal point, one can never be sure that the other player expects him to do his part in that equilibrium. Similar reasoning applies to the game in Figure 4.6 and indeed to all focal-point arguments.

The game in Figure 4.7 is called a game of *pure coordination* since players' interests perfectly coincide.[17] In such games, each person involved is better off if everybody makes the same decision, and in a coordination equilibrium no one would have been better off if any one player had decided differently. If we turn to Figure 4.7, it seems obvious that common knowledge of rationality and of the structure of the game do not suffice to guarantee coordination, especially in the absence of preplay communication. This is not to deny that expectations can become coordinated through some other mechanism, psychological or other-wise. A similar point is made by David Lewis (1969) in his essay on convention. Interpreting conventions as equilibria of coordination games, he maintains that a given coordination equilibrium will be played because of its salience in the eyes of the players. What Lewis refers to as salience is a principle stating that if there is an action that in some way stands out from the others, then this action is likely to be taken. So if the players can recognize an action that is more obvious than the others, they should expect every other player to recognize that action as more obvious and choose accordingly.[18] In this way expectations become self-fulfilling and coordination is attained. For example, suppose you are calling someone on the phone and the call gets interrupted. If you do not know your caller well, you may have some doubt about who should call back. Coordination means that one calls and the other waits, so should you wait or should you call? Lewis would say that it all depends on custom and habit. If you made the call then, *ceteris paribus*, usually you expect the other to reciprocate. But it might be that your party is an important person of whom you are asking a favor, in which case it is generally expected that you call back. This is to say that your response will be sensitive to the context, the identity of the parties, and the knowledge that you and your party share the same cultural background. The last point is very important, for it can be extremely difficult to predict the reaction of somebody who does not belong to our culture. That a good deal of intelligence activity is devoted to in-depth analyses of foreign cultures and value systems testifies to the importance of understanding those whom we attempt to deter, support, or persuade. Without a shared background of values and expectations, one can never be sure that what in one's view appears as an obvious course of action is evident or even familiar at all to the other party.

Schelling's notion of what makes something a good focal point is in much the same vein, though his terminology is quite different. A focal point is a solution on which the players' expectations about what the other players will do agree. In other words, many games might provide some sort of clue as to not only what a player might do, but what a player can expect another player to do and what a player can expect another player to expect will be done. To use one of Schelling's examples, suppose a player and her partner are asked to write down a time of the day at which they will meet in a given location (no communication is allowed); they win if they both choose the same time of day. What Schelling found was that in almost all cases both players managed to write down twelve noon. This is not too surprising, since there are many clues that would make each player believe that this was the most obvious solution for both (it is an even hour, it is the midpoint of the day, it has a special name, and so on).

A few examples will better illustrate both the power and the shortcomings of salience and focal points. Suppose several players are each given a strip of paper with the following numbers:

$$2 \quad 6 \quad 5 \quad 8 \quad 10 \quad 1 \quad 9$$

They are then told that if every player in the group circles the same number, they will each win that amount in dollars. This game does not need either salience or focal points: if rationality is common knowledge, then the players will all choose 10, since this value maximizes every person's payoff. Suppose we now change the game such that if everybody in the group circles the same number, everybody gets five dollars. In this game there is no optimal solution, since all coordination equilibria have the same payoff to the players. What the players do have now is a clue: the 8, being the only number underlined, is a more obvious answer. Each will probably notice the uniqueness of the 8 in this respect; each player might consequently expect the others to notice the uniqueness of the 8 and might expect the other players to expect him to notice the uniqueness of the 8. The number 8 becomes a focal point, and in this case the expectations can become self-fulfilling. Thus a coordination solution can be reached despite the existence of multiple equilibria.

Finally, suppose instead that we give a group of players a strip of paper without that clue:

$$2 \quad 6 \quad 5 \quad 8 \quad 10 \quad 1 \quad 9$$

Now the players have a much more difficult task in determining which solution would be the most apparent to all the other players. Any number of criteria might be used: they could choose the first number (2), the last number (9), the middle number (8), the highest number (10), the lowest number (1), and so on. Evidently many valid clues may be used, each one bringing the player to a different choice of action. The point to be made is that though salience and focal points might be useful in solving coordination problems where rationality falls short, they will not always guarantee that a coordinated solution will obtain. More important, even if they always did, the prediction that a certain solution is a focal point and hence will be achieved cannot be generated from the austere assumptions of rationality and common knowledge thereof. As we already observed, salience and focal points are sensitive to the context and presentation of the game, as well as to the identities and cultural background of the participants. These notions are, in a sense, very similar to concepts like similarity that are difficult to formalize precisely because they are highly context dependent. Any pair of objects can be found to be similar in some respect and different in others, and the characteristics that we find relevant to a judgement of similarity depend upon the setting and the interests of the observer. We must conclude that even if notions like salience and focal point may often succeed in sorting out one particular Nash equilibrium, they cannot serve as a formal justification for convergence.

4.7. Unreasonable Equilibria

Thus far, we have established that for most games the rationality and knowledge assumptions we made in previous sections are not strong enough to reason to an equilibrium in a rigorous way. Nash equilibrium is supported by coherent and correct beliefs, but, unlike coherence, correctness is not a purely formal matter. One has to state explicitly some evidence that a player may plausibly have and that elicits the right kind of belief. Dominance, preplay communication, and focal points are but different ways to ground players' beliefs on some piece of mutual evidence. Of the three approaches, only dominance relies on information provided by the game, whereas the other two depend on factors—such as communication and shared perceptions of what appears to be conspicuous in a given setting—that are outside the scope of game theory. As I remarked at the outset of this chapter, I am trying to construct a general argument for Nash equilibrium from endogenous premises, that is, from assumptions regarding players' rationality and information about the structure of the game. An alternative way of bridging the gap between Nash equilibrium and the usual game-theoretic premises is to modify those premises, and the notion of rationality in particular. For example, if a rational player, besides being an expected utility maximizer, is also understood to be a cautious player, then he should avoid "risky" strategies, and consequently should not be believed to play them by an opponent who knows he is rational in the appropriate sense. This broader definition of rationality serves as evidence in forming players' expectations about what rational opponents will do, so players' beliefs are further constrained by the requirement that they cohere with a more encompassing view of how rational players act.

Besides, further restrictions on beliefs are one possible solution to the drawbacks traditionally associated with the Nash equilibrium concept. One of them is the lack of uniqueness, in that many games have several equilibria, so that it may be difficult to predict which equilibrium (if any) is actually played. Another problem is that some equilibria are plainly unreasonable, but the concept of Nash equilibrium is too weak to rule them out. By "unreasonable equilibrium" we mean that an equilibrium strategy may involve an irrational move on the part of a player. As an example, consider in Figure 4.8 a variation of Figure 4.2 in which strategy I is only weakly dominant for Robinson.

In Figure 4.8 we may confidently predict that Robinson will pick strategy I, since it guarantees him a payoff of 2 (which is better than 1) in case Friday plays L, and if Friday chooses I instead, I guarantees Robinson as much as L. For Friday, in turn, it is enough to know that Robinson is rational to expect him to choose I with probability 1. Therefore Friday will always choose L. The combination of strategies (I, L) is the obvious solution to the game, but it is not the unique equilibrium. Another equilibrium is (L, I), since if Friday believes that Robinson will choose L he will respond with I, while if Robinson believes that Friday will choose I he will be indifferent between L and I, and so indeed L is a best reply, too. But is (L, I) a credible solution? Since it is never worse for Robinson to choose I instead of L, there is no ambiguity over what each player should expect the other to do. It is irrational for Friday to expect Robinson to

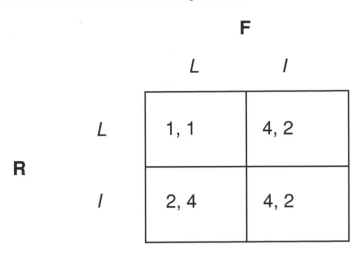

Figure 4.8

pick strategy L, since Robinson has no reason to believe that Friday expects him to play L and every reason to believe otherwise, and this should be obvious to both. But rationality simply demands that one plays a best reply against one's consistent beliefs, so both Nash equilibria in Figure 4.8 are rationalizable.

In order to identify and eliminate unreasonable equilibria, as well as to predict behavior as precisely as possible, several refinements of the Nash equilibrium concept have been proposed. In the normal form, refinements can be understood to formalize a notion of cautiousness, meaning that one should never be certain about the opponents' choices. A rational player, that is, is also a prudent player, and one way to formalize this notion is to assume that there is always a small probability that a player will make a mistake, which has the consequence that every pure strategy can be chosen with a positive probability. Then a Nash equilibrium is also a *perfect equilibrium* if it is stable with respect to small perturbations in the players' strategies—that is, if each player's equilibrium strategy is a best reply to the opponent's strategy and to some slight perturbation of that strategy (Selten, 1975).

Consider again the game in Figure 4.8. Assume that for some unspecified reason the players have agreed to play the equilibrium (L, I); if Robinson has a small doubt that Friday may play L (for example, even if Friday wants to pick I, his hand may tremble with probability $\varepsilon > 0$, so that he chooses L instead), then it is better for Robinson to switch to I. The same reasoning applies to Friday, so neither of them will expect the other to keep the original agreement to play (L, I). Indeed, the only stable (perfect) equilibrium is (I, L). The idea behind perfect equilibrium is to treat full rationality as a limit case: since a

Column

		L	L	D
	L	1, 1	4, 2	-3, -3
Row	I	2, 4	4, 2	-5, -5
	D	-6, -6	-5, -5	-8, -8

Figure 4.9

rational player may make a mistake, an equilibrium strategy must be optimal not only against the opponent's expected strategy, but also against some very small probability that the opponent makes a mistake and chooses something else instead. Another way to interpret "prudent play" is the following: suppose preplay communication is allowed and Robinson announces he is going to play L. Should Friday believe him? It is apparent that even if Robinson does not intend to play L, he has an incentive to convince Friday he will do it, so as to induce Friday to play I. Moreover, were Friday not to be convinced, Robinson would always be safe by picking I. Since both players can replicate each other's reasoning, it is mutual knowledge that Robinson's commitment to L is unbelievable. A prudent player can thus be understood to be a player who would never enter into an agreement to play a given equilibrium when it is evident that he has no good reason to play his part in it.

The concept of perfect equilibrium, however, does not succeed in eliminating all intuitively unreasonable equilibria. Consider next an enlarged version of the game in Figure 4.8, where each player has an additional, strictly dominated strategy available (D) (see Figure 4.9).

The game in Figure 4.9 has two pure strategy equilibria: (L, I) and (I, L). If the players agree to play equilibrium (L, I) and both expect mistake D to occur with greater probability than mistake I (respectively, L), then also (L, I) is a perfect equilibrium. But it seems rather odd that an equilibrium that is unreasonable under a set of circumstances becomes reasonable (perfect) when something as irrelevant as a dominated strategy is added to the game. The problem seems to lie with the mistake probabilities. In fact, (L, I) is a perfect equilibrium only if the probability of mistake D is greater than the probability of another mistake. It might be argued that if the players are rational, they should try hard to prevent costly mistakes, and consequently they should never expect mistake D to occur with greater probability than mistake L (respectively, I). The idea that rational players will make a more costly mistake with a smaller probability than a less costly one underlies the concept of *proper equilibrium* (Myerson, 1978). In the game in Figure 4.9, if the players make rational mistakes only (I, L) survives as a proper equilibrium.

Perfect and proper equilibrium are only two among several refinements of Nash equilibrium. In both cases, unreasonable equilibria are ruled out by extending the definition of rationality to include some form of prudence in the way of an acknowledgment of possible mistakes and of the different costs involved in these mistakes. Note that, in order to work, both concepts of perfect and proper equilibrium must implicitly assume that it is common knowledge among the players that they are rational in this broader sense, and that they use this knowledge in selecting their equilibrium strategies. A more general question that should be addressed is why a player who presumably incurs costs in preventing costly mistakes would not try to avoid mistakes altogether. It might be argued that even if it is costly to avoid mistakes, a player is always trading off costs and benefits, so that it would not be surprising to have some probability of mistakes at the optimum. But then a model of the game should explicitly contain this relevant piece of information. Moreover, it is doubtful that full rationality is compatible with mistakes. The longer a game is played, the smaller the chance that mistakes are random and uncorrelated, as is assumed by perfection and properness. And if in fact mistakes are correlated, a rational player should be able to learn from past experience and modify his behavior.

Common knowledge that rational players play cautiously will sometimes yield a unique prediction. But in many other games multiplicity persists, pointing to the ad hoc nature of refinements. As a way to avoid what is ad hoc in refinements like properness, one may require an equilibrium to be robust against all possible small mistakes. This more stringent stability criterion (it is called *strict perfection*) has been put forward by Kohlberg and Mertens (1986). Strict perfection, however, may be too strong. Let me illustrate this point with the example shown in Figure 4.10.

Here strategy A is always best for Column, so one expects it to be part of the equilibrium. Under this circumstance, what is Row's best reply? Being cautious,

Column

		A	B	C
	U	1, 1	1, 0	0, 0
Row				
	D	1, 1	0, 0	1, 0

Figure 4.10

Row will assign small probabilities to Column's making a mistake and playing B or C instead. If the probability of mistake B is higher than the probability of mistake C, then only U is a best response for Row; if the probabilities are reversed, then only D is a best response. Both (U, A) and (D, A) are perfect equilibria with respect to some mistake probabilities, but they are not jointly stable against all possible mistakes.[19]

Note that strict perfection, while preserving the concept of prudence underlying some refinements, also requires the players to employ, whenever possible, iterated elimination of dominated strategies. Since a prudent player does not choose a weakly dominated strategy, and since both rationality and prudence characterize the players and this fact is common knowledge, iterated elimination of weakly dominated strategies can be carried out. In Figure 4.10, for example, B is strictly dominated by A for Column, so we can delete B and obtain the reduced game shown in Figure 4.11.

In the game in Figure 4.11, D weakly dominates U for Row, so the unique solution is (D, A). But in the original game C is strictly dominated as well, and deleting C instead of B yields the game in Figure 4.12.

In the game in Figure 4.12, (U, A) is the unique solution. The problem is exactly that what we would expect Row to do depends on which of Column's dominated strategies we eliminate first.[20] The solution to the original game must contain both (U, A) and (D, A), and so it cannot be single-valued. Stability thus interpreted implies that the object of the theory is a set of equilibria rather than a unique equilibrium, a result that obviously impairs predictability and suggests that there might be a tradeoff between attaining greater predictive power and ruling out unreasonable beliefs.

The Kohlberg-Mertens criterion of stability imposes additional restrictions on beliefs beyond those involved in Selten's and Meyerson's refinements. Since it

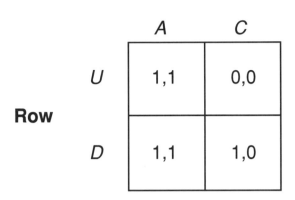

Column

	A	C
U	1,1	0,0
D	1,1	1,0

Row

Figure 4.11

Column

	A	B
U	1,1	1,0
D	1,1	0,0

Row

Figure 4.12

implies iterated elimination of dominated strategies, their criterion requires beliefs to be consistent with common knowledge of rationality. And when weakly dominated strategies are present, it requires beliefs to be consistent with common knowledge of rationality and prudence. Though the stable set is seldom a singleton, the Kohlberg-Mertens's restrictions on beliefs are sometimes powerful enough to eliminate all intuitively unreasonable equilibria, which is not

Column

		L	R
	A	5, 1	0, 0
Row	B	0, 0	2, 4
	C	3, 3	3, 3

Figure 4.13

always the case for perfect or proper equilibria.[21] To see the point, consider the game in Figure 4.13.

The game in Figure 4.13 has two Nash equilibria in pure strategies: (A, L) and (C, R). They are both proper equilibria, in that if Row expects Column to play strategy R with high probability, then to make mistake B is less costly than to make mistake A. So if Column himself assigns a higher mistake probability to B than to A, it makes sense for him to play R. But this reasoning is plainly inconsistent with the assumption that players have common knowledge of their mutual prudent rationality. Common knowledge of rationality implies that it is common knowledge that Row will eliminate strategy B, which is strictly dominated by C. At this stage, a prudent Column will choose strategy L, which is safer than R in case Row plays A. (C, R) is thus inconsistent with prudent rationality being common knowledge. What is important is that neither perfect nor proper equilibrium puts any restrictions on players' beliefs beyond internal consistency. The stability criterion fares much better, since it demands that an equilibrium survives perturbations in all directions. In our example, if Column assigns a greater probability to mistake A than to mistake B, it is better for him to play L; hence the equilibrium (C, R) does not survive a perturbation in this direction. So whenever iterated elimination of dominated strategies results in a unique equilibrium, that equilibrium is also stable against all perturbations —that is, it remains an equilibrium when tested against all sets of mistake probabilities.

	B_1	B_2	B_3
A_1	2, 4	5, 4	-1, 0
A_2	3, 4	2, 4	-2, 0
A_3	1, 2	0, 0	2, 2
A_4	0, 2	2, 0	0, 4

Figure 4.14

4.8. Is Common Knowledge Enough?

I have pointed out that in the normal form description of a game, common knowledge of the structure of the game and of their mutual rationality on the part of the players does not generally entail correct beliefs.[22] One possible solution involves restricting players' epistemic states by extending the notion of rationality to encompass prudent behavior (however defined). Those beliefs that are not consistent with common knowledge of prudence are then ruled out. Still, beliefs may remain indeterminate, this time because common knowledge is too strong a requirement. As an example, consider the case shown in Figure 4.14 (Samuelson, 1989).

Since mutual rationality and prudence are common knowledge, it is common knowledge that B_2 will be deleted, as it is weakly dominated by B_1. If B_2 is deleted, A_3 strongly dominates A_4, which is then eliminated. Now B_1 weakly dominates B_3, so B_3 is deleted, too. With B_1 as the only strategy left for the column player, A_2 is the best reply for the row player and (A_2, B_1) becomes the only reasonable equilibrium. However, since the column player assesses probability 1 that the row player is playing A_2, he will be indifferent between playing B_1 and B_2, since he will get a payoff of 4 either way. This reasoning can be replicated by the row player, which may now want to play A_1 in the hope of getting a payoff of 5. Although common knowledge of rationality and prudence permits recursive elimination of dominated strategies, it prevents players from reaching a definite conclusion about their mutual beliefs. Indeed, even if it may seem irrational to believe that column player will play strategy B_2 (which is weakly dominated by B_1), this choice becomes rational if considered from the viewpoint of the players' having common knowledge that A_2 will be chosen. This consideration, in turn, reinstates A_1 as a plausible choice. In this case, mutual beliefs remain indeterminate.

Another possible solution consists in assuming that the beliefs supporting a particular equilibrium are common knowledge among the players (Aumann, 1976, 1987). There are cases, however, in which not even common knowledge of beliefs yields a prediction about equilibrium play, as for example in mixed-strategy equilibria. As I argued earlier, any mixed-strategy equilibrium has the problem that each player is indifferent between all the strategies in the support of her mixed strategy. In this case, if priors are common knowledge, it is also common knowledge that no player has an incentive to play his equilibrium strategy, and consequently no player can predict what the other player will do.

One might argue that common knowledge of beliefs is neither more nor less plausible than common knowledge of rationality or utilities. If the game has chance moves, for example, it is commonly assumed that players have common knowledge of their beliefs concerning those moves, since there must be common knowledge of expected utilities. So why not assume that beliefs concerning the opponents' choices are common knowledge, too? I would argue that although in real life we often understand our opponents to be at least approximately rational and reasonably well informed, and guess more or less accurately their preferences, we seldom think of beliefs as being completely transparent. There are situations in which the relevant probabilities derive from public relative frequencies, much like the probability of an airplane crash or of having a child with Down's syndrome. In such cases, the probabilities are established by empirical means, so one would perhaps expect a well-informed person to know the odds and act accordingly. In the majority of cases of interest to game theorists, however, the pertinent probabilities—such as the probability that an opponent will play a given strategy—are subjective. More to the point, what is probable in this case is a proposition devoid of statistical background, and what we assess is a reasonable degree of belief in that proposition. For the subjectivist, probability is a relation between a statement and a body of evidence, but a given statement may have any probability between 0 and 1, on given evidence, according to the inclination of the person. From the subjectivist's viewpoint, since two players can assess different probabilities on the basis of the same information, the common knowledge assumption seems totally unwarranted, at least from a descriptive viewpoint (Kadane and Larkey, 1982, 1983).

It could still be argued that the relevance and suitability of the common knowledge assumption should be judged entirely on prescriptive grounds. If players were perfectly rational, the argument goes, their subjective probabilities would not be completely arbitrary. For example, in situations involving random devices with suitable physical symmetries, such as fair coins, all rational people can be expected to use the same probability distribution. Thus if rationality is common knowledge, it follows that in such circumstances people's priors will be common knowledge, too. Those who hold the so-called necessitarian view of probability think it is always possible uniquely to specify the subjective probabilities that a rational player can use in any given situation. In other words, probability represents a logical relation between a proposition and a body of knowledge: given a proposition and a body of evidence, there is only one degree of probability it has, relative to that evidence. In game theory, this view is often called the Harsanyi doctrine or, alternatively, the common prior assumption. The claim is that two individuals having access to the same information will necessarily come up with the same subjective probability assessment, and any difference in these assessments must be the result of differences in information. But what sort of information provided by the normal form justifies the common prior assumption? In Harsanyi's own words, "Most game theorists answer this question by constructing various normative 'solution concepts' based on suitable rationality postulates and by assuming that the players will act, and will also expect each other to act, in accordance with the relevant solution concept" (Harsanyi, 1982: 121). In this case mutually expected rationality is equated with joint adoption of a given solution concept, which in turn becomes the basis for a particular prior distribution. The missing step here is precisely a justification for the choice of a particular solution concept, a choice that should only be based on players' rationality and information about the structure of the game they are playing. We have already seen that in many games common knowledge of rationality and payoffs is not sufficient to predict that a given Nash equilibrium will be played, and so a fortiori it is a poor ground for the common prior assumption.[23]

If one thus rejects the idea of common priors, one is left with subjective probabilities that vary across people, not unlike their preferences and tastes. In this case, common knowledge of prior probabilities over the opponents' choices seems unwarranted even from a prescriptive viewpoint. Moreover, making players' priors common knowledge may be an unreliable basis for attaining a Nash equilibrium. Take as an example the game in Figure 4.1. Suppose that R believes that F plays I with probability 2/3, and F believes that R plays I with probability 1/2. Suppose further that these priors become common knowledge among the players. Since they are mutually inconsistent, how do the players proceed to revise their predictions in light of this piece of information? If it becomes common knowledge that F believes that R plays I with probability 1/2, it also becomes common knowledge that F will play L with probability 1, in which case R will respond with I. Conversely, if it is common knowledge that R believes that F plays I with probability 2/3, it is also common knowledge that

R plays *L* with probability 1. In which case *F* responds with strategy *I*. If the players start the game with mutually inconsistent priors, making them common knowledge does not guarantee that the subsequent process of belief-revision will converge to a set of stable beliefs (in the sense of condition *C*), hence to a Nash equilibrium.

It light of these considerations, the temptation is to conclude that the gap between individual rationality and equilibrium outcomes is unbridgeable. This, however, would be too hasty a conclusion. I have argued elsewhere (Bicchieri, 1993) that one way of explaining how a Nash equilibrium gets to be played is to suppose that players learn through repeated interactions which strategies are played by the opponents. A theory of learning in games explains how a player's beliefs about the environment (which includes the behavior of others insofar as it affects him) evolve until they have come to agree with the actual properties of the environment. This "agreement" means that players' expectations are correct. Once the players have learned to play in a given way, they may use this knowledge in a variety of different situations, provided those situations are sufficiently similar to the original one. A particular solution thus becomes an established behavioral regularity that people adhere to in subsequent games. Modeling learning dynamics and the conditions for convergence to an equilibrium are crucial steps toward providing an explanation of how some Nash equilibria become focal points, and hence have predictive significance. Such models would also supply a firmer foundation for Nash equilibrium.

Notes

1. This argument is found in von Neumann and Morgenstern (1944: 146–148).

2. To say that an event *E* is common knowledge among a group *G* means that each member of *G* knows *E*, and each knows that each knows *E*, . . . and so on ad infinitum (Lewis, 1969).

3. In general, I take the utilities to be von Neumann-Morgenstern utilities (1944), which also reflect each agent's decision under a situation of risk, but this additional assumption is not needed here.

4. The case in which players' randomizations are correlated is discussed in Aumann (1987).

5. It has been argued that in cases such as this other choice rules (e.g., *maximin utility, minimax loss, Hurwicza*, and others) that avoid using subjective probabilities are more suitable. But even if each of the alternative choice rules gives a definite recommendation on how to play, and some of them are attractive, none of them enjoys a privileged rational status. Furthermore, some of them are known to lead to irrational decisions in practical situations. For a discussion of these alternative choice criteria, see Luce and Raiffa (1957: ch. 13) and also Radner and Marschak (1954).

6. It would be more accurate to say that the conclusion of a practical syllogism is the intention to perform a given action, and not the action itself. Unless otherwise stated, I will equate intending to act with acting, assuming that there are no impediments to realizing one's intentions.

7. There are cases in which a belief is trivially stable, but may not be correct. Just consider a two player game where player 2 is indifferent between his actions. To be extreme about it, let's say

that player 2's payoff is 1, regardless of the actions player 1 chooses. Now if player 1 learns 2's beliefs about 1's actions, this gives him no information whatsoever about what 2 will do. Thus it cannot possibly affect his belief about 2's action. Yet surely 1's belief about 2's action need not be correct. If we rule out such cases, stable beliefs are always also correct beliefs.

8. Hereinafter I shall use "equilibrium" to refer to the class of Nash equilibria.

9. One important virtue of Nash equilibrium is that for games with a finite number of pure strategies and finitely many players, a Nash equilibrium always exists, at least in mixed strategies (Nash, 1951).

10. In particular, Harsanyi proves that under certain conditions every mixed-strategy equilibrium is a limit of some sequence of pure strategy equilibria in some sequence of games in which all payoffs are slightly randomly perturbed and each player gets the exact information only about his own payoffs.

11. On this well known point, a classic reference is Luce and Raiffa (1957: 75).

12. Von Neumann and Morgenstern make the same point when they state "Imagine that we have discovered a set of rules for all participants—to be termed as 'optimal' or 'rational'—each of which is indeed optimal provided that the other participants conform. Then the question remains as to what will happen if some of the participants do not conform. If that should turn out to be advantageous for them—and, quite particularly, disadvantageous to the conformists—then the above 'solution' would seem very questionable" (1944: 32).

13. A Pareto optimal outcome is one such that there exists no other cell that can improve the outcome for one player without worsening it for the other player.

14. For a definition of risk dominance, see Harsanyi and Selten (1988).

15. Note that there is a different and stronger argument for Pareto optimality in the case of preplay communication. In this case the players should not be content to agree on play that is Pareto-dominated by another possible self-enforcing agreement. However, suppose that the players in Figure 4.6 are able to meet and communicate before play, assuring each other that they will play (T, L). Should they trust each other? Aumann (1987) argues that the answer is no. Regardless of his own play, Column gains if Row plays T, so even if he intends to play R it is in his best interest to assure Row that he will play L. Both players are aware of this possibility, which makes it less obvious that they expect their pledges to be believed. Even if (T, L) seems a more likely outcome, it remains possible that they play (B, R).

16. Those who have proposed "symmetry arguments" would deny this claim. See, for example, Davis (1985).

17. Perfect coincidence of interests means that players have the same payoffs in every cell.

18. To see that salience is not a version of the clone assumption, consider the difference between the following cases. In one case a player has good reasons for choosing a given action and consider those reasons so obvious and visible that he believes they must be obvious and visible to all. In the second case, a player thinks that his propensity to choose a given action signals an equal propensity in the other player.

19. In the game depicted in Figure 4.10 there are several equilibria that survive mistakes in all directions: they are all the combinations of strategies in which Column plays A and Row randomizes over his pure strategies.

20. Note that if we try to avoid the order problem by eliminating both B and C at once, we are still left with multiple equilibria.

21. This result is established in Kohlberg and Mertens (1986: 1029).

22. As we have seen, the case of strictly dominated strategies is different: the choice of such a strategy would be plainly irrational, since a strictly dominated strategy is not a best response to any possible subjective assessment.

23. I should mention here two attempts to model the process by which players come to have

correct beliefs about each other's strategy choice. Harsanyi and Selten's "tracing procedure" and Skyrms's "rational deliberation" are models in which players start with common knowledge of their probability distributions over strategies and then keep revising them according to rules that are common knowledge, too. If the process converges, they prove that it converges to a Nash equilibrium. In these approaches, however, we are still left with the problem of explaining how rational players get the common priors from which deliberation begins. Cf. Harsanyi and Selten (1988) and Skyrms (1989, 1990).

References

Aumann, R. J. (1976). "Agreeing to Disagree." *Annals of Statistics* 4, 1236–1239.

———. (1987). "Correlated Equilibrium as an Expression of Bayesian Rationality." *Econometrica* 55, 1–18.

Aumann, R. J., and A. Brandenburger. (1991). "Epistemic Conditions for Nash Equilibrium." Working paper, Harvard Business School.

Aumann, R. J., Y. Katznelson, R. Radner, R. Rosenthal, and B. Weiss. (1983). "Approximate Purification of Mixed Strategies." *Mathematics of Operations Research* 8, 327–341.

Bernheim, D. (1984). "Rationalizable Strategic Behavior." *Econometrica* 52, 1007–1028.

Bicchieri, C. (1987). "Rationality and Predictability in Economics." *British Journal for the Philosophy of Science* 38, 501–513.

———. (1988). "Strategic Behavior and Counterfactuals." *Synthese* 76, 135–169.

———. (1992). "Two Kinds of Rationality." In N. De Marchi (ed.), *Post-Popperian Methodology of Economics*. Norwell, MA: Kluwer.

———. (1993). *Rationality and Coordination*. New York: Cambridge University Press.

Binmore, K., and Brandenburger, A. (1990). "Common Knowledge and Game Theory." In K. Binmore (eds.), *Essays on the Foundations of Game Theory*. London: Basil Blackwell.

Brandenburger, A. (1989). "The Role of Common Knowledge Assumptions in Game Theory." In F. Hahn (ed.), *The Economics of Information, Games, and Missing Markets*. Cambridge: Cambridge University Press.

Davis, 1.H. (1985). "Prisoners, Paradox, and Rationality." In R. Campbell and L. Sowden (eds.), *Paradoxes of Rationality and Cooperation*. Vancouver: University of British Columbia Press.

Harsanyi, J. (1965). "Bargaining and Conflict Situations in the Light of a New Approach to Game Theory." *American Economic Review* 55, 447–457.

———. (1966). "A General Theory of Rational Behavior in Game Situations." *Econometrica* 34, 613–634.

———. (1973). "Games with Randomly Disturbed Payoffs: A New Rationale for Mixed Strategy Equilibrium Points." *International Journal of Game Theory* 2, 1–23.

———. (1982). "Solutions for Some Bargaining Games Under the Harsanyi-Selten Solution Theory, I: Theoretical Preliminaries; II: Analysis of Specific Bargaining Games." *Mathematical Social Sciences* 3, 179–191, 259–279.

Harsanyi, J. and R. Selten. (1988). *A General Theory of Equilibrium Selection in Games.* Cambridge, MA: MIT Press.

Jeffrey, R. (1965). *The Logic of Decision.* New York: McGraw-Hill.

Kadane, J. B., and P. D. Larkey. (1982). "Subjective Probability and the Theory of games." *Management Science* 28, 113–120.

———. (1983). "The Confusion of Is and Ought in Game theoretic Contexts." *Management Science* 29, 1365–1379.

Kohlberg, E. (1989). "Refinement of Nash Equilibrium: The Main Ideas." Mimeo.

Kohlberg, E., and J. F. Mertens. (1986). "On the Strategic Stability of Equilibria." *Econometrica* 54, 1003–1037.

Kreps, D. (1990). *Game Theory and Economic Modelling.* New York: Oxford University Press.

Lewis, D. (1969). *Convention.* Cambridge, MA: Harvard University Press.

Luce, R. D., and H. Raiffa. (1957). *Games and Decisions.* New York: John Wiley.

Myerson, R. (1978). "Refinements of the Nash Equilibrium Concept." *International Journal of Game Theory* 7, 73–80.

Nash, J. (1951). "Non-cooperative Games." *Annals of Mathematics* 54, 286–295.

Pearce, D. (1984). "Rationalizable Strategic Behavior and the Problem of Perfection." *Econometrica* 52, 1029–1050.

Radner, R., and J. Marshak. (1954). "A Note on Some Proposed Decision Criteria." In R. M. Thrall et al. (eds.), *Decision Processes.* New York: John Wiley.

Roth, A., and F. Schoumaker. (1983). "Expectations and Reputations in Bargaining: An Experimental Study." *American Economic Review* 73, 362–372.

Samuelson, L. (1989). "Dominated Strategies and Common Knowledge." Mimeo, Penn State University.

Selten, R. (1975). "Re-examination of the Perfectness Concept for Equilibrium Points in Extensive Games." *International Journal of Game Theory* 4, 22–55.

Schelling, T. (1960). *The Strategy of Conflict.* Cambridge, MA: Harvard University Press.

Skyrms, B. (1989). "Deliberational Dynamics and the Foundations of Bayesian Game Theory." In J. E. Tomberlin (ed.), *Epistemology, Philosophical Perspectives* (vol. 2). Northridge: Ridgeview.

———. (1990). *The Dynamics of Rational Deliberation.* Cambridge, MA: Harvard University Press.

Tan, T., and S. Werlang. (1986). "On Aumann's Notion of Common Knowledge: An Alternative Approach." Working paper 85–26, University of Chicago.

van Damme, E. (1983). *Refinements of the Nash Equilibrium Concept.* New York: Springer Verlag.

———. (1987). *Stability and Perfection of Nash Equilibrium.* New York: Springer Verlag.

von Neumann, J., and O. Morgenstern. (1944). *Theory of Games and Economic Behavior.* Princeton, NJ: Princeton University Press.

Barton L. Lipman

Comments on Bicchieri: The Epistemic Foundations of
Nash Equilibrium

Introduction

Though economists were present at the birth of game theory,[1] the subject has
been introduced to the profession at large only in the last twenty-five years or
so. In this comparatively short period of time, it has become a part of virtually
every economist's bag of tricks, an important part of the curriculum in most
major Ph.D. programs, and, I believe, a much more widely used tool (by
microeconomists at least) than the traditional competitive equilibrium theory.

I think there are two important reasons why game theory has swept economics. First, standard competitive theory did not seem to allow much room for
discussing institutions. Yet casual observation suggests that the rules of price
determination vary widely across markets and that these rules are quite important. Prices of groceries do not seem to be set in the same way as prices on the
stock market or prices of rare diamonds, for example. Game theory, by its very
nature, allows a clean and clear way of asking what properties a given institution—that is, a given game—will have and why one institution might work
better in a particular setting than another. Second, many situations of interest are
characterized by small numbers of strategically interacting agents, where one
simply cannot appeal to "perfect competition." Once techniques were developed
for studying such situations, the deluge of applications began. Takeover bids,
union negotiations, entry deterrence, research and development competition,
optimal labor contracts, optimal taxation, location decisions, auctions, elections,
monetary policy, and stock market prices are just a few of the topics that have
been studied in the last fifteen years using game theory.

As the applications have spread, more questions have arisen about the fundamental basis of game theory. Many of these issues have been raised by economists, others by philosophers. (I should emphasize that this is one area of
economics that has been strongly influenced by philosophers, including David
Lewis, Michael Bacharach, Brian Skyrms, William Harper, Bicchieri, and many
others.) In her chapter, Bicchieri summarizes and adds to the debate.

In this discussion, I will offer my own views on these issues, taking Bicchieri's
chapter as a starting point. First I discuss the issue of prediction in game theory,
summarizing Bicchieri's arguments and offering a different perspective. Then I

turn to learning and whether, as Bicchieri suggests at the conclusion of her essay, an analysis of learning can resolve the problems in justifying Nash equilibrium. To make my points as strongly as possible, I wear my "hard-nosed real-world economist" hat, a hat even my best friends have rarely seen me wear. Finally, I remove the unfamiliar garment for a few concluding comments.

Prediction in Game Theory

The primary question Bicchieri focuses on is "What justifiable predictions can we make regarding the outcome of a game?" To answer this question—or even to be able to recognize an acceptable answer if we saw one—we must clarify a crucial point: what justifies a prediction? Empirical or experimental evidence? Axioms on individual behavior? Axioms on group behavior? I don't think anyone would disagree with what an ideal answer to this question would be. If we could have it, who would not want a justification that had a clear, unambiguous axiomatic basis, where those axioms are simple, compelling, and empirically verified? However, we will never find such a strong way to justify our predictions.

Bicchieri, naturally, does not ask for justification quite as strong as this. Instead, her focus is on whether we can find a general criteria, one that uses only information in or justifiable by the normal form of the game, to justify our prediction. As she puts it, "What we are interested in is whether what is generally specified in a model of strategic interaction is enough for the parties correctly to infer what the others will do, as well as for the theorist to predict that a specific solution will obtain." As Bicchieri convincingly argues, we will never see strong predictions with this kind of justification either.

I will briefly summarize a few of Bicchieri's observations on this point. First, it is well-known that the two clearest axioms we might try to use to justify our predictions—namely, common knowledge of the game and common knowledge of rationality—are not very helpful. These two assumptions imply only that each player must use a *rationalizable* strategy in the sense of Bernheim (1984) and Pearce (1984).[2] Unfortunately, this criterion is very weak, ruling out nothing at all in many games of interest.

What further conditions would we need to generate the prediction that the players play a Nash equilibrium? Aumann and Brandenburger (1991) have proven that if players have a common prior—that is, if the Harsanyi doctrine holds—and if each player's beliefs are common knowledge, then we can predict a Nash equilibrium. (As they show, we do not actually require common knowledge of the game and of rationality in this case: mutual knowledge of each suffices.) However, as Bicchieri notes, assuming common knowledge of beliefs seems to be rather a grand leap of faith, rather akin to assuming Nash equilibrium from the outset. (She also criticizes the common prior assumption, but I will defer discussing this for now.)

Alternatively, we may try to justify Nash equilibrium by viewing it as a necessary but perhaps not sufficient condition for an acceptable theory. If we wish to study agents who themselves understand our theory of their behavior, then the theory must not be self-refuting—that is, its recommendations should be followed even if the theory itself is common knowledge. Clearly, only a Nash equilibrium could have this property. This argument is sometimes referred to as the *Book of Nash story*—though I do not know who coined that term. However, as Bicchieri notes, the Book of Nash story seems to presume that the prediction is unique. Otherwise, it begs the question of how the players would come to recognize *which* Nash equilibrium they should play.

What should economists and game theorists conclude from this? To my mind, the fact that we cannot answer Bicchieri's question as well as we would like means that we need to ask an easier question. Less flippantly, if we cannot justify our predictions in an ideal manner, what, then, is good enough? In large part, this depends on why one wants predictions in the first place. Game theory can be used in economics for at least two distinct purposes. First is what I will call the *classical usage* for lack of a better term. By this, I mean the traditional use of models for both *positive* and *normative* purposes. By positive models, I refer to those analyses that specify in reasonable detail some situation of interest as a game and then use game theory to try to predict what will happen. By normative, I mean the attempt to determine what kinds of institutions are socially "good" in light of the positive analysis of various alternatives.

More recently, Aumann (1987), Rubinstein (1991), and others have argued that game theory also has what I will call a *conceptual usage*—that is, game theory can be used to help us understand the incentives and considerations present in strategic settings. Put differently, what we learn may not be a specific prediction about the real world, but instead we may gain general insight into the nature of strategic interaction. I will defer comments on this usage of game theory until my conclusion.

Returning, then, to the classical usage, what is the proper form of justification for our predictions if we wish to use game theory to make normative or positive statements about the real world? Presumably, empirical or experimental results indicating that Nash equilibrium predicts well would be as useful or more useful than anything. Since Bicchieri does not discuss such evidence and since I am not particularly well-informed on the subject, I will not discuss it further.[3]

So let us turn to theoretical criteria. Given that compelling, "general" axioms will not get us very far, presumably we would be willing to fall back on reasonable axioms that reflect our view of how the real world works. In her quest for more "ideal" axioms, Bicchieri seems to reject this as a basis for justification of

	L	R
L	1,1	0,0
R	0,0	1,1

Figure 1

a prediction. For example, she emphasizes that a criterion like common knowledge or correctness of beliefs "is not a purely formal matter," reminding the reader that she wishes to "construct a general argument for Nash equilibrium from endogenous premises—that is, from assumptions regarding players' rationality and information about the structure of the game." Similarly, she asks, "What sort of information provided by the normal form justifies the common prior assumption?" Clearly, the answer to this question is "none." However, an economist studying, say, the interaction of firms in a particular industry, may feel quite strongly that these firms have interacted enough in the past to have shared perceptions in a variety of senses, possibly including common priors or common knowledge of beliefs. In light of this, he may feel perfectly justified in using Nash equilibrium to predict. Put differently, when using game theory for prediction in a real world situation, it seems natural to change Bicchieri's question from "How would we predict the outcome of a game played exactly once?" to "In a real-world setting describable by such a game, what would we predict would happen?"

To illustrate this point, consider the simple example shown in Figure 1, sometimes called a *pure coordination game*. This game has two Nash equilibria (in pure strategies)—namely, where each player chooses action L and where each player chooses action R. It is easy to see that this means that both strategies are rationalizable for both players. To rationalize, say, action L for player 1, simply suppose he expects 2 to play L, justifies this to himself with the belief that 2 expects him to play L, and so on. So rationalizability does not eliminate anything. Similarly, the symmetry of the situation makes it quite clear that no reasonable theory will include one of the two Nash equilibria without including the other. Thus the Book of Nash story does not seem to help us either.

On the other hand, suppose we think of this game as representing the problem of which side of the street to drive on. No one really cares whether all drivers drive to their right or all to their left—as long as coordination on one of these two choices is successful. With the exception of the occasional error, most of us most of the time manage to coordinate on an equilibrium with our fellow drivers. We may have adjustment difficulties when traveling, but we do manage to solve them. In short, the hypothesis of Nash equilibrium seems to do quite a good job of predicting in this case. Note that it does not predict *which* action the players will coordinate on. But given the symmetry of the game—and the fact that we do see different forms of coordination in different countries—this is not terribly surprising.

To put the point differently, when we write down a game to describe a particular social situation, we do not have an easy way to incorporate all aspects of the situation. We are forced to omit a description of the cultural setting and may choose to omit the history of the interaction. Once these relevant details are gone and we analyze the bare bones of a normal form, the very details that tell us how players' expectations are formed have been lost. Hence perhaps we should not be surprised that the normal form does not tell us how players figure out what to do. Perhaps, in light of this, we should not object to putting that coordination of expectations into our equilibrium notion.

Of course, it would be better if we could *derive* this bringing together of expectations endogenously. This would have the advantage of giving us a better understanding of how—indeed, whether—common knowledge of beliefs or similar conditions are achieved. This is precisely Bicchieri's conclusion: that we should model the learning process. I discuss this possibility in the next section.

As a final comment on prediction, it seems worth noting that for the classical usage of game theory, the assumption of common priors seems quite reasonable—almost unavoidable, in fact. Presumably, our prediction about a game is a probability distribution that we (the analysts of the game) believe to be "the" correct distribution. But if the players do not have a common prior, they will not agree on what the correct distribution is. So where are we to get this distribution from? Put differently, it seems to me that the notion of prediction requires a notion of objective probability. Furthermore, it seems unreasonable (if not downright selfish) for the game theorist to keep these objective probabilities for himself and not to share them with his players.

Learning and Nash Equilibrium

Can models of learning provide better justification for a prediction in game theory? There has been a great deal of work on this issue in recent years. While it is beyond the scope of this essay to survey this work, I would recommend the papers of Fudenberg and Levine (1991), Kalai and Lehrer (1991), Young (1992), and Kandori, Mailath, and Rob (1992). Each of these papers proves a result that can be interpretted as saying that under certain conditions, players eventually learn to play a Nash equilibrium. However, each obtains this result by imposing some external "consistency"—precisely what we had hoped to avoid.

Can one generate Nash equilibrium from learning behavior without imposing some kind of consistency of beliefs exogenously? I do not think so. If we insist on the kind of strong justifications for our assumptions on learning that we tried unsuccessfully to use to justify Nash equilibrium, we will get no further than we did before.

To see the point concretely, suppose that we reanalyze the pure coordination game of the previous section. Let us suppose that we are not satisfied with my earlier assertion that the players should know which equilibrium is appropriate in a given situation. Instead, they must learn this. So suppose that we have two players and we are going to repeat the game n times (for some large n) to give them a chance to learn. We wish to know whether they will ultimately converge to Nash equilibrium. Clearly, this depends on their initial beliefs and on how they learn.

Note that we now have changed the situation to a repeated game. A strategy will now specify what action a player uses as a function of the history of the game. Hence we must now solve a different, more complex game. Let us try to use only the assumptions Bicchieri wished to use to justify Nash equilibrium previously. So let us suppose that the payoffs and rationality of the players is common knowledge. With this alone, we can only say that the players will use repeated game strategies that are rationalizable. This, by itself, still says virtually nothing.

A critic might argue, quite reasonably, that I have cheated by not taking account of learning. This critic might argue along the following lines. Suppose we wish to rationalize the strategy for player 1 of always playing L no matter what. Clearly, this is optimal for him if he expects player 2 to always play L no matter what. But this justification ignores learing: in particular, it presumes that player 1 plans to play L even after having his beliefs proven wrong by observing player 2 playing R. What belief in this situation would justify this plan?

To see the point concretely and to construct a reply to this critic, let us simplify to the case of $n = 2$. A strategy must specify a first period action and a rule for choosing a second period action as a function of the opponent's first period action. Let σ be the strategy of playing L in the first period and also playing L in the second period no matter how the opponent behaved in the first period. Let σ' be the strategy of playing R in the first period, but playing L no matter what in the second period. It is not hard to see that if the opponent is using σ, then a best response is also σ. Similarly, if the opponent is using σ', the best response is also σ'. However, as our critic has noted, it seems quite unreasonable to justify player 1 choosing σ by saying that he expects player 2 to play σ: if 2 plays R, player 1's beliefs have been refuted, so continuing with the plan specified by σ is not obviously appropriate.

However, we can justify the choice of σ in the following way. Suppose 1 is not sure what 2 is doing. Let δ be the probability distribution over strategies which puts probability .999 on σ and probability .001 on σ'. Similarly, let δ' put probability .001 on σ and .999 on σ'. Now we can justify player 1's choice of σ by saying that his beliefs regarding 2's strategy are given by δ. Notice that with these beliefs, no matter what 1 sees 2 do on the first move, he believes that 2 will certainly play L on the second. Hence with these beliefs, it is optimal for 1 to play L on the second move no matter what. We can rationalize 1's beliefs by supposing that he places probability .999 on 2's beliefs being δ and probability .001 on 2's beliefs being δ'. We can continue in a similar fashion to construct an infinite chain of reasoning supporting 1's choice of the strategy σ, just as we did in the static case.

In short, the fact that the players observe one another's actions certainly complicates matters. But it does not seem to change the basic conclusion that we will not be able to rule out anything if we are only willing to make very basic assumptions like common knowledge of rationality.

Conclusion

I will finally remove my hard-nosed real-world economist hat for a final comment. If one views the role of game theory differently, one also gets a different perspective on Bicchieri's essay and on what we might get from an analysis of learning. I believe that much of the value of game theory comes not from prediction but from clarifying the roles and interactions of different incentives. Consider, for example, the classic paper of Kreps, Milgrom, Roberts, and Wilson (1992). They reexamine the finitely repeated prisoners' dilemma and its well-known conclusion that the only equilibrium is for both players to defect in every period. They show that this conclusion collapses if rationality is not common knowledge. If both players are rational but attach a small probability to the opponent being irrational, then cooperation can be achieved for almost the entire game. Does this result aid us in prediction? Perhaps, but this does not seem to be the main impact of the result. Instead, I would argue that their paper gives a clear picture of the importance of common knowledge of rationality and the possible advantages of being thought irrational.

If one looks at game theory this way, then one takes a completely different perspective on the purpose of Bicchieri's essay. The issue of "justifying" Nash equilibrium becomes as much a way of understanding what equilibrium means as it is a way of understanding when we should predict an equilibrium. Similarly, an analysis of learning may not strengthen our confidence in Nash equilibrium as a predictor of behavior, but I do believe it will improve our understanding of strategic interaction. At the very least, it will clarify the issues raised in the previous section regarding justification of strategies in a dynamic environment.

Notes

1. This claim is a slight exaggeration since the study of games does predate von Neumann and Morganstern (1944). See Aumann (1989) for a history of the subject.
2. Actually, both Bernheim and Pearce also imposed a requirement that each player viewed the others as statistically independent. See Brandenburger's (1992) survey for more details.
3. Though I will mention that Holt (1992), McKelvey and Palfrey (1992), and Slade (1991, 1992) are interesting papers on the subject.

References

Aumann, R. (1987). "What Is Game Theory Trying to Accomplish?" In K. Arrow and S. Honkapohja (eds.), *Frontiers of Economics*. Oxford: Blackwell.
———. (1989). "Game Theory." In J. Eaton, M. Milgate, and P. Newman (eds.), *The New Palgrave: Game Theory*. New York: Norton.
Aumann, R., and A. Brandenburger. (1991). "Epistemic Conditions for Nash Equilibrium." Working paper, Harvard Business School.
Bernheim, B. (1984). "Rationalizable Strategic Behavior." *Econometrica* 52 (July), 1007–1028.
Brandenburger, A. (1992). "Knowledge and Equilibrium in Games." *Journal of Economic Perspectives* 6, (Fall), 83–101.
Fudenberg, D., and D. Levine. (1991). "Steady State Learning and Nash Equilibrium." Working paper, MIT.
Holt, D. (1992). "An Empirical Model of Strategic Choice with an Application to Coordination Games." Working paper, Queen's University.
Kalai, E., and E. Lehrer. (1991). "Rational Learning Leads to Nash Equilibrium." Working paper. Northwestern University.
Kandori, M., G. Mailath, and R. Rob. (1992). "Learning, Mutation, and Long Run Equilibrium in Games." Working paper, University of Pennsylvania.
Kreps, D., P. Milgrom, J. Roberts, and R. Wilson. (1982). "Rational Cooperation in the Finitely Repeated Prisoners' Dilemma." *Journal of Economic Theory* 27 (August), 245–252.
McKelvey, R., and T. Palfrey. (1992). "An Experimental Study of the Centipede Game." *Econometrica* 60 (July), 803–836.
Pearce, D. (1984). "Rationalizable Strategic Behavior and the Problem of Perfection." *Econometrica* 52 (July), 1029–1050.
Rubinstein, A. (1991). "Comments on the Interpretation of Game Theory." *Econometrica* 59 (July), 909–924.
Slade, M. (1991). "Equilibrium Solution Concepts in Dynamic Games: An Empirical

Test of Price and Advertising Competition." Working paper, University of British Columbia.

Slade, M. (1992). "Sticky Prices in a Dynamic Oligopoly: An Empirical Investigation of Fixed and Variable Adjustment Costs." Working paper, University of British Columbia.

von Neumann, J., and O. Morganstern. (1944). *Theory of Games and Economic Behavior*. Princeton, NJ: Princeton University Press.

Young, P. (1992). "The Evolution of Conventions." Working paper, University of Maryland.

5 OBSERVING THE UNOBSERVABLE

David Schmidtz[1]

5.1. Field Data and Controlled Experiments

The problem of producing public goods by collective action takes the form of a prisoner's dilemma when the marginal return per unit of contribution is less than one unit to the contributor but more than one unit to the group. In that case, the group is strictly better off if a given unit is contributed rather than withheld, but an individual is strictly better off withholding that unit. Because group members decide as individuals rather than as a group, the assumption that individuals act to maximize personal wealth implies that individuals in a prisoner's dilemma situation will contribute exactly nothing.

But theory and practice have a way of diverging. In 1980 and 1985, Canada's New Democratic Party attempted to raise $200,000 and $250,000, respectively, in campaign contributions. They succeeded both times, with $1,300 to spare in the second case (Bagnoli and McKee, 1991: 351). In 1979, the Association of Oregon Faculties wanted to raise $30,000 to hire a lobbyist to represent them at the state legislature. They sought $36, $60, or $84 contributions, depending on salary, from all faculty in the state. The drive was successful (Dawes, Orbell, Simmons, and Van de Kragt, 1986: 1172). These organizations solicited donations

147

on the understanding that the money would be refunded if the target figure was not reached. Donors, in other words, had a money-back guarantee.

Why did these fundraising drives succeed? Was it the money-back guarantee? Unfortunately, we will never know. Of course, our problem is hardly unusual. Field experiments are almost always uncontrolled in the technical sense. That is, we want to hold all variables constant, except for a single target variable, so that we may learn how the outcome is affected specifically by changes in the target variable. But in the field, holding all other variables constant is next to impossible, which means there almost always will be a variety of explanations for the observed outcome. For this reason, assessing the importance of changes in the target variable (the fundraising mechanism in this case) is typically very difficult.

This is just one example of a traditional problem with the scientific approach to economics. When field data seem to disconfirm an applicable theory, it is often just as reasonable to reject the data as it is to reject the theory because the data are gathered under conditions that do not permit proper control over the set of possibly relevant variables. Nor is control the only problem. Some relevant variables, like the value people attach to the hiring of a state lobbyist, are not even *observable*, let alone controllable. In-principle testability has been a feature of most important theories in economics; that is to say, they have empirical content. Practical testability has been another matter entirely.

Laboratory conditions, however, offer the possibility of greater control, particularly over such ordinarily unobservable variables as preferences, knowledge endowments, and strategies of the agents involved.[2] To determine how behavior is affected by alternative institutions, we need controls for these key variables, which are not controllable or even observable in the field. In the laboratory, inherently private valuations can be stipulated by and hence known to the experimenter. That is, we can specify the resale value to each subject of a given unit at the same time as we strip the unit of all properties other than price and resale value. So valuations are private information in the sense that subjects do not know how much a unit is worth to other subjects. Nevertheless, the experimenter can, for example, see exactly how actual contribution levels compare with optimal contribution levels or how actual behavior compares with demand-revealing behavior. (In other words, do subjects offer as much as the unit is worth to them, or do they underbid?) We thereby learn about the strategies subjects employ. And because the experimental instructions are generally the only source of information subjects have about the nature of the experiment, knowledge endowments are well controlled too. Thus, the usual response to field experiments—that when a theory is not corroborated, something is wrong with the experiment—is not so easily defended as a response to data gathered in the laboratory.

5.2. The Isaac-Walker Design

A general (and hence powerful) model of the public goods problem has been tested in the laboratory by Isaac, Walker, and Thomas (1984) and by Isaac and Walker (1988). In these experiments, subjects (four or ten in a group) were given an initial endowment of tokens and asked to allot them between private and public exchanges. A token invested in the private exchange yielded one cent to the individual subject. A token invested in the public exchange yielded a sum to be divided equally among all subjects in the group. (The size of the sum was determined by the group's production function. Two such functions were used, both linear, yielding either 0.3 or 0.75 units per subject for each token invested in the public exchange.) A series of ten trials allowed subjects to learn that their single-period dominant strategy was to invest all of their income in the private exchange. Subjects were told in advance that the tenth period would be the final period so that their single-period dominant strategy would clearly be salient in the tenth period. (And in periods one to nine, for what it is worth, a set of zero contributions is the Nash equilibrium predicted by backward induction.)

The results of these experiments disconfirmed the prediction that investment in the public exchange in period 10 will be zero. Even in final periods preceded by what should have been ample opportunity to learn dominant strategies, contributions are positive and substantial, albeit suboptimal. Why do subjects contribute as much as they do? Why do they contribute anything at all? Since our set of assumptions implies a prediction that contributions will be precisely zero in period 10, the fact that this prediction is consistently wrong suggests that one of our assumptions is false. Because noncontribution is clearly a dominant strategy, a process of elimination locates the error in our behavioral assumption that subjects act so as to maximize personal income. The hypothesis that people will free ride whenever they have the opportunity is disconfirmed by experiments such as those conducted by Isaac and Walker.

So if subjects are not trying to maximize personal income, what are they doing? Perhaps some subjects simply do not behave strategically. That is, they may develop some expectation of how much of the public good will be produced and then simply contribute what they are willing to pay for that product. Some subjects may operate by rules of thumb (like "Make small contributions to charity") and thus may be oblivious to the incentives involved in particular situations.

Inability to understand the rules of the game could also lead some subjects to contribute, although one might expect that subjects who did not understand the situation would be more likely to sit back and contribute nothing. Moreover, the situation was by no means complicated. I think failure to comprehend does play a role in what we observe, but by the tenth period, only a very small one.

In any event, the nature of our concern about incomprehension in the laboratory is partly a matter of whether we mean to test descriptive theory or prescriptive policy. However much confusion there is in the laboratory, there is more confusion in more complicated environments. So the reality of incomprehension is something we have to be aware of when drawing conclusions about policy. (I will have more to say about the difference between tests of theory and tests of policy.)

Perhaps the interests of others enter into subjects' preference functions. That is, subjects prefer to benefit other subjects. Or some subjects may not exactly have a preference for benefiting other subjects but may not consider it permissible to fail to do their share, whatever they perceive their share to be. Some subjects, if they are wealth maximizers at all, may place certain constraints on what they will do to maximize personal wealth. In other words, the externalities involved in the decision to contribute or not may enter into subjects' decisions as part of their set of constraints, along with income constraints and so on. To use David Gauthier's (1986: 160ff) terms, many of those who contribute even in final periods may be constrained rather than straightforward maximizers.

Contributing positive but suboptimal amounts in experimental situations is sometimes described as *weak* free riding. This label can mislead because the phenomenon so named may not be free riding at all. As I use the term, *free riding* is an attempt to enjoy the benefits of other players' contributions without responding in kind. Some individuals may contribute suboptimally not because they are free riders, weak or otherwise, but because they are averse to being, so to speak, taken for a ride. Let us call the aversion to being taken advantage of an *exploitation problem*. Subjects with an exploitation problem seek some assurance that the pattern of contributions within the group will be fair before they will contribute what they judge to be their share. Alternatively, a person may be willing to participate in a joint venture on mutually profitable terms. A person's contributions, however, may be limited to a level such that the sum of investments in the public exchange can be expected to yield a return sufficient to repay his own investment. Unless the person receives reasonable assurance that other people will contribute enough to ensure that his own contribution will not be wasted on a hopelessly underfunded cause, the person may decide to save his money. This limitation is an *assurance problem*.[3]

5.3. A Theory About Prisoner's Dilemmas

That leaves us with a puzzle about how to distinguish between defections according to what motivates them. The problem is important for policy because whether a money-back guarantee affects contribution levels depends entirely on

		How many do the other three players contribute?			
		None	One	Two	All Three
How many do you contribute?	No	0	+0.3	+0.6	+0.9
	Yes	−0.7	−0.4	−0.1	+0.2

Figure 5.1. Prisoner's dilemma (only "your" net gains and losses are shown)

whether the assurance problem is a real cause of defection. There is a theoretical issue here as well, because the standard theory implies that a money-back guarantee should not make any difference. It should not make a difference because, if the situation is a prisoner's dilemma, then adding a money-back guarantee cannot change the fact that noncontribution is a dominant strategy.

Figure 5.1 depicts the incentive structure in the Isaac-Walker experiments. There are four players with identical payoff functions, one of whom I refer to as *you*. If you contribute a unit, you lose that unit and each player including you gains 0.3 units. Not contributing is a dominant strategy, for no matter how many of the others contribute, you are always at least as well off not contributing. Indeed, you are strictly better off not contributing.

So goes the standard analysis of the prisoner's dilemma. The way I have defined free rider and assurance problems, however, sheds a new light on the dilemma. As defined, these two problems are complementary and essential components of the prisoner's dilemma. In effect, they constitute the two "halves" of the prisoner's dilemma. From your point of view, the left side of the matrix (the lower left three cells in the case at hand) represents your assurance problem. You may be willing to contribute so that (assuming the others also contribute) you get an extra twenty cents. But without assurance that the others will contribute, contributing may get you seventy cents less rather than twenty cents more. This gap, reflected in the difference between your payoffs in the upper left and lower left cells, constitutes an assurance problem. The right side (the upper right three cells in Figure 5.1) of the matrix, by contrast, represents your temptation to free ride. If the others contribute, then you get twenty cents by returning the favor. But there is no need for you to return the favor. In fact, by withholding, you get ninety cents rather than twenty. Thus the gap between the payoffs of the upper right and lower right cells constitutes a free-rider problem.

Consider the effect of the money-back guarantee. It solves the assurance problem by raising negative payoffs in the lower left cells to zero. On my analysis, that eliminates one of the two reasons for noncontribution that jointly

		How many do the other three players contribute?			
		None	One	Two	All Three
How many do you contribute?	No	0	+0.3	+0.6	+0.9
	Yes	0	0	0	+0.2

Figure 5.2. Your payoffs after adding money-back guarantee

constitute the prisoner's dilemma and thus should lead some people at least to contribute more than they otherwise would have. On the standard analysis, adding the money-back guarantee should not make any difference, since it does not change the fact that not contributing is the dominant strategy.

As we can see in Figure 5.2, defection is still a dominant strategy. When I was working on my master's thesis, though, I had a theory that people are not particularly responsive to the existence of dominant strategies. On my analysis, the prisoner's dilemma incentive structure is constituted by a conjunction of free-rider and assurance problems, and I believed that each problem has a distinct practical effect. I also thought that the money-back problem could solve the assurance problem, at least in some cases, thus leading in practice to a greater willingness to contribute notwithstanding the fact that noncontribution would remain a dominant strategy.

5.4. How to Observe Motives

In devising a test of a policy of offering money-back guarantees, the problem I initially faced was to determine the empirical status of my hypothesis that prisoner's dilemmas are conjunctions of free-rider and assurance problems. If a person does not contribute to a public goods project, how would we ever know what her reason was? And why would we care? Does a person's reason for withholding actually matter, or is this merely a distinction without a difference? The task was to design an experiment in which the two different kinds of withholding did not look the same.

I was familiar with the Isaac-Walker experiments, for at the time I was a research assistant for the Economic Science Laboratory and was enrolled in a course on experimental economics taught by Mark Isaac. My term paper for that course was a proposal for an experimental test of the assurance problem. The proposal was based on a modified Isaac-Walker design. My method was to introduce a provision point into the Isaac-Walker design such that the good at stake became a *step good*—a good that cannot be provided at all until total contributions reach a certain critical level. Consider what happens if the provision point is set at 100 percent of the group's total endowment. In that case, free riding is impossible. If any subject withholds even a single token, then neither he nor anyone else can receive the group good. Because free riding is impossible, there is no way to be taken advantage of—hence no exploitation problem. Rational subjects have only two reasons to withhold: the assurance problem and failure to understand the incentive structure.

For purposes of comparison, suppose we combine the 100 percent provision point with a money-back guarantee (that is, a guarantee that contributions to the public exchange will be returned if the provision point is not met). In that case, *contribution* is a dominant strategy. So the presence of assurance problems in the former case (100 percent provision point) and their absence in the latter (100 percent provision point plus money-back guarantee) should account for any significant difference between contribution levels with and without the money-back guarantee. Thus, we can infer the empirical significance of the assurance problem and can distinguish this significance from that of free-rider problems and failures to understand.

Besides indicating the magnitude of the assurance problem, the modified Isaac-Walker design also tests, under laboratory conditions, the empirical effect of the money-back guarantee on voluntary mechanisms for funding public goods provision. Hence it constitutes a test of my theory about what leads people to defect in prisoner's dilemmas and, to a lesser extent, a test of the money-back guarantee as an economic policy. I will discuss this and one other modified Isaac-Walker design. First, however, I report results of two other laboratory research projects that also bear on the efficacy of the money-back guarantee and on the assurance problem's significance in public goods contexts. To my knowledge, these studies currently exhaust the experimental literature on the subject of money-back guarantees in the context of public goods production. (Section 5.7 explores the distinction between theory tests and policy tests and reports on a new Isaac-Walker design for testing voluntary contributions in large groups.)

5.5. Analyzing the Data

5.5.1. Bagnoli and McKee

Bagnoli and McKee (1991) sought to test the efficacy of a money-back guarantee in eliciting contributions in a public goods situation. Their groups consisted of either five subjects (seven groups in all) or ten subjects (two groups in all), with subjects having individual endowments ranging between seven and sixteen tokens. The decision space was continuous; subjects were allowed to contribute whatever portion of their endowment they desired. The production function was binary; the group good was exactly twenty-five tokens if the provision point was met and nothing otherwise. In the event of failure, contributions were returned to those who made them. The group good was divided among subjects according to a preset pattern. In some experiments, the division was equal. In two of the five-person experiments, subjects received from one to ten tokens as their share of the group good. This range was present within as well as across experiments. Individual endowments, the pattern of individual shares in the group good, and number of subjects were common knowledge. In all cases, the provision point was 12.5 tokens. (Subjects could contribute fractions of tokens.) The experiment consisted of fourteen periods.

The seven five-person groups met or exceeded the provision point in eighty-five of ninety-eight periods (fourteen periods in each of seven experiments). Total contributions were within a half token of the provision point in seventy-five of ninety-eight cases. Of the seven small groups, five earned 95 percent or more of the theoretical maximum for all fourteen periods taken together. (The theoretical maximum is the sum of individual incomes, plus the total value of the public good produced, minus the minimum cost of reaching the provision point.) Five of seven groups actually attained the theoretical maximum over the last five periods (thirty-three out of thirty-five periods in all) and a sixth was very close. The two ten-person groups met the provision point in seventeen of twenty-eight periods. They were at 95 percent efficiency over the last five periods, although it took longer for the pattern of contributions to converge on an equilibrium (Bagnoli and McKee, 1991: 359).

It is interesting that their design did not solve the free-rider problem at all; rather, it induced public goods provision in spite of an incentive structure with a built-in free-rider problem. The most pertinent feature of Bagnoli and McKee's institution seems to be its money-back guarantee as a solution to the assurance problem. Unfortunately, we cannot be certain of this. The extent to which solving the assurance problem was what led subjects to contribute in this experimental context remains unclear. For our purposes, it would have been ideal if the Bagnoli and McKee experiments had incorporated a control for the money-back variable. As it is, we do not know how much subjects would have contributed in this environment if they had not had a money-back guarantee. Hence, we have no way of knowing how much the money-back guarantee helped.

5.5.2. Dawes, Orbell, Simmons, and Van de Kragt

Dawes et al. (1986) explored how well contributions are promoted by two devices: the money-back guarantee and *enforced fairness*. The first device returns contributions to donors if the group fails to meet its provision point. This solves the assurance problem. The second device requires contributions from those who did not contribute if and when the group succeeds in meeting its provision point. This solves the free-rider problem, albeit nonvoluntarily.

Dawes et al. hypothesized that contributions are better promoted by enforced fairness. Their rationale is this: the success of the money-back guarantee can be undermined by people's expectation that it will succeed. Why? Because as subjects become more confident that the money-back mechanism will succeed, free riding comes to seem less risky for it seems increasingly likely that their own contribution is not needed. Thus, the more the money-back mechanism succeeds, the more reason subjects have to withhold. In contrast, as subjects gain more confidence in enforced fairness, the assurance problem becomes less troublesome, for it seems increasingly likely that their own contribution will be sufficient (and the design rules out free riding). So the more the enforced fairness mechanism succeeds, the less reason subjects have to withhold.

Groups in these experiments consisted of seven subjects, each endowed with $5. Their task was to decide individually whether to contribute their endowment to the group project. The decision space was binary; subjects had two options: contribute $5 or contribute nothing. The production technology was also binary; it produced $10 for each subject if the provision point was met and nothing otherwise.

In the money-back dilemma, contributions were returned if the provision point was not met. The free-rider problem remained, but the assurance problem apparently was eliminated. In the enforced fairness dilemma, noncontributors had $5 taken from them if the provision point was met. (In effect, there are no noncontributors when enforced fairness succeeds; enforced fairness is forced unanimity.) The assurance problem remained because those who contributed voluntarily would lose their money if the provision point was not met. But the free-rider problem had been eliminated. Two provision points were examined. The first required $15; three of seven people had to contribute. The second required $25; five of seven had to contribute. These experiments consisted of a single period. The process was not iterated. As a control, full dilemmas, having neither money-back nor enforced fairness features, were also run with provision points.

As Table 5.1 shows, contributions in the Dawes et al. study were substantially higher in the enforced fairness dilemma than in the full dilemma. Dawes et al. (1986: 1183) concluded there was no statistically significant difference between full and money-back dilemmas: "There is no ambiguity whatever about the success of the money-back guarantee device for eliciting contributions compared with the success of the enforced contribution device: the enforced contribution is superior." They also conclude that "Fear of loss through contributing is not the critical motivation underlying defection" (1988: 1183).

Regarding their conclusion about the insignificance of the difference between

Table 5.1.   Three dilemmas in Dawes et al. (percentage of subjects contributing)

	Provision Point = 3	Provision Point = 5
Full dilemma	51	64
Money-back dilemma	61	65
Enforced fairness dilemma	86	93

full and money-back dilemmas, we might note that the observed difference in the experiments with three-person provision points would have become statistically significant had the difference been replicated over a modest number of further trials. We might also note that if instead of looking at individual contributions, we look at the proportion of groups meeting the provision point, we get a slightly different picture. That is, eleven of twenty groups met their provision point in the full dilemma, whereas eleven of fourteen met their provision point in the money-back dilemma.

Regarding the difference found by Dawes et al. between money-back and enforced fairness dilemmas, their inference that fear of loss is not a critical motivation contradicts my hypothesis that the assurance problem is a major component of the public goods problem. But I believe their inference is invalid for the following reasons. First, enforced fairness does not function only by eliminating the chance to free ride. It also reduces the fear of loss by making it impossible for others to free ride. The design does not rule out the possibility that reducing fear in this way plays a critical role in the success of enforced fairness. Second, in the enforced fairness dilemma, unlike in the full or money-back dilemmas, there was no reason at all to fear that one's contribution would be wasted by virtue of being redundant. (Under the enforced fairness regime, when a subject's contribution is redundant, it would have been collected anyway, so it is not wasted in the way that redundant contributions are wasted in the money-back regime.) Thus, the enforced fairness device reduced fear in two ways, ways in which the alternatives did not, and either way might have helped the enforced fairness device to elicit contributions. Dawes et al. conclude that the superiority of the enforced fairness device shows that fear of loss is not a critical motivational factor, but this conclusion does not follow.

With respect to their claim that enforced fairness is the superior fundraising mechanism, an obvious issue is that enforced fairness is not a voluntary mechanism at all. We should not be too surprised that fundraising efforts are more likely to succeed when backed up by the threat of force. Suppose our faculty club wishes to raise money for the purpose of expanding the local museum. In one scenario, we agree to raise half a million dollars in order to get a matching grant from a large corporation, on the understanding that we will return faculty contributions if we fail to reach the half-million-dollar target. In an alternative scenario, we say we will try to raise a half million voluntarily, and if we succeed we will seize another half million from faculty members who have not contributed yet. Even if enforced fairness is more effective, it raises rather urgent questions: How do we get that kind of power, and what gives us the right to use it in that way?

Moreover, aside from questions of legitimacy and problems in implementation, the conclusion that enforced fairness is superior does not follow from the data in the first place. In the Dawes et al. design, the efficient levels of contributions were $15 (three out of seven) and $25 (five out of seven) respectively for the full dilemma. Because redundant contributions were wasted, efficiency was reduced by any contributions made in excess of these figures. The same is true of the money-back dilemma. In the enforced fairness dilemma, however, efficiency was not reduced by excess contributions: $35 was an efficient level of investment because meeting the provision point meant that $35 was taken in any event. Obviously, this level of investment was not likely to be approached by the money-back mechanism; matching the contribution levels of enforced fairness (i.e., 86 percent and 93 percent) would have required people in the money-back experiments to throw their money away. (Subjects would not be certain they were throwing their money away, which mitigates my criticism, but they would be aware of the possibility.) When we consider that the efficient contribution levels in the money-back experiments were 43 percent and 71 percent, respectively, rather than 100 percent, the actual money-back contribution levels of 61 percent and 65 percent begin to look respectable, to say the least. Dawes et al. find "no ambiguity whatever" in the superiority of enforced fairness. However, although subtle, the ambiguity is real.

Dawes et al. hypothesized that the efficacy of the money-back guarantee would be undermined by the expectation of its success. This is true in their design. But perhaps real-world money-back guarantees are not subject to the same kind of undermining. In their design, increasing expectation of success also increased the expectation that one's contribution would be wasted, for there were two ways for it to be spent in vain. Both undercontribution and *over-contribution* entailed wasted investment in their design. Thus, the expectation of success not only creates a free-rider problem—as it might do in the real world—but creates its own assurance problem as well, which seems unrealistic.

5.5.3. Isaac, Schmidtz, and Walker

Mark Isaac, David Schmidtz, and James Walker (1989) used four-person groups, each subject initially being endowed with sixty-two tokens. Each subject had a continuous decision space (which means that each could contribute zero, sixty-two, or any whole number of tokens in between). The value of the public good was $G(x) = 1.2x$ if the provision point was met and zero otherwise. For example, if the sum of individual contributions is $2, and if $2 meets or exceeds the provision point, then the value of the public good produced is $2.40 (but if $2 falls short of the provision point, then the value of the public good produced is zero). This value is divided equally among subjects, so that, for example, if the sum of individual contributions is $2, then each of the four subjects receives one-fourth of the resulting G, which in this case means one-fourth of $2.40. Because the public good production function is linear (i.e., since the number 1.2 is a constant) and continuous for all values of x that meet the provision point, there is no possibility of contributions being wasted by virtue of being redundant (that is, because 1.2 is greater than 1 and constant for all values of x, there is no possibility of overcontributing). If the provision point is not met, contributions are returned in the money-back experiments and are not returned (are simply wasted) in the experimental controls, which lack the guarantee.

Three different provision points were used. (In a fit of enthusiasm for technical terms, we called them high, medium, and low.) The high provision point (HPP = 248) represents 100 percent of the group's endowment. Thus, the high provision point treatment eliminated the free-rider problem. The high provision point money-back experiments eliminated both free-rider and assurance problems. The medium provision point (MPP = 216) represented the number of tokens sufficient to produce a return of at least sixty-five cents to each subject, thus ensuring that a given subject could contribute all sixty-two tokens and still make a profit if the provision point was met. The low provision point (LPP = 108) presented a provision level such that any subject making a contribution in excess of thirty-two tokens was not assured of earning a return worth more than thirty-two tokens even if the provision point was met. Thus, subjects contemplating a contribution of more than half their income had assurance problems even given the money-back guarantee.

Subjects knew in advance that the experiment would run for ten periods. In early periods, there was a pronounced tendency for the four subjects to each make contributions of approximately one-fourth of the provision point. Isaac, Schmidtz, and Walker (1989: 223) call this a *focal point* contribution, a level of contribution that seems somehow obvious (see also Schelling, 1960). Table 5.2 pools data from eighteen experiments, six with each provision point. In keeping with the convention of Isaac, Walker, and Thomas (1984), the individual contributions are separated into five size categories ranging from zero to sixty-two.

Notice that contribution levels increased in proportion to increases in the provision point level. This is rather odd, because one would intuitively think assurance problems would worsen as the provision point rises. Table 5.2 suggests that

Table 5.2. First-period individual contributions in Isaac, Schmidtz, and Walker,
no money-back guarantee (number of subjects contributing)

Size Range of Contributions	Low Provision Point (focal pt. = 27)	Medium Provision Point (focal pt. = 54)	High Provision Point (focal pt. = 62)
0	1	3	8
1–20	3	3	0
21–41	15	2	1
42–61	2	12	3
62	3	2	12
Total	24	24	24

Table 5.3. Final-period individual contributions in Isaac, Schmidtz, and Walker,
no money-back guarantee (number of subjects contributing)

Size Range of Contributions	Low Provision Point	Medium Provision Point	High Provision Point
0	19	20	19
1–20	1	0	1
21–41	3	0	0
42–61	0	3	0
62	1	1	4
Total	24	24	24

provision points may have served as focal points in early periods. As the experiment progressed, however, contributions usually collapsed completely. Table 5.3 shows the end-period result.

On the other hand, in three of the eighteen experiments (one for each provision point), contributions remained at higher levels than ever before observed in the general Isaac-Walker design. (The four contributions of sixty-two tokens in Table 5.3's data pool for the high provision point, for instance, all came from a single experiment.) Isaac, Schmidtz, and Walker's (1989: 228) conclusion is that without the money-back guarantee, the introduction of a provision point can dramatically increase contribution levels in a few cases, but generally does not succeed and probably makes matters worse. Thus, introducing the provision point itself made a difference, the extent of which depended on the contribution level at which the provision point was set.

Isaac, Schmidtz, and Walker found that Pareto-superior Nash equilibria tended to collapse to Pareto-inferior Nash equilibria. This was true with and without the possibility of "cheap riding" (contributing only the minimal amount necessary

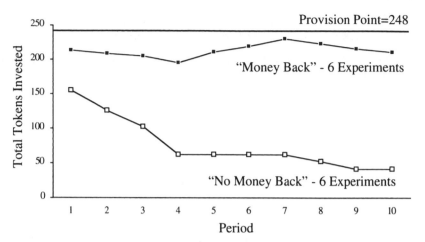

Source: Isaac, Schmidtz, and Walker (1989). Reprinted by permission of Kluwer Academic Publishers.

Figure 5.3   Mean number of tokens contributed in Isaac, Schmidtz, and Walker high provision point

to reach the provision point, given the expected pattern of contribution of the other members of the group). It does not appear to be dominance as such that causes the underprovision of public goods (Isaac, Schmidtz, and Walker, 1989: 229). Subjects' reasons for contributing are more complicated (and often considerably less rational) than that.

Introducing the money-back guarantee, however, made a substantial difference. Overall, success in meeting provision points went from 45 out of 180 to 93 out of 180 periods when a money-back guarantee was added. Figures 5.3, 5.4, and 5.5 compare average contribution levels for money-back versus no-money-back treatments on a per-period basis, for each of the three provision points.

These observations suggest that the assurance problem is observationally distinguishable from the free-rider problem and that it is a significant part of public goods problems. Further, the money-back guarantee that solves the assurance problem in theory also makes an empirical difference. Especially, note Figure 5.3. With or without the guarantee, the 248-token provision point renders exploitation and free riding impossible. The assurance problem is the sole reason for the difference between the money-back and no-money-back contribution levels. (Failures to understand presumably caused some of the failures to contribute in either case, but only the assurance problem can account for the *difference* between the two contribution levels.)

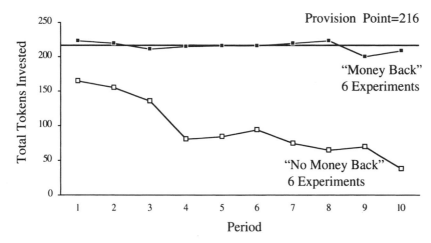

Source: Isaac, Schmidtz, and Walker (1989). Reprinted by permission of Kluwer Academic Publishers.

Figure 5.4   Mean number of tokens contributed in Isaac, Schmidtz, and Walker medium provision point

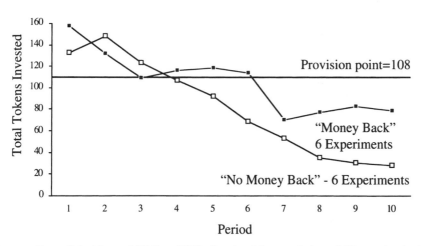

Source: Isaac, Schmidtz, and Walker (1989). Reprinted by permission of Kluwer Academic Publishers.

Figure 5.5   Mean number of tokens contributed in Isaac, Schmidtz, and Walker low provision point

Table 5.4. Guarantee versus no guarantee (number of periods in which groups met provision points)

	Money-Back	*No Money-Back*
Isaac, Schmidtz, and Walker	93/180	45/180
Dawes et al.	11/14	11/20
Bagnoli and McKee	85/98	no data

For practical purposes, imposing a provision point without the guarantee is a risky strategy. (Also, imagine people's reaction as you try to explain to them that you have decided not to produce any of the good but will not give their money back either.) Imposing a provision point together with a money-back guarantee appears to be a rather good idea, certainly better than simply asking for contributions. Table 5.4 shows the experimental success of the money-back guarantee in meeting provision points compared with that of the no money-back experimental controls.

In the money-back experiments with a high provision point, contributing sixty-two tokens was a dominant strategy. Contributing anything less was unquestionably a mistake, minimizing the subject's own income as well as that of the group. Nevertheless, it happened. Figure 5.3 shows the gap between the 248-token provision point and the line representing data from the money-back experiments. If all subjects had played their dominant strategies, there would have been no gap. In fact, however, in 56 out of 240 individual decisions made in the six ten-period high provision point experiments, subjects did not play their dominant strategy. Why? I have no truly satisfying answer, but we should note that nearly half of these failures to contribute occurred within a single experiment—one in which subjects reported responding to the group's initial failure by lowering their own bids either in frustration or in an attempt to prompt the others to action.

It also might have been important that those who irrationally made suboptimal contributions in the high provision point money-back experiments continued to earn an income of sixty-two tokens. (In contrast, those who contributed amounts between zero and sixty-two tokens in the no-guarantee, high provision point experiment lost their contributions, and the loss quickly taught them not to repeat their mistake.) Perhaps some subjects considered an income of sixty-two tokens per period perfectly satisfactory and for this reason felt no need to examine the possibility that *contributing* sixty-two tokens was actually a dominant strategy. This raises another question. It was assumed (at least by me) that a money-back guarantee would solve assurance problems without systematically affecting the amount of suboptimality attributable to simple failure to understand the game.

However, if a person could be hurt by his or her own misunderstanding in one game but could not be hurt in the same way in the other game, then perhaps my assumption is unwarranted. Perhaps there would be a difference in a person's tendency to learn from mistakes. If so, then this suggests that the gap between money-back and no-money-back experiments may understate the magnitude of the assurance problem. (Of course, because my main conclusion here is that the assurance problem is empirically significant, this possibility is not a threat.)

One thing the Isaac, Schmidtz, and Walker design does not do is allow subjects to observe each other's contribution within any given period. To the extent that they care about what other subjects are doing, they must respond to other subjects on the basis of cumulative information from past periods. In a given period, there is no way for them to learn about other subjects' intentions or to signal their own. In this respect, the Isaac, Schmidtz, and Walker design is a poor model of the telethon approach to fundraising, for example, because contributors to a telethon scheme have access to continuously updated information on what other contributors have so far pledged. Frequently, potential contributors also have information about *challenge pledges*—contributions promised pending the materialization of a certain level of contributions from others. (The fire department might challenge the police department, for example.) Of course, the main purpose of Isaac, Schmidtz, and Walker's experiments (from my point of view) was to verify the empirical significance of the assurance problem, and to show that the problem is observationally distinguishable from the free-rider problem. Our primary intent was to test theory, not policy. We were not out to test the efficiency of telethons. I will discuss the difference between tests of theory and tests of policy after taking note of recently completed experiments that do provide information about the efficiency of the telethon approach.

5.6. Contribution Patterns in Real Time

Robert Dorsey (1992) employed the basic design and incentive structure of Isaac, Schmidtz, and Walker. Dorsey's design, however, incorporates a major advance. It alters the decision-making environment in order to determine whether the decision-making process is sensitive to temporal factors and to the associated changes in the kind of information people have when making decisions. Dorsey's design gave subjects three minutes within each period to enter or update their contributions to the public exchange, in light of changing information about what the rest of the group had so far contributed in that period. This added time element reflects the kind of information and opportunity to update contributions that decision makers often have.

A second advantage of Dorsey's design over Isaac, Schmidtz, and Walker's

Table 5.5. The effect of real time (contributions as a median percentage of groups' total endowments; mean percentages shown in parentheses)

	Increase-Only Rule	*Increase-or-Decrease Rule*
No provision point	19.6 (23.12)	8.1 (11.53)
Provision point = 108	43.5 (34.78)	27.2 (26.99)

Source: Dorsey (1992: 277). Reprinted by permission of Kluwer Academic Publishers.

is that the extra information with which it provides subjects can alleviate assurance problems to some extent without resorting to provision points combined with money-back guarantees. This is so because a subject can easily see, given what other subjects have contributed, how much he or she can afford to contribute and still be assured of making a profit. Therefore, another way of solving the assurance problem (up to a certain contribution level) is to impose a rule that subjects can only add to previous pledges, not subtract from them. When subjects can add to or subtract from previous pledges, the assurance problem is present in full force.

By adding a provision point, Isaac, Schmidtz, and Walker also introduced a focal point, which meant that they needed to control for the possibility that the focal point rather than the money-back guarantee caused the rise in contribution levels. Because Dorsey's design dispensed with the need for a provision point, this control problem did not arise for him. Nevertheless, although Dorsey was able to design a fundraising mechanism that solved the assurance problem without introducing a focal point, he still wanted to test the effect of adding a provision point to what he called a "real time" environment—one with a time element that permits subjects to update contributions within periods. Unlike Isaac, Schmidtz, and Walker, who found that the provision point had a real but equivocal effect on contribution levels in the simultaneous game, Dorsey found that incorporating provision points in the real-time game had a substantial positive effect on contribution levels.

Dorsey contrasted the increase-only rule to a rule by which subjects could either increase or decrease commitments made previously in that period. In effect, the increase-or-decrease rule makes pledges nonbinding. Under such a rule, the temporal aspect of the real-time game does nothing to solve the assurance problem, even for last-second contributors. As we would expect, Dorsey found that in this environment contribution levels were much lower, sometimes collapsing entirely at the end of the three-minute period.

Table 5.5 reflects data gathered by Dorsey from sixteen experiments with the increase-only rule and eight experiments with the increase-or-decrease rule. In each treatment, half the experiments were run with no provision point and half

Table 5.6. Comparing Dorsey's increase-only and increase-or-decrease rules with Isaac, Schmidtz, and Walker (ISW) (contributions expressed as a median percentage of group's total endowments)

	Increase-Only	Increase -or-Decrease	ISW	ISW (money-back)
Provision point = 108	44.4	26.6	30.2	42.7

with a provision point of 108 tokens (equal to the low provision point of Isaac, Schmidtz, and Walker).

What we see is that adding a provision point in the real-time environment dramatically increases median contribution levels. (Even under the increase-or-decrease rule, the median contribution level was 27.2 percent with the provision point but only 8.1 percent without.) We also see that contribution levels are significantly higher under the increase-only rule than under the increase-or-decrease rule. Median contributions were roughly twice as high under the increase-only rule. Moreover, the real-time element itself makes a difference. Table 5.6 compares the data from Dorsey with data from Isaac, Schmidtz, and Walker. Isaac, Schmidtz, and Walker ran six experiments with 108 token provision points and another six experiments that also included a money-back guarantee against failure to meet the 108-token provision point. The median percentage of total tokens contributed in these experiments is presented in Table 5.6 for purposes of comparison.

As Dorsey notes, "Isaac, Schmidtz, and Walker, using identical parameters but without real time adjustments, reported that with a provision point of 108, only one experiment out of six achieved the provision point after the fourth period. With the real time environment, the provision point was reached at least once after the fourth period in eight out of 12 of the ten-period experiments" (Dorsey, 1992: 278).

Dorsey's real-time game is a different game. It has different rules, induces real people to play different strategies, and leads to different results. I once argued that the temporal factor (under an increase-only rule) could induce people to contribute more to a public goods project than they otherwise might. Against this, David Friedman (1987) argued that rational players in a real-time situation would wait until the last second. In the limit, everyone waits until the last second—thus, no one has any information about what anyone else is planning to do. "We all make our decisions in ignorance of what the rest are doing. We are back in the simultaneous game" (Friedman, 1987: 519). Dorsey's experiments, however, show that this is not how the temporal factor works. It may not be obvious that the real-time element has a bearing on the dominant strategy equilibrium, but nevertheless it does. When subjects have the opportunity within periods to lever up each other's contributions, the dominant strategy equilibrium is replaced by Nash equilibria. When players can respond to each other within a period, that means that a player's best strategy within the period—in terms of both what to contribute and *when*—depends on how other player's are prepared to respond during the period.

How, then, do we explain the fact that contribution levels rose when intraperiod decisions were made in real time? For one thing, the real-time element allows subjects to see whether total contributions are below the provision point at any particular moment during the period, while there is still time to do something about it. If we think of total contributions as being like a missile launched at the provision point, then the temporal factor allows players to use their contributions to guide the total toward the provision point. Without the temporal factor that allows subjects to adjust contributions, total contributions are like a ballistic missile. After the initial decision, no further control is possible. The analogy breaks down, however, when we use the increase-or-decrease rule, for with that rule, previous contributions can be withdrawn at a moment's notice. Contributions already announced are nonbinding and thus convey no real information about what adjustments will be required to meet the provision point as the period draws to a close.

I also suspect the increase-only format effectively converted the intraperiod game from a one-shot prisoner's dilemma to something that could be played as an iterated prisoner's dilemma. That is, a subject could contribute one penny, then step back until total contributions rose to a level sufficient to repay a one-penny contribution (say, four cents). Then the subject could contribute one more penny, wait until total contributions rose to a level adequate as a reciprocation for the subject's two-cent contribution, then take this as a cue to initiate another round by contributing one more, and so on. When Dorsey sequentially plotted intra-period contributions, the resulting curve in some cases showed just the series of regular small steps we would expect from such a strategy (Dorsey 1992: 279).

Whether this kind of strategy characteristically underlies the success of telethon fundraisers is far from clear, but it may be a part of it. Moreover, aside from the aspect of reciprocity permitted by the real-time environment, there is also the prospect of being able to make a decision with an assurance about the minimum level of total contributions one may expect, and this presumably is a big factor in both the Dorsey experiments and in the telethons that these experiments model.

Dorsey's results also have a significance that goes beyond their implications as a model of telethon fundraisers. Consider, for example, how it might be used to model negotiations over disarmament during the Cold War. Suppose the situation was as follows. (It might have been; I am not qualified to say.) The Soviet Union (circa 1988) had an approach to disarmament that suggests an attempt to capitalize on the incentives associated with the real-time element. They apparently were taking unilateral steps to disarm and demilitarize. As the United States government liked to stress, it is indeed true that these steps were very small. But small steps were precisely what the situation called for. The Soviets had a very pressing assurance problem and could not be expected to take larger steps unilaterally. If the cuts were genuine, then the United States might be (or might have been) best served by cutting its own military strength by slightly more than the Soviets cut theirs, so as to put the onus on the Soviets to maintain the momentum.

One major obstacle to successful negotiations in such situations is the problem of monitoring compliance. It is relatively easy to ensure that a given missile has been rendered inoperative; the big problem is to ensure that replacements are not secretly being built. But notice the structure of this monitoring problem. The problem is that we need to prevent playing by an increase-or-decrease rule. Both sides need assurance that the only available moves will be subtractions from the arms stockpile. Covert additions must be ruled out. The game will not run smoothly until we are in a position to play by a decrease-only rule with incentive properties equivalent to those of Dorsey's increase-only rule for monetary contributions.

For public goods problems involving a need to secure monetary contributions, a logical next step in the line of research begun by Isaac and Walker would be to compare a real-time provision point environment to one that added a money-back guarantee in the event the provision point was not met. Although the provision point induced greater contributions in the Dorsey experiments, it also featured an assurance problem because to initiate the incremental process of building up to the provision point, subjects had to accept the risk of never reaching it, thereby wasting whatever they had contributed. Solving this assurance problem with a money-back guarantee resulted in an increase of nearly 50 percent in median contributions (from 30.2 to 42.7 percent of total endowment) in Isaac, Schmidtz, and Walker. Combining the real-time and money-back features might lead to still higher contribution levels.

5.7. Theory Tests and Policy Tests

Experimental methods can be used to test both economic theory and economic policy. But as Charles Plott has pointed out, testing descriptive theory and testing prescriptive policy are two different things.[4] We must be careful not to confuse them because experimental methods serve different functions in these two roles and are subject to different problems. The function of a test of an economic prescription is to shift the burden of proof onto those who believe that a certain policy will have different effects in the rest of the world than it does in the laboratory. The result of such a test is by no means decisive, but if the policy does not work in the laboratory, this should at least lead us to question our reasons for prescribing the policy.

In contrast, the intent of a test of descriptive theory is to confirm or disconfirm a theory insofar as it yields testable predictions when applied to the experimental design. This is not to say that single tests are typically decisive. In fact, they seldom are. The point, rather, is that a descriptive theory can be confirmed or disconfirmed in a way that a prescriptive policy cannot.

For example, we might have a descriptive theory that people are exclusively self-interested. The data discussed in preceding sections, however, weigh heavily against the theory that people are exclusively self-interested. We may not want to say the data decisively refute the theory, but the theory is certainly misleading in a variety of laboratory situations in which people are called on to engage in collective action. At the same time, we might prescribe a policy of treating people as if they were exclusively self-interested when devising mechanisms for providing public services in large urban communities. Disconfirming the descriptive theory does not show that the prescriptive policy is false, or even that it is bad policy. Implementing the policy might, after all, yield just the results it was intended to yield in the particular kind of situation for which it was prescribed.

The pitfall to avoid in policy tests is careless extrapolation from the laboratory to situations that are different in kind. Laboratory simulations of large-scale policy problems are inevitably unrealistic. The possibility that some of the disanalogies will be relevant is inescapable. This is a problem inherent in any field of empirical research. But policy prescriptions are not intended to apply to laboratory situations. The laboratory policy test must be understood as essentially a *simulation* of the situation for which the policy was really proposed.

In contrast, the danger of inappropriate extrapolation does not arise in the same way for tests of theory. Disconfirmation in the laboratory is disconfirmation, period. We do not need to know if the experimental design is realistic: we just need to know if the theory applies to the design. One may suspect that the theory yields true predictions in other situations, but in any event, following up this suspicion requires one to modify the theory (preferably not in an ad hoc way) so that it is no longer systematically disconfirmed by what has been observed in the laboratory. Laboratory situations are real situations involving real people and real money. Theory tests in the laboratory are not "dry runs" in the way policy tests are. They are not mere simulations. Laboratory situations are themselves situations for which theories can have testable implications. Whether or not they simulate the real world, they are capable of disconfirming a theory, provided the theory yields testable implications when applied to them.

The possibility remains, however, that the theory will not apply at all in this sense. This is the real problem with tests of economic theory. If, for example, subjects receive unintelligible instructions, or if the monetary incentives are insignificant, then most economic theories will say nothing about what behavior we should expect to observe. The problem will not be that the situation is unrealistic. On the contrary, confused subjects and insignificant monetary rewards are features of many real-world situations. The problem will simply be that the theory has no testable implications under such circumstances.

One particular cause for concern when evaluating these experiments as a test of policy is that the experiments use small numbers. The conventional wisdom is that cooperation is easier to achieve in groups with small numbers. Would the results we got in groups of four and ten also be found if we had used groups of 40 or 100? Recent tests by Isaac, Walker, and Williams (unpublished) suggest that they would.

Isaac, Walker, and Williams ran tests with groups of 40 and 100. A second interesting feature of some of these experiments is that the ten-period sequences were spaced out over several days. Subjects left the lab between periods. (The periods themselves were not in real time. Subjects received information about contributions by the rest of the group only after the period was over.) Thus, subjects had to make an effort to enter a contribution. Following the first period, they were informed that if they did not show up at the laboratory for a given period, a default contribution of zero tokens would be invested for them. This feature adds another touch of realism that should interest those wanting to derive policy implications, for surely real-world defections sometimes are due not to greed or fear but rather to laziness or perceived inconvenience. Some people fail to contribute money not because they do not want to contribute money but rather because they do not want to spend the time and energy that it takes to contribute money. In many real-world situations, free riding saves time.

Under these conditions, Isaac, Walker, and Williams (unpublished: 10) discovered that with a marginal per capita return of 0.30—the same rate of return used in Isaac, Schmidtz, and Walker's groups of four, "groups of size 40 and 100 allocate more tokens to the group account on average than do groups of size 4 and 10." The larger groups contributed 40 to 50 percent of their tokens in the early rounds and 35 to 40 percent of their tokens in round ten. Groups of four, in contrast, contributed 20 to 30 percent of their tokens in early rounds and 15 percent or less in round 10 (Isaac, Walker, and Williams, unpublished: fig. 6).[5] So these data are encouraging in terms of its policy implications for voluntary mechanisms in general, although the effect of money-back guarantees in particular on contribution levels in large groups remains to be seen.

5.8. Conclusion

Data from literally thousands of experiments show that many subjects contribute substantial amounts even when defecting is a dominant strategy. On the other hand, Isaac, Schmidtz, and Walker have also seen that subjects occasionally fail to contribute even when contributing is a dominant strategy. We could talk all day about what might have gone wrong with the experimental design, but what was really wrong was the subjects, and the subjects were typical.

Solving the assurance problem makes a substantial difference, but even a design that made optimal contributions a dominant strategy failed to elicit optimal contributions consistently. Still, the laboratory data yielded one interesting result that is clear: dominance as such is not what leads people to pick one strategy over another. The decision procedures people actually employ are much harder to characterize than that. Subjects contribute to public goods projects even when noncontribution is a dominant strategy. Their contributions, however, tend to be suboptimal because of free-rider, exploitation, and assurance problems. Also, some subjects probably fail to make optimal contributions simply because they fail to comprehend the request.

As a policy tool, money-back guarantees generally should, when feasible, be incorporated into attempts to fund public goods production by voluntary contributions. Of course, in many cases, it is fairly obvious that a certain fundraising effort will meet its target in any event. In these cases, there is no point in complicating the issue with a superfluous guarantee. In other cases, it is not at all obvious that the target will be met. For these cases, the money-back guarantee should be used, but the provision point must be chosen with great care. It must be set at a level of funding that could reasonably be considered both necessary and sufficient for the good in question to be successfully produced. In addition to the obvious point that a necessary and sufficient level of funding is the amount of funding we want in the first place, a provision point set at such a level will be taken more seriously by prospective contributors.

The disadvantage of setting a provision point at all is that if it is not met, the fundraisers end up with nothing. But if the provision point is set so that a funding level below it would be inadequate anyway, the disadvantage may not matter. When there is no natural provision point and the adequacy of funding is strictly a matter of degree, then the task for fundraisers is simply to maximize revenue. The evidence is that the combination of a well-chosen provision point and a money-back guarantee increases expected revenue. It does not guarantee increased revenues, however. Contributors, not fundraisers, get the guarantee.[6]

Notes

1. Associate Professor, Philosophy Department, Bowling Green State University, Bowling Green, OH 43403. This article expands and updates material originally appearing in Chapter 6 of David Schmidtz (1991), *The Limits of Government: An Essay on the Public Goods Argument*. Adapted by permission of Westview Press, Boulder, Co.

2. I borrow this point from Vernon Smith's address to the Public Choice Society annual meeting in 1988.

3. Note that if we were somehow to solve the free-rider problem that constitutes one essential component of the prisoner's dilemma on my analysis, we would be left with the assurance problem as the only reason for noncontribution. This game's payoff rankings would be that of an assurance game. That is, if free riding on other people's contributions was ruled out, we would have a situation in which people would prefer to contribute if and only if others were contributing as well. See Sen (1967).

4. This section is heavily indebted to Plott (1982). See also Roth (1986).

5. I do not know why average contributions were higher in the larger groups, but it occurs to me that, for a given marginal rate of return per contribution, constrained maximizers would tend to contribute more as group size rose. Constrained maximizers (as defined by David Gauthier) are players who contribute when reasonably certain that the resulting payoff will be higher than the baseline payoff of mutual defection. Note, then, that the group contribution needed to ensure a return in excess of the mutual defection payoff is not determined by group size. It is determined by the marginal rate of return. So if the marginal return for a dollar contributed is thirty cents, then a total contribution of $2.34 from the rest of the group lifts me above the baseline, regardless of how large the rest of the group is. If there are thirty-nine rather than three other people in the group, then I can be much more confident that there will be three other constrained maximizers (or contributors of any kind) among them. Thus, the presence of constrained maximizers is possibly why contributions rose with group size.

6. I want to thank Elizabeth Willott for helpful comments on an earlier draft of this essay.

References

Bagnoli, Mark, and Michael McKee. (1991). "Voluntary Contribution Games: Efficient Provision of Public Goods." *Economic Inquiry* 29, 351.

Dawes, Robyn M., John M. Orbell, Randy T. Simmons, and Alphons J. Van de Kragt. (1986). "Organizing Groups for Collective Action." *American Political Science Review* 80, 1171–1185.

Dorsey, Robert E. (1992). "The Voluntary Contributions Mechanism with Real Time Revisions." *Public Choice* 73, 261–282.

Friedman, David. (1987). "Comment: Problems in the Provision of Public Goods." *Harvard Journal of Law and Public Policy* 10, 505–520.

Gauthier, David. (1986). *Morals by Agreement*. New York: Oxford University Press.

Isaac, R. Mark, David Schmidtz, and James M. Walker. (1989). "The Assurance Problem in a Laboratory Market." *Public Choice* 62, 217–236.

Isaac, R. Mark, and James M. Walker. (1988). "Group Size Effects in Public Goods Provision: The Voluntary Contributions Mechanism." *Quarterly Journal of Economics* 103, 179–199.

Isaac, R. Mark, James M. Walker, and Susan Thomas. (1984). "Divergent Evidence on Free Riding: An Experimental Examination of Some Possible Explanations." *Public Choice* 113–149.

Isaac, R. Mark, James M. Walker, and Arlington W. Williams. (Unpublished). "Group Size and the Voluntary Provision of Public Goods: Experimental Evidence Using Large Groups."

Plott, Charles R. (1982). "Industrial Organization Theory and Experimental Economics." *Journal of Economic Literature* 20, 1485–1527.

Roth, Alvin E. (1986). "Laboratory Experimentation in Economics." *Economics and Philosophy* 2, 245–273.

Schelling, Thomas. (1960). *The Strategy of Conflict.* Cambridge: Harvard University Press.

Schmidtz, David. (1991). *The Limits of Government.* Boulder: Westview Press.

Sen, Amartya. (1967). "Isolation, Assurance, and the Social Rate of Discount." *Quarterly Journal of Economics* 81, 112–124.

Jeffrey Baldani[1]

Comment on Schmidtz: Observing the Unobservable

Until recently, many, if not most, economists were quite skeptical of the very idea of economic experiment. During the last decade, however, there has been a rapid growth in the number of papers published in experimental economics, and this growth has been accompanied by growing respectability for the field.[2] Yet respectability may or may not translate into relevance and impact. The practical test is whether the proliferation of laboratory experiments has informed or affected economic theory.

Whether experimental economics has an affect on economic theory depends on a number of issues and questions that are discussed in more detail below. First, what exactly can experiments test? Second, can experiments tell us anything independent of real world observation—that is, can experiments alone support or refute economic inferences? Finally, can experiments serve as the basis for policy recommendations? Before turning to general attempts at answering these questions, let us look at how these questions are raised in the experiments described in Schmidtz's essay.

Public Good Provision

The issues raised in Schmidtz's essay on experimental economics are in many ways parallel to those raised in Bicchieri's essay on "The Epistemic Foundations of Nash Equilibrium." An example will help to explain the common issues in these two papers. Consider a simplified variation of Schmidtz's experimental game in which there are two players each endowed with three tokens. Let the provision point for the game be four tokens and the marginal return, if the provision point is met, be 0.5. This simple form allows us to show the entire payoff matrix for the game as in Figure 1.

In this medium provision point game, token allocations that exceed the provision point are never equilibria. For example, the total surplus maximizing strategy pair (3,3) fails the Nash equilibrium test since each player has a unilateral incentive to defect to a lower contribution level. There are, however, three Nash equilibria where the provision point is met and also a Nash equilibrium with zero contribution levels. These are shown in **boldface** in Figure 2. In the

173

	Player 2's Strategies			
	0	1	2	3
Player 1's Strategies 0	0, 0	0, −1	0, −2	0, −3
1	−1, 0	−1, −1	−1, −2	2, 0
2	−2, 0	−2, −1	1, 1	1.75, 0.75
3	−3, 0	0, 2	0.75, 1.75	1.5, 1.5

Figure 1

	Player 2's Strategies			
	0	1	2	3
Player 1's Strategies 0	**0, 0**	0, −1	0, −2	0, −3
1	−1, 0	−1, −1	−1, −2	**2, 0**
2	−2, 0	−2, −1	**1, 1**	1.75, 0.75
3	−3, 0	**0, 2**	0.75, 1.75	1.5, 1.5

Figure 2

actual experiments reported by Schmidtz a similar, although very much larger, multiplayer game matrix would exhibit a plethora of possible Nash equilibria.

Now consider a laboratory test of this model. We might begin by asking what the model predicts—that is, what does economic theory tell us to expect as an outcome? The answer to this question is that game theory predicts that any of the four Nash equilibria might occur as experimental outcomes. Furthermore, as Bicchieri points out, game theory lacks any clear explanation of how the players would coordinate on a single equilibrium, so that nonequilibrium outcomes might also be observed even if players were rational in the sense that game theory assumes them to be.[3] Experimental results from testing this game would not, therefore, have any direct bearing on the validity of game theory or the Nash equilibrium concept.

This "problem" lies partly in the nature of economic theory and partly in the particular version of the experiment. Economic theory, as commonly used by economists, is (elegantly) built up from the principle of rational goal maximization. Sometimes theory, as in the example, is not sufficient to generate a testable prediction. In this case economists might resort to using behavioral rules of thumb to predict outcomes. One behavioral rule might be that a contribution level of two tokens is a natural focal point. Such behavioral rules may seem reasonable, but the rules lack theory status in the sense that they are not derived from basic principles of rational optimization.

Suppose that we run this experiment with human subjects and find that by far the most common outcome is zero contribution levels by all players. This is an

Player 2's Strategies

		0	1	2	3
Player 1's Strategies	0	0, 0	0, 0	0, 0	0, 0
	1	0, 0	0, 0	0, 0	0, 0
	2	0, 0	0, 0	1, 1	1.75, 0.75
	3	0, 0	0, 2	0.75, 1.75	1.5, 1.5

Figure 3

interesting result that confirms economists' prevailing belief that there will be underprovision of public goods. The experiment also indicates that the focal point behavioral rule does not seem to work in this particular experiment. Yet in a crucial way the experiment is tangential to testing theory since any result is, by default, consistent with game theory. In no case can the experiment directly lead to a rethinking or reformulation of theory.

It is important to recognize that I am focusing on a narrowly drawn description of the experiment as actual plays of particular game matrix. In other words, human subjects were presented with a payoff schedule in a laboratory setting and they made certain choices. There is also an interpretative description of the experiment as a test of whether the introduction of a provision point improves the level of contributions to a public good. This policy-oriented interpretation may or may not be a valid extrapolation from the narrow description. The issue of interpreting experimental results—testing theory versus testing policy interpretations—will be discussed in more detail below.

Going back to our example, consider the effect of introducing a money-back guarantee. The new game matrix is shown in Figure 3. There are no strictly dominated strategies in this game. Also, the definition of Nash equilibrium, which requires only that Nash equilibrium strategies satisfy a weak dominance property, allows for several possible equilibria to this game. If, however, we use the rule of iterated elimination of weakly dominated strategies (a rule that, as Bicchieri points out, may be problematic), we are able to successively eliminate strategies until there is a single strategy pair left.[4] This strategy pair is for each player to contribute two tokens. Game theory therefore makes a weak prediction of an equilibrium outcome to this game and the prediction is experimentally testable.

Suppose we test the new form of the game theory matrix in an experiment and find that in many cases the outcome is that the experimental subjects reach the provision point but that in some cases they do not. This result and the supposed result of the first experiment, without a money-back guarantee, are consistent with game theory. A strict, noninterpretive reading of the results is that in the second game there is a unique equilibrium choice. Thus, the coordination problem of the first game is not present in the second game.

An interpretive policy-oriented reading would focus on the effects of the money-back guarantee. There is not, however, a single explanation of why the guarantee works. The reason for this is that the interpretation of results depends on the experimental economist's interpretation of subjects' motives. As pointed out by Schmidtz, the second game may be viewed as solving an assurance problem or an exploitation problem. Subjects might be motivated by a fear of lack of cooperation or by considerations of potential unfairness. It is also possible that subjects are motivated by attitudes towards risk. Positive contribution choices in the second game are less risky than in the first game.[5] Finally, it may be the case that the relevant change is that the second game solves the coordination problem inherent in the multiple equilibria of the first game. My point is that theory alone is insufficient to draw out these motivational issues and the particular experiments may therefore not be up to the task of directly testing the underlying economic theory. The problems here may be inherent, or the problems may simply suggest that further variations in experimental design are in order.

Before turning to a more general discussion of experimental economics, let me emphasize that, despite the caveats mentioned above, the experiments described in Schmidtz's chapter are interesting attempts at discovering, in the laboratory, what may be difficult or impossible to observe in the field. The experiments may not be perfect, but then neither is the theory being tested. In any case, the experiments are well designed and raise important issues concerning the provision of public goods. Well-thought-out experiments such as these help to explain economists' growing acceptance of and respect for experimental methods.

General Assessment

This section focuses on three questions: (1) What can experiments test? (2) what can experiments tell us that real world observation cannot? and (3) do experiments have policy relevance?

These general issues are somewhat difficult to deal with in the abstract. Experimental methods have been applied to several fields of economics and general comments on these questions may or may not represent the progress made in specific fields or particular experiments. Nonetheless, there are certain common themes that are raised by experimental economics as a method of empirical inquiry. My remarks below are (an admittedly incomplete) attempt to elucidate some of these themes.

What Do Experiments Test?

In the natural sciences experimental evidence and paradigm shifts are inextricably linked. There may be a chicken and egg problem of whether evidence or theory changes first, but what is notable is that paradigm shifts do occur. In contrast, economics has seen little change in the dominant paradigm of rational maximization.[6] Despite an increase in the level of mathematical sophistication, modern textbooks closely follow the basic paradigm and methods pioneered a century ago in Marshall's *Principles of Economics.* Whether this is due to the "correctness" of the dominant paradigm, to its simple elegance, or to the prejudices of economists is hard to say. My point is simply that laboratory experiments will almost certainly never alter this basic paradigm. Thus, experiments in economics will never play quite the same role as in the natural sciences.[7]

If the economic paradigm is, in some sense, carved in stone then perhaps one could expect that experiments could provide tests of competing theories. This is probably too ambitious a task. First, theoretical models are usually complex and are descriptive of complex situations. Laboratory tests are necessarily simple. For instance, it would be difficult, if not impossible, to test theories of international trade that model interactions between consumers, firms, and governments. The same can be said for macroeconomic theories. Second, theoretical predictions often differ depending on the values of parameters. Experimental methods in economics (as opposed to the natural sciences) are not generally realistic or accurate enough to reliably test or calibrate quantitative parameter values.

While tests of paradigms or of entire theories are problematic, experimental economics can still play a role in testing. Experiments are well suited to testing components of theories, especially components that are relatively simple and can be easily varied in the laboratory.[8] Schmidtz's tests of different provision points and of the introduction of money-back guarantees are good examples of the types of components that can be tested. Related examples would, in Schmidtz's words, include changing the incentive structure by introducing "challenge grants or allowing communications of contribution levels."

In my view, the most important feature of component testing is that experiments provide a vehicle for the study of different institutional structures. Economists have, until recently, paid little attention to the role of institutions. The fiction of a Walrasian auctioneer who costlessly equilibrates supply and demand has allowed economic theory to gloss over the practical workings of real-world markets and the fiction of the firm as a profit-maximizing black box has substituted for a theory of economic organization and behavior. These omissions have been rectified to some extent by recent theoretical attention to transaction cost theory. Advances in theory about institutions are, however, much less testable by econometric techniques than other components of economic theories. Institutions do not vary in the systematic *ceteris paribus* way that generates the data points needed for econometric analysis.

Not all institutional features can be modeled experimentally. Experiments still face simplicity constraints on the nature of instructions to subjects and on interactions between subjects. Yet many features such as those described in Schmidtz's essay can be fruitfully modeled. A final note of caution is in order here: experimental methods do not necessarily allow us to interpret why institutions matter or why some institutional features are more effective than others. More precisely, it is difficult to infer subjects' motives and reasons for reacting differently to different institutional settings.[9]

What Can Experiments Tell Us That Real-World Observation Cannot?

The title of Schmidtz's chapter—"Observing the Unobservable"—is experimental economics' claim to fame. If we could obtain adequate real-world observations or econometric data, few economists would see a need to conduct laboratory experiments. I would even go a bit further and argue that if there were a conflict between information from real-world observation and experimental data most economists would choose to believe the former. Fortunately, this rarely seems to be the case. Experimental evidence has generally been consistent with real world observation.

Experiments that are used as a window on the unobservable must be carefully set up and narrowly interpreted. An inability to confirm the experimental evidence with real-world observation greatly increases the credibility hurdle of an experiment. In particular, any time that an experiment indicates the efficiency or functionality of a particular institutional arrangement, the evidence will have to overcome the neo-Darwinian argument that if an institution is effective then it would already exist (and could be studied) in the real world. One could raise precisely this issue with the money-back guarantees. Schmidtz cites two examples in the introduction of his essay, but these examples are, to my knowledge, unusual and atypical.

The success of guarantees in a lab setting accentuates the question of why guarantees are not widespread in the real world. It could be that guarantees are effective only in the lab. It could be that there are practical problems in implementing guarantees in the real world. Or it might be the case that guarantees are effective but that real-world fund-raisers have somehow failed to discover this. Economic theory's strong emphasis on rationality would tend to discount this last possibility. In any case these types of issues will arise whenever our empirical evidence consists solely of laboratory experiments.

Institutions are not the only unobservable features that can be controlled and observed in the lab. Lab experiments allow close control over the knowledge endowments, strategy sets, and reward structure for experimental subjects: factors not easily observed or controlled for in real-world observation. A caveat here is that experimenters often seem to replicate the theoretical assumption that agents have a "willingness to pay schedule."[10] Experiments attempt to control for preferences by introducing monetary reward schedules that often have no direct real-world parallel. For example, in contributions to public goods campaigns (such as PBS) most of us do not explicitly think in terms of marginal returns on contributions or how the effectiveness of a given contribution depends on others' contributions. Is playing the game matrix then equivalent to a decision to contribute to PBS? It is at least debatable whether experimental monetary payoff schedules (and variations of those schedules) can substitute for real-world preferences. Indeed, some of the results of the experimental literature indicate that monetary payoffs and preferences are not the same—that is, that individuals for various reasons do not always choose actions that maximize their monetary payoffs.

Do Experiments Have Policy Relevance?

Whether experiments have policy relevance depends on two separate issues. The first is whether experimental results can validly be extrapolated into conclusions about the efficacy of various policies. The second issue is whether the policies themselves are relevant or practical. For example, economic theory shows the optimality of lump-sum, as opposed to activity-based, taxes. We might design lab experiments to demonstrate this proposition, while realizing that the method of lump-sum taxes could never actually be implemented in the real world.

Schmidtz captures the prevailing view of experimental economists in his claim that "lab policy tests must be understood as a simulation of the situation for which the policy was really proposed." This is, however, somewhat problematic. How do we judge the accuracy of a simulation? Can we even establish clear objective criteria for evaluating the applicability of a simulation? When can we rely on simulations in formulating actual policies? Experimental economics should rightly avoid overreaching claims of real-world applicability, but it needs to make some claims about when its results can be extrapolated. I should note that these same issues and questions apply both to economic theorizing about policy issues and to the use of economic theory in focusing experimental design. To be fair, experimental economics should not be held to any higher standard than economic theory.

My own experience in running computer-based business simulation games is instructive as to some of the potential pitfalls of extrapolating from simulations. In 1990 I ran training programs in market economics for Czechoslovakia enterprise managers. The simulation game results showed striking differences in the behavior of older more senior managers and the behavior of younger lower-level managers. Senior managers were unwilling to undertake risky strategies or investments, while junior managers were often aggressive competitors. My purpose was to train managers and not to suggest policies. Nevertheless, it struck me at the time that, if I had run the simulation with only one or the other group of managers, my prognosis for the success of the economic transition and my evaluation of policies would have been seriously incomplete.

A real problem in extrapolating from the laboratory to the real world is that policy issues are almost always difficult and complex. This makes simulation problematic. It also means, in many cases, that experiments test only a part of a policy issue with no assurance that experimental results on an isolated component can be neatly fitted into the more complex real-world setting. Simulations may give precise answers to narrowly focused questions without providing credible guidance to how larger issues should be resolved.

The other policy testing issue is whether the policies and institutional variations tested in the lab are too artificial to apply in the real world. When does the combination of a provision point and a money-back guarantee make sense? I may be unimaginative, but I do not believe that many fund-raising organizations would find the ideas particularly useful. On the other hand, the experimental results can be considered valuable as long as there are some real-world fund-raising campaigns that can benefit from the experimental insights. In other words, some practical specific policy application rather than sweeping policy generalizations should be the criterion for success.

Conclusion

The narrowest claim that can be made for experimental economics is that it allows us to observe the choices that subjects make—given a specific strategy set, a specific reward structure, and a specific set of rules in a laboratory setting. This narrow claim is so limited as to render experimental economics irrelevant to applied economic theory and observation. What has happened over the past few years is that broader and more significant claims (including observing the unobservable) have come to be accepted by economists. Experiments remain an imperfect substitute for real-world observation, and few economists are willing to discard theories simply because they aren't fully validated by laboratory experiments. Nevertheless, it isn't very risky to predict that experimental methods will continue to improve and experimental results will become more accepted as a tool of the economist's trade.

Notes

1. Associate professor of economics, Colgate University.

2. For overviews of experimental economics see the two volumes of collected journal articles edited by Vernon Smith (1990, 1991). The 1990 volume is a chronologically ordered overview with papers from numerous authors. The 1991 volume consists of papers by Smith (and his coauthors) organized by experimental topic.

3. Technically, Bicchieri's essay focuses on one-shot games, while Schmidtz's experiments are repeated games. Nonetheless, Bicchieri's claim that game theory does not explain coordination in one-shot games extends to the repeated game format. By this I mean that there is little or no formal theory of how players coordinate or which equilibrium will be chosen in a repeated game format. In fact, repeating a stage game can often expand the number of possible equilibria.

4. Game theory textbooks seem to be split, often with little discussion, on whether to use iterated elimination of strictly dominated strategies or iterated elimination of weakly dominated strategies to solve for equilibrium. See, for example, Rasmussen (1989) (weakly dominated strategies) and Gibbons (1982) (strictly dominated strategies).

5. This may also open up issues of whether subjects are expected utility maximizers or instead, as shown in numerous experiments, seem to make decisions under some form of prospect theory.

6. I refer here mainly to microeconomics. The Keynesian revolution might be viewed as a paradigm shift. Even in macroeconomics the analogy to the natural sciences is weak. It seems (at least to this microeconomist) that no amount of real-world data will ever conclusively settle macroeconomic debates.

7. At best, lab experiments might point out anomalies that don't fit the basic paradigm. The very term *anomalies* is instructive as to how economists view evidence. For some examples see past issues of the *Journal of Economic Perspectives* with Richard Thaler's column titled "Anomalies." These brief articles covered facts, experiments, and situations that seemed to contradict the standard paradigm.

8. See Smith (1989) for the distinction between composite tests using real-world data and component tests using laboratory data.

9. One possibility opened up by replicable experimental testing is that of testing differences between groups of subjects. Frank, Gilovich, and Regan (1993) provide evidence that economists and economic students may fit the economics model more closely than other subjects. At least some of their evidence points to systematic differences in motivations between different groups of subjects.

10. For example, Plott (1982: 1487) states: "The key assumptions are that the individual prefers more money to less, has no attitude toward the commodity or situation other than the advantages created by potential resale and that the individual fully understands the terms of resale. If these conditions hold, the redemption and cost schedules are limit price schedules for the subjects."

References

Frank, Robert, Thomas Gilovich, and Dennis Regan. (1988). "Does Studying Economics Inhibit Cooperation?" *Journal of Economic Perspectives* 7(2), 159–172.

Gibbons, Robert. (1982). *Game Theory for Applied Economists*. Princeton, NJ: Princeton University Press.

Plott, Charles. (1982). "Industrial Organization Theory and Experimental Economics." *Journal of Economic Literature* 20, 1485–1527.

Rasmussen, Eric. (1989). *Games and Information: An Introduction to Game Theory*. New York: Basil Blackwell.

Smith, Vernon. (1989). "Theory Experiments and Economics." *Journal of Economic Perspectives* 3(1), 151–170.

———. (1990). *Experimental Economics*. Brookfield, VT: Edward Elgar.

———. (1991). *Papers in Experimental Economics*. New York: Cambridge University Press.

6 PARMENIDES AND THE CLIOMETRICIANS[1]

Margaret Schabas

Since it is a changing world that we are studying, a theory which illumines the right things now may illumine the wrong things another time. This may happen because of changes in the world (the things neglected may have grown relatively to the things considered) or because of changes in our sources of information (the sorts of facts that are readily accessible to us may have changed) or because of changes in ourselves (the things in which we are interested may have changed). There is, there can be, no economic theory which will do for us everything we want all the time.

—Sir John Hicks (1981)

6.1

John Hicks's recognition of a "changing world," as described in the above quote, is a commonplace disclaimer among economists, particularly when confronted with the relative triumphs of natural scientists. But in what sense does the world change when it comes to economic inquiry? Neoclassical economists, having ascertained the current equilibrium state, maintain that one can make predictions to future equilibrium states. Time thus enters in as a dimension of

183

the analysis. But strictly speaking, the world does not change in a way that would upset the theory, as Hicks had intended. To the contrary, such analyses are predicated on the assumption that ourselves, our knowledge about the world, and the world itself—both physical and social—are fixed. An answer seems to be forthcoming from economic historians. Surely they attend to the vicissitudes of time, to new modes of thinking or beliefs that either directly or indirectly shape and alter our economic activities? This chapter argues that cliometricians— the dominant group of economic historians in the English-speaking world since the 1960s—have attempted to do what Hicks claims cannot be done: they have established a general all-purpose economic theory "which will do for us every- thing we want all the time." In short, they have eliminated the possibility of a changing world.

To support this claim, let me first provide a brief outline of the new economic history, noting some of its strengths and weaknesses, particularly on the subject of models and realism. To bring out the deep-seated commitment to universal rationality, I then discuss a classic study in cliometrics, *Time on the Cross*. Section 6.4 develops this theme in connection with the Hempelian model of historical explanation and the Davis and North analysis of institutions. Then, as a means of getting a grip on the question of change, I assimilate the rich insights of Ian Hacking's work and relate this to the question of laws in economic theory.

When political economy emerged as a distinct form of inquiry, arguably in the mid-eighteenth century if not before, it was steeped in historical reasoning. One might quibble with this claim; Adam Smith's appeals to that "early and rude state" of the deer and beaver hunters is hardly good history, at least by our standards. But the important thing to grasp is that explanations of economic laws and properties, such as money, prices, and markets, were offered historically. By the early nineteenth century, however, political economy had acquired a distinc- tively axiomatic, deductive cast, particularly in the work of Jean-Baptiste Say, David Ricardo, and Nassau Senior. Some opposition appeared in the 1830s, with strong appeals for a more inductive approach. But it was only in the 1860s and 1870s that economic history emerged as a distinct field, with the explicit aim of counteracting what some viewed as the excessive abstractions of mainstream theory (see both Kadish, 1989, and Koot, 1987). By the end of the last century, thanks to the contributions of Gustav Schmoller, T. E. Cliffe Leslie, and Arnold Toynbee, economic historians could be found in the far corners of the learned world. But economic history has remained a subfield to this day. The vast majority of economic literature, particularly in North America, is still primarily deductive and ahistorical.

In 1958, two young economists named Alfred Conrad and John Meyer (1958) published an article that unleashed the "New Economic History" or "Cliometrics," as it was quickly dubbed.[2] Briefly, the new approach called for the systematic use of quantitative estimates to replace the sort of loose qualitative claims that were tolerated up to that point. It also privileged counterfactual reasoning as a means of isolating some of the grander opportunity costs of nations or other collectivities and, most important, invited the widescale use of neoclassical models drawn from consumer choice theory and the theory of the firm. In almost every respect, cliometricians had abandoned the program of reform that had motivated economic historians a hundred years before. Their enthusiasm for neoclassical techniques spelled the end of economic history as a haven for opposition.

This did not come about without some resistance. In the next decade, much ink was spilled by economic historians on the merits and demerits of cliometrics. But it is fair to say that by the 1970s, cliometrics had become the orthodoxy.[3] The main point of contention was not the use of quantitative reasoning per se. One need only read works by traditional economic historians, such as T. S. Ashton, David Landes, or Phyllis Deane, to see that many questions were settled by appealing to quantitative measures—for example, regional rates of births and deaths, patents procured, and the availability of credit. The difference between the old and the new schools on the issue of numerical analysis was a matter of degree rather than of kind.

Counterfactual reasoning also held a place in historical narrative long before cliometrics, though never with quite the same emphasis. Cliometricians believed that they could systematize the counterfactual, perhaps even isolate the optimal counterfactual.[4] One of the most fanciful was broached by Robert Fogel, who subtracted the railway from the American economy and imagined a world with extensive canals in the prairies, not to mention a thermally controlled Erie canal for winter transport.[5] Fogel made some calculations that purported to demonstrate the insignificance of the railroad, for example, as an aid to westward migration. His grandest result was the estimation that economic growth without the railway (gross national product in 1890), would have been reduced by less than 5 percent, assuming that a canal and road system was developed instead of the railway. This is not nearly as much as traditional historians had implied when they paid tribute to the railroad as the key factor in American economic expansion.

Interesting critiques of counterfactual reasoning in cliometrics can be found in books by Peter McClelland (1975) and Jon Elster (1978), as well as the debates they sparked. There seems little point in covering that ground again. Suffice it to say that there are too many question-begging steps involved in attempting to ascertain the most proximate alternative world, and too little evidence to know how to bound the counterfactual. As Elster (1978) points out, there is a serious problem of ascertaining the right branching point, not to mention the arbitrary terminal date to the branch. It might make sense to subtract the railroad in 1830 and assume that everything unfolded as we knew it up to 1890, but that makes loose cannons of such timely inventions as refrigeration and the internal combustion engine. If necessity is the mother of invention, then presumably both of these would have spread much sooner, and the economy would have been altogether different.

Since there is no such thing as the optimal counterfactual, the decision as to which one to pursue will depend on the problem at hand and on the disposition of the historian. Perhaps, the more entrenched the received view being challenged, the more grandiose the counterfactual. Nevertheless, there are no clearcut rules of thumb. Cliometricians may be uneasy with the prospect that some judgments must remain subjective. A main feature of their search for an objective history is to let the facts speak for themselves, whatever that might mean.

In many respects, of course, they do. What could be more exact than the data of a marketplace—the prices and quantities of commodities exchanged? The ledgerbooks of every bank clerk and accountant, of every customs officer and tax collector, are ample grist for the cliometrician's mill. But gathering and compiling such data is costly, even with the aid of computers. Moreover, as in econometrics in general, in running regressions it is not strictly permissible to reuse the same data. One can divide the data set into two or more groups to circumvent this limitation. Nevertheless, as Fogel (1966: 652) admits, "It is often true that the volume of data available is frequently below the minimum required for standard statistical procedures." Lance Davis (1990: 5) has remarked that many cliometricians rely too heavily on extant data and put most of their effort into devising "clever but hopelessly misspecified models." Moreover, he notes that in the United States "funding for economic history has gotten much more difficult to come by, and funding for archival research almost impossible to obtain." Sooner or later cliometricians may have to confront the problem of data scarcity, particularly in well-trodden regions.

6.2

Cliometrics may have highlighted the problem of the paucity of data, as well as the subjective judgments that enter into the pursuit of counterfactuals, but the main point of contention centers on the use of neoclassical models. Insofar as the models of production and consumption are comparatively static in character and thus say nothing about the path taken from one equilibrium point to the next, it is highly presumptuous to think that history might move in a similarly punctuated manner. There is also an unwarranted reliance on linear models. Econometricians have devised numerous methods for obtaining nonlinear functions, but cliometricians, by and large, stick to the simpler method of least squares.

Furthermore, much reliance is placed on old stalwarts such as the Cobb-Douglas production function. Cliometricians must simply assume this function is an apt representation in order to proceed with their analysis. But again, there are problems in settling the question of returns to scale over time. To use the function requires an a priori commitment to one of three options (decreasing, constant, or increasing returns to scale), but until the historical research is done, it is hard to know which commitment to make. As C. H. Lee (1977: 52, 92) has pointed out, it is critical to know this, since the function is not homoscedastic. With larger firms, the error term that represents entrepreneurial skill, organizational efficiency, and technological differences, ought to matter more.[6]

In using models, one might accept such arbitrary commitments for the sake of explanatory insight. As Allan Gibbard and Hal Varian (1978: 665–666) have maintained, many economic models are simply structured stories or caricatures of which no single proposition is strictly true.[7] It is not just a matter, as in some scientific models, of omitting the more complicated features of a situation, frictions, and the like. Most economic models, by focusing on a select number of salient features, necessarily distort. They are more like political cartoons than photographs with areas covered up. No single line of the face in the cartoon would correspond to a photograph of the statesman undergoing ridicule, but the overall picture has an uncanny resemblance and offers much insight.

There is, I submit, a deep tension in cliometrics between instrumentalism and realism that results from the wedding of neoclassical models and historical practices. Whereas many economists readily purchase the instrumentalism of Milton Friedman, historians tend to be realists by bent, insofar as they avoid theoretical constructs. This is not a question of the existence of the external world or the possibility of accessing the past. Instrumentalists can be fully committed to a correspondence theory of truth and the aspiration that some of the theoretical claims map onto the real world. Friedman's sort of instrumentalism is distinguished by deeming the theoretical constructs to be explanatory instruments with no commitment to their existence. An economist appeals to unobservable utility states, for example, to motivate the theoretical analysis but is agnostic about whether or not they are real. Economic historians, by and large, tend to eschew explicit theoretical constructs, whether about human behavior or Durkheimian social facts. They might grant that the past, strictly speaking, exists only in their minds and on paper, but they nevertheless ground their discourse in facts and proceed as though each study ought to better approximate the actual events that in fact transpired. While archival work is rarely duplicated, there is enough common ground for corrective mechanisms to spring into place. As Jonathan Hughes (1991: 24) has remarked, "Just publish a mistake sometime and see how long it takes to get caught."

Factual fidelity will no doubt persist as a desideratum of historians, both economic and noneconomic. But there is considerable space between using the occasional fact and attempting to achieve photographic realism. The peculiar feature of cliometricians, assuming that Gibbard and Varian are correct about economic modeling, is that they accumulate massive data sets but use them to test models that are by definition too stylized to correspond to the world as it actually is. A simple example would be an historical analysis of a particular industry, such as brewing or paper making, and the heavy reliance on the Cobb-Douglas production function, which necessarily blurs over all of the fine-grained details of technology and organization. The question, then, is why cliometricians believe that they have a more tenacious grip on the past and thus are more open to empirical confirmation or falsification than their predecessors? They might flaunt their extensive data, but their use of neoclassical models presents serious limitations to claims of realism. The heavy reliance on counterfactuals simply augments the problem. As critics of Fogel's study of the railway have pointed out, it is difficult to verify or refute his analysis since it deals with an imaginary world. Because no one in his right mind would deny that the railway was a feature of American economic development in the last century, to subtract it altogether is de facto to move out of the realm of empirical verification.

Are cliometricians, like many neoclassical economists, in fact instrumentalists at heart? Can they do historical research and still purchase the Friedmanian arguments out of convenience? My informal survey of the field suggests that they are not content to take this line of reasoning. For one, the cliometrician does not score points by making sound predictions or retrodictions. Fame is garnered primarily by discrediting the received view, such as the critical role of the railroad in American economic development. For another, they seem bent on infusing neoclassical economics with as much realism as its slender shoulders can support. Lance Davis and Douglass North's (1971) work on institutions is a good case in point. The neoclassical apparatus is still the point of departure, but if more contingent rules (their definition of institutions) could be injected into the discourse, economics would be much the better. To quote North (1990: 400) in a recent overview of the subject:

> Neoclassical economic theory was not intended to account for such poor performance [of Third World economies], and it doesn't. It simply assumes away all the relevant issues. It is institutions that provide the key constraints and therefore shape incentives, and it is the path of institutional change that is determining the evolving performance of economies. Institutional theory focuses on the critical problems for development of human organization and the problems of achieving cooperative solutions to human interaction.

Cliometricians have thus taken on a serious burden. They have placed themselves in the position of complicating the models of neoclassical economics in the name of greater realism and relevancy. But can they do this and not rock the foundations? I will return to this question henceforth, but first it will help to look more closely at an example of cliometric reasoning.

6.3

One of the most celebrated and most controversial contributions to cliometrics is Robert Fogel and Stanley Engerman's *Time on the Cross* (1974). The book is divided into two volumes; the first contains the narrative and assumes little background knowledge of economics; the second contains the "evidence and methods" and thus assumes familiarity with neoclassical economics and elementary econometrics. Fogel and Engerman undoubtedly anticipated a hostile reaction (though probably not to the extent that actually transpired) and bent over backwards in the book to underscore their primary wish to portray an enobled black culture in antebellum America. Gone is the stereotypical figure of the cruel slavemaster, whipping and raping at every turn and governed by romantic pledges of prestige and honor. And precisely because these barbaric conditions were not prevalent, the typical slave was not inclined to protest by acting indolently or irresponsibly. Rather, in the effort of Fogel and Engerman (1974: vol. 1, 8–9) to discover "what really happened . . . [and thus] expose many myths that have served to corrode and poison relations between the races," we find a much more harmonious plantation with both groups committed to the virtues of labor and thrift.

In order to advance their new interpretation, Fogel and Engerman acknowledge the need to invoke "behavioral models whose relevance seemed dubious" and to transmute "some of the most passionate and personal of human issues into such cold, sterile terminology that they could hardly be recognized." But as they also emphasized, "the real question is whether quantitative methods have produced a more accurate and complete portrayal of slavery than was previously available" (vol. 2, 19). I shall not attempt to answer that question here. Suffice it to say that their research dug deeply into the fabric of the southern plantation and challenged many conventional wisdoms about the inefficiencies of slavery and the noncohesiveness of the black family.

Given the geographical features of the south, plantation agriculture and slave gangs were the most efficient means of production. In fact, the authors estimate that the slave plantations were anywhere from 19 to 53 percent more efficient than their Northern counterparts (depending on the age of the unit), and 34 percent more efficient than free Southern agriculture (vol. 1, 196, 209). "There is no evidence that economic forces alone would have soon brought slavery to an end without the necessity of a war or some other form of political intervention" (vol. 1, 5). Indeed (vol. 1, 4),

Slavery was not a system irrationally kept in existence by plantation owners who failed to perceive or were indifferent to their best economic interests. The purchase of a slave was generally a highly profitable investment which yielded rates of return that compared favorably with the most outstanding investment opportunities in manufacturing.

Plantation owners also recognized that slavery was most productive if their slaves were well-fed and clothed and encouraged to form stable families. "The belief that slavebreeding, sexual exploitation, and promiscuity destroyed the black family is a myth. The family was the basic unit of social organization under slavery" (vol. 1, 5). The rape of slave women was infrequent (only 1 to 2 percent of white men fathered slaves) because slaveowners realized that intimacy with slave women undermined the cohesive of the black family and was thus counterproductive. "Distraught and disgruntled slaves did not make good field hands. Consequently, most planters shunned direct interference in the sexual practices of slaves, and attempted to influence fertility patterns through a system of positive economic incentives, incentives that are akin to those practiced by various governments today" (vol. 1, 84). Quite literally, reason was no longer the slave of the passions.

Throughout their discourse, Fogel and Engerman have ascribed contemporary canons of rational behavior to slaveowners. They were profit maximizers, capable of calculating the costs and benefits of the plantation system "with as much shrewdness as could be expected of any nothern capitalist" (vol. 1, 73). In fact, their emphasis on the slaveowner's good treatment of slaves suggests that this group was remarkably ahead of its time, rivaled perhaps only by the humanitarian programs of Robert Owen.

But do these analyses by Fogel and Engerman, and all their attempts to redeem black history, also impute full-fledged rationality to the slaves? Presumably the sustainability of the plantation system depended on the cooperation of the slaves. If they had wished to undermine it, more effort would have been put into rebellions. Instead, it appears that the majority of slaves accepted the (albeit unfortunate) constraints of the system, and made the best of things. A sizeable number—25 percent of the male slaves—were upwardly mobile, either on the plantation (the majority of nonowner managers on large plantations were black) or in the towns (many urban blacks became artisans). Some acquired money and engaged in market transactions. One, named Aham, managed to amass enough capital to set up a homestyle bank (vol. 1, 152). Others, the law notwithstanding, acquired considerable education, another sign of the relative well-being of slaves and, more importantly, of their desire to maximize their well-being.

But what would it mean for every slave to be a rational economic agent under such a system? We must look to those areas of their life in which they could make genuine choices. Presumably their labor-leisure tradeoff was calculated and optimal, both by the day and over the course of a lifetime. In their exposure of "the myth of the incompetent slave," the authors emphasize the quality and efficiency of black labor, which could be possible only if they had the means to live long and healthy lives and be rewarded for voluntary contributions. Hence, we find an economic ladder in place for slaves to climb, from field hand to artisan to overseer. Fogel and Engerman make much of the fact that the life expectancy for slaves approximated that of white European peasants at the time and that few slaves committed suicide. Black children and the elderly worked on the plantation, but their tasks were less arduous than the ones faced during adulthood. Slaves were purchased for use, not for investment purposes, and slaveowners devised means to employ their slaves profitably throughout the life-cycle (vol. 1, 75). The authors also establish that the diet of the average slave "exceeded modern (1964) recommended daily levels of the chief nutrients" (vol. 1, 115) and that their clothing and housing were good by the standards of the time. Hence, the average slave was not as exploited, either materially or psychologically, as has commonly been supposed. "Over the course of his lifetime, the typical slave field hand received about 90 percent of the income he produced" (vol. 1, 5–6).

The area in which slaves appear to have exercised the most choice is reproduction. Fogel and Engerman go to great lengths to demonstrate that most slave women waited until they were married (about twenty years old) to bear children, and that they were able to space these children at appropriate intervals (if only because they were breastfeeding for a year per infant). Quite surprisingly, there were relatively few illegitimate births. Teenage girls were carefully watched by their parents, and premarital sex was severely discouraged. Nor were slavegirls so malnourished as to be unable to bear children until their twenties. With much dexterity, Fogel and Engerman use extant data on the height and weight of teenage slavegirls to show that their menstruation began at the normal age of thirteen.

From a purely economic standpoint, why would it matter if slaves married at thirteen, as opposed to twenty years of age? Fogel and Engerman recognize that certain decisions (say, to run for public office) were not open to slaves. But surely the one to reproduce was. Presumably, the slaves had worked out their life-cycle earnings, seen that they would be exploited by 10 percent over their lifetime, and decided to withhold that much labor power for the next generation to make up the difference. Or perhaps they were willing to tithe their income (implicitly) for the caretaking services of their owners? After all, they did not have to undertake the normal search costs for employment, face unemployment, or even decide on what food and clothing to purchase. A 10 percent tax is not much to pay for a cradle-to-grave welfare system.

Fogel and Engerman do not draw this last set of inferences, but they might have, given their commitment to the neoclassical model of rationality. It is not my intention here to judge whether or not they are right in following out this line of analysis, only to show that it involves some very strong assumptions. Once one opens the door to this line of reasoning, it is difficult to know where to stop. Possibly, buried somewhere in their analysis is a shadow price for freedom itself.

6.4

What lies at the heart of the cliometrics movement is the implicit assumption that human rationality has remained the same over the centuries. In order to apply the theory of consumer choice or the firm, cliometricians must accept all of the behavioral assumptions of neoclassical economics. Agents have complete, transitive, and continuous preferences; they are essentially self-interested maximizers without the human frailties of sympathy or regret or weakness of the will. Thus we have the phenomenon of the rational slave, or the rational, risk-averse peasant, adopting a pattern of scattered field plots the way an investor will purchase a portfolio of stocks and bonds.[9] All of this, particularly in light of the many critiques by Amartya Sen (1979) and Jon Elster (1983), strains credulity. How can cliometricians painstakingly collect data before passing judgment on comparative modes of production, yet accept unquestioningly the view that peasants in the fifteenth century had quasi-concave utility functions?

Interestingly, at almost the same time that cliometricians were sorting out their terrain, philosophers of science were debating the legitimacy of the Hempelian model of explanation for a pursuit such as history.[10] Hempel first published his schema in 1942, but most of the reaction to it vis-à-vis the discipline of history was clustered in the 1960s. Like cliometrics, Hempel and his followers maintained that history uses the same modes of explanation as the established sciences. Both movements appear in retrospect to be heavily indebted to positivism.

More significantly, both groups put much emphasis on rational agency in historical explanation. To understand why Caesar crossed the Rubicon, or Hitler invaded Russia, one must see that when a rational agent (in general) is in a situation of a certain kind (military aggression), the rational action is just what happened. It was, in short, the best course of action given the known set of goals and constraints. Hempel is willing to accept that historical agents might act irrationally, but that these acts would be explained away by noting disturbing causes (for example, extreme fatigue, emotional strain, intoxicants). The rationality principle still holds, even if the action is nondeliberative as in the case of riding a bicycle. It is a given that such "behavioural dispositions [were] acquired through a learning process whose initial phases did involve conscious reflection and deliberation" (Gardiner, 1974: 105).

Cliometricians adopt much the same pattern of reasoning, as we saw in *Time on the Cross*. They are essentially Hempelians and are unlikely to renounce their allegiance to the rationality principle. Nevertheless, in dealing with other cultures, places, and times, it might be useful to consider the possibility that different canons of rationality were operative.[11] Lorraine Daston (1988: 121–122) has found that municipalities selling annuities in fifteenth-century and sixteenth-century Europe took no note of the age of the annuitant, even though the Romans had bequeathed them Ulpian's table that correlated age with price. Her analysis of this practice does not assume that these statesmen were ignorant of their hefty interest payments. Rather, they had different attitudes to risk; life was a lottery at any age. This seems to me a good instance of flexibility on the part of a historian. Daston's study calls for a historicized theory of rationality, based on a careful perusal of the record.

The Davis and North appeal to institutions might appear to be tugging cliometrics in the same direction. But they have effectively just pushed the possibility of attending to genuine change and development one step further away. Institutions are defined as a set of rules—political, social, and legal—for governing economic behavior. Given that cooperation is costly (one of the more salient messages from the prisoner's dilemma), institutions induce mechanisms to minimize the costs of cooperation. In principle, they change only to keep the economy close to its most efficient point. As economies grow, the need for more extensive and distant systems of cooperation increases in tandem. There is, they grant, a period of disequilibrium as the institutions change to take stock of these disruptions. But with a proper model of institutional innovation, they should be able to predict the kind of institutional change given an external shock, as well as the period of time it would take to restore equilibrium. To quote North (1978: 386),

> Successful economic growth is the story of the evolution of more complex institutions that make possible cooperative exchange relations extending over long periods of time amongst individuals without personal knowledge of each other. Institutional reliability means we can have confidence in outcomes increasingly remote from our personal knowledge, an essential requirement to realizing the potential of modern technology, which entails immense specialization and division of labor.

North concludes his essay by declaring that the economic historian is thus the central theoretician of the profession, because of his or her acknowledgment of institutions. But his analysis of institutions is ultimately ahistorical, in that it eliminates the possibility of the sort of genuine change in the Hicksian sense, the kind that would ever upset the orthodox theory. His call to assimilate institutions into economic analysis has in effect leveled one more feature of the economic landscape that might have drawn attention to historical ruptures. In their *Economics of Slavery*, Conrad and Meyer (Tuma, 1971: 32) recognized this move early one:

> The economist seeks to establish theories with at least some generality and timelessness. He is interested therefore in the systematic, repetitive aspects of economic behavior. . . . The economic historian, in sum, should seek the limited generalization that is the objective of all science: only if that course is adopted can economic history expect to influence the development of economics.

6.5

It is worth noting a few additional developments on the philosophical horizon that will be familiar to readers here but may also help to provide a fresh glance at the debate. Since the work of Nancy Cartwright, it has become strikingly apparent that the majority of scientific laws are riddled with ceteris paribus clauses and thus, strictly speaking, do not hold true. But this may not be such cause for concern since, as she argues forcefully, "the truth doesn't explain much." To some extent, this insight was already enunciated by Milton Friedman, in his much misunderstood 1953 essay on "The Methodology of Positive Economics" (Cartwright, 1983: Essay 2).[12] We must remain content with models that capture some selected but hopefully salient features of the world and that yield sound predictions. The lack of strict veracity of the behavioral assumptions is of no concern. Managers of firms may be no more capable of calculating marginal costs and revenues than billiard players can solve the laws of mechanics.

Daniel Hausman (1992: 162–169) has offered a telling critique of this line of argument, with his delightful analogy to automobile mechanics.[13] It may be a helpful way to predict the future performance of a car by taking it for a road test, but it would also help to look under the hood. Insofar as economists have resisted attempts to probe into human psychology, and even gloss over the details of utility as a mental state, they have made themselves much more vulnerable to a breakdown somewhere down the road. The truth might not explain very much, but eliminating falsehoods might prove more fruitful as a long-run strategy.

Another development in the 1980s was the revival of a Baconian appreciation for experimentation as a means to escape the problems of the theory-ladenness of observation. Ian Hacking, Peter Galison, and Allan Franklin helped us to see that experimental findings have a resiliency that survives paradigm shifts. If one wishes to cling to realism, then it is through a hands-on approach to science. Use instruments, produce new effects, and hope that one is still unearthing the same entities. But this emphasis on experimentation, as a means of isolating the more persistent strands of our theoretical webs, has also helped to clarify the extent to which physicists, for all intents and purposes, now live in a different world than their predecessors. Almost all of the phenomena they study are produced in the laboratory. Very few, if any, are lying around ready to be picked like cherries on a tree.[14]

Recall the apology offered by Hicks for the shortcomings of economists as scientists. Indeed, in another book (Hicks, 1979: 39), he suggests that we have only recently come to see the extent of the problem: "the economics world, it has become increasingly obvious, is inherently in a state of flux." But is that any more or less the case for the natural scientists? Certainly in the biological realm growth and decay are everpresent; arguably the physical realm is also always turning over. Some of the key phenomena—heat, electricity and light—are naturally elusive. True, when we look at the world of the astronomer, things appear to be fairly stable, at least by our human dimensions.

But what matters is the world that we know and perceive. In this respect, the world of the natural scientist has changed more dramatically, primarily due to the use of scientific instruments. A hundred years ago, the astronomer did not have the elaborate telescopes and space probes or satellite photography to aid her inquiries. She may fervently believe that the same laws governed the astronomical world a hundred years ago, and all of the accumulated evidence lends weight to this view. But what she *knows* of that world, what she actually perceives, has drastically altered.

In physics, the case for a fluctuating world may be even stronger. As Ian Hacking has forcefully argued, the study of naturally occurring phenomena passed away a couple of centuries ago. Physicists study effects produced in the laboratory—the photoelectric effect, the Hall effect, the Zeeman effect. Artifice has worked its way into every nook and cranny of the physicist's world. As Hacking (1991: 239) remarks in a recent essay review of *Leviathan and the Air Pump*, "The truths of science have long ceased to correspond to the world, whatever that might mean; they answer to the phenomena created in the laboratory." And as a persistent style of reasoning, the experimental method becomes "self-authenticating." "It can't help but get at the truth because it determines the criteria for what shall count as true."

By contrast, economists may study a world of much greater constancy than they are traditionally willing to concede.[15] The primary virtue of cliometricians thus far has been one not of offering historical narrative and thus emphasizing change but of highlighting uniformities. To some this is grounds for suspicion. But let us put aside our preconceptions for the moment and consider the possibility that the economic world we know may actually have more robust patterns than the physical world.

To put it most forcefully, are there in fact any new kinds of phenomena that the neoclassical economist studies today that were not around in the seventeenth century? I set that block of time because it marked the emergence both of modern science and full-fledged capitalism, at least in parts of Western Europe, particularly England and the Netherlands.[16] Let me make it clear, too, that I am only comparing relative rates of change within two realms. At one level, everything in the economy is new, although that claim could be made, mutatis mutandis, about the world studied by the natural scientist. At another level, the physicist and possibly the economist might maintain that nothing has ever changed.[17] We have simply acquired better and more precise means of understanding the same world.

For the physicist, the astronomer, the chemist, and the biologist the answer to my question seems to be that there are many new kinds of phenomena, and by this I mean not just more chemical elements or biological species but entirely new explanatory concepts. Think of radioactive decay, black holes, isotopes, or chromosomes. But for the economist, once capitalism had taken hold, all of the key elements have remained more or less the same: factor markets, central banking, joint stock companies, insurance brokers, government bonds, not to mention the much more extensive phenomena pertaining to commodity markets and money. Of course, there have been countless technological inventions over the last four centuries or the last four millenia, for that matter. But economists treat technological change as one parameter in their models. Other variables, such as population, information, or wealth, also change but, like technology, are generally collapsed into a single parameter of the model.

My point, admittedly undersubstantiated, is that economists have been studying pretty much the same object, with the same basic features, for several centuries. Yes, the economy has grown and, at a certain level of detail, exhibits ever new data such as prices and other sorts of information. But, at least in comparison to the natural sciences, the explanatory concepts into which the data are grouped have evolved at a much slower rate. Were William Petty or John Locke alive today, they would most likely recognize the domain of discourse of the contemporary economist, with its emphasis on national income accounting, interest rates, inflation, and unemployment. One would like to presume the same of physicists, but the parts have changed so much that I doubt if seventeenth-century natural philosophers would find much familiar ground.[18]

Furthermore, the majority of the laws still upheld by contemporary economists were detected before the twentieth century: the law of supply and demand, Gresham's law, the quantity and velocity of money, the law of diminishing returns, Say's law, Engel's law, Walras's law, to name a handful. In our own century, most attempts to grasp at new nomologicals, the Phillips curve for example, have proved illusory.[19] Stefano Zamagni (1987: 104) has noted, in his insightful commentary on "economic laws" in the *New Palgrave*, that "the list of generally accepted economic laws seems to be shrinking." Of course, some philosophers and economists might argue that there are no laws in economics. Philosophers of science have certainly experienced numerous headaches in attempting to set out the conditions that demarcate laws from other categorical claims. This is not the time and place to embark on a long digression. Whatever one's epistemological predilections, let us concede for the time being that there are laws in economics if only because economists call them laws. It may well be that relatively few if any have been discovered (or decreed) in recent times because there are, in fact, no such laws in the economic realm. Nevertheless, economists, for better or for worse, still adhere to many of the traditional laws laid down in previous centuries.[20]

Hacking has given us a useful dualism—to wit, natural and artificial phenomena. It seems that the operative point of demarcation lies in the presence of the human hand in contributing to the occurrence of any given phenomenon.[21] By contrast, economic theory seems to be rooted in a single world. In neoclassical theories, there is no distinction between natural and artificial phenomena. Arguably, all of the phenomena are artificial, in the sense that they are partly or wholly made by humans. They are all products of human agency in the material world, and insofar as such agency remains fairly constant, so do the phenomena that are generated.[22] Some examples of stable features of the economic world might be the exchange ratio of gold to silver (hovering in the vicinity of 1:16) and business cycles (roughly every ten years), to which might be added a couple more—the real interest rate for peacetime developed economies (in the vicinity of 3 percent, allowing for temporary aberrations) and the patterns of consumption that conform to Engel's law.

Still, these pale in comparison to the numerous constants in physics—the gravitational constant, the permeability coefficients in electricity and magnetism, Avogadro's number, and so on. But again, as Hacking reminds us, these constants are contingent on the apparatus we use. There is nothing in the natural realm that comes to us directly in numerical form. Hicks was confused on this point. He makes the claim that some of the above economic constants are "artificial," in contrast to such things as the temperature at absolute zero or the number of chromosomes in the human zygote (his examples). But I fail to see how these are any more or less natural than the price of gasoline or the interest rate. In each case, it is we who impose the quantitative measures. Nature does not present itself to us in tidy numerical form like the price list at the fishmonger's. The only thing to be said in favor of measurements in the natural sciences is that they are considerably more constant, granted our apparatus. But if similar numerical constants can also be found in the economy, I fail to see how one could be more or less reliable than the other. It strikes me that there is nothing as salient in the physical realm, and as obviously numerical, as the interest rate in the economic realm.

6.5

To conclude briefly, cliometrics overshadowed traditional economic history within a decade or two of its formation. Detailed quantitative analysis has its place, but it might be worth recalling R. G. Collingwood's (1974: 37) remark that "statistical research is for the historian a good servant but a bad master." The egalitarian thrust of *Time on the Cross* has blurred this distinction to the point where everyone is both a servant and a master. The heavy reliance on neoclassical behavioral assumptions has undercut the customary allegiance of historians to a realist perspective and, more significantly, to the agenda originally set by economic historians to address a serious methodological imbalance in the discipline overall. Economic historians are effectively providing additional confirmations of current neoclassical theory.

It is now frequently maintained by economists that they do not set out to discover new laws. Rather, they construct models, or refine their measurements of the key parameters of the economy (see, for example, Gibbard and Varian, 1978: 676). Ironically, economic historians may have been one of the last groups of economists, prior to the advent of cliometrics, to actively seek laws.[23] Now they seek additional confirmations, in different times and places, of the same patterns of efficient production and exchange identified by neoclassical economists. For this reason, some see them as the best custodians of economic knowledge. As Donald McCloskey (1978: 28) has remarked: "Cliometricians are among the most vigorous appliers of economics, but their balancing devotion to historical standards makes them careful of facts and mindful of milieu to an extent honored in economics only in presidential addresses."

We have, in sum, a Parmenidian economic world. The flux of everyday life is illusory. Homo economicus has never evolved, at least since the emergence of capitalism and possibly long before that. Jevons (1905: 197) certainly believed as much when he made the following remark in an 1876 address on "The Future of Political Economy": "The first principles of political economy are so widely true and applicable, that they may be considered universally true as regards human nature. . . . I should not despair of tracing the action of the postulates of political economy among some of the more intelligent classes of animals." One wonders why it took economic historians so long to catch on.

Notes

1. I wish to thank the following scholars for stimulating conversations on the subject: Avi Cohen, Lance Davis, Neil de Marchi, Robert Leonard, Claude Ménard, Mary Morgan, and James Woodward. My gratitude also to the efforts of my research assistant, Maria Vasilodimitrakis, and the funds provided by a York University Faculty of Arts Research Grant.

2. The term *cliometrics* was coined by Stanley Reiter in 1960, and much groundbreaking work was conducted by his colleagues at Purdue University, Lance Davis, and Jonathan R. T. Hughes, both of whom stumbled into the field because their chairman at Purdue University made it part of their teaching assignment (see interviews of Davis, 1990, and Hughes, 1991).

3. On the entrenchment of cliometrics, particularly in North America, see Williamson (1989).

4. For an interesting discussion of this, see Engerman's (1980: 164–167) critique of Elster.

5. To his credit, estimates of the cost of heating the Erie canal were actually undertaken in the nineteenth century (see Fogel, 1964: 224).

6. In *Time on the Cross*, Fogel and Engerman (1974: vol. 2, 54 n. 3) assume increasing returns to scale on the plantation and constant returns to scale in the cotton industry as a whole.

7. At one point Gibbard and Varian, (1978: 669) claim that "the only statements of most applied models in economics that are true exactly are truths with no empirical content, such as definitions and mathematical truths." And as Glymour (1985: 293) has argued, "statistical tests don't inform us as to whether or not a model is *approximately* true. They don't permit us to compare false models to determine which is closer to the truth."

8. Hughes (1991: 25) also maintains that this helps to eliminate the prima donna in the field: "The first time somebody is able to show demonstrably how wrong you are on a particular point, that really blunts the ego."

9. For a recent treatment of this figure, see McCloskey (1991).

10. See, for example, the essays by Carl Hempel, William Dray, and Maurice Mandelbaum in Gardiner (1974).

11. A classic source for this debate, in the context of anthropological inquiry, is Wilson (1970).

12. I am not suggesting that she borrowed the idea from Friedman, only that they arrive at similar positions on the nature of explanation.

13. Mary Morgan informs me that Trygve Haavelmo already used this analogy to make much the same point.

14. This is eloquently argued by Hacking (1983: ch. 13).

15. I realize that this raises additional questions. Why have economists maintained the contrary view, and why, if their world is indeed so constant, have they not made more headway in understanding it? Answers will have to wait another time and place.

16. I take as my definition of capitalism the establishment of markets for the factors of production, land, labor, and capital. Under feudalism, we find instances of rent, wages, and interest on loans, but these were not sanctioned by the reigning institutions. Under capitalism, they become paramount.

17. Charles Plott remarked to me that neoclassical economics held true for Cro-Magnon, and my impression is that he is not the only economist who holds this view.

18. The dimensions of physics have remained much the same: space, time, and force. But the entities that serve as placeholders are radically different, as can be seen in the substitution of gravitational fields for gravitating bodies.

19. Other possible candidates, though they have been subjected to much the same criticisms as

the Phillips curve, are Oken's law, Verdoorn's law, and the Laffer curve. Slutsky's equation seems to be the best example, although it is effectively a mathematical recasting of relata known in the nineteenth century. Price elasticities and the income and distribution effect were worked out by William Whewell, P. H. Wicksteed, and others. Most other patterns in contemporary economics take the form of conditions (such as Simon-Hawkins conditions or the Marshall-Lerner conditions).

20. The ones that have been discarded are mostly of a historical nature, such as the law of the falling rate of profit. Of all the economic laws, the one I believe that is least riddled with problems is the rich insight by Adam Smith that the division of labor is a function of the size of the market.

21. An entomologist studying beetles in her garden with the aid of a magnifying glass would still be studying a natural phenomenon. The beetle would be there whether she chose to examine it or not. But the photoelectric effect would not take place unless we had constructed and operated the requisite apparatus in the first place. The advent of economic laboratories suggests that a change may be in store. One main instigator, Charles Plott, has drawn a distinction between the markets in his laboratory and those in "the wild." But he also insists that the markets in his lab are not simulations of real markets, but genuine markets (see Plott, 1990: 902).

22. From a very different angle, Alan Nelson (1990) has made much the same point by answering no to the question of natural economic kinds.

23. At least, this seems to be an apt characterization of Alexander Gerschenkron's analysis of industrialization (see Sylla, 1989).

References

Andreano, Ralph L. (1970). *The New Economic History: Recent Papers on Methodology.* New York: John Wiley.

Cartwright, Nancy. (1983). *How the Laws of Physics Lie.* New York: Oxford University Press.

Climo, T. A. and Howells, P. G. (1974). "Cause and Counterfactuals." *Economic History Review* (2nd ser.), 27, 461–468.

Coats, A. W. (1980). "The Historical Context of the New Economic History." *Journal of European Economic History* 9, 185–207.

Collingwood, R. G. (1974). "Human Nature and Human History." In Patrick Gardiner (ed.), *The Philosophy of History.* Oxford: Oxford University Press.

Conrad, Alfred H., and John R. Meyer. (1958). "The Economcs of Slavery in the Ante Bellum South." *Journal of Political Economy* 66, 95–130.

Cook, Karen Schweers, and Margaret Levi (eds.). (1990). *The Limits of Rationality.* Chicago: University of Chicago Press.

Daston, Lorraine J. (1988). *Classical Probability in the Enlightenment.* Princeton, NJ: Princeton University Press.

Davis, Lance. (1990). "An Interview." *Newsletter of the Cliometric Society* 5 (2), 3–10.

Davis, Lance, and Douglass North. (1971). *Institutional Change and American Economic Growth.* Cambridge: Cambridge University Press.

Elster, Jon. (1978). *Logic and Society: Contradications and Possible Worlds.* New York: John Wiley.

———. (1983). *Sour Grapes: Studies in the Subversion of Rationality.* Cambridge: Cambridge University Press.

Engerman, Stanley L. (1980). "Counterfactuals and the New Economic History." *Inquiry* 23, 157–172.

Fogel, Robert W. (1964). *Railroads and American Economic Growth*. Baltimore: Johns Hopkins University Press.

———. (1966). "The New Economic History: Its Findings and Methods." *Economic History Review* 19(3), 642–656.

———. (1970). "Historiography and Retrospective Econometrics." *History and Theory* 9, 245–264.

———. (1975). "The Limits of Quantitative Methods in History." *American History Review* 80, 329–351.

———. (1990). "An Interview." *Newsletter of the Cliometric Society* 5(3), 3–8.

Fogel, Robert W., and Stanley L. Engerman. (1974). *Time on the Cross*. Boston: Little, Brown.

Friedman, Milton. (1953). "The Methodology of Positive Economics." In *Essays in Positive Economics*. Chicago: University of Chicago.

Gardiner, Patrick (ed.). (1974). *The Philosophy of History*. Oxford: Oxford University Press.

Gibbard, Allan, and Hal Varian. (1978). "Economic Models." *Journal of Philosophy* 75, 664–677.

Glymour, Clark. (1985). "Interpreting Leamer." *Economics and Philosophy* 1, 290–294.

Gould, John. D. (1969). "Hypothetical History." *Economic History Review* 22, 195–120.

Hacking, Ian. (1983). *Representing and Intervening*. New York: Cambridge University Press.

———. (1988). "On the Stability of the Laboratory Sciences." *Journal of Philosophy* 85, 507–514.

———. (1991). "Artificial Phenomena." *British Journal for the History of Science* 23, 235–241.

Hausman, Daniel M. (1992). *The Inexact and Separate Science of Economics*. Cambridge: Cambridge University Press.

Hicks, John. (1979). *Causality in Economics*. Oxford: Blackwell.

———. (1981). *Wealth and Welfare*. Cambridge, MA: Harvard University Press.

Hughes, Jonathan R. T. (1991). "An Interview." *Newsletter of the Cliometrics Society* 6(3), 3–26.

Intrilligator, Michael. (1969). *Frontiers of Quantitative Economics*. Amsterdam: North-Holland.

Jevons, William Stanley. (1905). "The Future of Political Economy." In Henry Higgs (ed.), *The Principles of Economics and Other Papers*. London: Macmillan.

Kadish, Alon. (1989). *Historians, Economists, and Economic History*. London: Routledge.

Koot, Gerard M. (1987). *English Historical Economics, 1870–1926*. Cambridge: Cambridge University Press.

Latsis, Spiro (ed.). (1976). *Method and Appraisal in Economics*. New York: Cambridge University Press.

Lee, C. H. (1977). *The Quantitative Approach to Economic History*. London: Martin Robertson.

McClelland, Peter D. (1975). *Causal Explanation and Model Building in History, Economics, and the New Economic History*. Ithaca: Cornell University Press.

McCloskey, Donald N. (1978). "The Achievements of the Cliometric School." *Journal of Economic History* 38, 13–28.

————. (1991). "The Prudent Peasant: New Findings on Open Fields." *Journal of Economic History* 51, 343–355.

Morgan, Mary S. (1990). *The History of Econometric Ideas*. New York: Cambridge University Press.

Nelson, Alan. (1990). "Are Economic Kinds Natural?" In C. Wade Savage (ed.), *Scientific Theories*. Minneapolis: University of Minnesota Press.

North, Douglas C. (1978). "The Achievements of Economic History: Comments on Papers by McCloskey, Cohen, and Forster." *Journal of Economic History* 38, 77–80.

————. (1990). "Institutions and Their Consequences for Economic Performance." In Karen Schweers and Margaret Levi (eds.), *The Limits of Rationality*. Chicago: University of Chicago Press.

Plott, Charles R. (1990). "Will Economics Become an Experimental Science?" *Southern Economic Journal* 57, 901–919.

Schabas, Margaret. (1986). "An Assessment of the Scientific Standing of Economics." *Proceedings of the Philosophy of Science Association* 1, 298–306.

Sen, Amartya K. (1979). "Rational Fools." In Frank Hahn and Martin Hollis (eds.), *Philosophy and Economic Theory*. Oxford: Oxford University Press.

Sylla, Richard. (1989). "Patterns of European Industrialization: Rethinking Gerschenkron's Hypothesis." *Newsletter of the Cliometric Society* 4(2), 3–6.

Temin, Peter. (1974). "Methodology and Evidence in Economic History." *Economic Inquiry* 12, 415–418.

Tuma, Elias H. (1971). *Economic History and the Social Sciences*. Berkeley: University of California Press.

Williamson, Jeffrey G. (1989). "The Future of Economic History: A View from North America." *American Historical Review* 94, 291–295.

Wilson, Bryan (ed.). (1970). *Rationality*. New York: Basil Blackwell.

Zamagni, Stefano. (1987). "Economic Laws." In John Eatwell et al. (eds.), *The New Palgrave: The Invisible Hand*. London: Norton.

A. W. Coats

Comments on Schabas: The Nature and Significance of the "New" Economic History a Response to "Parmenides and the Cliometricians"

My reactions to Margaret Schabas's stimulating and provocative chapter are disturbingly mixed. While I agree with a good many of her specific observations and assertions, and have some sympathy with the general thrust of her argument, the choice of cliometrics to exemplify certain general methodological and philosophical issues strikes me as doubly unfortunate—because cliometrics was a unique and essentially transitory episode in the development of economic history as an academic discipline and because Schabas's account of it is misleadingly selective.

Of course I appreciate that Schabas is primarily concerned with using cliometrics as a convenient peg on which to hang her general case. But there is a real danger that the peg may in fact be a straw man—to use an excruciatingly mixed metaphor.

Contrary to Schabas's claim, although cliometrics may have "overshadowed traditional economic history within a decade or two of its formation," this is true only of the United States. It is certainly not true that its exponents have constituted "the dominant group of economic historians in the English-speaking world since the 1960s." Without quibbling about the precise meaning of "dominant," I fear that Schabas has been taken in by the cliometricians' loud, sometimes belligerent, and oft-repeated propaganda.[1] Intellectual revolutions rarely spread so swiftly. As an economic historian with a strong professional interest in economic methodology, I was teaching in an English university both before and after cliometrics burst upon the transatlantic scene in the late 1950s, and I can testify that the vast majority of my professional peers were equipped neither intellectually nor technically to take effective advantage of the new wave, even had they been inclined to do so. On the contrary, most of them viewed the new economic history with a combination of bewilderment, scepticism, and even hostility.[2] None of these sentiments was entirely commendable; but they were understandable, given the cliometricians' vigorous initial overselling of their claims. Even now, any suggestion that economic history in Britain is dominated by cliometrics can be dispelled quickly by perusing the *Economic History Review*, one of the leading scholarly periodicals in the discipline. And, I believe, much the same is true of the Commonwealth and the Scandinavian countries, which have long been distinguished centers of economic history research.

The situation was, however, very different in the United States where, for a time, the cliometricians swept all before them, for reasons I have discussed elsewhere (Coats, 1980, 1990).[3] Even so, it is crucial to recognize that as a group the "new" economic historians were not homogeneous, and the early phase of missionary overenthusiasm and exaggeration soon gave way to a more sober and balanced outlook. Schabas distorts the record by focusing so heavily on the work of Robert Fogel, the new economic history's most spectacular, energetic, and untypical practitioner, and on *Time on the Cross*, by Fogel and Stanley Engerman (1974), the movement's most spectacular, but unique, literary product.[4] Fogel far outreached other cliometricians in his deployment of large-scale counterfactual models—the least plausible of that controversial species. Hence it is no surprise that one critic spoke of his "daredevil impulse." *Time on the Cross*, unquestionably the most controversial economic history book ever published, made extraordinarily bold and, as it transpired, significantly overstated claims for the novelty, objectivity, and scientific validity of its authors' findings. These claims were quickly challenged, and on many points rejected, by a variety of competent critics.[5] It was at this time, the mid-1970s, that the new economic history can be said to have come of age. In the early years too much energy had been expended in overemphasizing the supposedly revolutionary break with the past and denigrating the achievements of earlier economic historians. *Time on the Cross* inaugurated a brief phase of bitter internecine warfare;[6] but in due course the cliometricians returned to the constructive work of developing their subject in accordance with the long-standing theoretical-quantitative tradition in American economics—especially that associated with Simon Kuznets, the National Bureau of Economic Research, and the Conference on Income and Wealth.

Schabas contends that the cliometricians "established a general all-purpose theory" that "eliminated the possibility of a changing world,"[7] and that "they had a deep-seated commitment to universal rationality." Yet this theory, and this commitment, were firmly "established" in economics long before cliometrics was even heard of. Historians of economics, including Schabas, are well aware of the long-standing objections to these features of mainstream classical and neoclassical economics. For example, leaders of the nineteenth-century German historical school accused the classical economists of "cosmopolitanism" and "perpetualism"—that is, the presumption that their theories were true of all times and all places. Several decades later the aggressive British economic historian, William Cunningham, made essentially the same point—albeit in less sweeping terms—in attacking his outstanding Cambridge colleague, Alfred Marshall; and Thorstein Veblen's oft-quoted American caricature of the hedonistic psychology presupposed in conventional economic analysis was specifically designed to ridicule and undermine the orthodox economists' "commitment to universal rationality," in what he saw as a post-Darwinian "world in flux."[8]

So what, then, differentiated cliometrics from "good old economic history," to cite Max Hartwell's apt description? Was it simply the clarity, force, and occasional extremism of the cliometricians' claims, or the fact that they were, for the most part, economist historians, rather than historians concerned with the economic past? Schabas correctly observes that with respect to numerical analysis the two species of economic history differed only in degree rather than in kind. Even so, the difference was striking. The cliometricians believed, and rightly, that there were vast, largely untapped statistical sources directly bearing on the history of the American economy; and they were eager to use state-of-the-art methods of processing and analyzing this data, methods unknown to most of the earlier economic historians. In this respect American economic history was largely catching up with American economics. Yet contrary to Schabas's account, the problem of data quantity often proved less serious than the problem of data quality; and for some cliometricians the urge to be quantitative (and therefore "scientific") led—as in economics—to an uncritical use of these source materials. This was especially obvious in some parts of *Time on the Cross* because the authors were so determined to push their enquiries, often ingeniously, into topics hitherto regarded as beyond the conventional boundaries of economics.

Schabas is on shaky ground in asserting that the new economic historians sought "photographic realism," or that "they let the facts speak for themselves"— whatever that means (McCloskey, 1981: xvii, 4–5; 1987: 11). In some instances, of course, the discovery, compilation, and interpretation of quantitative data took precedence over theorizing, for as Fogel once observed, the aim of the new economic history was to put American economic history on a "sound quantitative foundation." But this did not entail any abandonment of theory. Indeed, one of the basic differences between the "good old" and the "new" economic history was the latter's *explicit* use of economic theory—as against the looser tacit or implicit theorizing often to be found in the earlier economic history literature (Fogel, 1983: 6, 9).[10] And it is difficult to think of an American cliometrician of the past thirty years or so who was not, in one way or another, aware of and reliant on static neoclassical price theory as the appropriate analytical starting point.

There is room for debate as to whether the cliometricians could or should have developed their own theory, especially if, as Conrad and Meyer suggested, they hoped and expected to "influence the development of economics."[11] But on the whole they were net borrowers from contemporary economics and eager to be viewed as the economists' scientific and professional equals. (The fact that British economic history had for so long developed in quasi-independence from economics helps to explain the slow and reluctant acceptance of cliometrics in that region.)

In my view the "heart" of the econometrics movement was not "the implicit assumption that human rationality has remained the same over the centuries," but a particular conception of how economic history, and perhaps history in general, could be made "scientific." It was this, as much as explicit theory, techniques, and a naive belief in the statistical testing of hypotheses, that differentiated the new from the old economic history.

By far the most original and stimulating part of Schabas's essay is the section wherein she compares two "worlds," as known to and perceived by natural scientists and economists respectively. This raises fundamental epistemological and ontological questions that extend far beyond the cliometricians' world, questions that cannot be discussed briefly here. Hacking's observations about laboratory life and the consequences of the advanced technology available to natural scientists have no counterpart in late twentieth-century economics, which is only just beginning to develop a limited body of interesting and reasonably well-established experimental data.[12] In economics these days, methodological fashions rise and fall so readily that it is hazardous to generalize about the current state of knowledge. Even if economics has more "constants" than natural science—a point I feel Schabas somewhat overstates[13]—its relatively primitive gropings with more time-sensitive species of analysis (such as nonlinear, path-dependent, and irreversible processes; uncertainty; imperfect information; and the like) reveal that the discipline already has more "flux" than it can handle. Of quite a different order, however, is the possibility that if Schabas is correct, economists have yet another reason why they should abandon their long-standing urge to emulate physics, the "icon of scientificity." As recently suggested by Philip Mirowski (1989), in his provocative study *More Heat Than Light*,[14] economists have in any case been aping an outmoded nineteenth century conception of physics. If they attempted to take late twentieth-century physics as their model, they would be in even deeper trouble.

Notes

1. This is obviously a matter of judgment, depending in part on whether a broad or narrow definition of cliometrics is employed. One can acknowledge that cliometric conceptions and methods have made valuable and permanent contributions to economic history, without accepting either the movement's initial inflated claims or the view that it has dominated or completely transformed the subject, even in the United States. However, in developing her case, Schabas focuses on its more extreme and untypical manifestations.

In the following account *cliometrics* and *new economic history* will be treated as synonymous.

2. See, for example, the papers on "The Future of the New Economic History in Britain" by Jonathan R. T. Hughes, R. M. Hartwell, Barry Supple, and R. C. O. Matthews, in McCloskey (1971: 401–433). See also the editor's introduction (1971: 3). For a later assessment see Coleman (1987: especially 122–126).

Unlike the United States, there was no open intergenerational conflict over cliometrics among British economic historians.

3. On the "cultural warfare" among American economic historians resulting from the cliometricians' efforts to tear the fabric of traditional history to shreds, see Fogel (1983: 65). One traditional historian interpreted the cliometricians' message as: "Retool, rethink, conform, or be plowed under" (Fogel, 1983: 65). In this balanced essay, Fogel acknowledges the cliometricians' dependence on traditional methods, adding that overreliance on "mathematical wizardry or computer magic" sometimes led to embarrassing failures. He confirms that "The anticipated rout of traditional historians has not materialized and history has not been transformed into a science" (Fogel, 1983: 67). But the effect of cliometrics on economic history has, however, been considerable.

4. Schabas ignores the important fact that at the memorable Williamstown meeting in 1957, A. H. Conrad and J. R. Meyer produced two papers—the one she mentions on "The Economics of Slavery in the Ante-bellum South" and another, more general treatment of "Economic Theory, Statistical Inference and Economic History." It is arguable that the latter was the more significant of the two, given the subsequent development of cliometrics. Both were reprinted in their collection of essays (Conrad and Meyer, 1964). Note the word econometric in their title. Cf Donald McCloskey's recent survey (1987). This title implies, incorrectly, that all economic history is now econometric.

5. In addition to a long series of reviews, at least one of book length, the most accessible source is a collection of papers by Paul A. David et al. (1976). Many of the serious criticisms of *Time on the Cross* have never been directly answered by its authors. Moreover, the passage Schabas cites on p. 190, supposedly a discovery of *Time on the Cross*, simply summarizes the main conclusion of Conrad and Meyer's article published seventeen years earlier. Incidentally, Fogel and Engerman (1974: vol. 2, 160–160) did in fact refer to a shadow price for freedom.

6. Donald McCloskey has commented amusingly, that "The violence surrounding *Time on the Cross* is only the latest and largest in a series of intellectual muggings," adding that "In common with street crime, political purges and scholarly controversy in other fields, the violence is greatest among the closest neighbors." Cf. McCloskey (1981: 11–12). In the foreword to this volume Barry Supple wisely observes that controversy among the new economic historians has been due both to their felt "need to proselytize" and to their striving "with fierce enthusiasm to satisfy two sets of scholarly standards—those of economic theory and of historical evidence" (McCloskey, 1981: ix). The desire to achieve academic recognition and status by participating actively in the contemporary so-called quantitative-scientific revolution in economics was a major influence. Generally speaking, cliometrics has become much less controversial in the past decade or so.

7. The meaning of the second half of this statement is unclear to me. It confuses three possibilities: the practical usefulness of the cliometricians' models, intellectual discussions about how the economic world really is and how it should be represented in models, and methodological arguments about the way to find out about the world using those models (adapted from Morgan 1991: 244).

Most, but not all, of the cliometricians seem to have been epistemologically innocent. They were, as Schabas recognizes, essentially positivists (if that term still means anything), drawing on contemporary static neoclassical price theory. For a characteristically illuminating comment see Parker (1973: 13): "The new work justified the ways of the price system to men. And rightly so. If a model of an economy with flexible prices does not test out in early nineteenth century America, where, one wonders, is it to be used? The great constructive contribution of their work lay . . . in its shadowy adumbration of the machinery of a growing competitive economy. A sympathetic imagination can pick up the noise of growth behind these essentially static tableaux." But, as Schabas observes, the cliometricians too often seemed satisfied with models "by definition too stylized to correspond to the world as it actually is." They made little or no use of nonlinear models and took no interest in what is nowadays sometimes referred to as "real" historical time. Unfortunately, despite a tremendous investment of intellectual resources, the economists of the period were unable to develop a satisfactory theory of economic growth. See, for example, the magisterial survey article by Hahn and Matthews (1964: 779–902).

8. Schabas's concluding quotation from Jevons demonstrates that the commitment to rationality was no new phenomenon. However, she correctly emphasizes the cliometricians' unusually clear, explicit, and far-reaching use of that concept.

9. McCloskey implies that prior to 1957 economic historians made virtually no use of economic theory. This is wrong.

10. To quote McCloskey (1981: 14), a leading spokesman for cliometrics: "'Theory tells us' is as foolish in its own way as 'the facts say.'" I doubt that the new economic historians were as naive as Schabas implies.

11. Whether the economic historians' "limited" generalizations are liable, even able, to influence the development of economics is at least debatable.

12. However, some of the cliometricians' significant contributions to economic history were directly dependent on the availability of high-speed computers.

13. Her "admittedly undersubstantiated" discussion turns partly, if not largely, on matters of definition. Constancy in the economist's subject matter needs to be considered in relation to the problems addressed, rather than in quasi-absolute terms.

14. The subtitle is *Economics as Social Physics, Physics as Nature's Economics*.

References

Coats, A. W. (1980). "The Historical Context of the 'New' Economic History." *Journal of European Economic History* 9(1) (Spring), 185–207.

———. (1990). "Disciplinary Self-Examination, Departments and Research Traditions in Economic History: The Anglo-American Story." *Scandinanvian Economic History Review* 38(1), 3–18.

Coleman, D. C. (1987). *History and the Economic Past: An Account of the Rise and Decline of Economic History in Britain*. Oxford: Clarendon Pres.

Conrad, A. H., and J. R. Meyer. (1964). *The Economics of Slavery and Other Studies in Econometric History*. Chicago: University of Chicago Press.

David, Paul A., et al. (1976). *Reckoning with Slavery: A Critical Study in the Quantitative History of American Negro Slavery*. New York: Oxford University Press.

Fogel, Robert W. (1983). "'Scientific' and Traditional History." In Robert William Fogel and G. R. Elton, *Which Road to the Past? Two Views of History*. New Haven: Yale University Press.

Fogel, Robert W., and Stanley L. Engerman. (1974). *Time on the Cross*. Boston: Little, Brown.

Hahn, F. H., and R. C. O. Matthews. (1964). "The Theory of Economic Growth: A Survey." *Economic Journal* 74 (December), 779–902.

McCloskey, Donald W. (ed.). (1971). *Essays on a Mature Economy: Britain After 1840*. Princeton, NJ: Princeton University Press.

———. (1981). *Enterprise and Trade in Victorian Britain: Essays in Historical Economics*. London: George Allen and Unwin.

———. (1987). *Econometric History*. Basingstoke, Hants.: Macmillan.

Mirowski, Philip. (1989). *More Heat Than Light: Economics as Social Physics, Physics as Nature's Economics*. Cambridge: Cambridge University Press.

Morgan, Mary. (1991). "The Stamping Out of Process Analysis in Econometrics." In Neil de Marchi and Mark Blaug (eds.), *Appraising Economic Theories: Studies in the Methodology of Research Programs*. Aldershot, Hants.: Edward Elgar.

Parker, William N. (1973). "Through Growth and Beyond: Three Decades in Economic and Business History." In Louis P. Cain and Paul J. Uselding (eds.), *Business Enterprise and Economic Change: Essays in Honor of Harold J. Williamson*. Kent, Ohio: Kent State University Press.

Z 11 - 35

D 21,

7 OPTIMALITY ARGUMENTS AND THE THEORY OF THE FIRM

Harold Kincaid

7.1. Introduction

In the last decade or so economists have started tackling the difficult but largely ignored task of developing a real theory of the firm. Of course, sociologists and organizational theorists have studied the firm for decades. And economists always had a theory of the firm. However, that theory was largely a black box: it said little more than that firms would maximize profits and that the behavior of the firm would be determined by the familiar neoclassical production function. That account was not just abstract but also unrealistic. It generally assumed that managers and owners were one, that management had complete and more or less costless information about the productivity of employees, that management decisions were carried out without cost and completely, that contracts for inputs could completely specify the conditions of their use, and so on. The new economic work on the firm is exciting precisely because it tries to avoid such assumptions. Instead, recent economic models try to extend the standard maximizing under constraints approach to explain these real world phenomena. As a result, it is an important step toward both making neoclassical theory richer, more realistic, and more testable and toward bringing a powerful theory to an area where the piecemeal approaches of sociology and organizational theory have dominated.

This chapter examines some of these recent developments. My main concern throughout shall be the evidence for recent models of the firm—both what evidence has so far been adduced and what kind of evidence economists need to provide if they want relatively well-confirmed theories. Though I discuss a number of different issues related to evidence and confirmation, my main topic concerns evidence based on claims about optimality. Advocates of recent work on the firm claim over and over again that various economic practices "exist in order to promote" profitability, individual self-interest, efficiency, and so on. Their evidence for these claims is in large part an argument that these practices would be optimal. Indeed, the vast majority of recent work on the firm consists in developing models of what would be optimal and then showing that such models are consistent with certain real world situations. These "optimality arguments" and "in order to" explanations raise issues that have been discussed in other contexts by philosophers of science and biologists.[1] I try to extend that work to theories of the firm. Are such functional explanations legitimate? When are optimality arguments for them compelling? Do they require mechanisms to be convincing? I try to point out what optimality arguments require to succeed and then look in detail at different models of the firm in light of them.

The chapter is organized as follows. Section 7.2 sketches some general ideas about models and confirmation. Section 7.3 uses those ideas in analyzing optimality arguments and pointing out the general kind of obstacles they face. Section 7.4 then looks at transaction cost, implicit contract, and principal-agent models of the firm as well as some other work that falls under no single rubric. Section 7.5 draws some general morals about what the role of models is and should be in the theory of the firm—and by implication in economics more generally. Throughout my discussion will be neither complete nor definitive; my main goal is rather to raise and partly clarify some important questions about the theory of the firm, questions that have implications for the practice of economics in general.

7.2. Models and Confirmation

To help us assess recent work on the firm, it will be useful to first outline two basic morals about confirming models—namely, that (1) successfully deducing predictions from a model counts for little unless it can be shown that no other model predicts or predicts as well those same facts and that the model in question is reasonable given what else we know and (2) models that involve simplifications, idealizations, abstractions, and the like are only well confirmed if we can show that it is the substantive claims of the model, not the literally false simplifications, that are responsible for its predictive success. While these morals may not be universally accepted by methodologists, they are widely accepted and can be given very strong rationales. I explain these claims and their rationales below, focusing in particular on how they fit into a Bayesian account of confirmation. Both these specific claims and the Bayesian account will prove very useful in thinking about theories of the firm.

Philosophy sometimes learns from its failures. One failed account of confirmation was that labeled hypothetical deductivism.[2] In its simplest form, hypothetical deductivism said that a theory was confirmed by a given piece of evidence if it predicted it and disconfirmed if it did not. An obvious first problem with this view was that if hypothesis H entails evidence E, then so does H conjoined with any other claim. So if general relativity entails the extent to which light bends around the sun, then so does general relativity and the proposition that Ronald Reagan is a transvestite. Of course, this problem looks like a philosopher's trick, one that further restrictions ought to eliminate. While there may be ways to get around this particular problem, the general problem it points to seems fatal: many different theories can predict the same phenomena, so a successful prediction need not favor by itself any one of them. The idea here is that confirmation requires more than successful prediction; it also requires ruling out competing explanations. Until we do the latter, then the predictive success of our hypothesis is quite inconclusive.

If confirmation requires ruling out competitors, then a second stricture follows—namely, picking the most predictive model from a set of stupid models does not count for much. Showing that your model explains a range of facts and that no other model in some specified set does is not enough. We need to further show that the set of models we considered is likely to contain the true one—at least given what else we know. So predictions from a model confirm only to the extent that we (1) rule out competitors and (2) have a model that is relatively plausible given our background knowledge.

A second basic moral is that predictions from models count in their favor only to the extent that we can show that the substantive claims of the model, not its simplifications, account for its predictive success. Simplifications and idealizations are, of course, rife in all science. However, if we want to establish that the basic processes described by our model are in fact operative processes in the real world, then we have to do more than simply derive successful predictions. We also have to show that our success is not simply the result of a lucky but false assumption. Since we know that entirely false theories can successfully predict, we need to show that it is our model that deserves the credit of successful predictions, not the deviations from reality that it incorporates.

Both of these morals have an obvious rationale in Bayesian confirmation theory, and I want to point them out because the Bayesian approach will later give us a nice tool for analyzing optimality arguments.[3] The Bayesian approach assesses the extent to which a given piece of evidence E supports an hypothesis H by employing the probability calculus. One natural way to interpret probability in this context is as a measure of confidence or degree of belief. Thus claiming that $p(H/E) = .5$ (read "the probability of H given E equals .5") is claiming that one has as much confidence that H is true as it is false, given E. Bayes's theorem then gives us a way to determine how much a piece of evidence E should increase our confidence in H. That is determined by applying Bayes's theorem:

$$p(H/E) = \frac{p(H) \times P(E/H)}{p(E)}$$

where $p(H)$ is our confidence in H given our background knowledge minus E, $p(E/H)$ is our confidence in E assuming H is true, and $p(E)$ is how probable we believe that evidence to be on any hypothesis. Bayes's theorem is of course a trivial result of the probability calculus, and well-known arguments show that violating it leads to incoherence.

The Bayesian account of confirmation thus evaluates any given test by asking how plausible was the hypothesis to begin with, how probable is the evidence given the hypothesis (where the probability is 1 if H entails E) and how likely we were to see the evidence no matter what. All these judgments are based on our background knowledge. If $p(H/E)$ is greater than $p(H)$, E helps confirm H; if it is less, then it disconfirms H. The more $p(H)$ exceeds .5, the more it is confirmed.

Of course, in many cases estimating the needed probabilities is extremely messy. There are ways to deal with such problems. However, these problems are unimportant if what we want from the Bayesian approach is a framework for thinking about confirmation rather than precise quantitative assessments. And I think that for this more limited goal Bayesian confirmation theory does fairly well. In particular, it gives us a clear explanation of our two morals about confirmation.

Consider first the claim that no hypothesis is well supported until competing accounts are ruled out. The probability of the evidence come what may, $p(E)$, is equivalent to $p(E/H) \times p(H) + p(E/\text{not } H) \times p(\text{not } H)$. So an expanded form of Bayes's theorem is

$$p(H/E) = \frac{p(H) \times p(E/H)}{p(H) \times P(E/H) + p(\text{not } H) \times p(E/\text{not } H)}.$$

This version makes it quite clear that if a model, H, entails the evidence, H can nonetheless still be quite weakly confirmed. If any other alternative entails E as well, then $p(H/E)$ is not increased over $p(H)$. In short, evidence counts less toward our hypothesis if alternative hypotheses entail it as well. Similar reasoning shows that making successful predictions from a stupid model or assessing a hypothesis against straw competitors count for little. Bayes's theorem takes into account not only whether H entails E ($p(E/H)$) but also the prior plausibility of H and its rivals. If H is implausible, it gets little credit for a successful prediction. If all the competing hypotheses that we consider are implausible as well, that means important hypotheses have been left out (since H and all its competitors must sum to one).

The Bayesian account also explains our moral about simplifications. Imagine that a given model, H, together with auxiliary simplifying assumptions $A1 \ldots An$ entail the evidence. Nonetheless, H may not be well supported by E. One of the auxiliary assumptions, call it $A1$, is that the idealizations of our hypothesis or model are sufficiently close to reality to permit inferences about real processes. One catchall competitor to our hypothesis H is thus that H is false, that $A1$ is false, and that (not H and not $A1$) together entail E. So unless we have evidence to show that $A1$ is plausible, $p(E/\text{not } H \text{ and not } A1)$ need not be low and thus $p(H/E)$ need not be high, even though our model predicts the new evidence.

7.3. Functional Explanations and Optimality Arguments

Much recent work on the theory of firm provides *functional* explanations—explanations of economic practices by reference to the function they serve. Moreover, much of that work is supported by optimality arguments. In brief, economists describe a model, show that some existing practice would be optimal according to the model and then conclude that the practice exists in reality because of its optimal effects. In this section I discuss functional explanations and optimality arguments in general—how they work and their strengths and weaknesses. This background and that of the previous section is then applied to models of the firm in the next section.

When economists—or biologists or sociologists for that matter—claim that some practice exists "in order to" bring about some end, they are usually providing functional explanations. Functional explanations of course have a checkered history, but there is nothing inherently wrong with their modern variants. A functional explanation along the lines of "A exists in order to B" commits us to at least the following claims:

1. A causes B.
2. A persists because it causes B.

Claim 1 is straightforward but is not enough. As economists and biologists use functional explanations, they are not simply claiming that A has a function in the sense of playing some causal role. Rather, they are claiming that A exists in order to play that role. Claim 2 helps capture this second idea, and the basic thought is also simple enough: it says that A's causing B results in A's continued existence. For example, some finches on the Galapagos islands have short, thick beaks in order to crack the thick seeds in their environment. That entails that (1) those beaks actually do effectively crack the large seeds and (2) large-beaked birds survive and reproduce in part because they have the beaks they do. Construed this way, functional explanations are a particular type of causal explanation and to that extent uncontroversial.

Functional explanations in biology generally invoke natural selection mechanisms. However, the general account given above is silent on mechanisms: it does not say how A's causing B makes A persist, only that it does so. In the social sciences, functional explanations may rest on (1) purely intentional accounts—accounts where individuals see that A causes B and promote A for that reason, (2) differential sorting processes that make no essentially appeal to conscious choice, and (3) a complex mix of both processes. Thus functional explanations in economics might rest on individuals maximizing, on the differential selection of corporate strategies that come about entirely by chance, and various combinations of these processes.

Functional explanations are frequently supported by optimality arguments, both inside economics and out. Optimality arguments are considerably more controversial than functional explanations, at least when the latter are construed as ordinary causal claims. Optimality arguments work like this: they try to show that some trait A is the optimal way to bring about B and then conclude that A exists in order to B. More specifically, optimality arguments for "A exists in order to B" make three assumptions:

1. We have identified all possible ways to bring about B.
2. A is the best of the possible ways to bring about B.
3. There is some mechanism ensuring that the best possible way to bring about B comes to exist (or persists once it does exist).[4]

So in optimality arguments we argue that A exists in order to B by showing that an existing practice A is the best possible way to bring about B, assuming that some processes exists picking out the optimal.[5] When we establish all three assumptions, then we are in effect showing that A causes B and persists because it does so: in short, we are confirming the components of a functional explanation.

It useful to think about these optimality arguments in Bayesian terms. Let the hypothesis, F, be that a given practice A exists in order to B. That hypothesis is, in fact, a complex hypothesis assuming at least that A causes B, that the set of possible ways to bring about B contains members $al \ldots an$, that A is the best way in X to bring about B, and that there is some mechanism ensuring that the best route to B exists. Call the first subhypothesis the *causal* component, C, the second subhypothesis the *possibility* hypothesis, P, the third the *optimality* hypothesis, O, and the last the *mechanism* hypothesis, M. The alternative hypothesis is thus simply that the conjunction of these four claims is false—that is, not F. The evidence, E, for a functional explanation of course can vary. At its most minimal, it is simply that A exists or persists. More compelling evidence thus would both be evidence consistent with the four subhypotheses and inconsistent with their denial.

So an optimality argument depends on the value of all the factors in Bayes' theorem. That is, an optimality argument is stronger when

$p(C$ and P and O and $M)$ is high.
p $(E/C$ and P and O and $M)$ is high.
p not $(C$ and P and O and $M)$ is low.
p $(E/\text{not}$ $(C$ and P and O and $M))$ is low.

Obviously, when any of the assumptions for the functional explanation are improbable, the composite hypothesis is improbable as well (since $p(A + B) = p$ $(A) \times p(B)$ for independent events). Similarly, the minimal evidence that A exists is likely to be compatible with many alternative hypotheses, and thus $p(E/\text{not } F)$ is unlikely to be low when such evidence is all we have. As we cite evidence supporting a mechanism, supporting an account of possible ways to bring about B and so on, $p(E/\text{not } F)$ declines proportionally and $p(F/E)$ increases proportionately. Thus in the broadest terms, an optimality argument is weak evidence insofar as we fail to show that the trait or practice in question brings about the desired effect, that the practice is the best way to do so, and that there is a mechanism picking the best way.[6]

7.4. Recent Models of the Firm

Recent work on the firm aims to provide a realistic description and explanation—at least compared to earlier neoclassical work—of how the firm behaves.[7] Such accounts take into consideration the complex internal structure of firms and the complex environment they face. Among the important facts such accounts seek to explain are these: Why do many firms often promote primarily from within? Why do firms choose to produce a particular input rather than to buy it on the open market—in short, what explains vertical integration? Why do wages within a firm increase as we move up the hierarchy of authority? Why do firms have the kind of hierarchical authority structures they do? How do those authority structures and wage differentials relate to the objectives of the firm as a whole? In short, recent work tries to explain the internal structure of the firm and how that structure relates to the overall behavior of the firm.

I want to look first at the perhaps most developed recent work on the firm—namely, the transaction costs account as found in its best-known representative, Williamson (1975, 1985). Williamson argues that the technical costs of production are only part of the explanation for why firms behave as they do. Standard neoclassical models ignore the costs involved in bargaining over prices and carrying out contracts. However, in the real world these processes are not costless. The resources required for negotiating and policing contracts are what Williamson calls *transaction costs*. According to Williamson, three factors determine when transaction costs play a significant role: asset specificity, uncertainty, and frequency of exchange. When a supplier, for example, must make investments that cannot easily be switched to other uses, then a "holdup" problem arises. When the investment is made by the seller, for example, after an initially agreed upon price, the buyer is in a position to demand a lower price, since the supplier cannot take his investment elsewhere and prefers a lower price to the loss of sunk costs. If all future contingencies could be known costlessly, such problems could be eliminated by appropriate contracts. However, contracts are inevitably incomplete, and bargaining over and writing detailed contracts for every known contingency is generally costly. Finally, these two factors—asset specificity and uncertainty—have greater importance the more frequent such exchanges are between two parties.

Williamson uses this analysis to then answer all the questions we posed above about the firm. Inputs are produced inside the firm rather than acquired in an external market when and because they minimize transaction costs. Firms have hierarchical authority structures because such governing processes minimize transaction costs. Unions exist in those industries where they help minimize transaction costs. Internal promotion exists for the same reasons.

Williamson's explanations are clearly functional in form: he claims over and over again that the structure of the firm exists in order to minimize transaction costs. There is no gainsaying the suggestiveness of Williamson's approach, and his emphasis on transaction costs is an important step toward a more realistic theory of the firm. Should we, however, believe that Williamson has more or less successfully explained the structure of the firm? I think not. To successfully explain, his account must cite the real causal factors at work; to identify those factors, our evidence needs to meet the basic conditions cited in previous sections. However, it seems clear that Williamson's work as it now stands frequently fails to meet those conditions.[8]

The basic problem is that the evidence for transaction cost explanations is predominately story telling. Using his general model, Williamson derives implications that he shows are consistent with some select set of facts. More specifically, he identifies the ways in which various existing practices reduce certain transaction costs or shows that differences in practices are consistent with differences in transaction costs. However, to confidently explain, we need more than such consistency: we need to rule out the most plausible competing explanations. It is here than Williamson's evidence is weak.

Let me explicate some of those weakness by focusing more specifically on the requirements for successful optimality arguments. Williamson's evidence is overwhelmingly of this kind: he claims that a particular practice optimally reduces transaction costs and concludes from that claim that the practice exists in order to do so. For these inferences to be well confirmed, we thus need both to have a high level of confidence that we have identified all the significant costs and benefits and that there is some mechanism picking out practices with the benefits we cite. On both counts, Williamson's work faces large obstacles that at this point have not been overcome.

Consider first Williamson's account of why hierarchical authority structures are the dominant form of organization. Williamson (1985: ch. 9) describes six different possible authority structures:

- *The putting-out system* The entrepreneur owns raw materials and coordinates production by independent labors using their own tools and workshops.
- *Federated system* The entrepreneur leases the workspace and tools to individual workers producing different intermediate products, with the workers contracting among each other over the price of their particular input and output.
- *Communal system* A group of workers owns a plant in common, but each worker produces the entire product alone and receives the resulting profit from his or her individual efforts.
- *Peer group system* Same ownership and production as the communal, with each worker paid according to the total group output.
- *Inside contracting system* Management provides work location, equipment, raw materials and sells final product; the production process is subcontracted to nonemployees who hire their own labor.
- *Authority system* The factory is owned by a capitalist who hires labor that "stands ready to accept authority" of the owner.

Williamson analyzes the transaction costs involved in each of these forms, finds that the authority system has the lowest transaction costs, and concludes that the authority system exists in order to minimize transaction cost. This analysis is taken by him to refute the "radical" account—namely, that hierarchy exists to ensure control by capitalists.

Williamson's discussion here is a classic use of optimality argument: a list of possibilities is produced, relative optimality is determined in a model, and existing practices are shown to be optimal and thus presumed to exist for that purpose. Not surprisingly, this account also faces the problems that typically plague optimality arguments:

- *Uncertainty about possibilities*   The six different arrangements do not exhaust all the logically possible combinations, so we need to know that these six are the only possibilities. We also need to know that these six were in fact real possibilities. Without this information, the value of $p(P)$—what we called earlier the "possibility hypothesis"—is diminished and the strength of Williamson's case is correspondingly diminished.

- *Uncertainty about costs and benefits*   Williamson gives a rough accounting of some of the costs and benefits. Conclusive evidence would of course provide a precise measure of all the costs. It is clear, however, that Williamson ignores some important costs. In particular, he assumes that the commands of the central authority are carried out more or less without cost.[9] In the real world that is arguably not the case, at least in large hierarchies. Managers have to negotiate and fight to get decisions carried out that conflict with the interest of those lower in the hierarchy—just as they have to exert effort to obtain the information needed to make decisions when that information may bear negatively on the interests of employees. Similarly, those lower in the hierarchy will exert time and resources toward influencing any central authority. Such costs—called "influence costs" by Milgrom and Roberts (1980)—also are ignored by Williamson. Until we measure costs like these, we can have little confidence in Williamson's claim that the authority system is the optimal among the six—in particular, that it is more efficient than the inside contracting system. So we can have little confidence that $p(O)$—the optimality subhypothesis—is very high. And if we think hierarchies have other costs that Williamson misses, then we would not expect to find that hierarchical firms survive or that their primary function is to reduce transaction costs, assuming that we think there is some mechanism picking out the optimal. So doubts about correct specification of the costs are also doubts about $p(E/M)$ and thus about $p(E/F)$, where M is the hypothesis that there is a mechanism picking out the optimal, F is Williamson's functional explanation, and E is the evidence that hierarchy exists.

- *Uncertainty about mechanisms*   There are at least three different difficulties that arise when we ask how confident we should be that the appropriate mechanism exists:

  1. A mechanism working by the differential survival and founding of firms—the kind of mechanism mentioned by Williamson—selects firms as whole.

However, a firm structure that minimizes transaction costs may not be the most efficient way of doing other things. So what a selective mechanism would pick, assuming one exists, might not be that structure which minimizes transaction costs.[10]

2. If we do not assume that managers and owners are the same individuals and do assume that every employee pursues their own self-interest, then there will be selective process operating *at the level of individuals* that may push in different directions from selection for firms. What promotes the survival of the firm and what promotes the interests of managers and employees are identical only under special conditions. If those conditions do not hold, then the actual function of hierarchy will be the result of these two different processes. The optimal for the firm would not be expected.

3. Relatedly, the six possible organizational forms described by Williamson are not all subject to the same kind of selective process. In particular, the putting-out system involves *individuals* who are comparing the return on their labor and tools on their own premises against other ways that their labor might be employed; the authority system, on the other hand, allegedly outcompetes other *corporate* strategies. This makes comparing their relative efficiencies less than obvious. Individuals may have asset-specific skills and skill-specific assets such that no alternative use of their labor is better for them even if the authority-structured firm is the most efficient large-scale organizational way to produce the product in question. So the putting-out system might persist because it promotes individual self-interest, even though in the abstract the hierarchical firm involves a more efficient use of labor.

These three difficulties make it hard to assign a very high value to $p(M)$ or to $p(E/F)$ (recall the reasoning above from the uncertainties about cost).

My point here is not simply to raise skeptical questions nor to claim that Williamson's work is inherently flawed. Rather, it is to point out some of the empirical issues that may need to be resolved for Williamson's optimality arguments to carry much force. Given the unresolved issues sketched above, it is hard to avoid the conclusion that our confidence in Williamson's account of hierarchy should be quite low. In our Bayesian terms, the value of $p(C$ and P and O and $M)$ is low, for we are multiplying already low values. And if we think there are unmeasured costs and different mechanisms, then we would not predict that firms minimize transaction costs simpliciter. So $p(E/F)$ is low (where F is Williamson's functionalist hypothesis). More optimistically, pointing out these uncertainties is also pointing what might be done to better confirm Williamson's suggestive models—namely, precisely measuring complete costs and identifying real historical processes that select efficient firms.

It will not do, however, to argue as Williamson (1988) has done that his functional explanations are at least relatively plausible since other, nonfunctional explanations have not been established either. Even if we bought the implausible assumption that we should assign equal probabilities to hypotheses about which we are ignorant,[11] it would not follow that the functional-nonfunctional explanations would get equal weighting. The nonfunctional explanation is in fact a host of different hypotheses—for example, appeals to power relations, normative factors, historical contingency, and so on and combinations thereof are some possibilities. Moreover, Williamson's explanation focusing on transaction costs is only one possible efficiency account, as the unmeasured costs cited above suggest. So it is unwarranted to suggest, as Williamson does, that his accounts must be at least relatively plausible because of such burden of proof considerations. Only a careful and detailed measuring of costs and benefits and clear evidence that an appropriate mechanism exists will do.

I think these kinds of uncertainties hold generally for transaction cost explanations. To avoid seeming to pick on Williamson's most fanciful accounts, let's look briefly at some of the better empirical work that Williamson cites as supporting his claims—namely, that of Joskow. Joskow (1985, 1987, 1991) has tried to go beyond the generally anecdotal evidence Williamson cites. Looking at the coal market, Joskow measures differences in asset specificity to see if they are associated with the different practices that transaction cost models would expect. Investment in coal mines can sometimes involve paradigm cases of asset specificity—for example, when a coal mine and power plant are built at the same site and transportation of coal in and out of the site is costly. Joskow measures contract length, on the thought that long-term contracts will avoid the holdup problem associated with asset specificity. He does indeed find the expected correlations.

Joskow's results are certainly more telling than much of the piecemeal evidence Williamson cites. However, some of the same basic problems surface here as well. Let me mention three potential uncertainties in Joskow's data:

- A first worry is simply that high asset specificity, according to Williamson, does not necessarily entail long-term contracts rather than vertical integration. In fact, Williamson's general emphasis suggests that the latter rather the former should prevail because of the transaction costs involved in writing long-term contracts. Joskow, however, finds that long-term contracts are more common and to that extent his work disconfirms the transaction cost explanation.
- The transaction cost account would entail long-term contracts if the degree of uncertainty could be shown to be small, for in that case long-term contracts could be written to deal with the holdup problems. However, Joskow

does not control in his regressions for degree of uncertainty, though he cites informal evidence that it should be extensive. Thus we are left wondering why long-term contracts prevail rather than vertical integration, since it is the latter that at least the informal evidence suggests should be present if transaction costs are the main factor involved. Since vertical integration is not predominate, then we have to worry that there is some other factor involved other than transaction costs and thus that long-term contracts may not exist primarily because they minimize transaction costs.

- Similarly, if we knew that vertical integration had high costs—either in terms of scale considerations, skills specific to the mining industry that power companies might not have, or the costs of internal command—then we might expect long-term contracts rather than vertical integration. Joskow despairs, however, of measuring such variables; yet without doing so, we have left out potentially important costs, costs that might help explain Joskow's results in a way that would be consistent with the transaction cost perspective.

These problems all involve doubts that Joskow has fully measured the relevant costs. Until we have evidence about those costs, Joskow's work falls short of providing a compelling case for the transaction cost explanation. In fact, without those costs, his work threatens to disconfirm Williamson's work as much as it supports it, for Joskow's data does not find that vertical integration predominates when in fact it should. Nonetheless, Joskow's data surely does suggest that transaction costs must be playing some role, but turning that suggestion into a well-confirmed explanation requires, it would seem, considerably more investigation.

Though Williamson's approach is sometimes labeled "neoinstitutionalist," it should be clear that Williamson has as much in common with standard neoclassical models of the firm as he does with purely sociological approaches. After all, appeals to transaction costs are really simply a claim that the neoclassical black-box theory of the firm ignored important costs. Williamson is in many ways just applying the constrained maximizing approach to decisions affecting firm structure. I want to look next at some work by Rosen (1982, 1991) on firm structure that also involves a fairly straightforward extension of the neoclassical approach. Rosen is out to explain why there are (1) differences in responsibility, arranged generally in a hierarchical fashion inside the firm, and (2) differences in compensation according to responsibility. His answer comes by examining how more talented managers would ideally be distributed within and between firms. In an elegant analysis he shows that the most efficient assignment would put those with greater managerial talent at higher positions of authority within firms and shift the most talented managers to the largest firms. Greater managerial talent means greater productivity of those supervised, so increases in responsibility according to managerial talent is the optimal use of resources. Rosen's result thus has strong intuitive appeal. Rosen (1991: 87, 85) believes that his approach "will improve our understanding" of the firm and that it "can support extremely large salaries for top-level managers of large firms on marginal productivity grounds alone."

Rosen thus presents a functional explanation—hierarchies of responsibility and compensation exist to maximize profits. His evidence is (1) the fact that hierarchies exist and (2) a model that entails they are optimal. Should we believe on these grounds that salary and authority differentials exist to maximize efficiency? There are reasons to be skeptical, since Rosen arguably ignores important costs and benefits and since there is real doubt whether the needed mechanism is present. Consider, for example, the following possibilities:

- High salaries might correlate with seniority rather than ability, with promotions coming from the most senior. Why? Paying wages at a rate above marginal product in the latter part of an individual's job tenure could provide a strong incentive to not "shirk" or could result from an "implicit contract" (discussed below) where the wage reflects an insurance element.[12]
- Determining the real ability of managers, especially the ability in different jobs across firms, may be costly. If the costs are sufficiently high, then even if managers are rewarded according to ability, it may be only their ability relative to other internal candidates. If so, we would not necessary know that differences between firms in compensation should be explained by differences in ability. In short, the costs of obtaining reliable information about managers from other firms may make an inter firm market unviable or at the least unable to ensure that the optimal matches are made. So we might have reason to doubt that the requisite mechanism exists. Further difficulties along these line will be discussed below when we look at principal-agent models.
- Long-term employees may come to have skills and knowledge that are independent of their "managerial ability" and that cannot be transferred across firms. Such asset specificity would undercut any easy inference that the best managers are sorted to the largest firms. It would also give a place to contingent facts about individual's work history, since some entry-level jobs may be more conducive to acquiring such skills than others.[13]

All these factors may be present at once, and there are many more that could be mentioned. Until they are ruled out, we can have little confidence that Rosen has described all the main costs and benefits and little confidence that a mechanism exists picking out what he claims is optimal. So at this point we should have little faith in Rosen's claim to have "increased our understanding."

Let me turn next to another recent approach to explaining the internal structure of firms and its affect on firm behavior—the principal-agent model used by Fama (1980). Traditional black-box neoclassical theory assumed that ownership and control of the firm were concentrated in one person or function. Of course, this assumption is not generally true, and it is has often been claimed that the separation of ownership and control implies that firms should behave quite differently from the classical firm of neoclassical theory. Fama's work is one of the first recent attempts to incorporate such complexity into the neoclassical picture. His goal is to explain managerial compensation and the behavior of firms when managers are agents, but not principals, by delineating the effect of market forces on managers and owners pursuing their individual self-interests.

Fama analyzes a model with (1) owners who diversify their investments and thus have no strong interest in directly managing the firm and (2) managers who are not owners but derive their compensation by competing in the market for managerial talent. Fama identifies at least the following potential economic forces: (1) competition between firms, in particular between firms where managers and owners are one and firms with separation of functions, (2) the market for managerial talent, at all levels in the managerial hierarchy, (3) the market for outside directors, and (4) the effects of potential takeovers.

These forces, he argues, all will tend to ensure that managers are rewarded according to their marginal contribution to firm success. Since the separation of management and ownership has survived in a competition between firms with different structures, separation must contribute to efficiency. Since managerial rewards are determined by the market for managerial talent and since a manager's contribution to firm success determines his or her desirability, managers will be rewarded according to their success. In particular, managers who try to rest on past successes and shirk during their current contract will be found out when they change jobs; as a result, there will be a kind of ex post settling up that reduces their compensation and ensures that they receive their marginal product. Furthermore, lower-level managers depend for their marketability on the success of those above them in promoting shareholder profits. Consequently, they will have incentives to monitor top management performance as well. The threat of outside takeovers and the desire of outside directors on the board of directors to maximize their market value also will provide forces to ensure that management maximizes firm profits.

Thus where separation of ownership and control exists, it does so because it maximizes firm survival. Managerial salaries exist in order to reward the efficient; rewarding efficient factors exists to ensure firm profitability. So separation of ownership and control does not call for revision of the neoclassical account of firm behavior, rather it is the mechanism bringing about that behavior.

As with the other work discussed above, our confidence in Fama's explanations should be a function of our confidence that has correctly identified the main possible costs and benefits and our confidence that there exists the relevant mechanism picking out the optimal. On both counts, I suggest, we have reason to be cautious on the following grounds:

- The market for managers may not accurately "see" each manager's marginal product, for that requires knowing much more than overall firm success (which may be public knowledge): it requires an accurate assessment of manager behavior and the effects of that behavior. Not only is the latter not easily seen by other firms, but managers themselves have incentives to exaggerate their contribution. Moreover, management contributions are often team products, with all the room for cheating that they involve.[14]
- "The owners" need not be a homogeneous group with common interests (Holstrom and Tirole, 1988). Different time preferences, degrees of risk aversion, and so on may make it hard to identify some common interest; public-goods-type problems can prevent the optimal collective interest from emerging. So inferences about how managers would be forced to behave by self-interested owners investing in the best alternatives can be shaky because in actual practice "the owners" are not a homogeneous force.
- In general, competitive forces *between firms* and those *between individuals* need not pull in the same direction. So, for example, (1) markets may judge middle-level managers by the success of their units and thus managers may have incentives to promote those units in ways that a detrimental to the firm as a whole, (2) Fama's ex post settling up, which equates reward and marginal product does not ensure efficient *firms*, for as Fama describes it the settling up can happen when a manager takes his next job with another firm; thus the original firm may not then get the efficient use of its resources—efficient use on average across firms does not entail efficient use within firms, at least without further arguments; (3) managers pursuing their self-interest may have clear reasons to fight takeovers in ways that are not optimal for the shareholders, a possibility the data suggests is real (Dann and De Angelo, 1980); and (4) if the market for managers supports frequent job changes, managers may maximize their price by pursuing short-term firm success at the expense of long-term success.

What do these possibilities show? They do not show that Fama is wrong to look at principal-agent models of the firm or that the forces he describes could not explain the real world. But they do show—to the extent that they are real possibilities—that we should have very little confidence that Fama's model, as is, explains anything. Since Fama has not ruled out or otherwise shown insignificant these complicating variables, the consistency of his model with some select facts about firms tells us very little. We just do not know whether Fama's mechanisms are the real causal processes at work. Given the above complications, it is going far beyond the evidence to say as does Fama that "it is probably safe to conclude that the general phenomenon [of managerial markets, takeover markets, and so on]" explains why managerial salaries and managerial control separate from ownership persist.

Another recent body of work on the firm emphasizes the idea of *implicit contracts*.[15] Implicit-contract theory seeks to explain facts that are puzzling on the traditional neoclassical picture of the firm—for example, long-term employment and rigid wages. If labor is purchased in a fully competitive spot market, then price should be set at a level that clears the market at any given moment. When conditions change and a worker's marginal value product drops below that which the employer can obtain by hiring different labor in the labor market, either wages of current employees are reduced or old labor fired and new labor hired. However, real labor markets show neither the wage flexibility or the turnover in employment that this model implies.

Implicit contract theory seeks to explain such phenomena by incorporating more complexity into the wage bargain. Workers, so the story goes, are risk averse, or more so than employers, because they cannot diversify their human capital across many uses at once. Thus workers have an interest in obtaining insurance for those circumstances where their declining marginal product would call for wage cuts or unemployment. However, private insurance companies will find it hard to offer the insurance workers desire because they do not have accurate information about worker productivity or about the real reasons for worker firings—thus creating severe moral hazard problems and making effective private insurance impossible. Employers do have such information and may find it advantageous to offer insurance as part of the wage bargain. Thus the full wage of workers includes two components: the traditional price of labor reflecting its marginal product at the moment and an insurance payout or premium, depending on conditions at the time. Since such arrangements are seldom part of explicit employment contracts, economists infer that these arrangements are part of an "implicit contract"—an understood agreement that is nowhere written down. So long-term employment and inflexible wages exist in order to provide insurance to risk-averse workers.

As with other recent work on the firm, implicit-contract theory runs into fairly obvious problems both about its estimate of costs and benefits and the probability that the requisite mechanism exists. Worries about mechanisms surface as soon as we ask how implicit contracts are enforced. Explicit contracts have legal backing; implicit contracts do not. Thus there needs to be real incentive to ensure their enforcement. Implicit contracts over the conditions of work can be enforced by threats of quitting and firing. However, these mechanisms won't work for implicit contract theory, for it wants to explain quitting and firing itself. Why, for example, would workers not renege on implicit long-term contracts when their wages were below their marginal productivity, or, conversely, why wouldn't employers renege and fire workers when their marginal product dropped below their wage?

The upshot is that we can easily tell a story showing that the needed mechanism would not exist. In our Bayesian terms, $p(M)$ is lowered and $p(\text{not } F)$ correspondingly increased. Advocates of implicit contract theory might try to avoid such difficulties by adding further factors to the wage determination process—for example, the costs of switching jobs or reputation effects.[16] But as it stands now, we probably should have little confidence that the needed mechanism actually exists. It certainly will not do, as some have suggested, to defend implicit contract theory on the grounds that it is an "as if" explanation (Rosen, 1985: 1149). If economists want real explanations—explanations that identify the main causal processes and tendencies—then they must show that the deviations of their models from reality are not responsible for what successful predictions those models make. So to show that long-term employment and inflexible wages exist because of their contribution to efficiency and so on, we cannot simply deduce those phenomena from an abstract model. We must also show that the mechanism presumed by that model is at work; consistency with a few select facts is not enough to establish that conclusion, for other mechanisms may be equally plausible.

Implicit contract models also ignore numerous potential costs and benefits. Firm-specific investments in human capital, the transaction costs of either searching for and finding new employment or finding new labor, the greater information that firms have about current employee's productivity compared to the uncertainties about new employees, the contributions of long-term contracts to employee cooperation, and so on could potentially be involved in long-term employment and rigid wages. Until these factors are assessed, we should little confidence that the insurance element captures all or even the main benefits involved. Moreover, we could use these other factors to construct an alternative mechanism explaining long-term contracts and rigid wages, and such a story would seeming have as much or more a priori plausibility as the implicit contract mechanism.[17]

So far I have raised problems specific to particular models of the firm. In closing this section, let me briefly mention one general obstacle that all these models face. Throughout my discussion above, I assumed that the main competing explanations were always economic. Yet there is plenty of evidence that noneconomic factors play a role in shaping firms (see, for example, Granovetter, 1986). Noneconomic accounts are thus potential competing explanations. Purely sociological explanations probably have a very low prior probability. However, there is no reason that "sociological" and economic factors cannot operate at the same time—that particular practices can exist in part because of their contribution to profits or self-interest and in part because of other social causes. Such mixed explanations are much more serious competitors for any economic model of the firm. In principle, then, all the above models of the firm need also to rule out or factor in the role of social variables as well. Economists implicitly recognize this need when they include, for example, beliefs about "fair" wages as a variable in wage determination.[18] Thus the difficulties pointed out above are further magnified by the potential role of noneconomic social factors.

7.5. Some Tentative Morals for Economists

One obvious moral from the discussion of the last section is that developing idealized models and showing them consistent with a few generic facts is not enough—at least not enough to provide a relatively well-confirmed explanation of actual firm behavior and structure. To ensure that we are picking out real causal processes, we need to rule out competing explanations of the phenomena we predict. For most of the work on the firm discussed here, this means paying careful attention both to costs and benefits and to mechanisms. Identifying some efficiencies of a practice is not enough to show that it exists to promote efficiency. We need instead a full accounting, one that shows other potential costs and benefits are not present. Ruling out such competing explanations requires at the same time ruling out competing accounts of the relevant mechanism. As the many plausible stories discussed above show, the same practice can potentially be brought about in diverse ways—even assuming that it must exist for some efficiency reason or other. Ruling out those competing stories requires in particular attention to the level or kind of mechanism being invoked. Carefully identifying benefits to firm survival may not be enough, if we also expect that there are processes acting at the level of individuals. There is no a priori guarantee these two kinds of mechanisms must work in the same direction or have the same effects. So a well-confirmed model of the firm relying on optimality evidence must give us good reason to believe that total result of firm and individual-level processes is one picking out the optimal.

Have I set the standards here too high? Doesn't all science involve simplifications and model building? Indeed it does, but not all simplifications and models are of a piece. When models abstract from potentially relevant causes, then successful predictions from those models leave us with a quandary, for we do not know how to mete out credit and blame. Success could be due our model having captured the main causal process, or it could simply be the lucky result of false assumptions. Thus we can be sure idealized models really explain only if we show that our models are sufficiently close to reality. How do we go about arguing that our model describes a real process, despite its simplifications? There are numerous concrete methods for achieving this goal, but all work by trying to show that the simplifications are not causing a spurious positive result. Some of those methods are (1) showing that improvements in accuracy bring improvements in prediction, (2) showing that results hold up when different simplifying assumptions are used, (3) showing that the deviations of the model's idealizations from reality are random or unsystematic, (4) showing that past experience indicates that the kind of simplifications made in the model usually do not cause trouble, (5) showing that the model holds up across diverse data, testing situations, and so on, despite the simplifying assumptions it makes, and (6) showing that we have good independent evidence that a mechanism exists connecting the major variables in our model, and so on. Some such methods are essential to rule out the ever-present worry that the simplifying assumptions of our models are confounding our results.[19]

So if models of the firm ignore important costs and benefits and if they ignore the complexity of real-world mechanisms, we cannot defend those models by simply claiming that models are essential to good science. Models are essential, but models *explain* only when we use procedures like those listed above to show our models are reliable. We can see in principle at least what this would mean for the models of the firm discussed above. For example, we would like to know that as they provide a more complete account of the costs and benefits, they produce more reliable predictions. In the case of Joskow's work, for example, that would mean finding a measure for uncertainty and the associated costs and then showing that the transaction costs model can predict when vertical integration is favored over long-term coal contracts and vice versa—or finding some measure for the costs of vertical integration and then showing the transactions model provides better predictions when those costs are factored in. We would also like to know, for example, that as both individual-level and firm-level competitive processes are included, our models make more accurate predictions. Such steps would then increase our confidence that the models in question do capture important causal processes, despite their simplifications.

Unfortunately, these kinds of steps have not generally been taken by those working on the theory of the firm. Even though many of the difficulties I raised in the last section are ones that can be drawn from the current economics literature itself, defenders of the various models discussed above often claimed that their particular model increases our understanding, describes significant economic factors influencing the firm, or explains real world phenomena.[20] Those optimistic conclusions are unwarranted, for they far outstrip the evidence provided. There is an unfortunate tendency—in this work and in economics in general—to slip from plausible claims about a model qua model to claims about having explained the real world. To do so is to ignore some absolutely crucial steps—providing the empirical evidence that the model picks out the main processes operative in the world, that simplifications of the model do not undercut its predictive success, that alternative explanations of the data are implausible. Not matter how elegant and mathematically tractable a model is, simply postulating it and seeing its consequences provides no real explanation.

As an aside I should note that this moral has important implications concerning policy pronouncements. Many of the articles discussed in the previous section made policy recommendations—or welfare claims—based on their models.[21] Given how far those models are from being carefully confirmed, any policy recommendation is suspect. Of course there is nothing wrong with pointing out what the policy implications would be *if the model was the true one.* Unfortunately, economists do not necessarily couch their recommendations in such guarded terms—again they shift from implications about the model to implications about the real world without doing the hard empirical work need to make the transition. To the extent that economists do not make clear the highly tentative nature of their policy prescriptions, they do the profession a disfavor by opening it up to the charge of ideological bias.

The demand for careful empirical confirmation is the hallmark of good natural science, and it is one economics avoids only at its peril. However, if work on the firm is representative—and I suspect it is—much more weight seems to given inside the profession to model development than empirical specification and confirmation. Far more effort has gone into developing new models of the firm than has gone into providing well-confirmed applications of specific models to real-world situations. Model development thus threatens to become an end itself rather than what it should be—the means to producing carefully tested explanations of real economic processes.[22]

Model development of course need not be an obstacle to progress. Models can serve many functions besides directly explaining the real world: they can help test for consistency, they can make complex phenomena mathematically tractable, and so on. More important, perhaps, they can also play an important role in remedying the weakness pointed out in the previous section in at least the following two ways: (1) Producing many different models of the firm helps point out exactly what variables may need to be considered and what alternative explanations need to be ruled out. The very reason optimality arguments for any particular theory are unconvincing—because there are reasonable unmeasured costs and alternative mechanisms—is also a reason to hope that model development will contribute to progress in the long run. The more ingeniously and extensively economists develop different models, say, of internal labor markets, the better will be our grasp of the variables any convincing explanation must consider. (2) Model building can play a crucial part in showing when simplifications are reasonable and when they are not. If the assumptions of a model vary widely and the main predictions of the model hold up despite those changes, then we can have some confidence that our model picks out a real causal process. In Leamer's (1983) terminology, we can use models to show our inferences are "sturdy." However, models will serve these two roles well only if they are part of an ongoing process to explain real world events with carefully confirmed and tested accounts.

I want to finish by drawing one last moral from our discussion of work on the firm, this time a moral about what successful explanations of the firm may look like. The moral is that successful explanations of the firm are likely to be a piecemeal affair. Given the diversity of potential costs and benefits that different firm structures may have, we perhaps should not expect there to be any one general overarching explanatory theory of firm structure and behavior.[23] Rather, explanation will lie in the details—in taking the general processes the models tell us might be relevant and showing case by case exactly how particular practices come to be. Furthermore, it is in such case by case detail that sufficient evidence will be found to conclusively rule out some accounts and prefer others. The work by Joskow, for example, is a good start on such explanations for specific instances of vertical integration.

Here economics can perhaps take a lesson from evolutionary biology and ecology. Natural selection is not a unitary force like gravity but an abstraction from innumerable physically different environments interacting with biologically different organisms. As a result, theories in evolutionary biology and ecology outline the basic variables in broad strokes; however, explaining and confirming requires looking at unique realizations and combinations of those variables in local detail. That process does not come easy and requires careful collection of data and careful ruling out of competing hypotheses.[24] Since theories of the firm also invoke selective processes and deal with complex combinations of variables, we might expect successful models of the firm to proceed in a parallel fashion. As long as economists do not confuse model development and investigation with the separate process of concrete explanation—something biologists on the whole have successfully avoided—then we can view the new models of the firm as an exciting first step toward progress in economic science.

Notes

1. For a discussion of optimality arguments that inspired my approach here, see Kitcher (1987: 77–102). I discuss functional explanations and their evidence in much more detail in Kincaid (1990, forthcoming: ch. 4).

2. For criticisms see Glymour (1980: ch. 2) and Achinstein (1985).

3. For an account of the Bayesian approach see Howson and Urbach (1989).

4. "All possible ways" here is of course vague. In the economics case, if the mechanism involved is differential survival, then all possible ways can just be all the ways historically that have been present. The picture then is that competition allows the best of the existing options to persist. If the mechanism is conscious selection, then "the possible ways" probably needs to be more broadly conceived as "economically possible for rational agents." In this latter case, practices would not just *persist* because they were optimal, but would also have to come to exist because they are optimal.

5. A similar argument strategy can also be based on claims about stability by arguing that some trait must exist to serve a particular function because it is a stable strategy in a competitive process—that is, a "local" optimum that would not be dislodged once established. Stability arguments are not nearly as prevalent in work on the firm as are optimality arguments, so I do not discuss them here; nonetheless, all the same basic points made optimality arguments can be easily adapted to stability arguments.

6. The demand for mechanism here is *not* the result of some general claim that no causal process is established until the mechanism is. That general claim seem to me of dubious sense—what is "the" mechanism, since there are indefinitely may levels of mechanism involved in most causal claims?—and highly counterintuitive, since we make all kinds of well-confirmed explanatory causal claims without knowing the underlying mechanism (for example, I can know that the baseball broke the window without knowing anything at all about the quantum mechanical details that were the underlying mechanism in that process). Mechanisms are needed in optimality arguments because their evidential force presupposes some relevant mechanism exists—and even here what we need is evidence that there is a mechanism, not necessarily evidence about what "the" mechanism is, whatever that is supposed to mean.

7. For an overview of recent work, on which I draw below, see Holstrom and Tirole (1988).

8. The discussion that follows is in part inspired by Milgrom and Roberts (1988, 1989).

9. Such complications are not entirely unrecognized by Williamson, especially in his most recent work, but they are not incorporated in the analysis discussed here nor in many other of his accounts.

10. This is a common recognized problem in confirming evolutionary accounts in biology and is pointed out about evolutionary mechanisms in economics by Nelson and Winter (1982) and Winter (1991).

11. Williamson's burden of proof reasoning here is essentially the same as that given for the "equiprobability" assumption sometimes invoked in Bayesian decision theory under ignorance. The basic problem is that from the fact that how do not know how probable two theories are it does not follow that they are or can reasonably be treated as though they are equally probable. For a summary of criticisms of that assumption, see Resnik (1987: ch. 2).

12. See Lazear (1979) for a discussion of the former explanation; references for the implicit contract accounts are given below.

13. For worries along these lines see Granovetter (1986).

14. Problems of the former kind are discussed by Nelson and Winter (1982) and Winter (1991).

15. For surveys see Manning (1989) and Tzannatos and Rosen (1985).

16. For suggestions along these lines see Bean (1984) and Holstrom (1981), respectively.

17. Yet a further difficult for implicit contract theory concerns in what sense there can be implicit contracts at all. This is a thorny issue that raises a host of questions beyond the purview of this paper.

18. For models along these lines see Akerlof and Yellen (1988). Of course, once a narrow definition of rational self-interest is given up for a broader conception that requires only maximizing preferences, where the preferences can range over anything, then the "economic" approach potentially loses some of its bite, for much of the explanatory work is being done by the preferences themselves, which economics has nothing or little to say about. So it is unconvincing to claim (as

do Milgrom and Roberts, 1989: 449) that the standard constrained maximizing approach can handle such variables as norms and so on by adopting the broad definition of self-interested behavior. Obviously these are complex issues that require more careful attention I can give them here.

19. For a more detailed discussion of such requirements see Hausman (1981: ch. 7) and Kincaid (forthcoming: ch. 3).

20. Perhaps these models of the firm offer an explanation "in principle" or a "potential explanation" in some (yet to be clarified) sense. However, a potential explanation is not a real one, and descriptions of how the world might work will explain how the work does work only if we can show that the real world and the possible one are sufficiently "close"—that is, that the differences between the two do not prevent the mechanism in the potential model from acting in the real world. Showing that, however, requires answering all the kinds of doubt I have raised about the different accounts of the firm.

21. For example, Manning (1989) argues based on his model that governments should not intervene to make wages less rigid.

22. One crucial where there has been insufficient model building, so far as I can see, is in picturing how individual-level mechanisms and firm-level mechanism interact. Typically, models of the firm assume either that some process picks optimal firm strategies or that some process picks what is optimal for individuals pursuing their self-interest under constraints, but do not explore how the two might interact. Given the lack of clarity in work on the firm about mechanisms, these seems an area where models for models sake might well be fruitful.

23. A point also argued by Joskow (1991: 134).

24. Economists might draw some inspiration both about what has to be done and what can be done to really confirm functional explanations from looking at Endler (1986).

References

Achinstein, Peter. (1985). "The Method of Hypothesis." In P. Achinstein and O. Hannaway (eds.), *Observation, Experiment and Hypothesis in Modern Physical Science*. Cambridge: MIT Press.

Akerlog, George, and Janet Yellen. (1988). Fairness and Employment.'' *American Economic Review* 78, 44–49.

Bean, C. (1984). "Optimal Wage Bargains." *Economica* 51, 141–149.

Dann, Larry, and Harry DeAngelo. (1988). "Corporate Financial Policy and Corporate Control." *Journal of Financial Economics* 20, 87–127.

Endler, John. (1986). *Natural Selection in the Wild*. Princeton, NJ: Princeton University Press.

Fama, Eugene. (1980). "Agency Problems and the Theory of the Firm." *Journal of Political Economy* 88, 288–307.

Glymour, Clark. (1980). *Theory and Evidence*. Princeton, NJ: Princeton University Press.

Granovetter, Mark. (1986). "Labor Mobility, Internal Markets, and Job Matching: A Comparison of the Sociological and Economic Approaches." *Research in Social Stratification and Mobility* 5, 3–39.

Hausman, Daniel. (1981). *Capital, Profits and Prices*. New York: Columbia University Press.

Holstrom, Bengt. (1981). "Contractual Models of the Labor Market." *American Economic Review* 71, 308–313.

Holstrom, Bengt and Jean Tirole. (1988). "The Theory of the Firm." In R. Schmalensee and R. Willig (eds.), *Handbook of Industrial Organization*. Amsterdam: Elsevier.

Howson, Colin, and Peter Urbach. (1989). *Scientific Reasoning: The Bayesian Approach*. LaSalle, Illinois: Open Court.

Joskow, Paul. (1985). "Vertical Integration and Long-Term Contracts: The Case of Coal-Burning Electric Generating Plants." *Journal of Law, Economics and Organization* 1, 33–88.

———. (1987). Contract Duration and Transactions Specific Investment: Empirical Evidence from Coal Markets." *American Economic Review* 77, 168–185.

———. (1991). "Asset Specificity and the Structure of Vertical Relationships: Empirical Evidence." In O. Williamson and S. Winter (eds.), *The Nature of the Firm*. New York: Oxford University Press.

Kincaid, Harold. (1990). "Assessing Functional Explanations in the Social Sciences." *PSA 1990* 1, 341–355.

———. (1995). *Philosophical Foundations of The Social Sciences*. Cambridge: Cambridge University Press.

Kitcher, Philip. (1987). "Why Not the Best?" In J. Dupre (ed.), *The Latest on the Best: Essays on Evolution and Optimality*. Cambridge: MIT Press.

Lazear. (1979). "Why Is There Mandatory Retirement?" *Journal of Political Economy* 87, 1261–1284.

Leamer, Edward. (1983). "Let's Take the Con Out of Econometrics." *American Economic Review* 73, 31–43.

Manning, Alan. (1989). "Implicity-Contract Theory." In David Sapsford and Zafiris Tzannatos (eds.), *Current Issues in Labor Economics*. New York: St. Martin's Press.

Milgrom, Paul, and John Roberts. (1988). "Economic Theories of the Firm: Past, Present and Future." *Canadian Journal of Economics* 21, 444–458.

———. (1989). "Bargaining Costs, Influence costs, and the Organization of Economic Activity." In J. Alt and K. Shepsle (eds.), *The Foundations of Political Economy*. Cambridge: Harvard University Press.

Nelson, Richard, and Sidney Winter. (1982). *An Evolutionary Theory of Economic Change*. Cambridge, MA: Harvard University Press.

Resnik, Michael. (1987). *Choices: An Introduction to Decision Theory*. Minneapolis: University of Minnesota Press.

Rosen, Sherwin. (1982). "Authority, Control and the Distribution of Earnings." *Bell Journal of Economics* 13, 311–323.

———. (1985). "Implicit Contacts: A Survey." *Journal of Economic Literature* 23, 1144–1175.

———. (1991). "Transaction Costs and Internal Labor Markets." In O. Williamson and S. Winter (eds.), *The Nature of the Firm*. New York: Oxford University Press.

Williamson, Oliver. (1975). *Markets and Hierarchies*. New York: Free Press.

———. (1985). *The Economic Institutions of Capitalism*. New York: Free Press.

———. (1988). "Economics and the Sociology of Organization." In G. Farkas and P. England (eds.), *Industries, Firms and Jobs*. New York; Plenum Press.

Winter, Sidney. (1991). "On Coase, Competence and the Corporation." In O. Williamson and S. Winter (eds.), *The Nature of the Firm*. New York: Oxford University Press.

Marina Bianchi

Comments on Kincaid: Optimality Arguments and the Theory of the Firm

The merit of the new institutionalist theory of the firm, and of transaction cost theory in particular, is that of having rediscovered the organizational and "micro-micro" aspects of the firm's behavior. But an additional merit, too easily over-looked, is that it has emphasized that the main feature of the firm is its flexibility. In transactions costs theory, for example, the presence of asset specificity and limits on rationality require the firm's decisions to be adaptable over time. The firm's internal contract system, which is only partially specified and can be modified along with the new information flow, then allows the firm to adapt toward future, and as yet unknown, events. This flexibility is also what marks the difference between firm and market transactions. Purely market transactions require an ability to specify contracts at every future date, an ability that exceeds simple human powers if the future is uncertain, and human behavior opportunistic and governed by asset specificity. Coase's and Williamson's contractual relation-ships save on the effort and costs of forecasting future contingencies by simply allowing the specificity of contracts to vary. Choice can be deferred until more information and new skills are acquired (see Loasby, 1991: 117–120). The firm represents an organization that, as Simon concisely defines it, economizes on rationality.

Within this different perspective, not only is the firm's behavior not of the sort described by the traditional theory, that of optimizing with perfect foresight, but firms exist just because they need *not* be perfect optimizers. The degree of rationality that is required of the market to efficiently coordinate the allocation of resources, actually makes the market inefficient when compared with the alternative organization of the firm. Paradoxically, firms acquire superior effi-ciency by being only limitedly rational. In an ever-changing world, this lesser requirement on the firm's decision-making processes seems a powerful insight.

A problem with this approach is the following. Is this representation of the firm's behavior simply a new insight, albeit a powerful one, or does it constitute a theory, alternative to the traditional one? In other words, do the new models of firm structures present a set of propositions, which can be testable and rule out alternative and competing explanations?

This is the question addressed by Kincaid's chapter. Starting with his analysis of transactions costs theory, his main point is this. Since the allocative superiority of the firm's over the market's transactions lies in the reduction of transactions costs that firms enable, it is crucial for this representation of the firm's behavior to give an exact specification and measure of the costs that should account for the relative advantage enjoyed by this organizational form. Nor is this all of course. The transactions costs view actually deduces from the efficiency of the firm the reason for its being and persisting. By ascribing functions to the firm the theory also tells us why firms are there. The new approach therefore not only must specify and measure all the possible costs of the firm's efficient structure, but must also identify all the alternative and competing forms of contractual arrangements and show that the firm has been effectively selected against them as the most efficient. Only if it does that may it lay claim to the title of alternative theory.

Kincaid uses a Bayesian procedure of confirmation to show that transactions costs theory fails to provide evidence for all the various steps of its functionalist assumptions. In particular, the possible costs of hierarchical firm structure are left unmeasured and, more important, there is silence about the selective mechanism that should have prized the firm over alternative competing organizational forms. Kincaid extends the same procedure to other functionalist explanations of some relevent features of firm organization (salary and authority differentials, separation of ownership and management, implicit contracts) and shows that here too costs and benefits, and the mechanism picking out the optimal, are left unspecified. The upshot is that we seem to have little basis for our confidence in the claims of the new institutionalist approach to the firm to be a well-specified alternative theory or a reliable one.

It is true that such a heavy burden of proof has never been imposed on traditional theory. However, since the new theory of the firm founds its claim to superior explanatory power just on its ability to capture concrete firm behavior and real-world institutional settings, this stronger requirement is legitimate. If it were otherwise, there would be a strong temptation to regard the new representation as simply tautologous, since an extra cost can always be defined and added (or subtracted) in order to guarantee the firm's greater efficiency as compared with the market. Coase (1991) rejects this sort of criticism. Still, unless costs and mechanisms are specified, as Harold Kincaid strongly emphasizes, the theory rests on unstable ground.

Despite these serious weaknesses in the transactions cost approach, the new theory should not be dismissed as completely ill-founded. First of all, Kincaid says, the multiplication of specific models of firms' institutional solutions help us to identify the variables involved and to select alternative explanations. Second, the vary absence of an overall model of firm structure suggests that "successful explanations of firms are likely to be a piecemeal affair"—locally and case-by-case detailed, as Kincaid appropriately remarks.

I share entirely this line of reasoning, with some qualifications to be expressed in the course of my further discussion. I shall try therefore to complement Kincaid's chapter with a different line of reasoning. In particular, by continuing to focus on the transactions costs version of the literature on the firm, I shall try to "test" this theory not on empirical grounds but on its theoretical value. Through a different route, I will reach rather similar conclusions to those expressed in Kincaid's paper.

Let us imagine that we have in fact measured all the relevant costs necessary to firm organization, explored all the potential alternatives, and detected the process of selection. Can we then say that we have a positive theory of the firm based on transaction costs economy and efficient competitive mechanisms? In other words, does the theory tell us all we want to know about the firm's decision processes?

Williamson's hierarchical and planned firm stuctures are organizationally different from the traditional firm for the reasons we have previously recalled. But the environment in which the firm operates is left unchanged. In Williamson, and even more in the analyses based on property rights, or on principal-agent explanations, the "market" is perfectly competitive, "as if" populated by atomistic firms. No strategic considerations among firms intervene. The same strategic elements that are present in those transactions that allow for opportunistic behavior and that are responsible for the firm's decision to vertically integrate, play no role in the strategic interplay among firms. Interrelations among firms leave the single firm's decision process unaffected.

This is odd. What happens if we try to fill this logical lacuna and introduce strategic elements into the competitive process that firms engage in? Recent analyses, both historical and analytical (Chandler, 1990; Best, 1990; Auerbach, 1988), stress the different nature of competition when firms are of the type described by the new theory. It is not the old theory of monopoly power with its rent-seeking behavior and social inefficiency that Williamson correctly criticizes. It is something different.

For example, Chandler's historical reconstruction of the most successful firms in the United States, England, and Germany, starting from the end of the last century, clearly shows a pattern in the strategic moves of these dominant firms. This pattern is represented by a three-pronged set of investments that provided these firms with economies of scale and scope, with a vertically and horizontally integrated structure and, most important, with a central board of directors that constituted the decisional mind of the new organization. This set of investments was decisive not simply because it precipitately reduced unit costs but also because it gave these new emergent firms a prime-mover advantage over the others. Again, the advantage of these first movers was not based simply on efficiency gains, but on an accumulation of knowledge, skills, and abilities that was much more difficult to acquire, reproduce or imitate. As Chandler (1990: 34) remarks, "While the latecomer's production managers were learning the unique characteristics of what was a new or greatly improved technology . . . the first mover's managers had already worked out the bugs in the production processes. They had already become practiced in assuring prompt delivery. They knew how to meet customers' special needs and to provide demonstrations, consumer credit, installation, and aftersales repair and maintenance." Moreover, such "advantages" made it easy for first movers to nip challengers in the bud to stop their growth before they acquired the facilities and developed the skills needed to become strong competitors. And such advantages could be and often were "used ruthlessly" (Chandler, 1990: 35).

When competition is strategic, Chandler's examples show, firms' competitive weapons consist in their ability constantly to gain a comparative advantage and to alter in their own favor market opportunities. To do this firms have to create the organizational conditions and abilities that allow for new competitive moves to be discovered and explored. The multidivisional and managerial modern firm structure seems an answer to this problem. In this different perspective, therefore, efficiency alone does not suffice anymore to assure the firm's survival. Any new move from a rival firm can outcompete the perfectly efficient firm taken in isolation.

Edith Penrose (1959) saw this point with extraordinary clarity. She pointed to the growth of the firm as its main goal, and she ascribed this growth mainly to the firm's ability to develop and exploit firm-specific skills, information, and knowledge. This pool of firm-based resources and abilities for Penrose is never entirely utilized, is never in equilibrium, and represents a constant source for new opportunities to be developed and explored. The firm's growth, for its part, favors this multiplicity of uses of resources. "In the long run the profitability, survival, and growth of a firm does not depend so much on the efficiency with which it is able to organize the production . . . as it does on the ability of the firm to establish one or more wide and relatively impregnable 'bases' from which it can adapt and extend its operation in an uncertain, changing and competitive world" (Penrose, 1959: 137).

If we allow firms to act strategically and the market to reflect always new organizational changes, it is clear that Williamson's transactions costs analysis does not represent the complexity of the firm's decision processes.

First, decisions activated uniquely by transactions cost economies and market inefficiencies, do not respond to the difficult task of anticipating, preventing and outcompeting rivals' new moves. We need to take into account different organizational abilities. One of these is the firm's ability to create firm-distinctive knowledge and abilities.

Second, if this is true, then contrary to Williamson's analysis, the creation of firm-specific assets is the result, rather than the precondition, of the firm's growth. Kincaid says the same thing when he notices, in reference to Rosen's work, that long-term employees may acquire skills and knowledge that are firm-specific and therefore not easily transferable across firms. Every firm, in a sense, is unique, and on this uniqueness rests its strategic strength.

Third, in the strategic framework, as we have seen, transaction costs, even if perfectly measured, are not enough to account for a firm's successes and evolution. But the reverse is also true. Even if they were enough to fully represent the firm's behavior, unfortunately they *cannot* be measured. Williamson is able to introduce different degrees of allocative efficiency in different institutional settings because he limits his analysis to a static exercise. He compares two, or more, contractual arrangements, such as the market and the firm and intermediate contractual forms, as if they were present, fully developed and always accessible alternatives. But if firms are pushed by their very growth, and by their strategic position, to introduce constantly new opportunities and to modify their decisional constraints, the terms of comparison are much less definite. Better, they are not independent. If a buyer, for example, by deciding to "make" alters the conditions of "buying," and vice versa, the relative transactions costs involved in the two decisions can no longer be identified. Williamson's failure to give a complete account of relative decision costs and mechanisms rests in this case on the fact that these costs are in fact unmeasurable. They depend on decisions that alter the conditions under which they should be measured.

There is a final argument I wish to address. This argument represents a line of defense of the new theory of the firm that, in a certain sense, ousts both criticisms that many decisive costs are left unspecified and unmeasured, and that some others are unmeasurable. The argument is that, even if costs are not or cannot be completely accounted for, we can rely on a mechanism that connects and compares known and unknown costs and that favors the more efficient. The mechanism is the process of selection that invisibly does the job of our conscious reconstruction of costs and benefits and that actively selects through trial and error the more beneficial institution. The result is that we can still be confident of the relative efficiency of the market and the firm, "as if" we had exhausted and calculated all the possible elements of comparison.

To the considerations raised by Kincaid on this topic, I want to add these final observations. Even in a very simplified strategic setting such as those problem situations of social interaction represented as games, that players, by following their individual efficiency rule and by repeating the game, select the most efficient outcome, is not at all guaranteed. Moreover, even when selected, the more efficient solution may not be stable and may require a complex system of incentives to enforce it. Such systems do not simply arise as the result of spontaneous selection. Things change if we allow the players an ability to learn, to recognize and discover errors, and consequently to introduce new moves that change the original problem situation in a possibly more favorable way. The process of evolution cannot be charged with the task of reaching unintendedly what we cannot reconstruct by calculation. For the end point is not known and cannot possibly be judged efficient (or inefficient). As Hayek points out, we can only judge any new situation "from below." In this way we are simply left with a process of evolution that does not guarantee efficiency but represents an ability to adapt, to adjust, and to learn from errors. This conclusion is not far removed from recent experimental analyses of evolutionary processes, where simple ecological models of competitive reproduction show that it is the error maker who can outcompete a perfectly reproducing rival. This happens even if it is better at every instant *not* to make errors. Therefore "evolution does not lead to optimal behavior, because evolution concerns not only 'efficient performance,' but also the constant need for new discoveries" (Allen, 1988: 107). Exactly like the successful competitive firms portrayed by Chandler.

The moral to be drawn from this discussion is this. Efficiency alone is not a good way to explain the organizational specificity of the firm, nor is the association of efficiency with functionalist arguments enough to explain the firm's existence and persistence. Efficiency measures are either left unspecified or are unspecifiable, and the link between selection and efficiency is hard to maintain. This does not lead to the conclusion that efficiency does not matter; it is simply that its field of application has to be exactly specified and accounted for. When all is said and done, though, efficiency cannot be extended to the explanation of the firm structure as a whole. My answer to the original question, then, whether the new theory of the firm, based on its ability to economize on rationality, provides an alternative model of this institutional form, coincides with Kincaid's conclusions. The new theory gives an account of some aspects of the firm's decision processes, but for an account of the complexities of these processes we must rely on specific and piece-by-piece history.

As recognized by the new theory the firm's flexibility is important. What has still to be explored is the flexibility that comes from the firm's ability to learn, to adapt, and to respond strategically to those changes of circumstances that the same firm has caused to come into being.

References

Allen, P. M. (1988). "Evolution, Innovation and Economics." In G. Dosi et al. (eds.), *Technical Change and Economic Theory*. London: Pinter.
Auerbach, P. (1988). *The Economics of Industrial Change*. Oxford: Basil Blackwell.

Best, M. H. (1990). *The New Competition: Institutions of Industrial Restructuring.* Cambridge, MA: Harvard University Press.

Chandler, A. D., Jr. (1990). *Scale and Scope: The Dynamics of Industrial Capitalism.* Cambridge, MA: Belknap Press.

Coase, R. H. (1991). "The Nature of the Firm: Meaning." In O. E. Williamson and S. G. Winter (eds.), *The Nature of the Firm: Origins, Evolution, and Development.* Oxford: Oxford University Press.

Loasby, B. J. (1991). "Efficient Institutions." *Quaderni di Storia dell economia Politica,* IX, 2–3, vol. I, pp. 115–132.

Penrose, E. T. (1959). *The Theory of the Growth of the Firm.* Oxford: Oxford University Press.

8 ECONOMIC MODELS IN DEVELOPMENT ECONOMICS

Daniel Little

This chapter explores and evaluates the use of mathematical models in development economics, particularly computable general equilibrium (CGE) models. Such models have become an increasingly important tool of analysis in development economics. They represent an intriguing and powerful device for making predictions about the behavior of complex national economies in response to a variety of kinds of shocks. They are used to evaluate the probable economic consequences of various policy interventions (such as currency devaluation or an increase in food subsidies), as well as to identify the macroeconomic properties of a complex national economy. Such models permit the economist to run simulations of various macroeconomic scenarios. They thus represent the opportunity to conduct "experiments" within economics.[1] And they provide an important basis for policy advice offered to national governments by development consultants and agencies. My perspective in what follows is the philosophy of social science. I will try to identify the criteria of validity and consistency that ought to govern the evaluation of such models, and to question the degree to which we can attach rational confidence in their results.

Consider a schematic example. Let M be a macroeconomic model of the Mexican economy. M takes a list of exogenous variables x_i and a list of endogenous variables y_i and parameters p_i. The model makes a set of causal assumptions

243

about how the exogenous variables affect the endogenous variables and what the intrasystem relations are. These assumptions are represented in the form of a set of equations defining the behavior of the endogenous variables in terms of the parameters and exogenous variables. The model employs econometric techniques to establish values for exogenous variables and parameters and their trends over time. And it imposes a set of closure rules. The equations are solved for a given set of values for the parameters and exogenous variables; this represents the equilibrium condition for the endogenous variables in this setting. The model can now be used to consider the possible effects of various counterfactual conditions: change in exchange rates, energy price shock, removal of trade barriers, and so on.

The central attraction of such models is their promise of providing a systematic representation of the interrelatedness of a modern competitive market economy. A national economy such as Mexico's is an extremely complex affair, involving dozens of sectors, thousands of industries, millions of workers, a variety of government economic policies, and a fluctuating international economic environment. And it is desirable to have some way of estimating the probable consequences of possible economic shocks—such as an increase in international petroleum prices, a fall in the price of coffee—and possible government policies—such as an increase in food subsidies or expenditure on primary education. Partial equilibrium analysis leads economists to concentrate on a single sector (such as agriculture) and ask some or all of these questions; but because of the interconnections within a complex market economy, partial equilibrium analysis is likely to miss important secondary effects. General equilibrium analysis is intended to capture these effects—for example, the effect on agriculture of rising cost of grain leading to higher wages in industry, leading finally to higher input prices for agriculture.

This chapter is primarily concerned with epistemological issues arising in relation to models of this sort. What standards should be used to assess the validity and reliability of such models? What are the truth conditions of a model? What inferences can be drawn from a valid, reliable model? What is the relation between the model and the underlying economic reality? How do we determine how good a simulation we have in a particular model? How well does it represent the underlying economic causal structure? How reliable are its predictions? These issues invoke current debates concerning scientific realism and empiricist philosophy of social science: to what extent may we judge that a model is true? And to what extent does the acceptability of a model turn on its predictive success?

8.1. What Is a CGE Model?

A computable general equilibrium (CGE) model is a distinctive kind of economic model. It is grounded in the fundamentals of microeconomics: the idea that a competitive market economy reaches an equilibrium of supply and demand, determined by the demand functions and production functions of consumers and firms. It is a *general* equilibrium model, in that it is designed to analyze and explore the intersectoral effects of price changes and demand shifts (unlike, for example, the partial equilibrium analysis familiar from microeconomics). It is an *applied* model (rather than a purely theoretical model), in two respects: (1) it is based on observed economic data for a particular national economy, and (2) it is designed to simulate the behavior of the modeled economy, permitting predictions and counterfactuals about that particular economy. It is a *simulation* model: in contrast to the simple stylized models often constructed to investigate the properties of market systems, CGE models are intended to capture the empirical details and specific economic characteristics of a given economy, with the goal of simulating the response of this economy to a variety of hypothetical shocks and policy interventions.[2] Though CGE models make use of econometric analysis, they are not econometric models: they are not primarily designed to discern causal regularities through statistical analysis of time-series data and are instead based on specific theoretical hypotheses about the workings of a market system (Hausman, 1992; Weintraub, 1979; Rosenberg, 1992). And finally, though CGE models are based on microeconomic mechanisms, they are often employed to probe traditional *macro*economic problems: aggregate effects of taxation, tariffs, and trade; distribution of income; levels of savings and employment; and the causes and effects of price inflation. CGE models thus bridge micro- and macroeconomics. These models are generally multisectoral representations of the modeled economy. They use microeconomic laws—essentially, a representation of the demand and supply systems, with a computed equilibrium state— to simulate a whole economic system. The model thus depends on microeconomic assumptions while leading to macroeconomic analysis and inferences.[3]

Conceptually a CGE model is fairly simple. An economy is assumed to be an equilibrium system in which various quantities affect other through competitive market mechanisms. Economic properties are the effect of large numbers of rational consumers and producers interacting through a system of prices. The level of income, preferences, and prices jointly determine aggregate demand; while the price of inputs and demand for output determines the profitability (and therefore quantity of output) for each firm and sector. The system is subject to constraints and conditions. The system reaches equilibrium through a process of adjustments by consumers and producers to the current price structure.

The model is designed to capture the equilibrium conditions and the mechanisms of adjustment for the system as a whole. Demand is disaggregated into a set of income groups; each group is assumed to have a homogenous demand and savings function. Production is disaggregated into a number of sectors; each sector is assumed to have a homogeneous production function and (usually) fixed coefficients of production. The model takes the form of a system of equations and parameters designed to represent the equilibrium conditions of a market economy: the settings of prices and quantities of product that balance supply and demand given an accounting of all sources of demand (private, export, and government). If there are as many equations as endogenous variables then it is possible to solve for one (or more) set of values for endogenous variables that satisfy the equilibrium conditions.

The mathematics involved in solving a large set of independent equations are involved but conceptually simple. The model consists of a set of equations in n unknowns (endogenous variables), along with m constants and parameters (exogenous variables). If there are sufficiently many independent equations (n) there may be one or more solutions to the equations: a setting for all n variables that satisfy the equations.[4] The equations can be solved algebraically or numerically. There are now computer programs commonly available that will arrive at numerical solutions to large systems of equations. Numerical programs use various successive approximation algorithms (such as the Newton method, the Levenberg-Marquardt method, or the MINPACK algorithms developed by the Argonne National Laboratory) that involve an initial "guess" set of values for the variables, and then successive modification of the variables until a solution is found to a stipulated level of tolerance. There are various obstacles to finding a solution: the algorithm may get trapped in a local maximum, or the algorithm may fail to converge to the specified level of tolerance within a reasonable number of iterations. But these problems do not raise significant conceptual issues. It is the economics that poses the difficulties.[5]

The equations of a CGE model fall into two general categories: accounting identities representing the requirement that prices must be such that supply equals demand, investment must equal savings, and so forth; and hypotheses derived from economic theory representing the model-builder's assumptions about the variables that adjust to bring the system into equilibrium. The latter represent the "closure rules" invoked by the model and may reflect a variety of economic hypotheses—classical, neoclassical, or structuralist economic theory. A medium-sized model may involve several hundred equations, variables, and parameters —an algebraic system vastly too large to solve by hand. However, it is now possible for desktop computers to solve models employing several hundred equations in a reasonable period of time. Whereas first-generation general equilibrium theory was forced to rely on complex algebraic manipulation of small linear systems of equations, it is now possible to compute numerical solutions for large models including both linear and nonlinear equations. It is possible to consider such questions as these: How would a decrease in the food subsidy in Egypt in the 1970s have affected employment and government deficits? How will a 10 percent increase in the cost of imported oil affect Argentina's level of employment? How would currency devaluation affect the nutritional status of Nicaragua's poor?

8.1.1. Baseline Data

Any applied model must incorporate a body of empirical data characterizing the state of the economy at a given time (the base solution of the model). The model then permits the analyst to run the economy forward in time according to different assumptions about the macroeconomic or policy environment. Base-year information is generally represented in the form of a social accounting matrix (SAM).[6] This is a multisectoral snapshot of the state of the economy at a point in time, indicating the flows of products and labor between sectors and into consumption and investment. The rows of the table represent deliveries of commodities or sources of income; the columns are uses of commodities or incomes. Table 8.1 provides a simple example of a three-sector SAM. In theory the SAM ought to reflect all flows of product and income through the economy. A SAM incorporates the input-output relations familiar from Leontief and Sraffa (the intersection of columns 1–3 with rows 1–3 in Table 8.1); data here allow computation of input-output coefficients for each sector (that is, the value of product from sector i used in the production of one dollar of product of sector k; last four lines of Table 8.1). A SAM can also represent information concerning the distribution of income across income categories, depending on the level of disaggregation of income represented in the table (peasant, worker, capitalist; columns 4–6 in Table 8.1). A SAM is constructed subject to strict rules of accounting consistency. Totals of corresponding rows and columns must be equal, and all values must be computed in constant prices. The information in a SAM is derived from a number of sources: input-output tables for sectors or industries; national accounts; and household surveys on patterns of consumer spending.[7]

The equations in a CGE model are intended to specify the functional relationships that obtain between the economic quantities identified in the SAM. These equations may be broken down into blocks representing different sorts of economic constraints or processes. First, we need a set of equations representing sectoral demand-supply balances. Imports and domestic production must equal domestic demand plus exports. Second, there will be a set of equations describing price formation of all goods. Different price rules may be employed, but a common form is the markup pricing rule, in which the price of a good is determined by the cost of all inputs plus a fixed markup rate; another common approach is "flex-price" determination (Taylor, 1979). Third, the model must represent a set of income distribution rules for different income groups. Fourth, we need equations defining expenditures by different social groups, breaking down expenditure into savings and consumption (frequently using the assumptions of the "linear expenditure system"). Fifth, since international trade is generally present in modern national economies we need to represent exchange rates, tariffs, and trade balances. Sixth, since government economic activity is

Table 8.1. A social accounting matrix: three sectors and three income groups

	Agriculture	Industry	Energy	Total	Farmers	Workers	Capital	Total	Government Exports	Exports	Invest	Total
Agriculture	13,587	84,181	8	97,775	7,561	23,876	27,715	59,152	137	3,199	11,122	171,385
Industry	26,497	441,198	10,777	478,473	33,571	309,272	351,521	694,363	70,657	29,398	221,412	1,494,303
Energy	6,815	29,956	22,245	59,016	406	4,064	6,223	10,694	1,732	6,183	796	78,420
Total	46,899	555,335	33,030	635,264	41,538	337,213	385,459	764,209	72,525	38,780	233,330	1,744,107
Farmers	41,203	0	0	41,203								41,203
Workers	31,338	326,465	14,324	372,127					40,264			412,391
Capital	49,987	514,946	0	564,933								564,933
Total	122,529	841,410	14,324	978,263					40,264			1,018,527
Net taxes	624	54,303	26,431	81,358	0	19,679	28,260	47,940				129,298
Imports	1,333	43,256	4,635	49,223	-335	-3,354	-4,595	-8,284	536	16,260	27,287	85,021
Savings					0	58,854	155,809	214,663	15,972	29,982	260,617	260,617
Total	171,385	1,494,304	78,420	1,744,108	41,202	412,391	564,933	1,018,527	129,298	85,021	260,617	3,237,570
Production coefficient	0.07928	0.05633	0.00010									
	0.15461	0.29525	0.13743									
	0.03976	0.02005	0.28366									
Labor coefficient	0.1829	0.2185	0.1827									

Source: Derived from Lustig and Taylor (1990: table 2.1).

Table 8.2. Blocks of equations in typical CGE model

I	Sectoral demand-supply balances
II	Price formation of all goods
III	Income generation rules for different groups
IV	Expenditures by different social groups (consumption and savings rates)
V	Exchange rates, tariffs, balance of payments
VI	Government revenues and expenditures
VII	Sectoral adjustment rules
VIII	Savings-investment balance

Table 8.3. Examples of functional forms for demand and production

Cobb-Douglas production function	$Q(K, L) = a* K^{\alpha} *L^{\beta}$
CES production function	$Q(K, L) = \gamma* (\delta* K^{-\rho} + (1 - \delta)* L^{-\rho})^{-\frac{1}{\rho}}$
Linear expenditure system	$c_{ij} = \theta_{ij} + \dfrac{\mu_{ij}}{P_i} \cdot \left(E_j - \sum_{k=1}^{3}(P_i \cdot \theta_{kj}) \right)$

almost always significant it is necessary to represent government revenues and expenditures. Seventh, the model needs to specify the rules according to which sectors within the economy are postulated to adjust to changes in supply and demand, changes in exchange rates, inflation, and so on. These are the closure rules of the model; they represent substantive causal hypotheses about how some variables affect others. Finally, the model needs to sum up savings flows and investment. Table 8.2 summarizes these points.

Central to the equilibrium analysis are the functions representing demand and supply. It is common to treat consumer and producer optimization processes separately; this permits separate treatment of demand and supply conditions, which can then be aggregated into a general equilibrium result (Mansur and Whalley, 1984: 80). The modeler is forced to make somewhat arbitrary decisions in choosing a functional form in which to represent demand and production. It is common to use either Cobb-Douglas functions or constant elasticity of substitution (CES) functions to represent utilities (demand) and cost (production). And consumer demand is often represented in the form of a linear expenditure system (see Table 8.3 for examples of each).

These equations are formulated in terms of a large number of economic quantities—prices, production levels, income, wages, investment, and so forth. These quantities can be broken down into *variables* and *parameters*. Variables are the economic quantities whose behavior is either taken to be determined by the equations of the model (endogenous) or to be determined outside the modeled system (exogenous). Parameters (such as elasticities, coefficients, and exponents) are quantities that determine the particular "shape" of the economic processes being modeled through the functions. If there are as many equations as independent variables, then there may be at least one solution of the system of equations for any given set of assignments to the parameters. Table 8.4 represents the relation between parameters, model, and variables; we can look at the model as a superfunction that maps settings of the parameters onto settings of the variables that satisfy the model equations given the parameters. It must be true that the solution values of the model for base-year parameter settings satisfy the SAM for the base year.

Once the functional form is chosen for production and demand functions, the modeler must arrive at a reasonable assignment of values to parameters. Roughly, this means setting the slopes, curvature, and intercepts of the respective functions so as to reproduce the SAM. Input-output coefficients, savings rates, tariffs, taxation rates, exports, and exchange rates are examples of some of the parameters for which it is necessary to provide values. Some of these are set by government policy—tariffs, taxation rates, and exchange rates. Others are intrinsic features of the economy at a given time—input-output coefficients or savings rates. The SAM permits computation of most of these parameters, while household surveys or other empirical sources must be consulted for others (for example, the level of subsistence consumption).

There are two basic approaches to the problem of estimating parameters: calibration and stochastic measurement. The first approach involves calibrating the model to base-year data. Here the basic procedure is to assume that the economy is in equilibrium in the base year: substitute base-year observations for the endogenous variables into the equations, and solve for the parameters. Mansur and Whalley point out, however, that the effectiveness of this procedure depends on the functional form chosen for the production and demand functions. Cobb-Douglas functions imply a unique set of parameters under this procedure; whereas CES functions require stipulation (or independent measurement) of estimates of elasticities of substitution in order to arrive at a unique set of parameters. And since the results of the model are highly sensitive to assignments of elasticities, an important possible source of model invalidity occurs at this point.

The second possible approach for setting the parameters of the model is to provide an independent econometric measurement of the needed parameters. The econometric approach requires that we use all available data to arrive at statistical estimates of parameters. On this approach the measurement of parameters requires time-series data—ideally, a time series of SAMs for the economy in question.[8]

The solution of the model describes the setting of the central economic quantities that represent the equilibrium condition for the economy, given the values

Table 8.4. Logic of simulation

Parameters p_i Exogenous variables x_i	=>	Model equations	=>	Solution setting of variables y_i

of the parameters and exogenous variables (Table 8.4). These quantities include, first, quantity and price information for each sector. These variables in turn permit calculation of income, consumption, and savings for each income group; government revenue, expenditure, and savings; and foreign expenditure, savings, and trade balance.

8.1.2. Substantive Economic Assumptions

A model of any process is only as good as the underlying theory on which it is based, and economic models are no exception. The principles that underlie economic models are of two broad sorts. First, there are a host of accounting identities that any economy in equilibrium must satisfy: supply must equal demand, savings must equal investment, income must equal consumption plus investment, and output of consumption-goods industries must equal domestic consumption plus exports. These identities are formally represented in the social accounting matrix described above.

Second, an economic model must embody assumptions about economic causation: which economic variables exert primacy within an economic system, and what is the functional form of their influence? Most broadly, assumptions at this level determine how equilibrium is restored after a shock and represent the economist's assumptions about dynamic processes in the short run and medium run. Assumptions at this level are described as the "closure rules" of the model, and they are critical to the behavior of the model. Adopting different closure rules will lead to substantial differences in the behavior of the model.

There are a number of different sets of economic assumptions that can serve as closure rules. Classical models take the wage and the rate of profit as endogenous. Neoclassical models take the production function as the starting point and determine prices, wages, and profits as the result of profit maximizing within a freely competitive market. Structuralist models take the institutional context of the economy as a constraining variable; they build into their models assumptions about the functional distribution of income.

Intermediate between these two levels of assumptions are the mathematics of input-output relations. Assume that there are n sectors of production and that various sectors use products of other sectors as intermediate goods; what level of production is required in each sector to satisfy intermediate and final demand? And what set of commodity prices represents an equilibrium in which supply and demand will be equal? It is common to assume linear production functions with fixed coefficients of production. Under these assumptions, it is possible to solve the quantity and price problem formulated above using simple matrix algebra. This construction takes the wage, the rate of profit (markup rate), and the level of final demand, and computes a price vector and a quantity vector for the n sectors.[9]

8.1.3. Static Versus Dynamic Simulations

So far we have considered a process of modeling that permits us to extrapolate current economic data forward one period on various counterfactual assumptions. It establishes the equilibrium conditions that correspond to a new setting of some of the exogenous variables. This is a static simulation, since it does not build in a representation of the processes of change that the economy is experiencing. It is possible to introduce dynamic considerations by performing a series of iterations of the model, updating exogenous variables (parameters) on the basis of a hypothesis about their behavior over time. For example, population change and productivity increase can be built into a dynamic simulation by indexing parameter values over time. It is possible to use econometric techniques to arrive at an estimate of the rate of increase in factor productivity over time; this regression can then be used to determine parameter values for factor productivity over a number of iterations. Likewise, we may want to build into a dynamic simulation a hypothesis about the direction of change of the real wage; this hypothesis may be based on extraeconomic factors such as the political strength of unions within given society. Chenery, Lewis, de Melo, and Robinson (1986a: 315) describe the dynamic features of their model in these terms: "Intertemporal linkage equations update exogenous variables and parameters that are dependent on policy choices and specify cumulative dynamic processes such as factor accumulation and productivity growth. The intertemporal equations provide all exogenous variables needed for the next period (four years later) by the CGE model, which is then solved for a new equilibrium." These intertemporal equations describe the behavior of such factors as labor force growth, capital stock growth, productivity growth, world market trends, and trends in savings rates—variables whose behavior is assumed to be independent of the economic processes modeled by the CGE simulation itself. It should be noted that the intertemporal equations are exterior to the CGE model itself; they represent an effort to model change in exogenous variables over time, which then serve as input to the CGE model for its static equilibrium. In the Chenery

Table 8.5. Lustig-Taylor model of Mexican food consumption policies

I	Prices for eight sectors	Flex prices for agriculture; markup pricing for nonagricultural sectors
II	Sectoral balances for eight sectors	
III	Consumer demand	Linear expenditure system
IV	Total income by income group	Income generation rules for each group
V	Total expenditure by income group	Income discounted by savings and taxation
VI	Final prices	Base prices plus commerce margin,
VII	Consumption of commerce	subsidies
VIII	Savings (government, foreign, private)	
IX	Investment-savings balance	

model, the simulation is run over four periods of five years each. The equilibrium condition for year 0 is solved; the exogenous variables are then updated for year 5 and the equilibrium condition is solved; and so forth through year 20.

CGE models are particularly common in development economics, and this discipline is centrally concerned with processes of change over time: structural transformation, technological change, population growth, capital formation, growth in educational resources, and economic growth. So it is essential to be able to provide dynamic analysis within the CGE framework. However, many of these dynamic processes are *not* purely economic; they depend on institutional change, political power, and other noneconomic factors.

8.1.4. A Sample Simulation

We are now ready to consider a sample simulation. Nora Lustig and Lance Taylor offer a CGE model to examine the effects of various policy interventions in Mexico aimed at improving nutritional status of the poor (Lustig and Taylor, 1990). Lustig and Taylor aim to compare the effects of (1) a direct income transfer to target groups, (2) a targeted price subsidy, and (3) a general price subsidy. They construct a social accounting matrix for the Mexican economy based on 1975 data (a simplified version of which is provided in Table 8.1 above). Their model represents eight domestic sectors (corn and beans, other agriculture, petroleum, fertilizers, food processing, industry, services, and commerce) and seven income groups (peasants, agricultural workers, agricultural capitalists, urban workers, urban capitalists, merchants, and urban marginals). The model is summarized in Table 8.5. The model contains ninety-two equations, but it can

Table 8.6. Simulation results

	δ Real Incomes (Peasants, Agricultural Workers, and Urban Marginals)	δ Trade Deficit	δ Government Savings
Income transfer	12.3%	16.6%	−59.7%
Targeted price subsidy	5.6	9.5	−30.6
General price subsidy	11.4	82.3	−269.6

be broken into a series of independent blocks. Given fixed production coeffi-cients and exogenous markup rates, the price equations can be solved independ-ently of quantity information. Consumer demand depends on prices and income; so blocks II through VII must be solved simultaneously. Closure is established through adjustment of activity levels, the trade gap, and income distribution to bring savings and investment into balance. The model is calibrated to reproduce the SAM data as its base solution. Lustig and Taylor use the model to run three policy experiments: an income transfer to peasants and agricultural workers, a targeted price subsidy, and a general price subsidy. The central results are de-scribed in Table 8.6; in general, each policy has the effect of increasing incomes flowing to the poor, but at the expense of increasing trade and government budget deficits. The general price subsidy leads to an explosion in trade and budget deficits and is practically infeasible. The targeted price subsidy is least costly in terms of fiscal and trade balance but has only about half the effect on incomes to the poor that are generated by direct income transfer.

8.2. Criteria of Adequacy

8.2.1. Evaluation

Let us turn to the problem of evaluating a CGE model. What standards of adequacy should be used to assess CGE models? And what forms of inference does this technique permit? Suppose we are presented with a CGE model of the Mexican economy that has been designed to evaluate the probable effects of a targeted food-price subsidy. We are told, let us suppose, that the model predicts that (1) income to the poor will increase by 5.6 percent over what it would have been absent subsidies; (2) the trade deficit will increase 9.5 percent; and (3) government savings will fall by 30.6 percent. We are to imagine ourselves in the position of policy maker with the power to decide whether or not to implement this subsidy. What sorts of questions should we entertain about this line of argument?

First, there is the straightforward policy question. If we take the simulation as an accurate representation of the economic reality confronting us—that is, we accept that the contemplated action will have these computed economic effects—then it is a question of social policy to determine whether the benefits of the policy outweigh the costs (improved nutrition for the poor versus higher trade and budget deficits). And here various lines of argument and analysis are available; it might be argued, for example, that the costs are limited to the short run and that the benefits of improved nutrition today will lead to an eventual improvement in workers' productivity that more than offsets these costs. Or it might be held that the resulting trade and budget deficits will so harm future growth as to worsen the welfare of the poor in the next period of time.

The harder question, however, is how we should determine whether the model can be relied on in the first place: that is, whether it is likely that the predicted effects will in fact occur if the policy is adopted. This is a general question of scientific rationality; the model, underlying data, associated computations, and predicted outcome constitute a complex scientific hypothesis that needs to be evaluated on rational grounds. How much confidence can we rationally have in the predictions of the model, given the details of construction and data-gathering on which these rest? Under what circumstances may we conclude that the model provides a good approximation to the workings of the existing economy?

8.2.2. What Sorts of Knowledge do CGE Models Purport to Offer?

Before we can decide what sorts of criteria ought to be used to evaluate a CGE model, we need a clearer idea of the purpose of such models. We have a start on answering this question in the fact that CGE models are *applied* models: they are designed to analyze the short-term and medium-term workings of specific empirically given economies. Moreover, they are intimately associated with policy concerns; they are commonly used to assess the probable consequences of alternative economic policies (such as taxation, tariffs, interest rates, and currency devaluation). These features mean that the empirical standards to be applied to CGE models are stringent; the models are intended to shed quantitative light on existing economies, so it is critical that the results of the model should approximate the behavior of the actual economy being modeled. And finally, CGE models are concerned with causal relations within a competitive market economy. Holding a vast range of institutional and situational details fixed, these models generally ask questions of the form: what would be the net effects of policy action A on economic variables X, Y, and Z? So CGE models are designed to provide *causal* knowledge about existing economic systems. This knowledge may take the form of a *prediction*: If Brazil's national bank devalues its currency by 6 percent, its coffee exports will increase by 5 percent. Or it may take the form of a *counterfactual* inquiry: What would have happened if (contrary to fact) such and so had occurred? Seen in this light, CGE models fit a familiar type of causal analysis: an effort to work out particular cause-effect relations based on a theory of the underlying general mechanisms. The model applies a general theory of the causal properties of a given kind of system (S) to a particular case (s). The theory is general equilibrium theory, and the causal properties in question are the probable effects on a new economic equilibrium induced by a given set of transformations to price, supply, or demand conditions.

How much precision is expected of CGE results? In the Lustig-Taylor model discussed above, the simulation results are reported to two decimal points; thus the three policy measures lead to government savings changes of −59.70 percent, −30.62 percent, and −269.58 percent (Lustig and Taylor, 1990: table 2.3). In their model of the aggregate effects of three different development strategies Chenery et al. (1986a: table 11.3) provide estimates of GDP growth rate: import substitution (5.7 percent), balanced strategy (6.2 percent), and export promotion (6.5 percent). The consumer of such models needs to exercise a skeptical eye, however, at such precision. Are these advanced as realistic estimates of probable results? Or are they notional estimates, indicating only order-of-finish comparisons between policies? The latter seems more plausible than the former; but this means that the actual prediction authorized by the model is that policy X will lead to a higher rate of growth than policy Y.[10]

In some cases CGE models appear to be designed for analytical rather than predictive purposes. In this kind of application the goal is to trace out the causal consequences of various strategies and shocks at a theoretical level. Thus Chenery et al. (1986a: 311–312) write, "We are interested in creating a stylized version of Korea for the purpose of comparative analysis, not in analyzing the strategic choices available to Korea in 1963."

8.2.3. Correspondence, Abstraction, and Realism

Science is generally concerned with two central semantic features of theories: truth of theoretical hypotheses and reliability of observational predictions.[11] Truth involves a correspondence between hypothesis and the world; while predictions involve statements about the future behavior of a real system. Science is also concerned with epistemic values: warrant and justification. The warrant of a hypothesis is a measure of the degree to which available evidence permits us to conclude that the hypothesis is approximately true. A hypothesis may be true but unwarranted (that is, we may not have adequate evidence available to permit confidence in the truth of the hypothesis). Likewise, however, a hypothesis may be false but warranted (that is, available evidence may make the hypothesis highly credible, while it is in fact false). And every science possesses a set of standards of hypothesis evaluation on the basis of which practitioners assess the credibility of their theories—for example, testability, success in prediction, inter-theoretical support, simplicity, and the like.[12]

The central concern of this article is the epistemology of economic models. But what does this amount to? The preceding suggests that there are several questions that fall within the domain of epistemology in this context. First, we can ask whether the model is a good approximation of the underlying economic reality—that is, the approximate truth of the model. Likewise, we can ask whether the model gives rise to true predictions about the future behavior of the underlying economic reality (subject to the time frame of the analysis). Each of these questions falls on the side of the truth value of the model. Another set of questions concerns the warrant of the model: the strength of the evidence and theoretical grounds available to us on the basis of which we assign a degree of credibility to the model: Does available evidence give us reason to believe that the model is approximately true, and does available evidence give us reason to expect that the model's predictions are likely to be true? These questions are centrally epistemic; answers to them constitute the basis of our scientific confidence in the truth of the model and its predictions.

It is important to note that the question of the approximate truth of the model is separate from that of the approximate truth of its predictions. It is possible that the model is approximately true but its predictions are not. This might be the case because the *ceteris paribus* conditions are not satisfied or because low precision of estimates for exogenous variables and parameters leads to indeterminate predictive consequences. Therefore it is possible that the warrant attaching to the approximate truth of the model and the reliability of its predictions may be different. It may be that we have good reason to believe that the model is a good approximation of the underlying economic reality, while at the same time we have little reason to rely on its predictions about the future behavior of the system. The warrant of the model is high on this account, while the warrant of its predictions is low.

Let us look more closely at the semantic properties of economic models: the relation between a model M and the underlying economic reality S. Note, to begin, that the relation between analysis and the economic reality is more complex than it first appears. Models are formulated on the basis of economic theory. The theory itself bears a referential relation to the world. That is, it is appropriate to ask whether general equilibrium theory is a true characterization of the workings of competitive market systems. And it is appropriate to assess the degree of warrant that we can attach to the general theory. So truth and warrant pertain to the general theory. Next we have the model of a particular economy. The model is designed to correspond to the underlying economic reality of the particular economy. Likewise, it is designed to implement the general theory, in application to the particular case. So in the case of the model we have several questions to ask—first, with respect to its adequacy as an implementation of the theory, and second, with respect to its correspondence to the underlying economic reality. Again, there are several distinct epistemic possibilities. We may attach high warrant to both the theory and the model, or we may have confidence in the theory but not the model. (The third possibility— confidence in the model but not the underlying theory—is the instrumentalist's position. But for reasons spelled out below, I find this implausible.)

Whatever position we arrive at concerning the possible truth or falsity of a given economic model, it is plain that this cannot be understood as literal descriptive truth.[13] Economic models are not offered as full and detailed representations of the underlying economic reality. For a model unavoidably involves abstraction, in at least two ways. First, the model deliberately ignores some empirical characteristics and causal processes of the underlying economic reality. Just as a Newtonian model of the ballistics of projectiles ignores air resistance in order to focus on gravitational forces and the initial momentum of the projectile, so an economic model ignores differences in consumption behavior among members of functional defined income groups. Likewise, a model may abstract from regional or sectional differences in prices or wage rates within a national economy.

The second form of abstraction is more distinctive of economic analysis. General equilibrium theory represents the general hypothesis underlying CGE models. But the application of the theory to a particular economy or policy problem is not straightforward. There is no canonical mode of representing the central economic quantities and processes. Thus utility functions can be represented in a variety of ways, and likewise with consumption and production functions. (As we saw above, the linear expenditure system is commonly used in CGE models to represent consumer demand, in large part because this is a highly tractable formulation. But there are alternative nonequivalent formulations available.) So a given model represents one out of many different possible ways of implementing the general theory; and in order to arrive at an overall judgment of the credibility of the model we need to assess the adequacy of its particular implementation of supply, demand, savings behavior, and the like.

It follows from this observation that the specifics of a given model are not deductively entailed by the economic theory that underlies it. Different model builders can have equal commitment to the general theory, while providing very different formulations of the central economic processes (such as utility functions, production functions, and demand functions). And the resulting models may have significantly different properties, giving rise to different predictions about the behavior of the economic system in question.

Another epistemically significant feature of economic models is the difficulty of isolating causal factors in real social or economic systems. Models (and economic theories as well, for that matter) are generally subject to *ceteris paribus* conditions. Predictions and counterfactual assertions are advanced conditioned by the assumption that no other exogenous causal factors intervene; that is, the assertive content of the model is that the economic processes under analysis will unfold in the described manner absent intervening causal factors. But if there are intervening causal factors, then the overall behavior of the system may be indeterminate. In some cases it is possible to specify particularly salient interfering causal factors (such as political instability). But it is often necessary to incorporate open-ended *ceteris paribus* conditions as well.

Finally, economic theories and models unavoidably make simplifying or idealizing assumptions about the populations, properties, and processes that they describe. Consumers are represented as possessing consistent and complete preference rankings, firms are represented as making optimizing choices of products and technologies, product markets are assumed to function perfectly, and so on. Suppose that our CGE model makes the assumption that the coefficients of production are constant. This implies that producers do not alter production technologies in the face of different price schedules for inputs. This assumption abstracts from producers' substitution behavior. But the model builder may argue that this is a reasonable approximation in a static model; whatever substitutions occur from one period to the next will be small and will have little effect on aggregate input-output relations.

Given, then, that models abstract from reality, in what sense does it make sense to ask whether a model is true? We must distinguish between truth and completeness, to start with. To say that a description of a system is true is not to say that it is a complete description. (A complete description provides a specification of the value of all state variables for the system—that is, all variables that have a causal role in the functioning of the system.) The fact that models are abstractive demonstrates only that they are incomplete, not that they are false. A description of a hockey puck's trajectory on the ice that assumes a frictionless surface is a true account of some of the causal factors at work: the Newtonian mechanics of the system. The assumption that the surface of the ice is frictionless is false; but in this particular system the overall behavior of the system (with friction) is sufficiently close to the abstract model (because frictional forces are small relative to other forces affecting the puck). In this case, then, we can say two things: first, the Newtonian model is exactly true as a description of the forces it directly represents, and second, it is approximately true as a description of the system as a whole (because the forces it ignores are small).

Consider, then, this account of the truth conditions of theories and models. An economic theory is true if and only if

1. The causal processes the theory identifies are actually at work in the real system, and
2. The real processes have approximately the causal properties postulated by the theory.

A model is said to be approximately true if and only if

3. Its characterization of the central economic processes is approximately true, and
4. The causal processes it ignores have little effect within the scope of analysis of the model.

This account takes a strongly realist position on economic theory, in that it characterizes truth in terms of correspondence to unobservable entities, processes, or properties.[14] The presumption here is that social systems generally— and economic systems in particular—have objective unobservable characteristics which it is the task of social science theory to identify. The realist position is commonly challenged by some economists, however. Milton Friedman's (1953) famous argument for an instrumentalist interpretation of economic theory is highly unconvincing in this context.[15] The instrumentalist position maintains that it is a mistake to understand theories as referring to real unobservable entities. Instead, theories are simply ways of systematizing observable characteristics of the phenomena under study; the only purpose of scientific theory is to serve as an instrument for prediction. Along these lines, Friedman argues that the realism of economic premises is irrelevant to the warrant of an economic theory; all that matters is the overall predictive success of the theory. But when we consider general equilibrium models, it is clear that a central part of the overall warrant of the models is the confidence that we have in the approximate truth of general equilibrium theory. If we were to doubt this theory, then we would have no reason whatsoever to rely on CGE models. The instrumentalist approach to the interpretation of economic theory, then, is highly unpersuasive as an interpretation of the epistemic standing of economic models. Instead, the realist position appears to be inescapable: we are forced to treat general equilibrium theory as a substantive empirical hypothesis about the real workings of competitive market systems, and our confidence in general equilibrium models is limited by our confidence in the approximate truth of the general equilibrium theory.

8.2.4. Warrant of Economic Models

Turn now to the problem of warrant: what sorts of evidence and theoretical arguments are available to permit us to assess the credibility of a given economic model? I approach this problem from two points of view: first, the antecedent warrant of a given model, and second, the a posteriori warrant of the model. The antecedent warrant of the model is a function of our assessment of its overall adequacy as an implementation of what we know about the causal processes that are being modeled, including particularly the relevant portions of economic theory. The a posteriori warrant of the model is our evaluation of the credibility of the model on the basis of a comparison between its results and relevant empirical data.

The general problem of the antecedent credibility of an economic model can be broken down into more specific questions concerning the validity, comprehensiveness, robustness, reliability, and autonomy of the model. I define these concepts in the following terms.

- *Validity* is a measure of the degree to which the assumptions employed in the construction of the model are thought to correspond to the real processes underlying the phenomena represented by the model.
- *Comprehensiveness* is the degree to which the model is thought to succeed in capturing the major causal factors that influence the features of the behavior of the system in which we are interested.
- *Robustness* is a measure of the degree to which the results of the model persist under small perturbations in the settings of parameters, formulation of equations, and so on.
- *Autonomy* refers to the stability of the model's results in face of variation of contextual factors.
- *Reliability* is a measure of the degree of confidence we can have in the data employed in setting the values of the parameters.

These are epistemic features of models that can be investigated more or less independently and prior to examination of the empirical success or failure of the predictions of the model.

Let us look more closely at these standards of adequacy. The discussion of realism above suggests that we may attempt to validate the model deductively, by examining each of the assumptions underlying construction of the model for its plausibility or realism. (This resembles Mill's "deductive method" of theory evaluation. See Hausman, 1981, for a discussion.) Economists are highly confident in the underlying general equilibrium theory. The theory is incomplete—or, in Daniel Hausman's (1992) language, inexact—in that economic outcomes are not wholly determined by purely economic forces. But within its scope economists are confident that the theory identifies the main causal processes: an equilibration of supply and demand through market-determined prices.

Validity can be assessed through direct inspection of the substantive economic assumptions of the model: the formulation of consumer and firm behavior, the representation of production and consumption functions, the closure rules, and the like. To the extent that the particular formulation embodied in the model is supported by accepted economic theory, the validity of the model is enhanced. On the other hand, if particular formulations appear to be ad hoc (introduced, perhaps, to make the problem more tractable), the validity of the model is reduced. If, for example, the model assumes linear demand functions and we judge that this is a highly unrealistic assumption about the real underlying demand functions, then we will have less confidence in the predictive results of the model.

Unfortunately, there can be no fixed standard of evaluation concerning the validity of a model. All models make simplifying and idealizing assumptions; so to that extent they deviate from literal realism. And the question of whether a given idealization is felicitous or not cannot always be resolved on antecedent theoretical grounds; instead, it is necessary to look at the overall empirical adequacy of the model. The adequacy of the assumption of fixed coefficients of production cannot be assessed a priori; in some contexts and for some purposes it is a reasonable approximation of the economic reality, while in other cases it introduces unacceptable distortion of the actual economic processes (when input substitution is extensive). What can be said concerning the validity of a model's assumptions is rather minimal but not entirely vacuous. The assumptions should be consistent with existing economic theory; they should be reasonable and motivated formulations of background economic principles; and they should be implemented in a mathematically acceptable fashion.

Comprehensiveness too is a weak constraint on economic models. It is plain that all economic theories and models disregard some causal factors in order to isolate the workings of specific economic mechanisms; moreover, there will always be economic forces that have not been represented within the model. So judgment of the comprehensiveness of a model depends on a qualitative assessment of the relative importance of various economic and noneconomic factors in the particular system under analysis. If a given factor seems to be economically important (for example, input substitution) but unrepresented within the model, then the model loses points on comprehensiveness.[16]

Robustness can be directly assessed through a technique widely used by economists, sensitivity analysis. The model is run a large number of times, varying the values assigned to parameters (reflecting the range of uncertainty in estimates or observations). If the model continues to have qualitatively similar findings, it is said to be robust. If solutions vary wildly under small perturbations of the parameter settings, the model is rightly thought to be a poor indicator of the underlying economic mechanisms.

Autonomy is the theoretical equivalent of robustness. It is a measure of the stability of the model under changes of assumptions about the causal background of the system. If the model's results are highly sensitive to changes in the environment within which the modeled processes take place, then we should be suspicious of the results of the model.

Assessment of reliability is also somewhat more straightforward than comprehensiveness and validity. The empirical data used to set parameters and exogenous variables have been gathered through specific well-understood procedures, and it is mandatory that we give some account of the precision of the resulting data.

Note that reliability and robustness interact; if we find that the model is highly robust with respect to a particular set of parameters, then the unreliability of estimates of those parameters will not have much effect on the reliability of the model itself. In this case it is enough to have "stylized facts" governing the parameters that are used: roughly 60 percent of workers' income is spent on food, 0 percent is saved, and so on.

Failures along each of these lines can be illustrated easily.

1. The model assumes that prices are determined on the basis of markup pricing (costs plus a fixed exogenous markup rate and wage). In fact, however, we might believe (along neoclassical lines) that prices, wages, and the profit rate are all endogenous, so that markup pricing misrepresents the underlying price mechanism. This would be a failure of validity; the model is premised on assumptions that may not hold.

2. The model is premised on a two-sector analysis of the economy. However, energy production and consumption turn out to be economically crucial factors in the performance of the economy, and these effects are overlooked unless we represent the energy sector separately. This would be a failure of comprehensiveness; there is an economically significant factor that is not represented in the model.

3. We rerun the model assuming a slightly altered set of production coefficients, and we find that the predictions are substantially different: the increase in income is only 33 percent of what it was, and deficits are only half what they were. This is a failure of robustness; once we know that the model is extremely sensitive to variations in the parameters, we have strong reason to doubt its predictions. The accuracy of measurement of parameters is limited, so we can be confident that remeasurement would produce different values. So we can in turn expect that the simulation will arrive at different values for the endogenous variables.

4. Suppose that our model of income distribution in a developing economy is premised on the international trading arrangements embodied in GATT. The model is designed to represent the domestic causal relations between food subsidies and the pattern of income distribution across classes. If the

results of the model change substantially on dropping the GATT assumption, then the model is not autonomous with respect to international trading arrangements.

5. Finally, we examine the data underlying the consumption functions and we find that these derive from one household study in one Mexican state, involving 300 households. Moreover, we determine that the model is sensitive to the parameters defining consumption functions. On this scenario we have little reason to expect that the estimates derived from the household study are reliable estimates of consumption in all social classes all across Mexico, and therefore we have little reason to depend on the predictions of the model. This is a failure of reliability.

These factors—validity, comprehensiveness, robustness, autonomy, and reliability—figure into our assessment of the antecedent credibility of a given model. If the model is judged to be reasonably valid and comprehensive, if it appears to be fairly robust and autonomous, and if the empirical data on which it rests appears to be reliable, then we have reason to believe that the model is a reasonable representation of the underlying economic reality. But this deductive validation of the model does not take us far enough. These are reasons to have a priori confidence in the model. But we need as well to have a basis for a posteriori confidence in the particular results of this specific model. And since there are many well-known ways in which a generally well-constructed model can nonetheless miss the mark—incompleteness of the causal field, failure of *ceteris paribus* clauses, poor data or poor estimates of the exogenous variables and parameters, proliferation of error to the point where the solution has no value, and path-dependence of the equilibrium solution—we need to have some way of empirically evaluating the results of the model.

8.2.5. Empirical Confirmation of a Model

The preceding provides an account of a variety of theoretical arguments and standards that can be employed to assess antecedent credibility for a given model. But we have seen that there is a substantial gap between a model's being judged adequate on these grounds and our being justified in relying on its predictions. In order to arrive at a reasonable confidence in the predictive adequacy of a model, therefore, we need to have ways of empirically testing the model.

Consider an analogy. Suppose that an engineer has designed a complicated mechanical device to be used in space. The device has not yet been built and ipso facto has not been used in space. The engineer wants to know how the device will behave when subjected to vibration in zero gravity. He therefore creates a computer simulation of the device that takes into account the device's known mechanical characteristics and the environmental variables known to be causally relevant to the performance of the device. The simulation model is validated along the lines suggested above: it is checked for validity, comprehensiveness, robustness, autonomy, and reliability. The simulation predicts that the device will continue to function according to design even if subjected to vibrations within a given range. How much confidence ought we have in this result? Relatively little, it would seem, until we have had some experience comparing the predicted results of the simulation with the actual behavior of the simulated device.

The most obvious approach to empirically evaluating a model is through direct evaluation of its predictions: compare the predictive results of the model with observed data. It is significant, however, that none of the dozen models contained in *Socially Relevant Policy Analysis* (Taylor, 1990) provide such post facto evaluation.

A second and less direct approach is to attempt to establish the empirical credentials of a class of models. Here the idea is to consider the predictive successes of a given type of CGE model in application to a range of specific economies. If a given model has been reasonably accurate in the past, this gives us some basis for confidence in its current application. (By analogy, suppose there are several different approaches to modeling weather phenomena. Models have been constructed for particular applications from each of the different approaches. We might argue inductively that the class of models with the greatest empirical success in the past is likely to continue to succeed in the future.) The problem with this approach is that each CGE model is tailored to the particular analytical questions the modeler is interested in answering; this means that there will be significant differences in the structure and details of models in different applications. As a result there will not generally be a track record of previous predictions that might establish the reliability of a given model.[17]

Another form of direct empirical test of a model or theory is an application of the "bootstrapping method" of confirmation (Glymour, 1980). We may evaluate various components of the model—its representation of the demand functions —by holding fixed other theoretical hypotheses, deducing demand behavior for the next period, and comparing the predicted results with that predicted by the target demand function.

It is possible to design an empirical test of a CGE model, then; but very little work has been done along these lines, and CGE models are not generally accompanied by substantial empirical argument designed to support the credibility of the model. (This stands in marked contrast to the econometrics literature, in which issues of empirical adequacy of findings have received substantial attention.)

8.3. Assessment

Let us now pull together some general conclusions on the reliability and validity of CGE models.

What is the basis for our antecedent confidence in the results of a CGE model? The most fundamental point concerns the degree of confidence we have in the underlying theory. Second, a given model can be examined in detail to determine the plausibility of its implementation of the underlying theory—the functional implementation of demand and supply conditions. And finally, it is possible to evaluate the empirical core of the model: the SAM on which it depends and the calibration of parameters and exogenous variables. So there is a general basis for confidence in CGE models: the theory is well confirmed, a given model can be validated as a reasonable implementation of the theory, and the empirical data used to establish the initial conditions of the simulation can be evaluated independently.

Epistemically, then, the situation of CGE models is this: If the theory accurately identifies the chief mechanisms of systems of the sort S, and if the model adequately represents the causal hypotheses of the theory, and if the observations of s are accurate and reliable, and if there are no significant countervailing causal factors—*then* we are justified in attaching credence to the causal assertions, counterfactual claims, and predictions of the model.[18] But note that each of these qualifications introduces its own uncertainties into the credibility of the resulting assertions. The theory may be incorrect or incomplete; the model may make damaging simplifications (to make the problem more tractable, perhaps); the description of the existing economy may be incorrect; and there may be unusual causal factors at work in this case that are not generally significant in systems of this sort.

If we can arrive at a general assessment about the reliability of CGE models, it is this. CGE models are powerful instruments of analysis that permit economists to represent a good deal of the complexity of a modern multisectoral economy. They permit the economist to explore the consequences of a general-equilibrium representation of an economy, representing the complex interconnections across industries, sectors, and income groups. As such, they promise to shed a good deal of light on the causal processes within such economies. At the same time, the predictions of such models are not highly reliable. This is not a consequence of such models being theoretically ill-conceived; on the contrary, as we saw above, the theoretical motivation for these models is compelling. But the gap between general theoretical principles, abstract and selective implementation of these principles in a particular model, and the net predictive consequences of the resulting model is substantial. It is quite possible that the predictions of a model that is antecedently credible will nonetheless be wide from the mark.

The only convincing way of confirming that a given model is a good simulation of a given economy is to empirically test is against data drawn from that economy. But in many of the contexts in which CGE models are relied on this is not possible; indeed, the whole purpose of formulating a CGE simulation is the difficulty or impossibility of deriving such data. The level of confidence that policy makers should attach to such predictions, therefore, is somewhat low. CGE models are a legitimate and useful way of probing possible economic effects, based on a representation of certain important aspects of the economy in question. They are most useful when they are used cautiously to explore intersectoral effects. But there is such a wide range of alternative and equally supportable formulations of the general principles, and such a high degree of sensitivity of outcomes to the settings of parameters and exogenous variables, that the predictions of such models must be regarded as speculative.

Finally, let us return to the idea of simulation as experiment. Do CGE simulations serve as "experiments" for economics? They do not, if we understand the idea of an experiment in anything like its usage in the natural sciences. An experiment involves a theory of the causal processes contained within a system S, a prediction derived from the theory about what effects a given kind of intervention P will produce, a controlled empirical situation that embodies the main characteristics of system S along with the experimenter's ability to produce P, and an empirical observation of the state of the system following P. The theory predicts an specific outcome and the experiment allows for an empirical test of that prediction. CGE simulations differ from this in that they lack the crucial empirical test. A CGE simulation allows us to formulate a prediction about what would happen to the system if a given intervention occurred. But this prediction does not have the empirical standing of an observation. So simulations are thought experiments, not genuine experiments with empirical import.

Notes

1. Thus Chenery, Lewis, de Melo, and Robinson, (1986a: 311) write, "Our approach is to use a CGE model of a single country as a simulation laboratory for doing controlled experiments designed to explore different development strategies." I express skepticism about this notion in the concluding section.

2. See Irma Adelman's useful discussion of simulation models in Eatwell, Milgate, and Newman (1990).

3. Sherman Robinson and Laura D'Andrea Tyson (1984) address this feature of CGE models.

4. Herbert Scarf pioneered a solution technique for general equilibrium models based on the Brouwer fixed-point theorem and a method of piecewise-linear approximations of the equilibrium condition. See Scarf (1984) for a presentation of the main outlines of his approach, as well as Michael Todd's companion essay (1984). Scarf's entry in the *New Palgrave: General Equilibrium* is useful as well (Eatwell, Milgate, and Newman, 1989). But since there are now available fast

computer algorithms for solving large systems of nonlinear equations, it is unnecessary to construct specialized solution techniques for general equilibrium models.

5. There are various software packages that implement solution algorithms for models involving large systems of equations. One such package is *Soritec: Integrated Econometric and Statistical Analysis System*. Medium-sized models can be implemented in *Mathcad*, a widely available and intuitive mathematics software package.

6. Lance Taylor's *Macro Models for Developing Countries* (1979) provides a detailed description of the structure and construction of social accounting matrix; the discussion here follows Taylor's.

7. Mansur and Whalley (1984) provide a substantial discussion of the difficulties confronting the construction of a "benchmark data set" for use in a general equilibrium model; see Scarf and Shoven (1984).

8. See Lawrence Lau's comments on Mansur and Whalley for defense of the econometric approach (Scarf and Shoven, 1984). Kevin Hoover has done very interesting work on the underlying epistemological assumptions of calibration methods (Hoover, 1992).

9. Note, however, the limitations of these assumptions.

10. Oscar Morgenstern's (1963) trenchant criticism of spurious precision in economic analysis is equally pertinent in this context.

11. Philosophers understand the concept of semantics as encompassing the relations between a sentence and the world: truth and reference (Tarski, 1983; Putnam, 1975). This understanding connects with the ordinary notion of semantics as meaning, in that the truth conditions of a sentence are thought to constitute the meaning of the sentence. For a good introduction to contemporary philosophy of science see Brown (1979) and Newton-Smith (1981).

12. See Hempel (1965a, 1965b), Glymour (1980), Lakatos (1978), Kuhn (1970), Newton-Smith (1981), Brown (1979, 1987), and Laudan (1977) for discussion of the nature of the standards of theory evaluation employed in different scientific disciplines.

13. Allan Gibbard and Hal Varian (1978) explore the idea of approximate truth in "Economic Models." See also Weston (1992) for a useful analysis of the logic of inference using approximate truths.

14. See Boyd (1984) and other essays in Leplin (1984) for a statement of scientific realism.

15. For more extensive discussion of Friedman's view see Rosenberg (1976, 1992) and Gibbard and Varian (1978). Positions comparable to Friedman's have been argued more recently by Robert Lucas, Jr. (1987: 45) and Charles Plott.

16. This appears to lie at the heart of the disagreement between neoclassical and structuralist economic theory; the structuralists argue that institutional features of an economy (features of the property system, historical strength of the labor movement) are causally significant, whereas neoclassical economists abstract from these features. See Taylor (1990) for extensive discussion of the structuralist viewpoint.

17. See James MacKinnon's thoughtful suggestions along these lines in his comment on Dale Jorgenson's CGE model of the U.S. economy (Scarf and Shoven, 1984).

18. Note the correspondence between this procedure and the hypothetico-deductive model of explanation.

References

Boyd, Richard N. (1984). "The Current Status of Scientific Realism." In J. Leplin (ed.), *Scientific Realism*. Berkeley: University of California Press.

Brown, Harold I. (1979). *Perception, Commitment, and Theory*. Chicago: University of Chicago Press.

———. (1987). *Observation and Objectivity*. Oxford: Oxford University Press.

Cartwright, Nancy. (1989). *Nature's Capacities and Their Measurement*. Oxford: Oxford University Press.

Chenery, Hollis, Jeffrey Lewis, Jaime de Melo, and Sherman Robinson. (1986a). "Alternative Routes to Development." In Hollis Chenery, Sherman Robinson, and Moshe Syrquin, *Industrialization and Growth: A Comparative Study*. New York: Oxford University Press.

Chenery, Hollis, Sherman Robinson, and Moshe Syrquin. (1986b). *Industrialization and Growth: A Comparative Study*. New York: Oxford University Press.

Chenery, Hollis, and T. N. Srinivasan (eds.). (1988). *The Handbook of Development Economics* (vol. 1). Amsterdam: North-Holland Press.

Eatwell, John, Murray Milgate, and Peter Newman (eds.). (1989). *The New Palgrave: General Equilibrium*. New York: Norton.

———. (1990). *The New Palgrave: Econometrics*. New York: Norton.

Friedman, Milton. (1953). *Essays in Positive Economics*. Chicago: University of Chicago Press.

Gibbard, Allan, and Hal Varian. (1978). "Economic Models." *Journal of Philosophy* 25, 664–677.

Glymour, Clark. (1980). *Theory and Evidence*. Princeton: Princeton University Press.

Hausman, Daniel. (1981). "John Stuart Mill's Philosophy of Economics." *Philosophy of Science* 48, 363–385.

———. (1992). *The Inexact and Separate Science of Economics*. Cambridge: Cambridge University Press.

Hempel, Carl. (1965a). "Studies in the Logic of Confirmation." In Carl Hempel, *Aspects of Scientific Explanation*. New York: Free Press.

———. (1965b). *Aspects of Scientific Explanation*. New York: Free Press.

Hoover, Kevin D. (1988). *The New Classical Macroeconomics: A Sceptical Inquiry*. Oxford: Basil Blackwell.

———. (1992). "Calibration and the Methodology of Quantitative Macroeconomics." Unpublished manuscript.

Kuhn, Thomas. (1970). *The Structure of Scientific Revolutions* (2nd ed.). Chicago: University of Chicago Press.

Lakatos, Imre. (1978). *The Methodology of Scientific Research Programmes: Philosophical Papers* (vol. 1). Cambridge: Cambridge University Press.

Laudan, Larry. (1977). *Progress and Its Problems*. Berkeley: University of California.

Leplin, Jarrett (ed.). (1984). *Scientific Realism*. Berkeley: University of California Press.

Lucas, Robert E., Jr. (1987). *Models of Business Cycles*. Oxford: Blackwell.

Lustig, Nora, and Lance Taylor. (1990). "Mexican Food Consumption Policies in a Structuralist CGE Model." In Lance Taylor (ed.), *Socially Relevant Policy Analysis*. Cambridge, MA: MIT Press.

Mansur, Ahsan, and John Whalley. (1984). "Numerical Specification of Applied General Equilibrium Models: Estimation, Calibration, and Data." In Herbert E. Scarf and John

B. Shoven (eds.), *Applied General Equilibrium Analysis*. Cambridge: Cambridge University Press.

Mathcad. (1992). Version 3.1. Cambridge, MA: MathSoft.

Morgenstern, Oskar. (1963). *On the Accuracy of Economic Observations* (2nd ed.). Princeton, NJ: Princeton University Press.

Newton-Smith, W. H. (1981). *The Rationality of Science*. Boston: Routledge & Kegan Paul.

Putnam, Hilary. (1975). *Mind, Language, and Reality*. Cambridge: Cambridge University Press.

Robinson, Sherman, and Laura D'Anchea Tyson. (1984). "Modeling Structural Adjustment: Micro and Macro Elements in a General Equilibrium Framework." In Herbert E. Scarf and John B. Shoven (eds.), *Applied General Equilibrium Analysis*. Cambridge: Cambridge University Press.

Rosenberg, Alexander. (1976). *Microeconomic Law: A Philosophical Analysis*. Pittsburgh: University of Pittsburgh Press.

———. (1992). *Economics: Mathematical Politics or Science of Diminishing Returns?* Chicago: University of Chicago Press.

Rosenberg, Nathan. (1982). *Inside the Black Box: Technology and Economics*. Cambridge: Cambridge University Press.

Scarf, Herbert E. (1984). "Computation of Equilibrium Prices." In Herbert E. Scarf and John B. Shoven (eds.), *Applied General Equilibrium Analysis*. Cambridge: Cambridge University Press.

Scarf, Herbert E., and John B. Shoven (eds.). (1984). *Applied General Equilibrium Analysis*. Cambridge: Cambridge University Press.

Soritec: Integrated Econometric and Statistical Analysis System. (1990). Springfield, VA: Sorites Group.

Tarski, Alfred. (1983) [1951]. *Logic, Semantics and Metamathematics* (2nd ed.). Indianapolis: Hackett.

Taylor, Lance. (1979). *Macro Models for Developing Countries*. New York: McGraw-Hill.

———. (1990). *Socially Relevant Policy Analysis: Structuralist Computable General Equilibrium Models for the Developing World*. Cambridge: MIT Press.

Todd, Michael. (1984). "Efficient Methods of Computing Economic Equilibrium." In Herbert E. Scarf and John B. Shoven (eds.), *Applied General Equilibrium Analysis*. Cambridge: Cambridge University Press.

Weintraub, E. (1979). *Microfoundations*. Cambridge: Cambridge University Press.

Weston, Thomas. (1992). "Approximate Truth and Scientific Realism." *Philosophy of Science* 59: 53–74.

Lance Taylor

Comments on Little: Economic Models in Development Economics

Economic discourse is theory driven; rarely does a simple appeal to evidence carry a debate. This intellectual bias is clearly illustrated by the ways in which computable general equilibrium (CGE) models are used. Contrary to the thrust of Daniel Little's chapter, these complicated contraptions are not primarily set up in "neutral" fashion to explain the data or numerically explore the possible repercussions of policy changes or institutional shifts. Rather, they are designed as quantified illustrations of their designers' conceptions of the economic world. Each model becomes a rhetorical tool, a means to expound in detail its builder's ideas about the key linkages in the "real" economy out there. Little's conclusion that CGE model "simulations are thought experiments, not genuine experiments with empirical import" is correct, but he arrives at it through philosophical categories. It may be of interest to illustrate his point directly by looking at the properties of one influential family of models, along with other CGE exercises for the developing world.

Since the mid-1980s there has been a flood of CGE computations of the putative effects of free-trade agreements, first the Free-Trade Agreement (FTA) between Canada and the United States and subsequently the North American Free Trade Agreement (NAFTA). Almost all the models were put together by orthodox (mainstream, neoclassical) economists, incorporating most or all of the following assumptions:

1. Full employment of resources exists in both (or all) trading partners;
2. Balanced trade, or at least prespecified trade deficits or surpluses, exists;
3. Investment demand in a country does not fall markedly when its trade is liberalized;
4. Even in oligopolistic industries, national prices will be largely determined by external prices under trade (that is, the "law of one price" approximately applies);
5. Consumer demands obey a specification due to Armington (1969), which means that consumers distinguish products by their countries (but not their firms) of origin;
6. Various functional forms with associated numerical parameters are specified to state these ideas in algebraic fashion.

The first five hypotheses strongly influence the qualitative nature of the trade models' results, but their importance is not quite captured by the evaluation criteria that Little emphasizes in his paper. He does stress the issue of parameter estimation summarized in assumption 6, but parameters and functional forms may prove to be of minor qualitative significance in a CGE simulation (although they will certainly affect the magnitudes—if not the signs—of the numbers that the computer cranks out). The first part of this comment is dedicated to establishing these points, and the second to drawing out their implications as they apply to developing country models more generally.

Maintained Hypotheses

The first two assumptions are built solidly into the orthodox argument for the gains from trade in its Ricardian, Heckscher-Ohlin, and "new trade theory" forms. They preclude any unpleasant outcomes from liberalization. Even if high-cost Country A opens market relationships with Country B, which can produce all commodities more cheaply, the full-employment assumption means that Country A's overall output cannot decline while balanced trade ensures that Country B cannot overrun all its partner's markets.

These twin axioms guaranteed that productive Portugal could not beat England out of both wine and cloth production in Ricardo's original numerical example.[1] Factor price shifts in favor of "abundant" production inputs serve the same balancing function in the Heckscher-Ohlin version, as do firms opening up and shutting down in the new trade theory (under an assumption that nonzero, pure profits cannot persist). In all these stories, resources are reallocated in the direction of less costly producers, generating more output and potential gains from trade.

In the Jargon, assumptions 1 and 2 are "closure" assumptions of a macroeconomic nature that must be imposed on CGE models. They cannot be deduced from the details of micro level (firm, household, or sectoral) behavioral specifications and must be incorporated explicitly or implicitly into a model's algebra to permit it to determine an equilibrium solution. From the foregoing discussion, it is clear that closure postulates will often determine the essential results of a simulation. For example, in CGE model runs of the effects of NAFTA, full employment and predetermined trade balances rule out massive relocation of Canadian factories or U.S. jobs south of their respective borders. In other words, free trade agreements *cannot* generate loud "sucking sounds" in H. Ross Perot's colorful phrase from his 1992 presidential campaign. Under alternative closures, the noise could prove to be deafening.

In Little's terminology, the "antecedent warrant" of the "validity" and "comprehensiveness" of the two dozen free-trade models that have been produced rests heavily on assumptions 1 and 2. These axioms have ample professional support, insofar as most economists are partisans of free trade, and full-employment/ balanced-trade hypotheses are built into the most widely quoted supporting theorems. Yet, as Perot pointed out on the talk shows and the stump, there is no compelling reason outside the world of international trade textbooks to believe that they are true. There have been numerous plant closings in Canada since the free-trade agreement was signed (whether due more to the FTA or to prolonged recession is by no means clear), and the results from NAFTA remain to be observed. If the outcomes of the agreements prove to be generally unfavorable to Canadian, U.S., or even Mexican interests, they may force trade economists to change their closure ideas, but then they would have been wrong for a very long time.

In shorter words, we arrive at two conclusions: First, closure assumptions are crucial to CGE methodology since they drive the *directions* of results that models produce; second, mainstream economists have strong preconceptions about closure that may not always be true (at least according to informed observers from outside the profession).

Assumptions 3 through 5 are contingent on a model's macro closure but can strongly influence the ways in which it works out. In practice, applied models often seem to depend on just a few key assumptions besides closure; the art of model design is to figure out what they are and how they work through the system. We can illustrate in the context of trade models with investment, oligopoly, and consumer demand specifications.

Assumption 3 presupposes a closure that permits an independent investment function to exist.[2] The way it is specified can strongly affect model behavior. For example, in a NAFTA scenario stressed by Blecker (1992), suppose that real capital formation stagnates in the United States after the agreement, as U.S. firms respond to new profit opportunities by diverting investment toward Mexico. The U.S. trade surplus (or savings minus investment at home) would increase, but its potential GDP growth rate and demand for its neighbors' exports could fall. Reduced stimulus by the dominant partner could easily prove severe enough to throw the smaller economies into long-term decline.

In Little's usage, Blecker's version of the investment function affects the "autonomy" of the model by determining context. More than a question of "reliability" is involved, since time series evidence cannot inform us about the investment behavior of U.S. firms under NAFTA because they were never in an analagous situation: one cannot answer statistical questions that are meaningless in terms of the economy's past experimental design. A model builder would just have to look at past U.S. investment patterns and guess about their future under NAFTA. He or she could always check "robustness" of a given set of investment parameters by sensitivity analysis, but the results could never be completely convincing. Most mainstream simulations rule out Blecker's scenario by postulating a full employment closure. Hufbauer and Schott (1992) allow less than full employment in the United States but don't consider major shifts in investment demand. At a more micro level than model closure, their specific assumptions guarantee positive benefits from freeing trade.

Assumption 4 about oligopoly pricing plays a similar role.[3] It was built into a pioneering new trade theory model by Stykolt and Eastman (1960), which in the long run had a profound effect on the debate regarding Canadian-American free trade. They argued that protection granted a sector with many potential product varieties would lead all its component firms to raise prices and profits, causing excessive entry in turn. The outcome after a zero-profit condition came into effect would be a congeries of small firms wiping up extra profits through inefficiency due to underutilized economies of scale. Such a situation was supposed to be the outcome of Canada's industrial protection. The solution? Free trade to cut Canadian prices via U.S. competition. Some firms would be "disciplined" into bankruptcy, permitting the survivors to reach efficient volumes of sales.

Stykolt-Eastman doctrine was built into a CGE model by Harris and Cox (1984), which "generated huge predictions of efficiency gains to Canada from tariff cuts—predictions that were undoubtedly influential in the Canadian government's determination to successfully negotiate its free trade agreement with the United States" (Hazeldine, 1990). As we have already observed, the Harris-Cox projections appear to be about 180 degrees off the mark.[4]

Why was their model so wrong? Its postulated big capital inflows into Canada (to be induced by abolishing a tariff structure that was in part set up to attract direct foreign investment in the first place) explain part of Harris and Cox's results, but their assumptions regarding oligopolistic pricing matter at least as much. As Hazeldine points out, there is no compelling reason to expect that reducing a tariff will end up cutting domestic market prices, once pricing behavior of the surviving producers is taken into account. Their own oligopoly becomes tighter, and arguably more likely to push for bigger markups instead of longer production runs.[5]

An Eastman-Stykolt outcome is even more likly under the Armington (1969) demand assumption that consumers distinguish commodities by their country of origin. One implication is that liberalization will shift demand across countries by only a few percentage points. On the other hand, if the number of domestic firms shrinks notably, the survivors can raise output and reap economies of scale: this form of rationalization explains some of the favorable results reported by Harris and Cox.

An alternative story more in keeping with the Cournot-Nash hypothesis about firm behavior often adopted in the industrial organization literature is that the survivors have to share the market with all remaining firms, domestic *and* foreign. In other words, the market share of the domestic industry may be broadly related to the number and sizes of its surviving firms. If, say, United States-based companies enter the Canadian and Mexican markets in force, then local survivors may find their market shares significantly curtailed. They may also be beaten out of exports if U.S. producers set up foreign manufacturing operations for their home market, as happened with new General Motors and Ford automobile engine plants in Mexico in the 1980s (which were directly managed, incidentally, from Detroit and not Mexico City or Monterrey). The fact that Mexican-built engines can be hidden under the hood circumvented Armington-style limitations to their export volumes.

As with investment functions and closure, these assumptions about oligopoly responses and demand patterns go a long way toward determining the qualitative properties of the trade models' results. They cannot readily be refuted from time series data, but then neither could hypotheses that would make the models generate different results. "Warrant" becomes not so much an empirical question as an affirmation of orthodox international trade theory's strong bias in favor of liberalizing trade. The CGE liberalization models just attached numbers to conclusions trade economists "knew" to be true all along.

CGE Models in Practice

The foregoing observations underline Little's basic point about CGE simulations: They *are* thought experiments, usually from a given theoretical perspective. More precisely, they are extensions of the back-of-the-envelope calculations that economists often do, perhaps slightly more credible because a model incorporates consistent accounting of macroeconomic data from its underlying social accounting matrix (SAM) and enforces mathematical consistency on the part of its user. From a practicioner's angle, these characteristics impart strengths and weaknesses that Little does not bring out.

One strength has to do with prediction, especially in developing economies. It is useful to contrast forecasts from a CGE model or SAM incorporating a few sectors, income categories, and financial flows with those from an econometric model, the principal competing methodology.

Even in countries with long, credible time series for the national accounts and ample input-output information, there is no compelling reason to believe in predictions from any one collection of equations from econometrics. As the volume of articles on (say) the U.S. macroeconomy in professional journals attests, any number of theoretical structures can be forced on a nation's one existing set of data with impressive goodness of fit. However, projections forward in time can diverge strongly, depending on the theory underlying each particular model. The same observation applies to developing countries, with the additional points that their time series are short and often unreliable, while their economies are subject to sharp structural breaks ranging from political revolutions through debt crises and roller coaster terms of trade. Equations statistically tied to past data become increasingly dubious as these drawbacks become stronger.

The implication is that if one is in the business of projecting an aggregate SAM (which is what economists do in practice, even when the relationship between the numbers in the SAM and the economy that they are supposed to mirror is tenuous at best), then starting from a matrix for this year and updating it under reasonable assumptions about what is going to happen next year will usually produce as good an economic forecast as anyone can expect. For reasons to be explained shortly, it may be best *not* to undertake this exercise with a formal model: playing with numbers subject to the accounting restrictions implicit in the SAM's spreadsheet may make more sense. But even this "methodology" is far closer to a CGE exercise than it is to basing projections on econometrics.

A similar observation applies to "backcasts" based on a CGE model or a SAM. Given the latter's accounting restrictions, it is easy to set a few variables to a previous year's values and let the bookkeeping identities grind out the rest. Subject to the vagaries of index number and aggregation problems, they will be very close to being "correct" because the accounting won't allow them to be otherwise.

Under forgiving closures such as a Keynesian one that predetermines previous years' investment demands, the same observation applies to a formal model's backward simulations (see Cardoso and Taylor, 1979). "Reliability" in the sense of tracking time series is fairly easy to establish for a CGE model; that is what calibration is about. Whether such a procedure heightens confidence about the model's conditional projections is another question. Many possible parameter settings can be contrived to fit the past, but all could be based on misleading theory.[6]

If its theory looks credible and it can track past data, then why not believe in a CGE model's results wholeheartedly? The basic reason is that it is likely to be too simple-minded. Consider, for example, a developing economy subject to a big external shock such as the debt crisis or plummeting terms of trade. We know from experience that it will react in several ways: inflation will speed up, output will fall, interest rates will rise, investment will decline, income and wealth distributions will become more regressive, external payments will go into arrears, and so on.

There are at least two problems with using a model to preassign the relative importance of these outcomes. First, a collection of closure axioms and behavioral equations at the level of detail that a model (probably better than its builder!) can comprehend will not capture all the disaggregated behavior that leads macroeconomic shocks to dissipate through specific channels. Each closure will tend to emphasize specific repercussions; a model builder, for example, can only assume that the trade deficit is exogenous or that it is not. At a more micro level, we have seen from the discussion of trade models that certain assumptions can have strong qualitative effects. Both aspects of any formal specification will tend to exaggerate the importance of some linkages and underestimate others because the reality is too complex to summarize in just a few equations.

Second, even if the model is well calibrated to the effects of past shocks, people's behavior will change: policy makers will behave differently (or believe in different economic theories), and other folks will try to avoid errors of the past. Moreover, it may well be that the nature of this year's shock differs radically from those of the past.[7] The details of any forecast of its effects are bound to be wrong.

Do these problems make CGE model results useless? Ideally not. For example, a model could be used to track the ability of each channel mentioned above to absorb a shock by itself, or to gauge the effects of possible compensatory combinations of policies. Such simulations would involve changes in both macro and micro causal assumptions, with appropriate sensitivity analysis of parameters. The goal would be to think through how the economy is likely to respond, not to make unconditional predictions. We return to thought experiments or back of the envelope calculations. If one doesn't get lost in the detail, then information is gained if the envelope is the size of a spreadsheet with a few dozen rows and columns—that is, a SAM. Unless the theory underlying the numbers is thoroughly wrong-headed (as it may be in the free trade agreement simulations), then contemplating how they bounce around under different assumptions can give insight—usually a precious commodity in and of itself.

Notes

1. "Cloth," of course, provided scale economies and technical progress that soon would have allowed England to overcome the lower real wages implicit in its original (according to Ricardo) absolute cost disadvantages. In history as opposed to Ricardian texts, English frigates parked in Lisbon's harbor played a substantial role in putting the observed system of specialization into place (Sideri, 1970).

2. Without going into great detail, in an economy with no foreign trade, full employment of resources, and explicit savings functions for each set of income recipients, there is "no room" in the macroeconomics for a full collection of sectoral investment functions since they would overdetermine the system by making the number of behavioral equations and accounting identities exceed the number of "reasonable" endogenous variables. In models open to trade, $N-1$ of N countries can have

independent investment functions so long as all trade deficits vary endogenously. For algebra and diagrams to back up these assertions, see Taylor (1990, 1991).

3. Contrary to some of Little's discussion, CGE models do not have to be based on competitive general equilibrium theory. Many follow Keynes and Kalecki into demand-driven closures with markup pricing, incorporate oligopoly behavior and market power, postulate increasing returns to scale, or otherwise violate Walrasian assumptions.

4. Traditionally, neoclassical numerical models had not cranked out big benefits from removing trade distortions. Welfare improvements were measured by general equilibrium analogs of the "little triangles" in the traditional demand-supply diagram; even in many dimensions, they remained stubbornly small. One reason that the Harris-Cox model got a lot of professional attention is precisely because it put Eastman-Stykolt oligopoly theory together with economies of scale and a favorable macroeconomic closure to project big welfare gains from Canadian free trade.

5. As in all industrial organization models, Hazeldine's conjectures depend on specific details of his specification, such as his Cournot-Nash assumption about national and foreign oligopoly pricing behavior. This hypothesis is not less "appropriate" than the collusive pricing rules postulated by Stykolt-Eastman and Harris-Cox; for example, the latter authors assume that the domestic price is some weighted average of import costs and a markup on domestic marginal cost. Hazeldine's point is that there is *no* good reason after liberalization *not* to expect that the local (and perhaps the foreign) markup rate will go up.

6. The observations in the text may help alleviate Little's concern about why the authors collected in Taylor (1990) did not compare the results of their models with observed data. In fact, some did, but since they had already calibrated their models to past SAMs and knew they could adjust exogenous variables to fit future ones pretty accurately, they did not bother to report the outcomes.

7. Recall, for example, how badly well-established econometric models predicted the stagflationary effects of the 1973 oil shock on the U.S. economy, basically because their builders had never thought to include the relevant cost-price and aggregate demand linkages in their specifications.

References

Armington, Paul S. (1969). "A Theory of Demand for Products Distinguished by Place of Origin." *International Monetary Fund Staff Papers* 16, 159–176.

Blecker, Robert A. (1992). "Trade and Investment Liberalization in North America: A Structuralist Macro Model of the NAFTA." Washington, DC: Economic Policy Institute.

Cardoso, Eliana A., and Lance Taylor. (1979). "Identity-Based Planning of Prices and Quantities: Cambridge and Neoclassical Models for Brazil." *Journal of Policy Modeling* 1, 83–111.

Harris, Richard, and David Cox. (1984). *Trade, Industrial Policy, and Canadian Manufacturing*. Toronto: Ontario Economic Council.

Hazeldine, Tim. (1990). "Trade Liberalization and Economic Welfare with Endogenous Market Structure." Vancouver: Department of Agricultural Economics, University of British Columbia.

Hufbauer, Gary C., and Jeffrey J. Schott. (1992). *North American Free Trade Issues and Recommendations*. Washington, DC: Institute for International Economics.

Sideri, Sandro. (1970). *Trade and Power: Informal Colonialism in Anglo-Portuguese Relations*. Rotterdam: Rotterdam University Press.

Stykolt, Stefan, and Harry C. Eastman. (1960). "A Model for the Study of Protected Oligopolies." *Economic Journal* 70, 336–347.

Taylor, Lance (ed.). (1990). *Socially Relevant Policy Analysis.* Cambridge, MA: MIT Press.

———. (1991). *Income Distribution, Inflation, and Growth.* Cambridge, MA: MIT Press.

Index